# Handbook of COMPUTER FUNDAMENTALS

**DR. NASIB SINGH GILL**

FIETE, PDS(Brunel, UK), Ph.D.(Computer Sc.), MBA

**Professor & Head,**
Department of Computer Science & Applications
**Director**, Directorate of Distance Education
**Director**, MDU Alumni
MAHARSHI DAYANAND UNIVERSITY, ROHTAK
HARYANA, INDIA

**KHANNA BOOK PUBLISHING CO. (P) LTD.**

Publisher of Science, Technology and Engineering Books

4C/4344, Ansari Road, Darya Ganj, New Delhi-110002
**Phone:** 011-23244447-48 **Mobile:** +91-99109 09320
**E-mail:** contact@khannabooks.com, sales@khannapublishers.com
**Website:** www.khannabooks.com, www.khannapublishers.com

**Price: ₹ 390.00**

**ISBN:** 978-93-82609-67-4

**Handbook of Computer Fundamentals** *by* N.S. Gill

First Edition: 2016
**Reprint Edition: 2025**

To view complete list of books, Please scan the QR Code:

*Published by:*
**Khanna Book Publishing Co. (P) Ltd.**
*CIN: U22110DL1998PTC095547*

Visit us at: **www.khannabooks.com**
Write us at: **contact@khannabooks.com**

Printed in India.

# DEDICATION

This book is dedicated to all
My Family Members,
My Relatives,
My Friends,
My Students,
&
All Beloved Readers.

The machine develops - but not on our lines. The machine proceeds - but not to our goal. We only exist as the corpuscles that course through its arteries, and if it could work without us, it would let us die.

**—E.M. Forster, The Machine Stops**

Since the computer is so fast, it needs a fast boss.

**—Donald Sanders, In Computers Today**

It is the capability of the computer for solving problems and making decisions that represents its real novelty and that poses the greatest difficulties in predicting its impact upon society.

**—Herbert A. Simon (Nobel Laureate)**

A ship in port is safe, but that is not what ships are for. Sail out to sea and do new things.

**—Admiral Grace Hopper, Computer Pioneer**

# Preface

If you are curious about computers, if you want to know how they work and what they can do for you, and if we wonder what a computerized world of the future would be like, this book will help you - whatever your education and background.

Today there is an ever-increasing awareness and curiosity about computers among people in all walks of life. In today's information age, knowledge of computer is a must. We feel mildly threatened by this new technology that is spreading fast, and have an inner urge to learn something about this new technology. Parents want their children to choose computer science as a subject in schools, youngsters enroll in large numbers in numerous computer professional classes and adults look for appreciation courses and books on computers.

While books on computer fundamentals are plenty in number, there are not many which give broad introduction to the computer covering its development, operation, applications and implications. This book is meant to fill this gap and is aimed at professionals, students and laymen who want to understand computers and network technology. While the presentation is kept simple, the coverage is wide - from the origins of computers to the prospects of future. Besides, the book well emphasizes on communication and computer networks. Moreover, Internet and Intranet have also been discussed up to a desirable depth.

Whether you are pursuing a career as an actuary, a social worker, an attorney, an accountant, a computer specialist, a sales manager, or virtually any other job, this book will prove to be beneficial. For most of you, this knowledge will be a fundamental prerequisite to performing your job.

This book is intended to serve for a variety of intermediate and advanced courses in computer science, computer application and computer engineering programmes including B.E./B.Tech., B.A/B.Com/B. Sc. (Pass Course), B.Sc.(Computer Science), B.Sc.(IT), BCA, BCAII, MCA, MCAII, M.Sc.(Computer Science), M.Sc.(IT), M.Tech.(CSE/IT), MBA, LLB and so on.

When readers enjoy what they read, they remember it. The text's friendly style encourages students to read and increase their comprehension.

I would like to point out in advance that this book has been written based on the work done by many people who have provided information directly or indirectly through their books, publications or lectures. However, references have been provided at the end of the book, from where the author has drawn material for use.

I would appreciate it if you, the reader would notify me of any errors or omissions in the book. Also if you would like to suggest improvements or to contribute exercises, I would be glad to hear from you. I will do my utmost to ensure that they are corrected and serve your purpose most appropriately.

### Key Features of the Book:

- The complete spectrum of computer fundamentals starting from historical evolution of computers to its successful usage among common men.
- Another important dimension of the book includes its opening from general concept of data communication to the extent of Internet & Intranet usage.

- The book also attempts to highlight the societal impacts of the computer technology.
- The language used in the book is lucid, is easy to understand, and facilitates easy grasping of concepts.
- The chapters have been logically arranged in sequence.
- The book is written in a reader-friendly manner both for the students and the teachers.
- Most of the contents presented in the book are in the form of bullets, organized sequentially. This form of presentation, rather than in a paragraph form, facilitates the reader to view, understand and remember the points better.
- The explanation is supported by diagrams, pictures and images wherever required.
- Adequate exercises have been given at the end of the every chapter.

## Readership

This book attempts to serve for a variety of intermediate and advanced courses in computer science, computer applications and computer engineering programmes including B.E./B.Tech., B.A/B.Com/B. Sc. (Pass Course), B.Sc.(Computer Science), B.Sc.(IT), BCA, BCAII, MCA, MCAII, M.Sc.(Computer Science), M.Sc.(IT), M.Tech.(CSE/IT), MBA, LLB and so on.

## Contents



**(Nasib Singh Gill)**

# Contents

CHAPTER 1

# Historical Evolution of Data Processing and Computing

## 1.1 INTRODUCTION

We all are familiar [illegible] subtraction [illegible] time but [illegible] explored the [illegible] with full accuracy [illegible]

The computer [illegible] applications of [illegible] appreciate the [illegible] payment of [illegible] processing, medical [illegible] extremely useful [illegible]

### Definition:

*A computer [illegible] the input [illegible] and store [illegible]*

It can also [illegible] the help of [illegible] (EDP). Computer [illegible]

The term data processing means

- Arithmetic and logical operations [illegible]
- To send and receive information [illegible]
- Arranging data in a specific order [illegible]

## 1.2 INFORMATION PROCESSING SYSTEM

A digital computer [illegible] with very high speed, in addition [illegible]

CHAPTER 1

# Historical Evolution of Data Processing and Computing

## 1.1 INTRODUCTION

We all are familiar with calculations in our day to day life. We apply mathematical operations like addition, subtraction, multiplication, etc. and many other formulae for calculations. Simpler calculations take less time but complex calculations take much longer time. Another factor is accuracy in calculations. So man explored the idea to develop a machine which can perform this type of arithmetic calculation faster and with full accuracy. This gave birth to a device or machine called **'computer'**.

The ***computer*** we see today is quite different from the one made in the beginning. The number of applications of a computer has increased, the speed and accuracy of calculation has increased. You must appreciate the impact of computers in our day to day life. Reservation of tickets in Air Lines and Railways, payment of telephone and electricity bills, deposits and withdrawals of money from banks, business data processing, medical diagnosis, weather forecasting, etc. are some of the areas where computer has become extremely useful.

### Definition:

> *"A computer is an electronic machine that operates under the control of instructions, that accepts the input data, processes or manipulates the given data according to the predefined instructions and stores the result for future use".*

It can also retrieve the stored results as and when required again. Now-a-days, data is processed with the help of computer. This modern technique to process data is known as Electronic Data Processing (EDP). Computer is also known as Electronic Data Processing machine.

The term data processing means:

- Arithmetic and logical operations on data to get required results.
- To send and receive information from one location to another.
- Arranging data into a specific order etc.

## 1.2 INFORMATION PROCESSING SYSTEM

A digital computer can store, process and retrieve data as and when desired. The computer processes data with very high speed. In addition to being very fast, computer is also very accurate in calculations. These are the main capabilities of the computer.

Therefore, we may define *computer as a device that transforms data into information.* Data can be anything like marks obtained by you in various subjects. It can also be name, age, sex, weight, height, etc. of all the students in your class or income, savings, investments, etc., of a country. Computer can be defined in terms of its functions. It can

- accept data
- store data
- process data as desired, and
- retrieve the stored data as and when required and
- print the result in desired format.

**Data processing** is the collection and manipulation of items of data to produce meaningful information. The term is often used more specifically in the context of a business or other organization to refer to the class of commercial data processing applications.

**Data processing** i.e. manipulation of data by a computer. It includes the conversion of raw data to machine-readable form, flow of data through the CPU and memory to output devices, and formatting or transformation of output. Any use of computers to perform defined operations on data can be included under data processing. In the commercial world, data processing refers to the processing of data required to run organizations and businesses.

Data processing may involve various processes, including:

- Validation – Ensuring that supplied data is "clean, correct and useful"
- Sorting – "arranging items in some sequence and/or in different sets."
- Summarization – reducing detail data to its main points.
- Aggregation – combining multiple pieces of data.
- Analysis – the "collection, organization, analysis, interpretation and presentation of data."
- Reporting – list detail or summary data or computed information.
- Classification – separates data into various categories.

## 1.3 DATA PROCESSING AND INFORMATION CYCLE

Data processing is simply the conversion of raw data to meaningful information through a process. Data is manipulated to produce results that lead to a resolution of a problem or improvement of an existing situation. Similar to a production process, it follows a cycle where inputs (raw data) are fed to a process (computer systems, software, etc.) to produce output (information and insights).

The Data Processing Cycle is a series of steps carried out to extract information from raw data. Although each step must be taken in order, the order is cyclic. The output and storage stage can lead to the repeat of the data collection stage, resulting in another cycle of data processing. The cycle provides a view on how the data travels and transforms from collection to

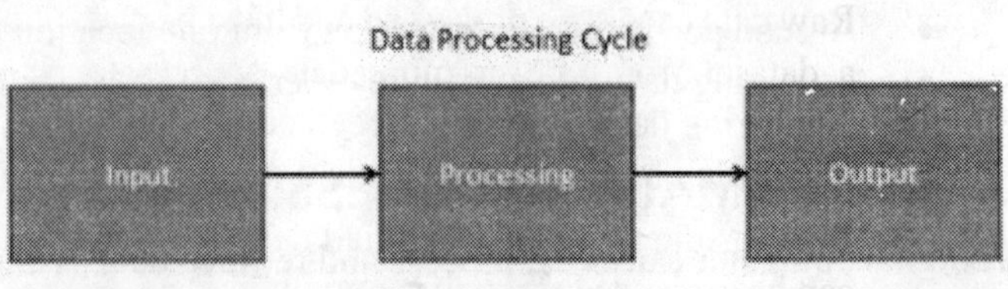

**Fig. 1.1:** Data Processing

interpretation, and ultimately, used in effective business decisions.

Generally, organizations employ computer systems to carry out a series of operations on the data in order to present, interpret, or obtain information. The process includes activities like data entry, summary, calculation, storage, etc. Useful and informative output is presented in various appropriate forms such as diagrams, reports, graphics, etc.

## Stages of the Information Cycle

1. **Collection** is the first stage of the cycle, and is very crucial, since the quality of data collected will impact heavily on the output. The collection process needs to ensure that the data gathered are both defined and accurate, so that subsequent decisions based on the findings are valid. This stage provides both the baseline from which to measure, and a target on what to improve.

   Some types of data collection include census (data collection about everything in a group or statistical population), sample survey (collection method that includes only part of the total population), and administrative by-product (data collection is a by-product of an organization's day-to-day operations).

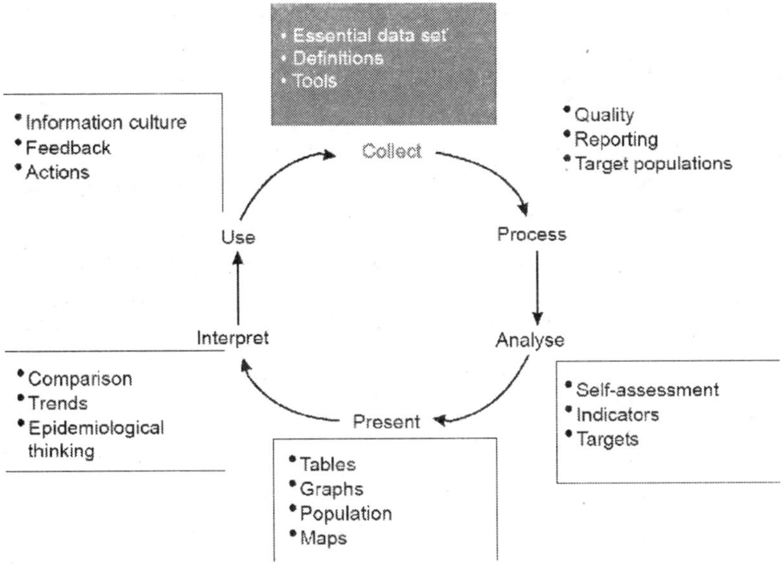


**Fig. 1.2:** Information Cycle

2. **Preparation** is the manipulation of data into a form suitable for further analysis and processing. Raw data cannot be processed and must be checked for accuracy. Preparation is about constructing a dataset from one or more data sources to be used for further exploration and processing. Analyzing data that has not been carefully screened for problems can produce highly misleading results that are heavily dependent on the quality of data prepared.
3. **Input** is the task where verified data is coded or converted into machine readable form so that it can be processed through a computer. Data entry is done through the use of a keyboard, digitizer,

scanner, or data entry from an existing source. This time-consuming process requires speed and accuracy. Most data need to follow a formal and strict syntax since a great deal of processing power is required to breakdown the complex data at this stage. Due to the costs, many businesses are resorting to outsource this stage.

4. **Processing** is when the data is subjected to various means and methods of manipulation, the point where a computer program is being executed, and it contains the program code and its current activity. The process may be made up of multiple threads of execution that simultaneously execute instructions, depending on the operating system. While a computer program is a passive collection of instructions, a process is the actual execution of those instructions. Many software programs are available for processing large volumes of data within very short periods.
5. **Output and interpretation** is the stage where processed information is now transmitted to the user. Output is presented to users in various report formats like printed report, audio, video, or on monitor. Output need to be interpreted so that it can provide meaningful information that will guide future decisions of the company.
6. **Storage** is the last stage in the data processing cycle, where data, instruction and information are held for future use. The importance of this cycle is that it allows quick access and retrieval of the processed information, allowing it to be passed on to the next stage directly, when needed. Every computer uses storage to hold system and application software.

## 1.4 HISTORY OF COMPUTING

In this chapter we will discuss the history of computing because it will give us the basic idea about the technological development trends in the past and its projection in the time to come. If we are interested to know about computers completely then we must start from the history of computers and look into the details of various technological advancements.

Man has developed from time to time various instruments to assist him in day-to-day calculation and for his data-processing needs. Depending upon the type of instruments used, the span of period has been split into following three ages:

- Dark Age (5000 B.C. - 1890 A.D.)
- Middle Age (1890 - 1944)
- Modern Age (Since 1944)

## 1.5 DARK AGE (5000 B.C. - 1890 A.D.)

In this age all the computing devices were manual-mechanical in nature and all the earliest data processing equipment were all manual-mechanical devices. We refer to the era when these machines were used exclusively as the Dark Ages of data processing. This age introduced the following devices.

### 1.5.1 Fingers

Perhaps the simplest calculating device which we can think of is our own fingers, which are certainly very easier and more portable. Even right now, children are taught by making use of fingers to add and subtract. This method of finger reckoning was widely used until a few centuries ago.

### 1.5.2 Abacus (5000 B.C)

Historian start the history of calculations with the Abacus and it was one of the simplest and earliest devices to aid arithmetic. Abacus was developed in China and was used by Greeks, Romans and Chinese. Abacus is nothing but a frame with beads strung on wires or rods. Abacus is shown in ***Fig. 1.3.***

**Fig. 1.3:** Abacus

Arithmetic calculations are performed by manipulating the beads strung on different wires. The abacus is still used world-wide. A skilled abacus operator can calculate even faster than a clerk using a desk calculator. It is still in use in India and some Western countries.

### 1.5.3 Napier's Bones (1617)

John Napier (1550-1617), a Scottish mathematician, brought about the next great step towards today's computers. Napier is known for something called Napier's Bones. His ***"bones"*** are a set of eleven rods with numbers marked on them in such a way that by simply placing the rods side by side products and quotients of large numbers can be obtained. Napier is also best known for the invention of logarithms, which in turn led to the slide rule. It has also been claimed that, Napier also introduced the decimal point into common usage and eliminated the use of notation to indicate fractional position.

### 1.5.4 Oughtred's Slide Rule (1632)

Although the slide rule appeared in various forms in Europe during the 17th century, its invention is attributed to the English mathematician William Oughtred. He is credited for two discoveries, both of which were forms of a slide rule. He introduced the circular slide rule and the rectangular slide rule. Basically a slide rule consists of two movable rulers placed side by side. Each ruler is marked off in such a way that the actual distances from the beginning of the ruler are proportional to the logarithms of the numbers printed on the ruler. By sliding the rulers one can quickly multiply and divide. Each of these instruments had a common accuracy of three digits.

### 1.5.5 Schickard's Calculator (1623)

Wilhelm Schickard, a professor at the University of Tubingen, Germany, built the first mechanical calculator in 1623. It could work with six digits, and carried digits across columns. It worked, but never made beyond the prototype stage.

### 1.5.6 Pascal's Calculator

Blaise Pascal (1623-1662) was a great French mathematician and was also the son of a mathematician and tax collector, Etienne Pascal. Blaise Pascal is most remembered among Computer Scientists as the inventor of the calculator.

In 1642, he presented this calculator his father to assist him. This calculator, called Pascaline, resembled the mechanical calculators used in 1940's. Pascal's Calculator is shown in ***Fig. 1.4.***

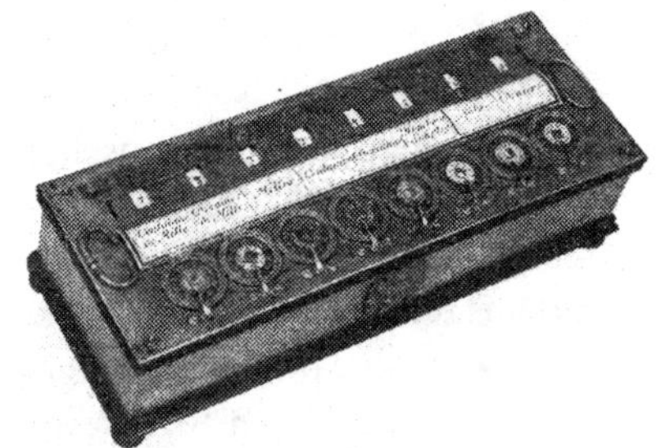

**Fig. 1.4:** Pascal's Calculator

It didn't end the contributions by Pascal. He also invented the syringe, the hydraulic press, and Pascal's law of pressure. Pascal built Pascaline based on the design described by Hero of Alexandria to add up the distance travelled by a carriage. The basic principle of his calculator is still used today in Water Meters and modern-day Odometers.

The automobile odometer is an example of a device that still uses a series of cogwheels to calculate data. Pascal's machine was improved by the philosopher and mathematician Leibnitz, whose "Wheel" could also perform multiplication and division. Leibnitz Wheel is shown in ***Fig. 1.5.***

**Fig. 1.5:** Leibnitz Wheel

### 1.5.7 Leibnitz's Steppard Reckoner

Leibnitz (1646-1716) was born in Saxony (now Germany). He was most associated with his contributions to Integral Calculus. In 1694, he invented the Steppard Reckoner. This was another calculator similar to that of Pascaline, except that this device used stepped cylinders, like a music box, rather than gears. Based on the decimal system this device could multiply and divide as well as add and subtract. Unfortunately, both this and the Pascaline were simple too complicated for mass production and so they remained one-of-a-kind.

### 1.5.8 Jacquard's Loom (1801)

Joseph Marie Jacquard (1752-1834) was born in Lyon, France. He was a stone mason and later a weaver. He introduced the Punched Card Loom in 1801. This device was a new type of loom for weaving cloth. Punched cards controlled its operation. Needles could pull threads through cards where there were holes and not where were no holes. Thus pattern were stored on punched-cards. The pattern woven by the loom was determined by the placement of holes in a control card - only those threads whose guiding hook encountered a hole in the card could enter the pattern is shown in ***Fig. 1.6.***

**Fig. 1.6:** Jacquard's Loom

### 1.5.9 Colmar's Arithmometer (1820)

Thomas de Colmar (1785-1870) invented his first Arithmometer in 1820. This was the first mass produced calculator. It did multiplication in much the same way as Stepped Reckoner but at the size of about a desktop was much smaller and easier to produce. With some assistance from the user could do division as well. This device was widely used, but the importance of it was the inspirations that it later caused.

### 1.5.10 Babbage's Difference Engine (1823)

Charles Babbage (1792-1871) realized in 1812 that many long computations consisted of operations that were regularly repeated. Following this, he designed a calculating machine called Difference Engine. Difference Engine is shown in ***Fig. 1.7.***

It is based on the principal that, for certain formulas, the difference between certain values is constant. A machine of this type was later adopted by insurance companies for computing life tables.

**Fig. 1.7:** Babbage's Difference Engine

### 1.5.11 Babbage's Analytical Engine (1833)

Charles Babbage (1792-1871) followed the difference engine with a much deeper and more general conception. This machine, never realized owing to the limited technology of the time, would have contained many features of present-day computers, including punched-card input, storage unit, arithmetic unit, printing unit, and control by a sequential program.

## 1.6 MIDDLE AGE (1890-1944)

In the Middle Age, all computing devices were electro-mechanical in nature. In other words, these worked mechanically with the help of electricity.

### 1.6.1 Hollerith's Tabulating Machine

The Middle Ages of data processing are said to have begun when Dr. Hollerith, a statistician with the U.S. Bureau of the Census, completed a set of machines to help process the results of the 1890 census. Using 3 by 5 inch punched cards to record the data, he consulted a box to sort the data and a manually fed, electromagnetic counting machine to tabulate the data. The 1890 census was processed in ¼ th time needed for the 1880 census. Hollerith left the Census Bureau to build and sell his own tabulating machines. His company was the forerunner of IBM Corporation. His successor at the Census Bureau, Dr. James Powers, also left to form his own company, which ultimately became Sperry Rand Corporation.

In 1908, Powers patented a 20-column punching machine. In the same year Hollerith developed a horizontal sorter whose rate was almost 275 cards per minute.

The speed and capabilities of punched-card machines continued to improve. Verifiers were invented to check that the right data were entered into the cards. Collators were invented to merge several sorted decks of cards into a single sorted deck. Electromechanical accounting machines were developed which could read cards containing both alphabetical and numerical data, perform simple arithmetic operations, and print the results.

**Fig. 1.8:** Dr. John Vincent Atanasoff

### 1.6.2 Atanasoff Berry Computer (ABC)

In 1939, Dr. John Vincent Atanasoff ***(Fig. 1.8),*** Professor of Iowa State University, and his student Mr. Berry assembled a prototype of the ABC to perform faster calculations.

A working model was launched by them in 1942.

## 1.7 MODERN AGE (SINCE 1944)

Computers changed over time; they improved in speed, power and efficiency. Those changes are recognized as a progression of generations of discoveries, each characterized by specific developments.

### 1.7.1 Mark I (1944)

Howard H. Aiken of Harvard University in 1937 designed a machine that could automatically perform a sequence of arithmetic operations and it was completed in 1944. It was named Mark I. It was an electromechanical (relay) device, like the calculators which preceded it. It contained 72 adding accumulators and 60 sets of switches for setting constants and was operated by means of switches, buttons, wire plugboards and punched tape. Information was represented by patterns of open and closed mechanical relays. It is, interesting to note that it measured 15 meter long, 2.4 meter high and 0.6 meter wide.

The average multiplication and division times were about 4 and 11 seconds respectively. The results were printed at the rate of one result per 5 seconds. The input and output were by punched cards and paper tapes. It is interesting to note that Dr. Aiken did not learn of Babbage's work until Mark I was completed.

## 1.8 COMPUTER GENERATIONS

The history of computer development is often referred to in reference to the different generations of computing devices. A generation refers to the state of improvement in the product development process. This term is also used in the different advancements of new computer technology. With each new generation, the circuitry has gotten smaller and more advanced than the previous generation before it. As a result of the miniaturization, speed, power, and computer memory has proportionally increased. New discoveries are constantly being developed that affect the way we live, work and play.

Each generation of computers is characterized by major technological development that fundamentally changed the way computers operate, resulting in increasingly smaller, cheaper, and more powerful and more efficient and reliable devices. Read about each generation and the developments that led to the current devices that we use today.

The tem generation indicates the type of technology used in the computer construction. As new technology was emerging, it was being used in the making of computer. The new technology improved the speed, accuracy and storage capacity of the computers. Different technologies have been used for computers in different times.

Therefore, computers can be divided into five generations depending upon the technologies used. **These are:**

1. First Generation (1946 – 1959)
2. Second Generation (1959 – 1965)
3. Third Generation (1965 – 1971)
4. Fourth Generation (1971- 1985)
5. Fifth Generation (1985 onwards)

### 1.8.1 FIRST GENERATION (1946-1959)

All subsequent computers after Mark I were all electronic. The early first-generation computers were powered by thousands of vacuum tubes. The first computers used vacuum tubes for circuitry and magnetic drums for memory, and were often enormous, taking up entire rooms. A magnetic drum, also referred to as drum, is a metal cylinder coated with magnetic iron-oxide material on which data and programs can be stored. Magnetic drums were once use as a primary storage device but have since been implemented as auxiliary storage devices.

The tracks on a magnetic drum are assigned to channels located around the circumference of the drum, forming adjacent circular bands that wind around the drum. A single drum can have up to 200 tracks. As the drum rotates at a speed of up to 3,000 rpm, the device's read/write heads deposit magnetized spots on the drum during the write operation and sense these spots during a read operation. This action is similar to that of a magnetic tape or disk drive.

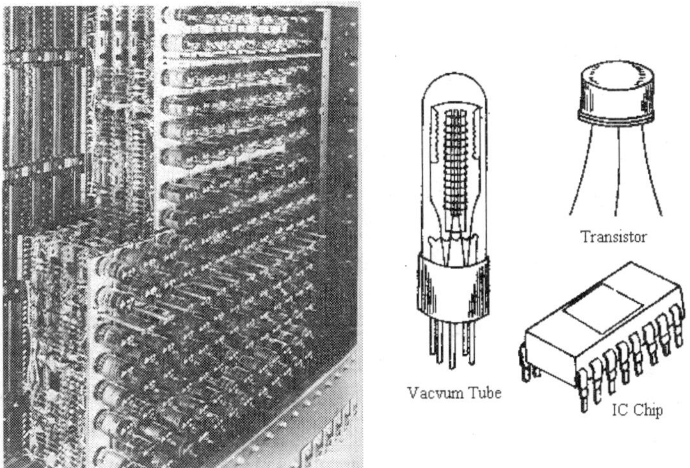


**Fig. 1.6:** Vacuum Tubes

They were very expensive to operate and in addition to using a great deal of electricity, generated a lot of heat, which was often the cause of malfunctions. First generation computers relied on machine language to perform operations, and they could only solve one problem at a time. Machine languages are the only languages understood by computers. While easily understood by computers, machine languages are almost impossible for humans to use because they consist entirely of numbers. Computer Programmers, therefore, use either **high level programming languages** or an assembly language programming. An assembly language contains the same instructions as a machine language, but the instructions and variables have names instead of being just numbers.

Programs written in high **level programming languages** retranslated into assembly language or machine language by a compiler. Assembly language program retranslated into machine language by a program called an assembler (assembly language compiler).

Every CPU has its own unique machine language. Programs must be rewritten or recompiled, therefore, to run on different types of computers. Input was based on punch card and paper tapes, and output was displayed on printouts.

## ENIAC

In 1946 John Mauchley and Presper Eckert developed Electronic Numerical Integrator and Calculator (ENIAC) at the Moore School of Electrical Engineering at the University of Pennsylvania. It was the first electronic calculator. It occupied a room measuring 9 meter × 15 meter and contained 18,000 vacuum tubes, 1500 relays and weighed 30 tons. Programs were loaded into the machine by a system of changing wired plugboards and using a series of manual switches. ENIAC performed 5000 additions per second. Credit for inventions relating to the electronic implementations of the ENIAC computer was disputed till 1974. A US Court later ruled that Mr. John Vincent Atanasoff, a former Professor of Iowa State College was the originator of the important new concepts.that led to the design of ENIAC. The Court concluded that Dr. Mauchley visited Mr. Atanasoff and visited the computer which he assembled in 1942 and got important ideas for the design of ENIAC.

## EDVAC

The Moore School and Ballistics Research Laboratory of US Army built the computer Electronic Discrete Variable Automatic Computer (EDVAC) which was based on John Von Neumann's ***(Fig. 1.9)*** ideas. Neumann was the first to introduce in mid-1940s the ***'Stored Program Concept'*** in the computer. EDVAC's storage capacity was 1024 words each of 44 bits each.

There was also an auxiliary storage of 20,000 words. The access time of primary storage varied between 0.48 to 384 ms. In the EDVAC, the computer program was fed into the storage unit by means of punched paper tape. The first program for EDVAC was written by John Von Neumann, which was a routine to arrange numbers in ascending order. Thus he showed that computers can be used for non-scientific computations.

**Fig. 1.9:** John Von Numann

## EDSAC

Another computer using internal storage, called Electronic Delay Storage Automatic Computer (EDSAC) was developed in 1949 at the University of Manchester (UK). EDSAC was of some significance since it was the first computer to contain a changeable program of instructions within its own memory.

## UNIVAC I

UNIVAC I and other similar computers were large because of the massive number of tubes required to operate the machines. The tubes themselves were large; they required a lot of energy and generated a great deal of heat. The computer's memory was stored on magnetic storage devices primarily magnetic tapes and magnetic drums. UNIVAC I is shown in ***Fig. 1.10.***

Most of the data were entered into the computer on punched cards similar to Jacquard's loom process. Output consisted of punched cards on paper, and machine and assembly languages were used to program the computers. however, a human operator physically had to reset relay switches and wiring before a program could be run.

**Fig. 1.10:** UNIVAC I

### Characteristics of First Generation

- Vacuum tubes
- Magnetic tape and magnetic drum for external storage
- Punched cards for input

- Punched cards and paper for output
- Machine and assembly languages
- Human operators to set switches

**Examples:** UNIVAC I, UNIVAC II, Datamatic 100, EDSAC, Burrough 2202, etc.

## Advantages

The main advantages of first-generation computers were:

1. These computers were the fastest of their time.
2. They were programmed using machine language.
3. The electronic digital computers were introduced due to the vacuum tube technology.

## Disadvantages

The main disadvantages of first-generation computers were:

1. Very big in size
2. Not reliable
3. Consumed large amount of energy
4. Constant maintenance required
5. More heat generated and air-conditioning was required
6. More costly
7. Very slow in speed (data processing)
8. It was difficult to programmed, because they used only machine language
9. Non-portable
10. Limited commercial use

## 1.8.2 SECOND GENERATION (1959-1965)

Transistors replaced vacuum tubes and ushered in the second generation computer. Transistor is a device composed of semiconductor material that amplifies a signal or opens or closes a circuit. Invented in 1947 at Bell Labs, transistors have become the key ingredient of all digital circuits, including computers. Today's **latest microprocessor** contains tens of millions of microscopic transistors.

Prior to the invention of transistors, digital circuits were composed of vacuum tubes, which had many disadvantages. They were much larger, required more energy, dissipated more heat, and were more prone to failures. It's safe to say that without the invention of transistors, computing as we know it today would not be possible.

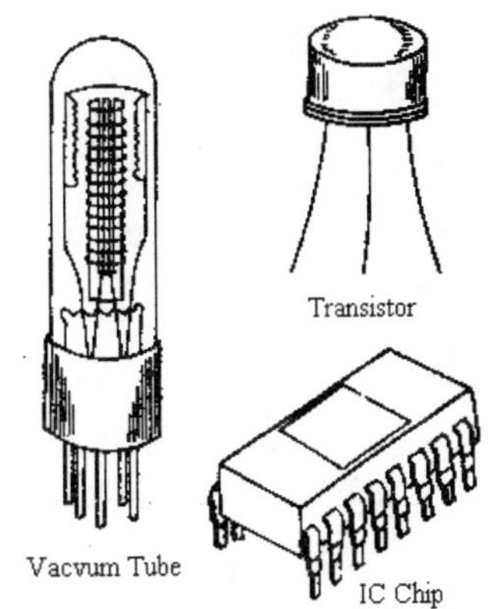

**Fig. 1.7:** Transistors

The transistor was invented in 1947 but did not see widespread use in computers until the late 50s. The transistor was far superior to the vacuum tube, allowing computers to become smaller, faster, cheaper, more energy-efficient and more reliable than their first-generation predecessors. Though the transistor still generated a great deal of heat that subjected the computer to damage, it was a vast improvement over the vacuum tube. Second-generation computers still relied on punched cards for input and printouts for output.

Second-generation computers moved from cryptic binary machine language to symbolic, or assembly, languages, which allowed programmers to specify instructions in words. High-level programming languages were also being developed at this time, such as early versions of COBOL and FORTRAN. These were also the first computers that stored their instructions in their memory, which moved from a magnetic drum to magnetic core technology.

The first computers of this generation were developed for the atomic energy industry.

## Characteristics of Second Generation

- Transistors
- Magnetic-core storage
- Magnetic tape and magnetic disk for external storage
- Punched cards and magnetic tape for input
- Punched cards and paper for output
- High-level languages- FORTRAN, COBOL, PL/I, BASIC and others
- Human operators to handle cards

**Examples:** Honeywell 200-, 400-, 800-series, IBM 7070/7080, CDC 1604, Burrough B5000 series, etc.

## Advantages

The main advantages of second-generation computers as compared to first-generation computers are:

1. Low in cost
2. Smaller in size
3. Fast in speed
4. Less heat generated More reliable and accurate in calculations
5. Consume low power etc.
6. Used for commercial purposes
7. Portable
8. Assembly language was introduced. This language is easy to write program than machine language

## Disadvantages

The main disadvantages of this generation computers were:

1. Air-conditioning required
2. Commercial production was difficult and these were very costly
3. Constant (or frequent) maintenance required
4. Only used for special purposes

## 1.8.3 THIRD GENERATION (1965-1971)

During this time integrated circuits with transistors, resistors, and capacitors were etched onto a piece of silicon. This reduced the price and size of computers, adding to a general trend in the computer industry of miniaturization. The development of the integrated circuit was the hallmark of the third generation of computers. Transistors were miniaturized and placed on silicon chips, called semiconductors, which drastically increased the speed and efficiency of computers.

A non-metallic chemical element in the carbon family of elements, Silicon - atomic symbol "Si" - is the second most abundant element in the earth's crust, surpassed only by oxygen. Silicon does not occur un-combined in nature. Sand and almost all rocks contain silicon combined with oxygen, forming silica. When silicon combines with other elements, such as iron, aluminium or potassium, a silicate is formed. Compounds of silicon also occur in the atmosphere, natural waters, and many plants and in the bodies of some animals.

Silicon is the basic material used to make computer chips, transistors, silicon diodes and other electronic circuits and switching devices because its atomic structure makes the element an ideal semiconductor. Silicon is commonly doped, or mixed, with other elements, such as boron, phosphorous and arsenic, to alter its conductive properties.

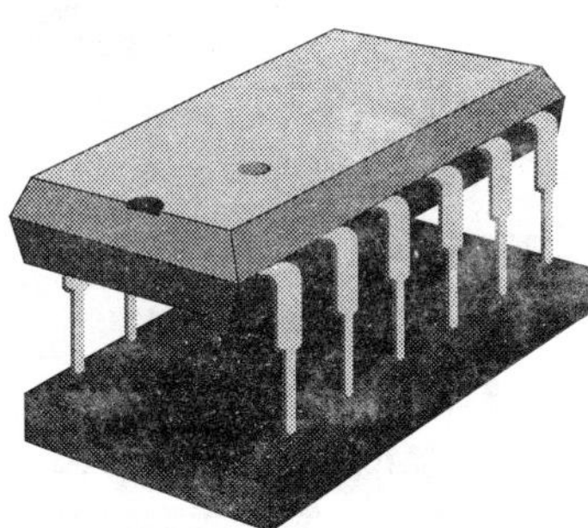

**Fig. 1.8:** Integrated Circuits

A chip is a small piece of semi conducting material (usually silicon) on which an integrated circuit is embedded. A typical chip is less than ¼-square inches and can contain millions of electronic components (transistors). Computers consist of many chips placed on electronic boards called printed circuit boards. There are different types of chips. For example, CPU chips (also called microprocessors) contain an entire processing unit, whereas memory chips contain blank memory.

Semiconductor is a material that is neither a good conductor of electricity (like copper) nor a good insulator (like rubber). The most common semiconductor materials are silicon and germanium. These materials are then doped to create an excess or lack of electrons.

Computer chips, both for CPU and memory, are composed of semiconductor materials. Semiconductors make it possible to miniaturize electronic components, such as transistors. Not only does miniaturization mean that the components take up less space, it also means that they are faster and require less energy.

Digital Equipment Corporation (DEC) introduced the Programmed Data Processor- 1 (PDP-1), which can be called the first minicomputer due to its relatively small size. It is classified as a third generation computer because of the way it was built, even though it was made before 1965. The PDP-1 was also the computer that ran the very first video game, called Spacewar.

The software industry came into existence in the mid 1970's as companies formed to write programs that would satisfy the increasing number of computer users. Computers were being used everywhere in business, government, military, and education environments. Because of the target market, the first software companies mostly offered accounting and statistical programs. This time period also had the first set of computing standards created for compatibility between systems.

E-mail originated sometime between 1961 and 1966, allowing computer users to send messages to each other as long as they were connected through a network. This is closely tied to the work that was being done on Advanced Research Projects Agency Network (ARPANET), networking technology and innovation that would one day bring the internet.

Fig. 1.9: 3rd Generation Computer (DEC's Program Data Processor)

## Characteristics of Third Generation

- Integrated circuits
- Improved disk storage
- Monitors and keyboards for input and output
- More high-level languages, including RPG and Pascal
- First complete operating system meant less involvement for human operators
- Family of computers introduced allowing compatibility
- Minicomputers used commercially
- **Examples:** IBM System/360, IBM System/370, Burrough 5700/6700, PDP-8 Series, PDP-11 Series, etc.

## Advantages

The main advantages of third-generation as compared to previous generations of computers were:

1. Smaller in size
2. Production cost was low
3. Very fast in computational power
4. More reliable
5. Low power consumption
6. Maintenance cost was low because failure rate of hardware was very low
7. Magnetic disk, used for external storage
8. More storage capacity
9. Easily portable
10. Easy to operate

11. Upgraded easily
12. Widely used for various commercial applications all over the world
13. Lower heat generated
14. High-level languages were commonly used
15. Many input/output devices were introduced such as mouse and keyboard etc.

### Disadvantages

The main disadvantages of third-generation computers were:

1. Air-conditioning required
2. Highly sophisticated technology required for the manufacturer chips

### Distinct Feature

Instead of punched cards and printouts, users interacted with third generation computers through keyboards and monitors and interfaced with an operating system, which allowed the device to run many different applications at one time with a central program that monitored the memory. Computers for the first time became accessible to a mass audience because they were smaller and cheaper than their predecessors.

## 1.8.4 FOURTH GENERATION (1971-1985)

The microprocessor brought the fourth generation of computers, as thousands of integrated circuits we rebuilt onto a single silicon chip. A silicon chip contained a CPU. In the world of personal computers, the terms microprocessor and CPU are used interchangeably. At the heart of all personal computers and most workstations sits a microprocessor.

Microprocessors also control the logic of almost all digital devices, from clock radios to fuel-injection systems for automobiles.

### Three basic characteristics differentiate microprocessors:

- **Instruction Set:** The set of instructions that the microprocessor can execute.
- **Bandwidth:** The number of bits processed in a single instruction.
- **Clock Speed:** Given in megahertz (MHz), the clock speed determines how many instructions per second the processor can execute.

**Fig. 1.10:** Microprocessor

In both cases, the higher the value, the more powerful the CPU. For example, a 32-bit microprocessor that runs at 50MHz is more powerful than a 16-bitmicroprocessor that runs at 25MHz. What in the first generation filled an entire room could now fit in the palm of the hand. The Intel 4004chip, developed in 1971, located all the components of the computer - from the central processing unit and memory to input/output controls - on a single chip.

Abbreviation of central processing unit, and pronounced as separate letters. The CPU is the brains of the computer. Sometimes referred to simply as the processor or central processor, the CPU is where most calculations take place. In terms of computing power, the CPU is the most important element of a computer system.

On large machines, CPUs require one or more printed circuit boards. On personal computers and small workstations, the CPU is housed in a single chip called a microprocessor.

### Two typical components of a CPU are:

- The arithmetic logic unit (ALU), which performs arithmetic and logical operations.
- The control unit, which extracts instructions from memory and decodes and executes them, calling on the ALU when necessary.

In 1981 IBM introduced its first computer for the home user, and in 1984 Apple introduced the Macintosh. Microprocessors also moved out of the realm of desktop computers and into many areas of life as more and more everyday products began to use microprocessors.

Computer technology had advanced so rapidly that computers could fit in something the size of a typewriter. These were called microcomputers, the first one being the Altair 8800. Many people acknowledge the Altair 8800 as the computer that sparked the modern computer revolution, especially since Bill Gates and Paul Allen founded Microsoft with a programming language called Altair BASIC–made specifically for the 8800.

A small company called Apple Computer, Inc. was established in 1976 and single handedly changed the industry forever. Steve Wozniak and Steve Jobs began to sell their Apple 1 computer that same year, and it quickly gained popularity. It came with a keyboard and only required a monitor to be plugged into the back of the system, which was a novel idea for computers at that time. The Apple II was released the next year and was the first mass produced microcomputer to be commercially sold, and also ushered in the era of personal computing.

In 1981, Microsoft Disk Operating System (MS-DOS) was released to run on the Intel 8086 microprocessor. Over the next few years MS-DOS became the most popular operating system in the world, eventually leading to Microsoft Windows 1.0 being released in 1985. In 1984 Apple introduced their Mac OS, which was the first operating system to be completely graphical. Both Mac OS and Windows used pull-down menus, icons, and windows to make computing more user-friendly. Computers were now being controlled with a mouse as well as keyboard. The first mouse was developed in 1981 by Xerox.

Software became much more common and diverse during this period with the development of spreadsheets, databases, and drawing programs. Computer networks and e-mail became much more prevalent as well.

The first truly portable computer, called the Osborne 1, was released in 1981. Portable computers like the TRS-80 Model 100 / 102 and IBM 5155 followed afterward.

Not all the computers of the time were small, of course. There were still being supercomputers built with the aim of being as fast as possible. These supercomputers were sold to companies, universities, and the military. An example of one such supercomputer is the Cray-1, which was released in 1976 by Cray Research. It became one of the best known and most successful supercomputers ever for its unique design and fast speed of 250 MFLOPS.

This generation was also important for the development of embedded systems. These are special systems, usually very tiny, that have computers inside to control their operation. These embedded systems were put into things like cars, thermostats, microwave ovens, wristwatches, and more.

As these small computers became more powerful, they could be linked together to form networks, which eventually led to the development of the Internet. Fourth generation computers also saw the development of GUI's, the mouse and handheld devices.

### Characteristics of Fourth Generation

- LSI and VLSI
- Magnetic disk most common external storage
- Introduction of microcomputers
- Fourth-generation languages (4GLs) emerged and application software for microcomputers became popular
- Microcomputers used - Compaq Deskpro 386
- Typical examples: Burroughs B7700 and HP 3000 minicomputers

### Advantages

The advantages of fourth-generation as compared to previous generation computers are:

1. Smaller in size
2. Production cost is very low
3. Very reliable
4. Hardware failure is negligible
5. Easily portable because of their small size
6. Totally general purpose
7. Air conditioning is not compulsory
8. Very high processing speed
9. Very large internal and external storage capacity
10. Used advanced input & output devices such as optical readers, laser printers, CD-ROM/DVD-ROM drives etc.

### Disadvantages

The main disadvantage of fourth-generation computers is:

1. Highly sophisticated technology required for the manufacturer of microprocessor chips.

## 1.8.5 FIFTH GENERATION (Beyond 1985 and till-date)

The changes that have occurred since 1985 are plentiful. Computers have got tinier, more reliable, and many times faster. Computers are mostly built using components from many different corporations. For this reason, it is easier to focus on specific component advancements. Intel and AMD are the main computer processor companies in the world today and are constant rivals. There are many different personal computer companies that usually sell their hardware with a Microsoft Windows operating system preinstalled. Apple has a wide line of hardware and software as well. Computer graphics have got very powerful and are able to display full three dimensional graphics at high resolution. Nvidia and ATI are two companies in constant battle with one another to be the computer graphics hardware king.

The software industry has grown a lot as well, offering all kinds of programs for almost anything you can think of. Microsoft Windows still dominates the operating system scene. In 1995 Microsoft released Windows 95, an operating system that catapulted them to a new level of dominance. In 1999 Apple revamped its operating system with the release of Mac OS X. In 1991 Linus Torvalds wrote the Linux kernel that has since spawned countless open source operating systems and open source software.

Computers have become more and more online orientated in modern times, especially with the development of the World Wide Web. Popular companies like Google and Yahoo! were started because of the internet.

In 2008 the IBM Roadrunner was introduced as the fastest computer in the world at 1.026 PFLOPS. Fast supercomputers aid in the production of movie special effects and the making of computer animated movies.

**Fig. 1.11:** 5th Generation Computer (Powerful Laptop)

Fifth generation computing devices, based on artificial intelligence, are still in development, though there are some applications, such as voice recognition, that are being used today. Artificial Intelligence is the branch of computer science concerned with making computers behave like humans. The term was coined in 1956 by John McCarthy at the Massachusetts Institute of Technology.

## Artificial intelligence includes:

- **Games Playing:** programming computers to play games such as chess and checkers.
- **Expert Systems:** programming computers to make decisions in real-life situations (for example, some expert systems help doctors diagnose diseases based on symptoms).
- **Natural Language:** programming computers to understand natural human languages.
- **Neural Networks:** Systems that simulate intelligence by attempting to reproduce the types of physical connections that occur in animal brains.
- **Robotics:** programming computers to see and hear and react to other sensory stimuli.

## Characteristics of Fifth Generation

- Development of true artificial intelligence
- Development of Natural Language Processing
- Advancement in Parallel Processing
- Advancement in Superconductor Technology

Currently, no computers exhibit full artificial intelligence (that is, are able to simulate human behaviour). The greatest advances have occurred in the field of games playing. The best computer chess programs are now capable of beating humans. In May, 1997, an IBM super-computer called Deep Blue defeated world chess champion Gary Kasparov in a chess match.

In the area of robotics, computers are now widely used in assembly plants, but they are capable only of very limited tasks. Robots have great difficulty identifying objects based on appearance or feel, and they still move and handle objects clumsily.

**Fig 1.12:** Artificial Intelligence

Natural-language processing offers the greatest potential rewards because it would allow people to interact with computers without needing any specialized knowledge. You could simply walk up to a computer and talk to it. Unfortunately, programming computers to understand natural languages has proved to be more difficult than originally thought. Some rudimentary translation systems that translate from one human language to another are in existence, but they are not nearly as good as human translators.

There are also voice recognition systems that can convert spoken sounds into written words, but they do not understand what they are writing; they simply take dictation. Even these systems are quite limited -- you must speak slowly and distinctly.

In the early 1980s, expert systems were believed to represent the future of artificial intelligence and of computers in general. To date, however, they have not lived up to expectations. Many expert systems help human experts in such fields as medicine and engineering, but they are very expensive to produce and are helpful only in special situations.

Today, the hottest area of artificial intelligence is neural networks, which are proving successful in a number of disciplines such as voice recognition and natural-language processing.

There are several programming languages that are known as AI languages because they are used almost exclusively for AI applications. The two most common are LISP and Prolog.

Few major projects of 5th generation computers include the following:

- **ICOT Project in Japan:** The Japanese ICOT project is regarded as a critical element in Japan's industrial performance. A central institute ICOT has been set up where basic research takes place. Advances in architecture are intended to lead to the development of parallel inference computers for the next phase of the research.
- **MCC Project in USA:** In order to keep up with the Japanese program, a group of IT corporations in the USA have set up the MCC (Microelectronic and Computer Technology Corporation). The MCC carries out research and advanced product development, and makes the results available to sponsor corporations for implementation. The sponsors include Digital Equipment Corporation (DEC), National Cash Register (NCR) and chip manufacturers Motorola and National Semiconductor.

- **DARPA Project in USA:** Much of the 5th generation research and development is being co-ordinated by the Defence Advanced Research Project Agency (DARPA). This agency allocates US Government funds to IT projects with the actual or potential military applications.
- **Espirit Initiative EC:** The Espirit program is the EC's response to the Japanese 5th generation initiative. It has a small central directorate, which sponsors projects carried out by consortia of corporations and universities in EC countries. The Espirit program is likely to merge into the wider EUREKA initiative, which aims to co-ordinate research and development in a number of high-technology fields.
- **Alvey Program in Britain:** The Alvey is the advanced Information Technology (IT) program in UK and has a central directorate which allocates state funds covering up to 50 % of the cost of approved projects. The program is centred on four key enabling technologies:
  - Software Engineering
  - VLSI Chip Architecture
  - Intelligent Knowledge Based Systems
  - Intelligent User Interfaces.

Fifth generation computers are supposed to be the ideal computers. The scientists are working to design such computers that will have the following features.

1. Having their own thinking power
2. Making decisions themselves
3. Having capabilities of learning
4. Having capabilities of reasoning
5. Having large capacity of internal storage
6. Having extra high processing speed
7. Having capabilities of parallel processing

### In these computers following technologies will be used:

- ULSIC (Ultra Large Scale Integrated Circuits) technology
- Artificial Intelligence (AI) technology also called the knowledge Processor. The AI means automatic programs that let the machines to think and decide themselves. The programming languages LISP (List Processor) and PROLOG (Programming with Logic) are used for artificial intelligence. The scientists at ICOT in Japan use the PROLOG to develop the Artificial Intelligence software.

## 1.9 EVOLUTION OF COMPUTING SYSTEMS

Computers have evolved from the fundamental principles of mathematical calculation and language processing. The computing systems of today are an outcome of the efforts and intellect of mathematicians, logicians, linguists and technologists from all over the world. Computer history comprises the evolutionary journey of computing systems, the timeline of operating systems as well as the history behind the development of a wide variety of computer software and hardware.

Here is a brief overview of the progress of computing technology from early days right up to the modern-day digital portable computers.

**Table 1.1:** 1940s Computing Systems

**1939 | Hewlett-Packard is founded in California**

Their first product was the popular HP 200A Audio Oscillator, used as sound effects generators for Walt Disney Pictures movie "Fantasia."

**1940 | Complex Number Calculator (CNC)**

Designed by researcher George Stibitz and completed by Bell Telephone Laboratories.

**1941 | Z3 computer / Bombe**

The Z3 was built by German engineer Konrad Zuse in complete isolation from developments elsewhere.
The Bombe was used to decrypt Nazi Military communications

**1942 | Atanasoff-Berry Computer (ABC)**

The ABC was designed and built by Professor John Vincent Atanasoff and graduate student Cliff Berry at Iowa State College

**1943 | Project Whirlwind / Relay Interpolator**

Project Whirlwind was a simulator to train bomber crews.
The Relay Interceptor assisted in testing its M-9 Gun Director.

**1944 | Harvard Mark-1 / Colossus**

The Harvard Mark-1 was a room-sized, relay-based calculator.
The Colossus was designed to break the complex Lorenz ciphers used by the Nazis during WWII.

**1945 | "First Draft of a Report on the EDVAC"**

Outlined the architecture of a stored-program computer, which would lead to the mainstream computers we know today.

**1946 | ENIAC / AVIDAC**

The ENIAC improved by 1,000 times on the speed of its contemporaries.

**1948 | IBM SSEC**

The Selective Sequence Electronic Calculator produced the moon-position tables used for plotting the course of the 1969 Apollo flight to the moon.

**1949 | EDSAC / Manchester Mark I**

The first practical stored-program computer.
The Manchester Mark I computer functioned as a complete system using the Williams tube for memory.

**Table 1.2:** 1950s Computing Systems

**1950 | ERA 1101 / SEAC / Pilot ACE**

ERA 1101 was the first commercially produced computer.
SEAC was the first computer to use all-diode logic.
Alan Turing's philosophy directed design of Britain's Pilot ACE

**1951 | MIT Whirlwind**

The first computer with a reliable OS, running 35 hours a week at 90-percent utility using an electrostatic tube memory.

**1951 | LEO / UNIVAC I**

Leo, England's first commercial computer, solved clerical problems. UNIVAC I, used by U.S. Census Bureau, was the first commercial computer to attract widespread public attention.

**1952 | MANIAC**

Based on John von Neumann's IAS computer at the Institute for Advanced Studies in Princeton, N.J.

**1953 | IBM 701**

IBM shipped its first electronic computer, the 701.

**1954 | IBM 650**

The IBM 650 magnetic drum calculator established itself as the first mass-produced computer, selling 450 in one year.

**1956 | MIT TX0**

The first general-purpose, programmable computer built at MIT with transistors.

**1958 | SAGE**

Semi-Automatic Ground Environment — linked hundreds of radar stations in the United States and Canada in the first large-scale computer communications network.

**1958 | NEAC 1101**

Japan's NEC builds the country's first electronic computer

**1959 | IBM STRETCH**

IBM's 7000 series mainframes were the company's first transistorized computers.

**Table 1.3:** 1960s Computing Systems

**1960 | DEC PDP-1**
The precursor to the minicomputer.

**1961 | IBM 1401**
The 1401 mainframe replaced the vacuum tube with smaller, more reliable transistors and used a magnetic core memory.

**1962 | LINC (Laboratory Instrumentation Computer)**
The first real time laboratory data processing machine.

**1964 | IBM System 360**
A family of six mutually compatible computers and 40 peripherals that could work together.

**1964 | CDC 6600**
The fastest computer of its time performed up to 3 million instructions per second - three times faster than the IBM Stretch.

**1965 | DEC PDP-8**
The first commercially successful minicomputer.

**1966 | ILLIAC IV**
The first large-scale array computer.

**1966 | HP-2115**
Hewlett-Packard entered the general purpose computer business with its HP-2115.

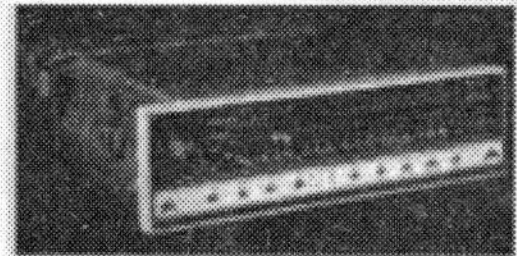

**1968 | Nova**
The Nova is introduced, with 32 kilobytes of memory, for $8,000.

**1968 | Apollo Guidance Computer**
The Apollo Guidance Computer made its debut orbiting the Earth on Apollo 7.

**Table 1.4:** 1970s Computing Systems

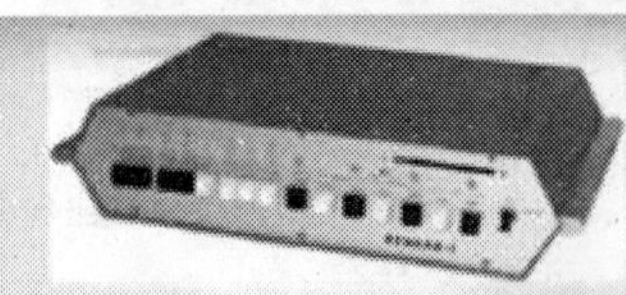

**1971 | Kenback 1**

The first personal computer, advertised for $750 in Scientific American.

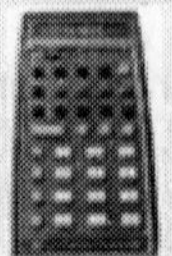

**1972 | HP-35**

The HP-35 was a fast, extremely accurate electronic slide rule with a solid-state memory similar to that of a computer.

**1973 | TV Typewriter / Micral**

The first display of alphanumeric text on an ordinary television set. The Micral was the earliest commercial, non-kit personal computer based on a micro-processor.

**1974 | Xerox Alto / Scelbi 8H**

The first work station with a built-in mouse for input. The first commercially advertised U.S. computer based on a micro-processor

**1975 | MITS Altair / Tandem-16**

The Altair was based on Intel´s 8080 microprocessor, and ran on BASIC. The Tandem was the first fault-tolerant computer, for online transaction processing.

**1976 | Apple I / Cray I**

Steve Wozniak designed the Apple I, later selling it with Steve Jobs. The Cray I was the first commercially successful vector processor.

**1977 | Commodore PET**

The Commodore Personal Electronic Transactor was the first of several personal computers released in 1977.

**1977 | Apple II / TRS-80**

The Apple II became an instant success when released in 1977. The TRS-80 was Tandy Radio Shack´s first desktop computer.

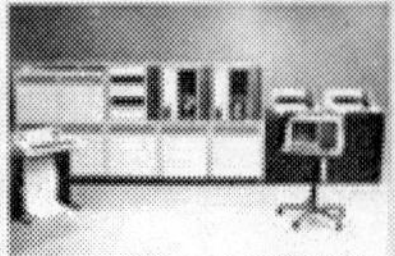

**1978 | VAX 11/780**

The VAX 11/780 had the ability to address up to 4.3 gigabytes of virtual memory, 100 times the capacity of most minicomputers.

**1979 | Atari 400 and 800**

Atari introduces the Model 400 and 800 Computers with gaming abilities.

**Table 1.5:** 1980s Computing Systems

**Table 1.6:** 1990s Computing Systems

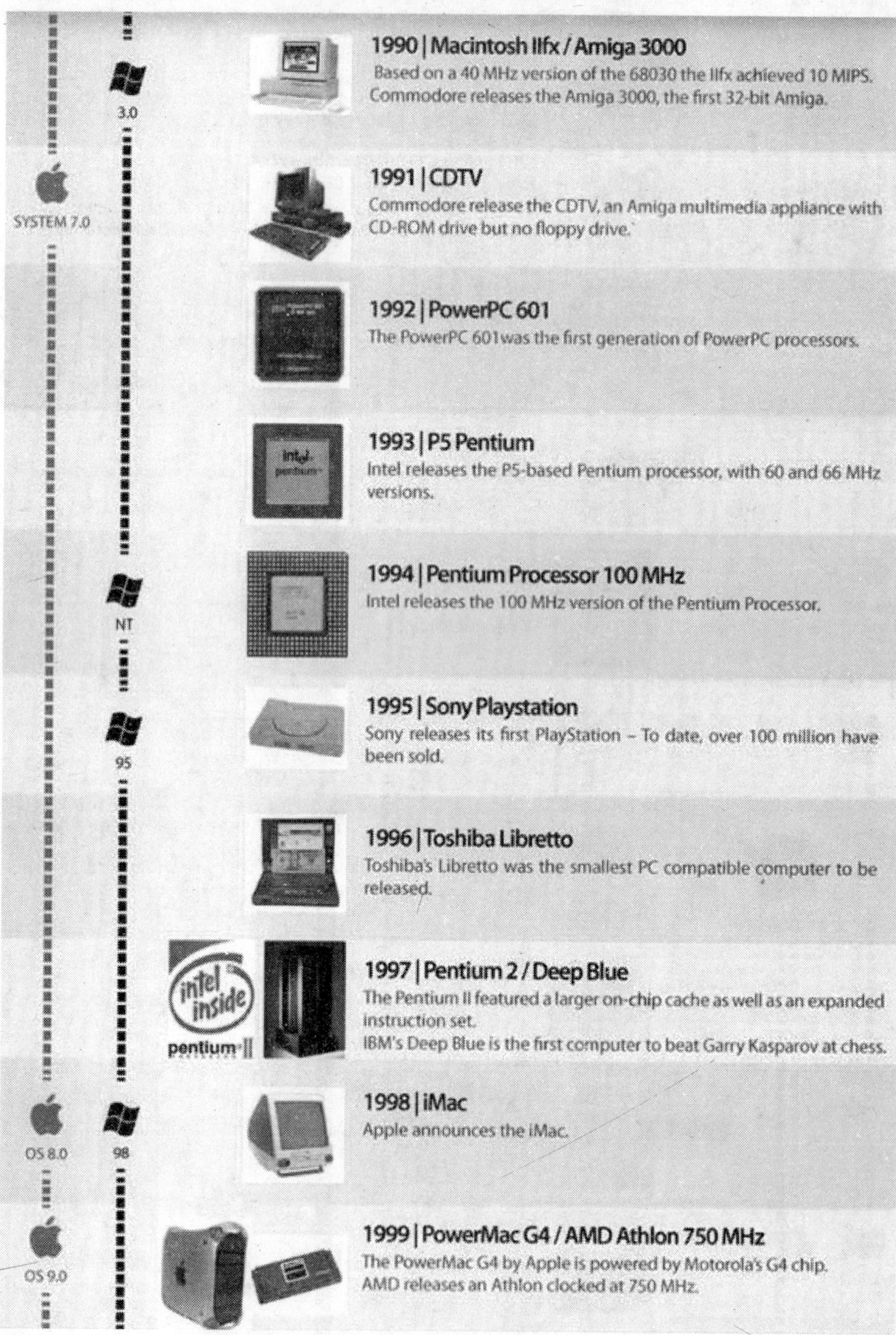

**1990 | Macintosh IIfx / Amiga 3000**
Based on a 40 MHz version of the 68030 the IIfx achieved 10 MIPS. Commodore releases the Amiga 3000, the first 32-bit Amiga.

**1991 | CDTV**
Commodore release the CDTV, an Amiga multimedia appliance with CD-ROM drive but no floppy drive.

**1992 | PowerPC 601**
The PowerPC 601was the first generation of PowerPC processors.

**1993 | P5 Pentium**
Intel releases the P5-based Pentium processor, with 60 and 66 MHz versions.

**1994 | Pentium Processor 100 MHz**
Intel releases the 100 MHz version of the Pentium Processor.

**1995 | Sony Playstation**
Sony releases its first PlayStation – To date, over 100 million have been sold.

**1996 | Toshiba Libretto**
Toshiba's Libretto was the smallest PC compatible computer to be released.

**1997 | Pentium 2 / Deep Blue**
The Pentium II featured a larger on-chip cache as well as an expanded instruction set.
IBM's Deep Blue is the first computer to beat Garry Kasparov at chess.

**1998 | iMac**
Apple announces the iMac.

**1999 | PowerMac G4 / AMD Athlon 750 MHz**
The PowerMac G4 by Apple is powered by Motorola's G4 chip.
AMD releases an Athlon clocked at 750 MHz.

**Table 1.7:** 2000s Computing Systems

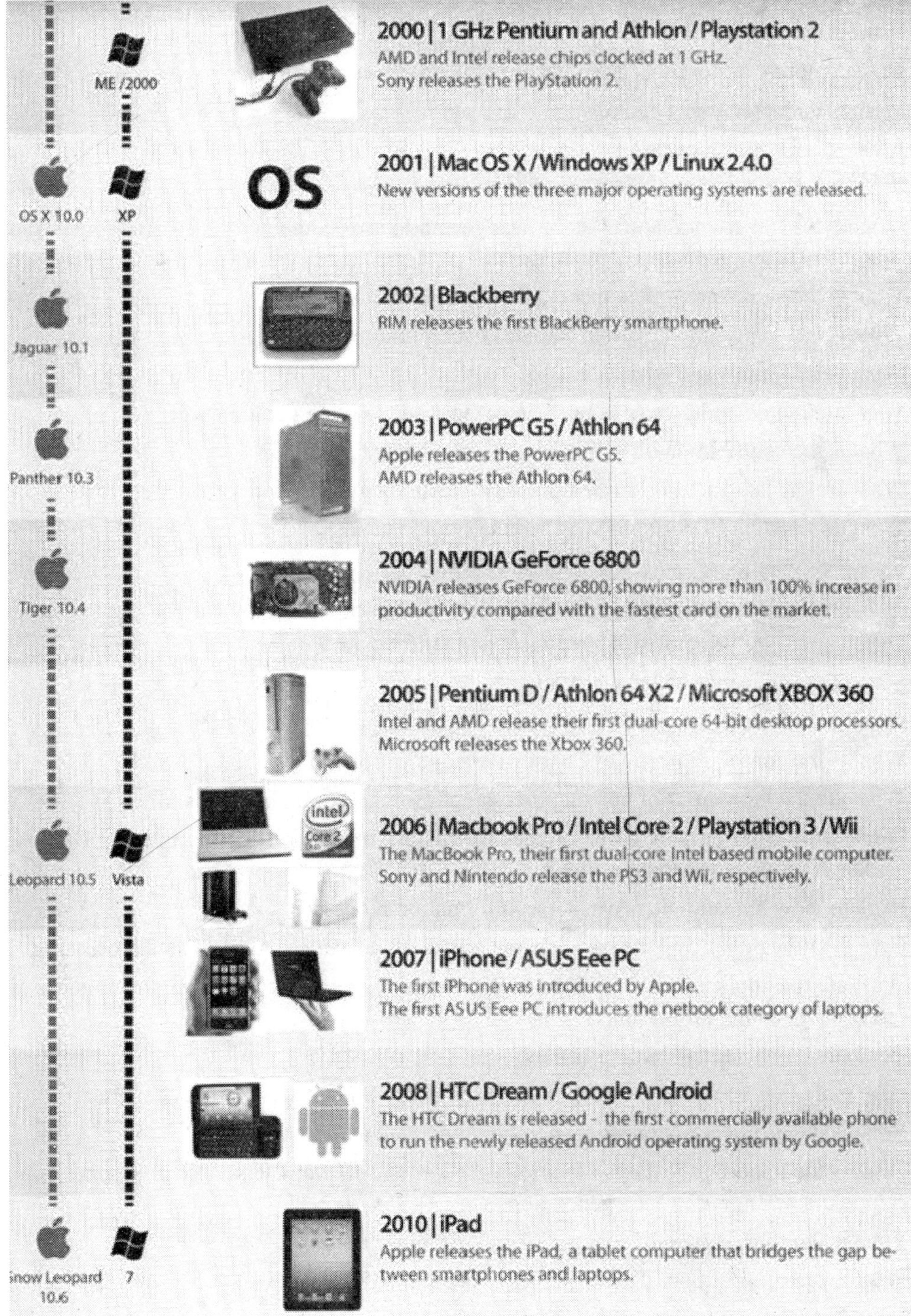

## EXERCISE

1. What is data processing?
2. How computer system acts as an information processing system?
3. What is data processing cycle?
4. What is information cycle?
5. What are different stages of information processing cycle?
6. Discuss the important features of various generations of computers. Also give some examples of computers belonging to each generation.
7. What is the stored program concept? Why is it important?
8. What is the contribution of John Napier to computing?
9. What is an Abacus and what is its use?
10. Why are microcomputers so popular in comparison to other computers?
11. What is the contribution of Blaise Pascal and what is Pascaline?
12. What are the latest trends in microprocessor technology? Explain.
13. What do ENIAC, EDSAC, EDVAC and UNIVAC stand for?
14. State the evolutionary stages of data processing.
15. State the contribution(s) due to John Von Neumann.
16. Differentiate the principles of Analytical and Differential Engine.
17. State the significance of Jacquard Loom?
18. Detail out the description of Mark I electromechanical computer.
19. What is the contribution due to Charles Babbage? Explain.
20. What are the limitations of human processing? How these can be removed?
21. Discuss the basis on which one divides the history of data processing into the Dark Ages, the Middle Ages and the Modern Ages.
22. Explain, how human-beings can act as information processor?
23. Give the time period and the basic characteristic of the Middle Ages of data processing.
24. What are the implications for information systems design of the statement that humans are serial rather than parallel processors?
25. Compare computer and human-beings.
26. Give three major innovations of 1st - , 2nd -, 3rd -, 4th - and 5th -generation computers.
27. What is the difference between a microcomputer and a microprocessor?
28. Discuss the important features of various generations of computers. Also give some examples of computers belonging to each generation.
29. What is the stored program concept? Why is it important?
30. What is the contribution of John Napier to computing?
31. How do analog computers differ digital computers?

32. State the criteria for classification of digital computers.
33. Is digital computer more accurate than analog computer? Justify your answer.
34. What are the operations that a computer is able to perform?
35. What is an Abacus and what is its use?
36. Why are microcomputers so popular in comparison to other computers?
37. What is a digital computer? Provide its anatomy and explain the functioning of such a computer through its block diagram.
38. What is the contribution of Blaise Pascal and what is Pascaline?
39. What are the latest trends in microprocessor technology? Explain.
40. What do ENIAC, EDSAC, EDVAC and UNIVAC stand for?
41. State the evolutionary stages of data processing.
42. State the contribution(s) due to John Von Neumann.
43. Differentiate the principles of Analytical and Differential Engine.
44. State the significance of Jacquard Loom?
45. Why should we go for computers?
46. Detail out the description of Mark I electromechanical computer.
47. What is the contribution due to Charles Babbage? Explain.
48. Comment on how computers are changing our traditional patterns of recreation.
49. What are different types of portable computers?
50. In terms of physical size, how are PCs categorised?
51. What is the difference between a microcomputer and minicomputer?
52. What are the limitations of human processing? How these can be removed?
53. Discuss the basis on which one divides the history of data processing into the Dark Ages, the Middle Ages and the Modern Ages.
54. Give the time period and the basic characteristic of the Middle Ages of data processing.
55. What are the implications for information systems design of the statement that humans are serial rather than parallel processors?
56. Compare computer and human-beings.
57. Give three major innovations of $1^{st}$ - , $2^{nd}$ -, $3^{rd}$ -, $4^{th}$ - and $5^{th}$ -generation computers.

CHAPTER 2

# Computers and Their Classification

## 2.1 INTRODUCTION

Let us begin with the word 'compute', which means 'to calculate'. We all are familiar with calculations in our day to day life. We apply mathematical operations like addition, subtraction, multiplication, etc. and many other formulae for calculations. Simpler calculations take less time but complex calculations take much longer time. Another factor is accuracy in calculations. So man explored the idea to develop a machine which can perform this type of arithmetic calculation faster and with full accuracy. This gave birth to a device or machine called **'computer'**.

## 2.2 COMPUTER

The ***computer*** we see today is quite different from the one made in the beginning. The number of applications of a computer has increased, the speed and accuracy of calculation has increased. You must appreciate the impact of computers in our day to day life. Reservation of tickets in Air Lines and Railways, payment of telephone and electricity bills, deposits and withdrawals of money from banks, business data processing, medical diagnosis, weather forecasting, etc. are some of the areas where computer has become extremely useful.

However, there is one limitation of the computer. Human beings do calculations on their own. But computer is a dumb machine and it has to be given proper instructions to carry out its calculation. This is why we should know how a computer works.

### Definition:

*"A computer is an electronic machine that operates under the control of instructions, that accepts the input data, processes or manipulates the given data according to the predefined instructions and stores the result for future use".*

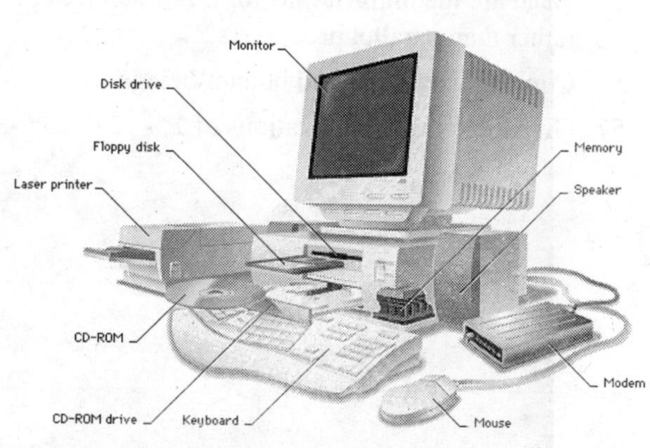


**Figure 2.1** Components of a computer

It can also retrieve the stored results as and when required again. Now-a-days, data is processed with the help of computer. This modern technique to process data is known as Electronic Data Processing (EDP). Computer is also known as Electronic Data Processing machine.

The term data processing means:

- Arithmetic and logical operations on data to get required results.
- To send and receive information from one location to another.
- Arranging data into a specific order etc.

A computer can store, process and retrieve data as and when desired. The computer processes data with very high speed. In addition to being very fast, computer is also very accurate in calculations. These are the main capabilities of the computer.

Computer is an electronic device. As mentioned in the introduction it can do arithmetic calculations faster. But as you will see later it does much more than that. It can be compared to a magic box, which serves different purpose to different people. For a common man computer is simply a calculator, which works automatic and quite fast. For a person who knows much about it, computer is a machine capable of solving problems and manipulating data. It accepts data, processes the data by doing some mathematical and logical operations and gives us the desired output.

Therefore, we may define *computer as a device that transforms data.* Data can be anything like marks obtained by you in various subjects. It can also be name, age, sex, weight, height, etc. of all the students in your class or income, savings, investments, etc., of a country. Computer can be defined in terms of its functions. It can

- accept data
- store data
- process data as desired, and
- retrieve the stored data as and when required and
- print the result in desired format.

You will know more about these functions as you go through the later sections.

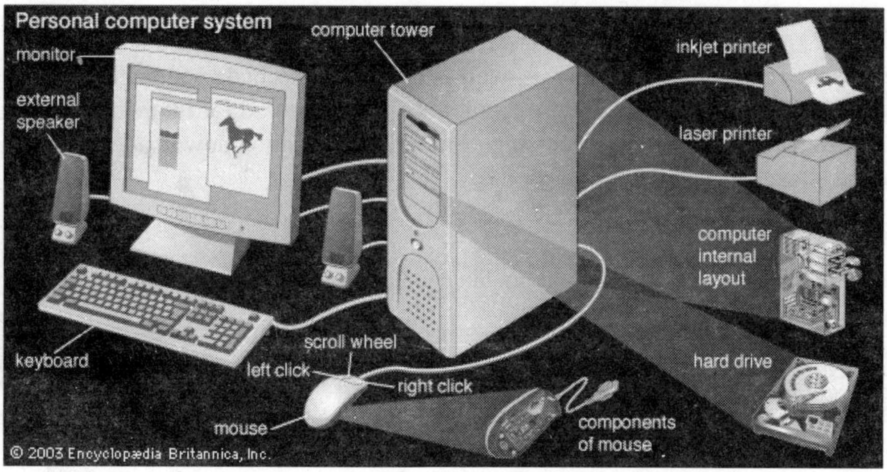


**Figure 2.2:** Basic Components of a Computer

## 2.3 CHARACTERISTICS OF A COMPUTER

Now-a-days computer is playing a main role in everyday life it has become the need of people just like television, telephone or other electronic devices at home. It solves the human problems very quickly as well as accurately. The important characteristics of a computer are described below:

### 1. Speed

The computer is a very high speed electronic device. The operations on the data inside the computer are performed through electronic circuits according to the given instructions. The data and instructions flow along these circuits with high speed that is close to the speed of light. Computer can perform million of billion of operations on the data in one second. The computer generates signals during the operation process therefore the speed of computer is usually measure in mega hertz (MHz) or gega hertz (GHz). It means million cycles units of frequency is hertz per second. Different computers have different speed.

### 2. Arithmetical and Logical Operations

A computer can perform arithmetical and logical operations. In arithmetic operations, it performs the addition, subtraction, multiplication and division on the numeric data. In logical operation it compares the numerical data as well as alphabetical data.

### 3. Accuracy

In addition to being very fast, computer is also very accurate device. it gives accurate output result provided that the correct input data and set of instructions are given to the computer. It means that output is totally depended on the given instructions and input data. If input data is in-correct then the resulting output will be in-correct. In computer terminology it is known as garbage-in garbage-out.

### 4. Reliability

The electronic components in modern computer have very low failure rate. The modern computer can perform very complicated calculations without creating any problem and produces consistent (reliable) results. In general, computers are very reliable. Many personal computers have never needed a service call. Communications are also very reliable and generally available whenever needed.

### 5. Storage

A computer has internal storage (memory) as well as external or secondary storage. In secondary storage, a large amount of data and programs (set of instructions) can be stored for future use. The stored data and programs are available any time for processing. Similarly information downloaded from the internet can be saved on the storage media.

### 6. Retrieving data and programs

The data and program stored on the storage media can be retrieved very quickly for further processing. It is also very important feature of a computer.

### 7. Automation

A computer can automatically perform operations without interfering the user during the operations. It controls automatically different devices attached with the computer. It executes automatically the program instructions one by one.

### 8. Versatility

Versatile means flexible. Modern computer can perform different kind of tasks one by one of simultaneously. It is the most important feature of computer. At one moment your are playing game on computer, the next moment you are composing and sending emails etc. In colleges and universities computers are use to deliver lectures to the students. The talent of computer is dependent on the software.

### 9. Communications

Today computer is mostly used to exchange messages or data through computer networks all over the world. For example the information can be received or send through the internet with the help of computer. It is most important feature of the modern information technology.

### 10. Diligence

A computer can continually work for hours without creating any error. It does not get tired while working after hours of work it performs the operations with the same accuracy as well as speed as the first one.

### 11. No Feelings

Computer is an electronic machine. It has no feelings. It detects objects on the basis of instructions given to it. Based on our feelings, taste, knowledge and experience: we can make certain decisions and judgments in our daily life. On the other hand, computer can not make such judgments on their own. Their judgments are totally based on instructions given to them.

### 12. Consistency

People often have difficulty to repeat their instructions again and again. For example, a lecturer feels difficulty to repeat a same lecture in a class room again and again. Computer can repeat actions consistently (again and again) without loosing its concentration:

- To run a spell checker (built into a word processor) for checking spellings in a document.
- To play multimedia animations for training purposes.
- To deliver a lecture through computer in a class room etc.

A computer will carry out the activity with the same way every time. You can listen a lecture or perform any action again and again.

### 13. Precision

Computers are not only fast and consistent but they also perform operations very accurately and precisely. For example, in manual calculations and rounding fractional values (That is value with decimal point can change the actual result). In computer however, you can keep the accuracy and precision upto the level, you desire. The length calculations remain always accurate.

## 2.4 CLASSIFICATION OF COMPUTERS

Though in general we use digital computers, however, present day computers may be classified into three categories:

- Analog
- Digital
- Hybrid

### 2.4.1 Analog Computers

Analog computers are computers which work on the basis of continuous measurement of physical quantities, e.g. pressure, voltage, current, temperature, current, length, etc. We can quote a number of instruments that work on the principles of an analog computers.

Limitations of Analog Computers

- These don't have logical facilities afforded by programming
- Don't have the ability to store data in large quantities
- Cost of implementation of computation is very high

***Examples***: Thermometer, Speedometer, Wall-clock, Voltmeter, Ammeter, etc.

### 2.4.2 Digital Computers

Digital computers are computers which represent data in terms of discrete number and processes data using the standard arithmetic operations. These computers directly operate on numbers and produce precise results. These are used in a unlimited number of applications. The basic differences between analog and digital computers are listed in ***Table No. 2.1.***

- We will be concerned with digital computers only because of the following reasons:
- The tasks that can be done on analog computers can also be done on digital computers while the reverse is not true.
- To understand the calculations made by an analog computer, some mathematical background is necessary, whereas digital computer can be used and understood without much mathematical background.

The digital computer is used extensively in many areas of application.

### 2.4.3 Hybrid Computers

Design features of Analog and Digital computers can be combined to create a Hybrid Computer. Such computers are used for special applications only. Examples of such computers include:

- Chemical Process Control
- Patient Monitoring System
- Electronic Calculating Scale
- Missile Guidance Computer
- Flight Simulators For Training Air-plane Pilots
- Petroleum Distillation Monitoring Systems

### 2.4.4 Difference between Analog and Digital Computers

**Table 2.1:** Analog Vs. Digital Computer

| S.No. | Analog Computers | Digital Computers |
|---|---|---|
| 1. | Represent continuous measurement of physical quantities e.g. rotation, voltage, temperature, etc. | Represent numbers by discrete coded patterns |

| S.No. | Analog Computers | Digital Computers |
|---|---|---|
| 2. | Accuracy is quite limited | Unlimited accuracy |
| 3. | Represent physical or mathematical quantities | Represent numbers, letters and other symbols |
| 4. | Data-storage scattered in various non-interchangeable devices | Data-storage concentrated in space, interchangeable and unlimited in duration |
| 5. | Distinct elements used for each operation | Identical elements used in sequence |
| 6. | Sets up analogy of problem | Breaks down problem into arithmetic operations |
| 7. | Best-suited to represent measurable quantities and simulate response of physical systems by mathematical analogies | Best suited to handle discrete random processes, statistical data, and numerical problems of business and scientific nature |
| 8. | Serves as model and mirrors relations of actual system | Digital computer compounds arithmetic data, unrelated to system it represents |
| 9. | Operations usually carried out in real-time of physical system | Time of operations usually does not correspond to real-time. |
| 10. | Relatively few devices used and easier programming | Many devices needed and difficult programming |
| 11. | Basic operation performed by relatively few 'single-purpose' devices (integrators, multipliers, magnitude-comparators, etc. | Operation performed by relatively many interchangeable arithmetic devices such as adders, registers, accumulators, etc. |

## 2.5 BASIC ANATOMY OF DIGITAL COMPUTER

Modern computer systems are available in numerous physical shapes and sizes, and truly speaking there is no end to it. Few of the shapes and sizes of computer system are given in ***Fig. 2.3*** and few others have already been discussed in the earlier portion of this chapter.

In Computer System, different parts of a computer are organized in such a way that, it helps to perform various operations to complete the given specific task. A computer is a sort of electric brain, which capable to solve mathematical problems with in movements or produce desired information or a controlling order.

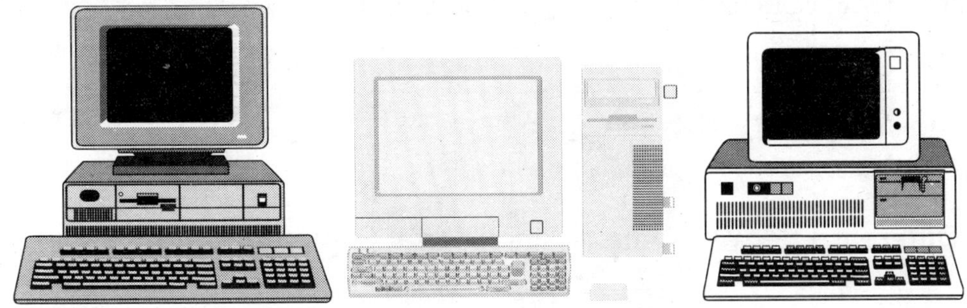

**Fig. 2.3:** Computer Systems

All the Modern electronic computer consists of three main components. These are indicated in the block diagram ***(Fig. 2.4).***

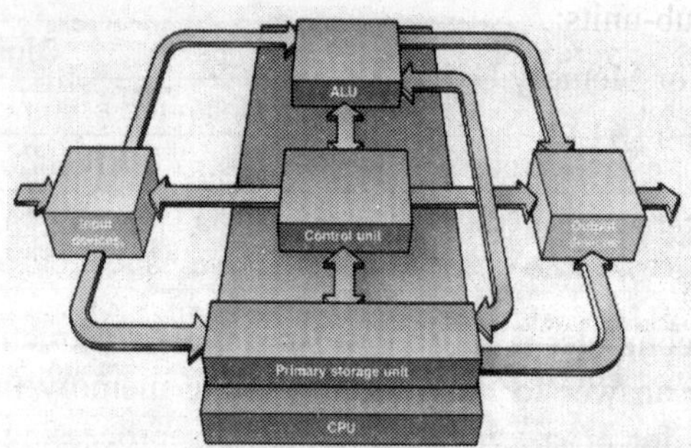


**Fig. 2.4:** Block Diagram of a Computer

Let us now study the organisation and function of each unit in detail.

## I. Input Unit

A unit provided to supply data to the computer is called ***Input Unit.*** This unit is also called Input Devices Unit and uses devices like mouse, lightpen, keyboard etc. to transfer data/information to the computer directly or may collect data on magnetic disks and tapes and later transfer it to the system.

Peripherals is the term applied to all devices that are connected to the CPU but are not part of the CPU. These include the Input/Output (I/O) and mass storage devices and other computer devices such as analog-to-digital converters. The collection of all peripheral equipments is called the computer configuration.

There are two types of peripherals given as under:

i. Off-line Peripheral and

ii. On-line Peripheral.

Auxiliary devices that are not directly connected to the CPU, such as keypunches, card sorters, and so on. These are called off-line devices. The term on-line devices refers to equipment that is connected to the CPU.

## II. Central Processing Unit (CPU)

This unit is called the brain or heart and soul of the computer system. It comes in different shapes viz. Vertical CPU, Mid-Tower, Horizontal CPU, etc. Few popular CPU types are shown in ***Fig. 2.5.***

(a) Mid Tower CPU (b) Vertical CPU

**Fig. 2.5:** Few Popular CPU Shapes

It has the following three sub-units:

i. Primary Storage Unit (or Memory Unit)
ii. Arithmetic & Logic Unit (ALU)
iii. Control Unit

### a) Primary Storage Unit

We are already aware that the computer is capable of storing data/instruction/information into it. Where does the data get stored? The answer to this question is the memory unit. Memory is a part of the microcomputer that holds data for processing, instructions for processing the data and information i.e. processed data.

As we have different types of data to be stored, this memory unit has four major logical areas, which are not shown in the figure to avoid complexity.

i. Input Storage Area: The input data does not straight away go to the processor. It is first stored in this area till the processor asks for it.
ii. Working Storage Area: ***'Working storage area'*** is like a sheet of scratch paper. When the data is being processed, there are some intermediate results that are not required as output but are required to obtain the output. Such results are stored in ***working storage area***.
iii. Output Storage Area: The final output is not taken by the output devices immediately but is stored in memory till the output device is ready to receive it. Thus an ***'output storage area'*** holds the finished results of the processing operations until they are released on the output device.
iv. Program Storage Area: In addition to above, the primary storage also contains a ***'program storage area'***. The instructions for data manipulation are stored in this area.

### b) Arithmetic & Logic Unit (ALU)

This unit is capable of performing arithmetic operations and logical operations on the data stored in storage area. The basic arithmetic and logical operations include addition, subtraction, multiplication, division, ORing, ANDing, NOT (complementing), increment, decrement, shifting, clearing operations, etc. The data is transferred to ALU for processing and the intermediate results and final results are transferred to the storage area.

### c) Control Unit

This unit controls the operation of each unit of computer system by issuing control signals on the basis of instructions provided to the computer as a program. So this unit can be called the central nervous system of the computer. This unit generates timing and control signals necessary for execution of instructions. It provides status, control and timing signals necessary for the operation of other parts of the CPU, memory, and I/O devices. It controls the entire operation of the computer. It is actually the control section of the CPU, which acts as the brain of a computer.

## III. Output Unit

The result generated by CPU is either transferred directly or from the output area of the memory to the output devices like visual display units (VDU) or printers, etc.

### Mass Storage Devices

The primary storage area of the computer is limited in size and is expensive. Only, the frequently required instructions are stored in it. To supplement this limited memory, we use auxiliary or secondary storage devices like magnetic tapes and disks. The data can be transferred to/from these devices by the processor at a very fast speed. But as compared to primary storage, secondary storage is slow. But the advantage of secondary storage devices is that apart from being cheap, they are transferable which primary storage is not. There is no limit to secondary storage memory. This can be compared to human beings who use a note-book or pocket-diary to store the notes to supplement the brain.

## 2.6 WORKING OF DIGITAL COMPUTER

In order to carry out the operations mentioned in the previous section the computer allocates the task between its various functional units. The computer system is divided into three separate units for its operation. They are (1) arithmetic logical unit, (2) control unit, and (3) central processing unit.

### 2.6.1 Arithmetic and Logic Unit (ALU)

**Arithmetic logic unit** is that part of the computer which performs the different logic operations and arithmetic calculations like addition, subtraction, multiplication and division. It is the high speed digital circuit that solves calculations and does comparisons.

After you enter data through the input device it is stored in the primary storage unit. The actual processing of the data and instruction are performed by Arithmetic Logical Unit. The major operations performed by the ALU are addition, subtraction, multiplication, division, logic and comparison. Data is transferred to ALU from storage unit when required. After processing the output is returned back to storage unit for further processing or getting stored.

#### Functions of Arithmetic Logic Unit

- Almost all the actions of the computer are done by it. It gets its data from a certain computer memory called **processor register.** After the data gets processed, its results get stored in output registers of the **arithmetic logic unit.**
- The **arithmetic logic unit** can perform integer arithmetic operations like addition, subtraction, etc.
- It can also perform bitwise logic operations like AND, OR, XOR, etc.
- The **arithmetic logic** unit performs bit-shifting operations like rotating or shifting a certain word to either the left or the right by a given number of bits. These can also be represented as divisions by 2 and also multiplications by 2. These are the simple operations carried out by the **arithmetic logic unit.**

### 2.6.2 Control Unit (CU)

The next component of computer is the Control Unit, which acts like the supervisor seeing that things are done in proper fashion. The control unit determines the sequence in which computer programs and instructions are executed. Things like processing of programs stored in the main memory, interpretation of the instructions and issuing of signals for other units of the computer to execute them. It also acts as a switch board operator when several users access the computer simultaneously. Thereby it coordinates the activities of computer's peripheral equipment as they perform the input and output. Therefore it is the manager of all operations mentioned in the previous section.

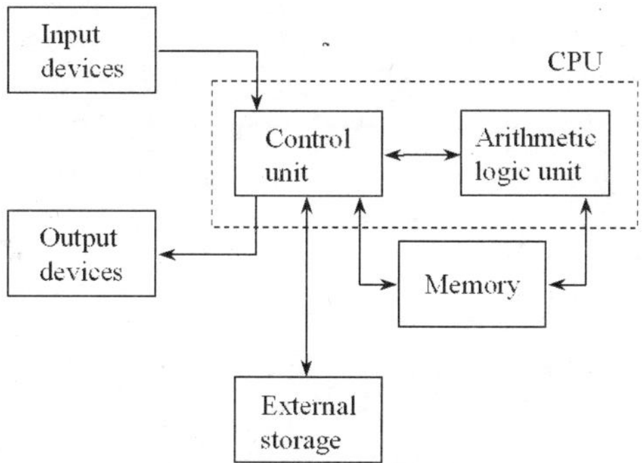


**Figure 2.6:** Control Unit

### Control Unit and Micro-program

There was a time when the manufacturing of **control units** was a difficult process, especially in designing it. But today the scenario has changed. A **control unit** is executed in the form of micro-programs which remain in control stores. There is a micro sequencer which chooses the words and certain portions of those words which directly manage the various computer parts. These parts are arithmetic and logic units, buses, instruction registers, registers and input/output. Today the latest computers may possess subsidiary controllers for every subsystem, which would be supervised by the main **control unit.**

### Functions of Control Unit

A **control unit** can be described as a sort of circuitry that supervises and controls the path of information that runs over the processor and organizes the various activities of those units that lie inside it.

- It carries out many tasks such as decoding, fetching, handling the execution and finally storing the results.
- It controls the execution of instructions in a sequential order.
- It guides the flow of data through the different parts of the computer.
- It interprets the instructions.
- It regulates the time controls of the processor.
- It sends and receives control signals from various peripheral devices.

A **control unit** is a major computer part which helps in the functioning of the central processing unit and in turn runs the whole computer.

## 2.6.3 Central Processing Unit (CPU)

The ALU and the CU of a computer system are jointly known as the central processing unit. You may call CPU as the brain of any computer system. It is just like brain that takes all major decisions, makes all sorts of calculations and directs different parts of the computer functions by activating and controlling the operations.

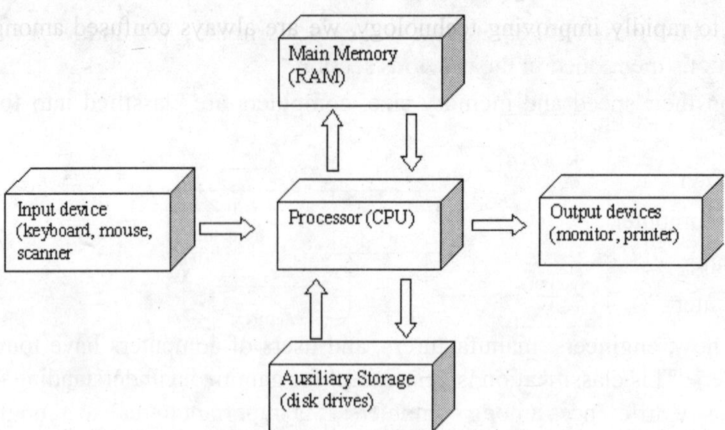


**Figure 2.7:** Computer Architecture

**The CPU is Also Known As:** processor, microprocessor, central processor, "the brains of the computer".

**Central processing unit (CPU),** principal part of any digital computer system, generally composed of the main memory, control unit, and arithmetic-logic unit. It constitutes the physical heart of the entire computer system; to it is linked various peripheral equipment, including input/output devices and auxiliary storage units.

The central processing unit (CPU) is the portion of a computer system that carries out the instructions of a computer program, and is the primary element carrying out the computer's functions. The central processing unit carries out each instruction of the program in sequence, to perform the basic arithmetical, logical, and input/output operations of the system. This term has been in use in the computer industry at least since the early 1960s. The form, design and implementation of CPUs have changed dramatically since the earliest examples, but their fundamental operation remains much the same.

Early CPUs were custom-designed as a part of a larger, sometimes one-of-a-kind, computer. However, this costly method of designing custom CPUs for a particular application has largely given way to the development of mass-produced processors that are made for one or many purposes. This standardization trend generally began in the era of discrete transistor mainframes and minicomputers and has rapidly accelerated with the popularization of the integrated circuit (IC). The IC has allowed increasingly complex CPUs to be designed and manufactured to tolerances on the order of nanometers. Both the miniaturization and standardization of CPUs have increased the presence of these digital devices in modern life far beyond the limited application of dedicated computing machines. Modern microprocessors appear in everything from automobiles to cell phones and children's toys.

## 2.7 CLASSIFICATION OF DIGITAL COMPUTERS

There is a wide variety of computers in the market today which differ in terms of physical size, price, capacity, and performance. The variety is so wide that it is sometimes difficult to see those elements that are shared by many computers and those elements that tend to differ among computers.

Computers are classified according to their data processing speed, amount of data that they can hold and price. Generally, a computer with high processing speed and large internal storage is called a big computer. Due to rapidly improving technology, we are always confused among the categories of computers.

Depending upon their speed and memory size, computers are classified into following four main groups.

1. Supercomputer
2. Mainframe computer
3. Mini computer
4. Microcomputer

For some time now, engineers, manufacturers, and users of computers have found it convenient to group these computers. This classification is very useful for gaining an understanding of the key elements of computer and the key differences among computers. It is important to realise, though, that these classes are not precisely defined. This is for two reasons:

- There is actually a spectrum of computer types, and the differences among computers within each of three classes are as great as the differences between neighbouring classes.
- Computer technology is evolving rapidly, so that the microcomputer of today is as powerful as the minicomputer of a few years ago, and the minicomputer of today is as powerful as the mainframe of a few years ago.

This classification implies differences between classes between in one or more characteristics. In the 1960s, before the microcomputer, there was a clear-cut distinction between minicomputers and mainframes. The most important characteristics that could be used to differentiate the two types of computers were:

- Speed
- Instruction sizes
- Number of CPU registers
- Word Length
- Main Memory Size
- Complexity of I/O modules
- Operating System Complexity
- Physical size
- Cost
- Virtual address space
- Secondary Memory Size
- Degree of Multiprogramming

### 2.7.1 Supercomputer

Supercomputer is the most powerful and fastest, and also very expensive. It was developed in 1980s. It is used to process large amount of data and to solve the complicated scientific problems. It can perform more than one trillions calculations per second. It has large number of processors connected parallel. So parallel processing is done in this computer. In a single supercomputer thousands of users can be connected at the same time and the supercomputer handles the work of each user separately.

Supercomputers are mainly used for:

- Weather forecasting.
- Nuclear energy research.
- Aircraft design.
- Automotive design.
- To control industrial units.

The supercomputers are used in large organizations, research laboratories, aerospace centers, large industrial units etc. Nuclear scientists use supercomputers to create and analyze models of nuclear fission and fusions, predicting the actions and reactions of millions of atoms as they interact.

A supercomputer is shown in ***Fig.2.8.***

**Fig. 2.8:** Super Computer

There is a need for computers to solve mathematical problems of real processes, such as occur in disciplines including:

- Seismology
- Meteorology
- Atomic Physics
- Aerodynamics
- Plasma Physics
- Fluid-dynamics
- Nuclear Physics

Typically, these problems are characterised by the need for high precision and a program that repetitively performs floating-point arithmetic operations on large arrays of numbers. Most of these problem into the category known as continuous-field simulation.

The supercomputer has limited use and because of its price tag has a limited market. Only a few dozen of these machines are operational, mostly at research centres and some government agencies with scientific or engineering functions. As in some current applications in aerodynamics and nuclear physics, absorbing more than two days of computing time on a contemporary supercomputer, are needed for a single problem. Thus the technology and performance of the supercomputer continues to evolve.

Supercomputers are specially designed to maximise the number of FLOPS. Seymour Cray ***(Fig.2.9)***, owner of Cray Research is known as the ***'Father of Supercomputers'***.

Today's supercomputers are not fast enough to simulate the airflow around an entire aircraft. Therefore, designers and builders of new air-planes simulate the airflow around separate parts of a plane. Thereafter, they combine the results to obtain an effective aerodynamic design. Thus the technology and performance of the supercomputer must continue to evolve.

**Examples:**

- CRAY X-MP/14, X-MP/24, X-MP/48
- CRAY Y-MP, Y-MPC
- CRAY 2
- CRAY 3
- ETA (EDC-ETA 10, ETA 20)
- C-DAC's PARAM
- NEC (NEC SX-3)
- IBM 3090 (with vector)
- Fujitsu (VP Series)
- Hitachi (HITAC S-300)
- PARAM,
- etc.

**Fig. 2.9:** Seymour Cray

## 2.7.2 Mainframe Computers

The mainframe remains a distinct class of computers and are very powerful large general purpose computers. Large organisations use mainframe computer (shown in ***Fig.2.10***). Some of the key differences between the high end of mainframe class and the high end of the minicomputer class are there. One of the most dramatic differences is the speed of the two classes.

Mainframe computers are also large-scale computers but supercomputers are larger than mainframe. These are also very expensive. The mainframe computer specially requires a very large clean room with air-conditioner. This makes it very expensive to buy and operate. It can support a large number of various equipments. It also has multiple processors. Large mainframe systems can handle the input and output requirements of several thousand of users. For example, IBM, S/390 mainframe can support 50,000 users simultaneously. The users often access then mainframe with terminals or personal computers.

Fig. 2.10: Mainframe Computer

A common measure of speed is millions of instructions per second (MIPS); this is the rate at which machine instructions are executed. However, the instruction sets of mainframes and super-minis are comparable , and so this is a fair comparison. Another dramatic area of difference is price.

**Examples:**

- DEC's VAX-8350, -8650
- HP 9000 Model 870S/400, Model 870S/300
- IBM 4300 Series (small to medium-size models)
- IBM 308X Series (large models)
- Latest model IBM 3090 Series (IBM 3090/600 installed in 1988)
- IBM Enterprise System/9000 Series
- ICL Series
- MEDHA Series
- Sperry Series; etc.

There are basically two types of terminals used with mainframe systems.

**These are:**

i. **Dumb Terminal:** Dumb terminal does not have its own CPU and storage devices. This type of terminal uses the CPU and storage devices of mainframe system. Typically, a dumb terminal consists of monitor and a keyboard (or mouse).

ii. **Intelligent Terminal:** Intelligent terminal has its own processor and can perform some processing operations. Usually, this type of terminal does not have its own storage. Typically, personal computers are used as intelligent terminals. A personal computer as an intelligent terminal gives facility to access data and other services from mainframe system. It also enables to store and process data locally.

The mainframe computers are specially used as servers on the World Wide Web. The mainframe computers are used in large organizations such as Banks, Airlines and Universities etc. where many people (users) need frequent access to the same data, which is usually organized into one or more huge databases. IBM is the major manufacturer of mainframe computers. The examples of mainframes are IBM S/390, Control Data CYBER 176 and Amdahl 580 etc.

### 2.7.3 Minicomputers

Minicomputers are faster and more powerful than microcomputers. The word-length of these computers is usually 32-bits or more. By the early 1960s, economic and technical factors combined to make small, inexpensive computers attractive for many applications. Many computing tasks could be accomplished with the less power than was then available on contemporary mainframe computers. For example, computers could be used to control some industrial or data acquisition process, such as checkout of the electronic system of a product on an assembly line. This type of task could be economically performed by a mainframe, but a small, relatively inexpensive computer could be used. While mainframe machines were run by staffs of operators, such costs could not be justified for the inexpensive minicomputer. Thus, direct interaction between the minicomputer and the user was required.

As the speed, instruction size, memory-size, and other characteristics of minicomputers increased with advancement in technology, its role changed. Many of the stand-alone or dedicated applications began to be performed by microcomputers. The minicomputer became a multi-user, or shared, system. Throughout the 1960s and 1970s, advances in technology led to the increasing functionality of the minicomputer. Instruction sets were enhanced to include operations on floating point numbers for scientific processing and on character strings for commercial applications. The availability of low-cost memory allowed a dramatic increase in the size of main memory attached to the minicomputer. The speed of instruction execution increased.

A minicomputer can support up to 64 or even 100 terminals. Minicomputers can support a greater variety of fast peripheral devices. Minicomputers are extensively used for multi-user and interactive applications in colleges, universities, research organisations, government organisations, industries and so on. These are also used for sophisticated real-time Industrial controls and interactive engineering design work.

#### Examples:

- Wipro S-68030V and S-68033V built around Motorola 68030 CPU
- HP 9000 series 800 (a Supermini) built around HP's VLSI RISC Processor
- HCL Magnum built around 68030 and 68040 CPUs
- IBM AS/400/B60 (installed in 1988)
- DEC's VAX 8842 (installed in 1988)
- Wipro LandMark 860 (a Supermini) built around Intel's 64-bit RISC processor i860 CPU, and so on.

The capabilities of a minicomputer are between mainframe and personal computer. These computers are also known as midrange computers.

The minicomputers are used in business, education and many other government departments. Although some minicomputers are designed for a single user but most are designed to handle multiple terminals. Minicomputers are commonly used as servers in network environment and hundreds of personal computers can be connected to the network with a minicomputer acting as server like mainframes, minicomputers are used as web servers. Single user minicomputers are used for sophisticated design tasks.

The first minicomputer was introduced in the mid-1960s by Digital Equipment Corporation (DEC). After this IBM Corporation (AS/400 computers) Data General Corporation and Prime Computer also designed the mini computers.

## 2.7.4 Microcomputer

The microcomputers are also known as personal computers or simply PCs. Microprocessor is used in this type of computer. These are very small in size and cost. The IBM's first microcomputer was designed in 1981 and was named as IBM-PC. After this many computer hardware companies copied the design of IBM-PC. The term "PC-compatible" refers any personal computer based on the original IBM personal computer design.

The most popular types of personal computers are the PC and the Apple. PC and PC-compatible computers have processors with different architectures than processors in Apple computers. These two types of computers also use different operating systems. PC and PC-compatible computers use the Windows operating system while Apple computers use the Macintosh operating system (MacOS). The majority of microcomputers sold today are part of IBM-compatible. However the Apple computer is neither an IBM nor a compatible. It is another family of computers made by Apple computer.

It is low-cost small digital computer. This type of computer contains a microprocessor as its CPU, a memory unit, input and output device(s). The word-length of these computers lie between 8 to 32-bits. These have a wide range of applications.

The microcomputer has become such a common part of everyday life that little need be said about it here. Home computers and personal office computers have proliferated, bringing computing power and literacy to more and more people.

On the basis of cost and performance, personal computers can be classified as:

- Personal Computer (PC)
- Personal Computer with Extended Technology (PC/XT)
- Personal Computer with Advanced Technology (PC/AT)
- Super AT or Super Micro

### 2.7.4.1 Personal Computer (PC)

PC is the simplest and cheapest type of personal computer. It uses Intel 8086/8088 as CPU, 640 KB RAM, 8KB ROM and normally two floppy disk drives. One of the drives is normally meant for holding bootable floppy diskette and the second one is used for holding the application package as well as for secondary storage. This type of computer does not contain any hard-disk. It is a single-user system. Its ROM can be extended from 8KB to 64 KB. It uses MS-DOS operation system. It may also employ 8087 math co-processor.

### 2.7.4.2 PC/XT

This type of computer contains hard-disk(s) as well as floppy disk drive i.e. 360 KB/1.2 MB. Its cost is obviously more than the PC due to additional components. It is also a single-user system. Its ROM can also be extended up to 64 KB. It also normally uses MS-DOS operation system. It may also employ 8087 math co-processor.

### 2.7.4.3 PC/AT

It contains 80286 as CPU, 640 KB RAM (can be expanded to 4 MB), 64 KB ROM (can be expanded to 128 KB), hard-disk drive and floppy-disk drive (360 KB/1.2 MB). Microprocessor 80286 is more powerful than the microprocessors of PC and PC/XTs. Up to 4 terminals can be connected to PC/AT to make it multi-user system by using XENIX as an operating system. Hard-disk capacity may lie in the range 20-80 MB. It uses 80287 math co-processor. Processing speed of PC, PC/XT and PC/AT lies in the range 1-5 MIPS.

### 2.7.4.4 Super AT (or Super micros)

These computers use a 32-bit CPU such as Intel 80386 or 80486. The processing speed of 80386 and 80496 may range from 3 to 5 MIPS and 12 MIPS at 25 MHz respectively. RAM size of these lie in the range 2-8 MB. In case of 80386 microprocessor, it can be extended up to 32 MB and in case of 80486 up to 64 MB. Hard-disk capacity of these lies in the range 200 MB-780 MB. Normally, UNIX is used as a multi-user operating system on these systems. 80386 CPU offers the connectivity up to 8-12 terminals whereas 80486 offers the connectivity up to 16-64 terminals.

Personal computers are available in two models. These are:

- Desktop PCs
- Tower PCs

A desktop personal computer is most popular model of personal computer. The system unit of the desktop personal computer can lie flat on the desk or table. In desktop personal computer, the monitor is usually placed on the system unit.

Another model of the personal computer is known as tower personal computer. The system unit of the tower PC is vertically placed on the desk of table. Usually the system unit of the tower model is placed on the floor to make desk space free and user can place other devices such as printer, scanner etc. on the desktop. Today computer tables are available which are specially designed for this purpose. The tower models are mostly used at homes and offices.

Microcomputers are further divided into following categories.

- Laptop computer
- Workstation
- Network computer
- Handheld computer

### 2.7.4.5 Laptop computer

Laptop computer is also known as notebook computer. It is small size (85-by-11 inch notebook computer and can fit inside a briefcase. The laptop computer is operated on a special battery and it does not have to be plugged in like desktop computer. The laptop computer is portable and fully functional microcomputer.

It is mostly used during journey. It can be used on your lap in an airplane. It is because it is referred to as laptop computer.

The memory and storage capacity of laptop computer is almost equivalent to the PC or desktop computer. It also has the hard dist, floppy disk drive, Zip disk drive, CD-ROM drive, CD-writer etc. it has built-in keyboard and built-in trackball as pointing device. Laptop computer is also available with the same processing speed as the most powerful personal computer. It means that laptop computer has same features as personal computer. Laptop computers are more expensive than desktop computers. Normally these computers are frequently used in business travelers.

#### 2.7.4.6 Workstations

Workstations are special single user computers having the same features as personal computer but have the processing speed equivalent to minicomputer or mainframe computer. A workstation computer can be fitted on a desktop. Scientists, engineers, architects and graphic designers mostly use these computers.

Workstation is an expensive and a very powerful machine used by engineers, scientists and other professionals such as artists, etc. who need to process a lot of data. People who need to execute complicated programs and display both work in progress and outputs graphically also make use of workstations.

These have advanced processors, more RAM and storage capacity than personal computers. These are usually used as single-user applications but these are used as servers on computer network and web servers as well.

Workstations use sophisticated display screens featuring high-resolution color graphics and operating systems such as UNIX, Windows NT, 95, 98 those permitted multitasking. Workstations also use powerful networking links to other computers.

Most significant feature of workstations is the powerful processor which churn out results much faster than the PCs.

**Examples:** *Sun-, Apollo-, Hewlett-Packard-, NeXT- and IBM-workstations.*

#### 2.7.4.7 Network computers

Network computers are also version of personal computers having less processing power, memory and storage. These are specially designed as terminals for network environment. Some types of network computers have no storage. The network computers are designed for network, Internet or Intranet for data entry or to access data on the network. The network computers depend upon the network's server for data storage and to use software. These computers also use the network's server to perform some processing tasks.

In the mid-1990s the concept of network computers became popular among some PC manufacturers. As a result several variations of the network computers quickly became available. In business, variations of the network computer are Windows terminals, NetPCs and diskless workstations. Some network computers are designed to access only the Internet or to an Intranet. These devices are sometimes called Internet PCs, Internet boxes etc. In home some network computers do not include monitor. These are connected to home television, which serves as the output devices. A popular example of a home-based network computer is Web TV, which enables the user to connect a television to the Internet. The Web TV has a special set-top box used to connect to the Internet and also provides a set of simple controls which enable the user to navigate the Internet, send and receive e-mails and to perform other tasks on the network while watching television. Network computers are cheaper to purchase and to maintain than personal computers.

### 2.7.4.8 Handheld Computer

In the mid 1990s, many new types of small personal computing devices have been introduced and these are referred to as handheld computers. These computers are also referred to as Palmtop Computers. The handheld computers sometimes called Mini-Notebook Computers. The type of computer is named as handheld computer because it can fit in one hand while you can operate it with the other hand. Because of its reduced size, the screen of handheld computer is quite small. Similarly it also has small keyboard. The handheld computers are preferred by business traveler. Some handheld computers have a specialized keyboard. These computers are used by mobile employees, such as meter readers and parcel delivery people, whose jobs require them to move from place to place.

The examples of handheld computers are:

- Personal Digital Assistance
- Cellular telephones
- H/PC Pro devices

### 2.7.4.9 Personal Digital Assistants (PDAs)

The PDA is one of the more popular lightweight mobile devices in use today. A PDA provides special functions such as taking notes, organizing telephone numbers and addresses. Most PDAs also offer a variety of other application software such as word processing, spreadsheet and games etc. Some PDAs include electronic books that enable users to read a book on the PDA's screen.

Many PDAs are web-based and users can send/receive e-mails and access the Internet. Similarly, some PDAs also provide telephone capabilities.

The primary input device of a PDA is the stylus. A stylus is an electronic pen and looks like a small ballpoint pen. This input device is used to write notes and store in the PDA by touching the screen. Some PDAs also support voice input.

### 2.7.4.10 Cellular phones

A cellular phone is a web-based telephone having features of analog and digital devices. It is also referred to as Smart Phone. In addition to basic phone capabilities, a cellular phone also provides the functions to receive and send e-mails & faxes and to access the Internet.

### 2.7.4.11 H/PC Pro Devices

H/PC Pro dive is new development in handheld technology. These systems are larger than PDAs but they are not quite as large as typical notebook PCs. These devices have features between PDAs and notebook PCs. The H/PC Pro device includes a full-size keyboard but it does not include disk. These systems also have RAM with very low storage capacity and slow speed of processor.

## 2.8 REASONS OF POPULARITY OF MICROCOMPUTERS

The microcomputers are very popular due to the following reasons:

i. Useful: They are very useful. By using microcomputers, individuals and small businesses can increase productivity or accomplish tasks that would ordinarily take too much time or too much effort to even attempt manually.

ii. Something For Everyone: Computers can be useful to a variety of people for a variety of tasks. they can be used to play games, teach children math, create new musical sounds, predict stck market trends, or serve as a handy reference resource.

iii. Inexpensive: They are very inexpensive. Families or home businesses can afford to buy a small system to use at home.

iv. Easy To Use: Microcomputers are relatively easy to use. Typically, people don't need to know how a computer actually operates internally to use one. Some computers are easy to use because many of the ready-to-use software packages have instructions that appear on the computer screen to guide you through the task at hand.

## 2.9 FUNCTIONAL SIMILARITIES OF COMPUTER SYSTEMS AND HUMAN BEINGS

We have already gone through the anatomy of a digital computer and functioning of a computer system using its various components. Besides, we are also well versed and aware with the functioning of human-beings using its various organs.

Processing of data by hand is satisfactory only when the amount of data to be processed is small and also the manual data processing is slow, monotonous and often subject to error. Human-beings utilises past experiences and intuitions for decision making whereas computer follows an algorithmic procedure. Human-beings as a decision maker utilises heuristic. Society will benefit most if complementary strengths of human beings and computers are utilised. Definitely, computers today have more intelligence than in the past and the strides are being made to increase machine capabilities.

The Newell-Simon model suggests that there are limitations on the ability of human as information processors:

- One set of limits concerns the processing of data and is directly related to short-term memory
- Another set of limits is the ability of humans to detect differences
- Humans are also limited in their ability to generate, integrate, and interpret probabilistic data.

Functional similarities of a computer system with human being is in the following ***Table 2.2.***

**Table 2.2:** Computer Vs. Human-being (Similarities)

| S. No. | Computer element | Purpose | Human-Being |
|---|---|---|---|
| 1. | Input | Used to receive data and instructions in computer-compatible form | Input to the system is through ears, eyes, mouth or nose |
| 2. | Main Storage | Used to hold input data and instructions temporarily before it is processed | Data and instructions are stored in brain and can be recalled whenever needed |
| 3. | Secondary Storage | Used as an extension to main storage and the contents stored in it are retained permanently | Use pocket-diaries, notebooks, etc. to store contents for permanent use. |

| 4. | ALU | Used to carry out arithmetic and logical computations desired in an instruction execution | Portion of our brain is used to carry out comparisons and calculations for helping out in logical judgements |
|---|---|---|---|
| 5. | Control Unit | Used to receive stored instructions in serial fashion and one at a time. Interpret each instruction and prompt its execution by one of the units like input, output, storage or ALU. | Our brain controls our mental or body actions on the basis of calculations and comparisons. Before taking any action, the old results stored in brain are also referred to and thus brain acts as a CPU. |
| 6. | Output | Used to give out results via a suitable device e.g. VDU, printer, plotter, etc. | Output is either in the form of a speech using mouth or some action e.g. writing, gesture, body language, etc. |

## EXERCISE

1. Discuss the important features of micro, mini, mainframes and super-computers.
2. What is a Computer? What capabilities does a computer possess?
3. What is the stored program concept? Why is it important?
4. How do analog computers differ digital computers?
5. State the criteria for classification of digital computers.
6. Is digital computer more accurate than analog computer? Justify your answer.
7. What are the operations that a computer is able to perform?
8. What are the fundamental components of a computer system? Which component of a computer system executes the program?
9. Why are microcomputers so popular in comparison to other computers?
10. What is a digital computer? Provide its anatomy and explain the functioning of such a computer through its block diagram.
11. What are the latest trends in microprocessor technology? Explain.
12. State the evolutionary stages of data processing.
13. What are the advantages and disadvantages of pen-based computing used by PDAs? For what type of applications would you use a PDA?
14. Why should we go for computers?
15. Detail out the description of Mark I electromechanical computer.
16. What are the applications for supercomputers and embedded computers which are affecting our lives?
17. How is a PC different from a Workstation?
18. Comment on how computers are changing our traditional patterns of personal communication.

19. What is the difference between a Laptop and a Sub-notebook Computer?
20. What is the Y2K problem?
21. What are the characteristics of a computer?
22. Do you think there is a continuing need to increase computer speed? Can you think of examples in which more speed would be desirable?
23. What is hybrid-computer? State its significance along with few important applications.
24. Why do embedded computers make tools more flexible?
25. Identify at least 3 examples of computer systems you have seen or used.
26. Is a computer more intelligent than human-beings? Justify your answer.
27. What is a PDA and for whom is it preferred?
28. Elucidate difference between micro-computers and mainframes.
29. The computer has had far-reaching effects on our lives. How has the computer affected your life?
30. What is a mainframe and what are its typical applications?
31. Identify two types of portable microcomputers and explain how they differ from each other?
32. What are supercomputers and where are they used?
33. Comment on how computers are changing our traditional patterns of recreation.
34. What are different types of portable computers?
35. In terms of physical size, how are PCs categorised?
36. What is the difference between a microcomputer and minicomputer?
37. What are the limitations of human processing? How these can be removed?
38. What are the implications for information systems design of the statement that humans are serial rather than parallel processors?
39. Compare computer and human-beings.
40. What is the difference between a microcomputer and a microprocessor?
41. What are Cellular Phones? Are these different from PDAs? Justify your answer.
42. What are hybrid computers? Give some examples.
43. What makes microcomputers popular?
44. What are laptop computers? What are its specific characteristics?
45. How do you compare human beings and computers?
46. What are workstations?
47. What are network computers? What characterises network computer?
48. How computers are useful in publishing?
49. What are uses of computers in health care?
50. How computers help in the field of education?

51. What are limitations of computers?
52. What are the main capabilities of computers?
53. What are the important characteristics of computers?
54. How computers may help in travelling?
55. How computers can help in business? Name some business applications.
56. How computers can be helpful in science and arts? Discuss.

# Number Systems and Their Interconversions

## 3.1 INTRODUCTION

A digital computer is an electronic machine that accepts a stream of symbols, stores them, processes them according to precise rules and produces meaningful output. Computers are used in scientific calculations, commercial and business data processing, air traffic control, space guidance, the educational field, and many other areas. The most important characteristic of a digital computer is its generality. It can follow a sequence of instructions, called a *program* that operates on given data.

In this Chapter we will discuss the Number Systems and representation of data in digital systems. There are two main categories of data:

(*i*) Numbers, and

(*ii*) Characters.

As mentioned earlier that internally in a digital system all data is represented by sequence of symbols where each symbol, called a bit, is either a 0 or a 1. The general properties of number systems, methods of their inter-conversions, complements and other data representation techniques are also discussed in this Chapter.

## 3.2 BASIC FEATURES OF DIGITAL SYSTEMS

Few basic features which are common to all digital systems are as under:

- All streams of input symbols to a digital system are encoded with two distinct symbols 0 (zero) and 1 (one), known as *binary digits* or *bits*. Bits can be stored and manipulated reliably and inexpensively using electronic circuits.
- The instructions for manipulating the symbols are to be properly specified so that a machine can be built to execute these. The instructions for manipulation are also encoded using *bits*.
- A digital computer has a storage unit which stores the symbols to be manipulated and the encoded instructions for manipulation of the symbols.
- Bit manipulation instructions are realized by electronic circuits.

## 3.3 NUMBER SYSTEMS

Number systems are very important to understand because the design and organisation of a computer depends on the number systems. The modern civilization is familiar with ***Decimal Number System,*** in which ten digits, namely 0 to 9 are used to represent any number. Now the *decimal number system* is used frequently in the field of Science and Technology. Once the famous Mathematician Laplace stated, "It is India that gave us the ingenious method of expressing all numbers by means of ten symbols, each symbol receiving a value of position as well as an absolute value, a profound and important idea which appears so simple to us now that we ignore its true merit."

Thus, the importance of a number system does not lie in the number of symbols used in it but what is important in it is the concept of face value (absolute value) and the place value (value of position) of a symbol. However, if instead of decimal system the binary number system, using two digits namely, 0 and 1, had been popular everywhere, the understanding of computer working would have been much easier. The binary number system is the one which is used in computers and is based on the fundamental concept of decimal number system. Various other number systems such as Octal System and Hexadecimal System (popularly known as Hex system) also use the fundamental concept of face value and place value.

The knowledge of number systems is essential for understanding of computers. The useful number systems discussed are:

- Binary Number System
- Octal Number System
- Decimal Number System
- Hexadecimal Number System.

### 3.3.1 Binary Number System

The **Binary Number System,** as the name suggests, consists of two digits namely, 0 and 1. These binary digits are called BITS. Thus, the word **BIT** stands for either of the binary digits, namely 0 or 1. Since this system uses two digits only, it has the **base** or **radix 2.** It may be noted that the base digit namely 2, is not the fundamental or basic digit of the system. Thus, all the numbers in binary system are written with the help of these two digits namely, 0 and 1. The positional value or place value of each digit in a binary number is twice the positional value of the digit on its right. This number system is identical to decimal number system with the base replaced by 2. The binary numbers are usually written with the base indicated as a subscript on the least significant digit (LSD). For example,

$$(101101.1011)_2$$

It can be represented as shown in Figure 3.1:

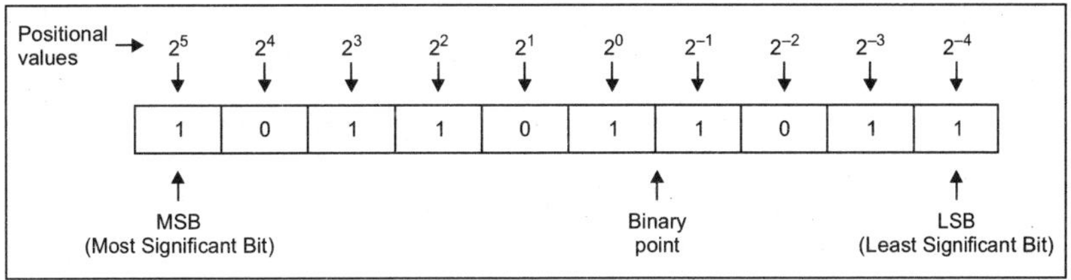


**Fig. 3.1** Binary number shown with positional values.

Here, the places to the left of the binary point are positive powers of 2 and places to the right are negative powers of 2.

The commonly used terms in coding of data in computer terminology are:

- ***BIT (BInary digiT):*** A binary digit is logical 0 or 1.
- ***Nibble:*** A group of four bits (binary digits) is called a Nibble. It is useful in coding the numeric data to hexadecimal form.
- ***Byte:*** A group of 8 bits make a byte. A byte is the smallest unit which can represent a data item or a character.
- ***Computer Word:*** A computer word, like a byte, is a group of fixed number of bits which varies from computer to computer but is fixed for each computer. The number of bits in a computer word is known as the **word size** or **word length.**

***Why is Binary Number System used in Computers?***

i. The circuits and switches in a computer have only two states, either on or off, which are represented by 1 and 0.

ii. Handling of two digits, that is, 1 and 0 is simpler, cheaper and more reliable.

iii. Every operation or activity that can be performed by decimal number system can also be done using binary number system, so it does not create any problem.

### 3.3.2 Octal Number System

This number system has **base** or **radix** 8. The basic digits of this system are 0, 1, 2, 3, 4, 5, 6 and 7. It may be noted that the base 8 is not the basic digit of the system. It is commonly used as a shorthand way of expressing binary quantities. Also the numbers represented in octal number system can be used directly for input and output operations.

The Octal Number System is also a positional value system, wherein each octal digit has its own value or weight expressed as a power of 8. For example,

$$(157246.3174)_8$$

It can be represented as shown in Figure 3.2:

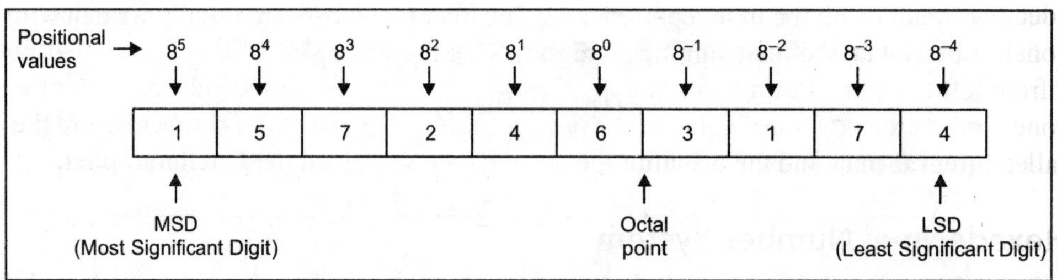


**Fig. 3.2** Octal number shown with positional values

Here, the places to the left of the octal point are positive powers of 8 and places to the right are negative powers of 8.

### 3.3.3 Decimal Number System

The decimal number system consists of 10 digits namely 0 to 9. A number written using these digits is called a decimal number. For example, the numbers 12876, –1024, 58.74, +768 are decimal numbers. Apart from these digits, the decimal point and ± signs may also be used in writing decimal numbers. The **base** or **radix** of the number system is the number of digits used in it. Since the decimal number system consists of 10 digits, the base of this system is 10. In a number system the base is not the fundamental digit of the system because fundamental digits in this system are 0, 1, 2, 3, 4, 5, 6, 7, 8, 9. The value of each digit in a number depends upon the following:

i. The face value of the digit, that is, the digit itself.
ii. The base of the system.
iii. The position of the digit in the number.

Thus, the magnitude of a number depends upon the digits of which it is made, position of the digits and base of the system. For example,

351479.8265

Since no base is mentioned, the base is taken as 10.

It can be represented as shown in Figure 3.3:

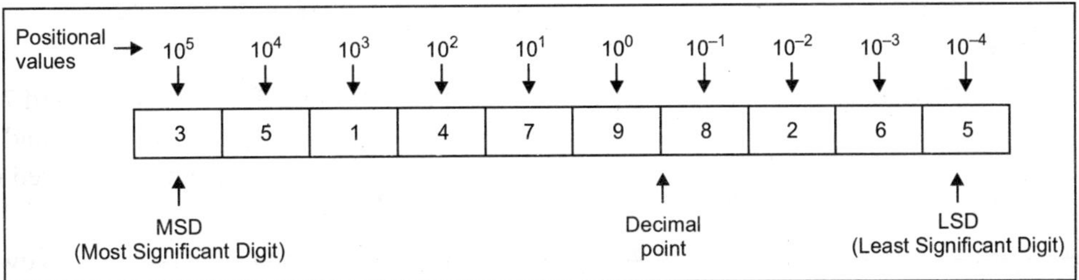


**Fig. 3.3** Decimal number shown with positional values.

Here, the places to the left of the decimal point are positive powers of 10 and places to the right are negative powers of 10.

In a decimal number as we move from right to left (starting with the digit before decimal point) the positional or place value of each digit is 10 times the positional value of the digit to its right and as we move from left to right (starting with the digit after decimal point) the positional value of each digit becomes one-tenth of the positional value of the previous digit. The part of the number before the decimal point is called **integral part** and the one after the decimal point is called the **fractional part.**

### 3.3.4 Hexadecimal Number System

The Hexadecimal Number System, popularly known as Hex System, has sixteen symbols and therefore has the **base** or **radix** as 16 or H. It is very well suited for big computers. The hexadecimal number system represents an information in the concise form. The sixteen symbols used in this system are:

0, 1, 2, 3, 4, 5, 6, 7, 8, 9, A, B, C, D, E, F

The equivalence between hex-numbers (Hexadecimal numbers) and decimal numbers is given below:

| Decimal | 0 | 1 | 2 | 3 | 4 | 5 | 6 | 7 | 8 | 9 | 10 | 11 | 12 | 13 | 14 | 15 |
|---|---|---|---|---|---|---|---|---|---|---|---|---|---|---|---|---|
| Hexadecimal | 0 | 1 | 2 | 3 | 4 | 5 | 6 | 7 | 8 | 9 | A | B | C | D | E | F |

Hexadecimal number system is also a positional value system, wherein each hexadecimal digit/letter has its own value or weight expressed as a power of 16. For example,

$$(6A9E83.C5BD)_{16}$$

It can be represented as shown in Figure 3.4:

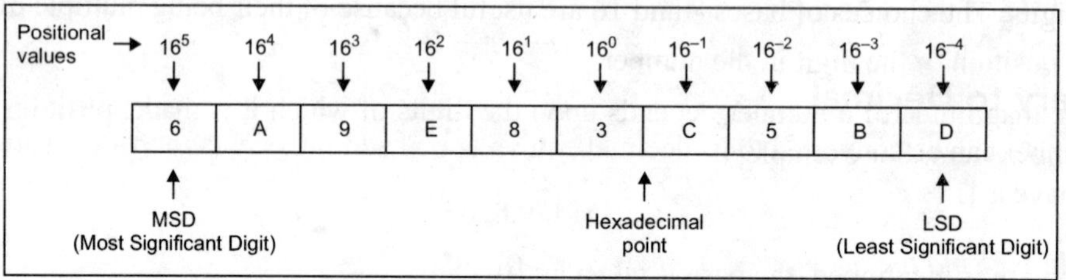


**Fig. 3.4** Hexadecimal number shown with positional values.

Here, the places to the left of hexadecimal point are positive powers of 16 and places to the right are negative powers of 16.

The Table 3.1 illustrates the relation between binary, octal, decimal and hexadecimal number systems:

**Table 3.1** Numbers with Different Bases

| Binary (base 2) | Octal (base 8) | Decimal (base 10) | Hexadecimal (base 16) |
|---|---|---|---|
| 0000 | 0 | 0 | 0 |
| 0001 | 1 | 1 | 1 |
| 0010 | 2 | 2 | 2 |
| 0011 | 3 | 3 | 3 |
| 0100 | 4 | 4 | 4 |
| 0101 | 5 | 5 | 5 |
| 0110 | 6 | 6 | 6 |
| 0111 | 7 | 7 | 7 |
| 1000 | 10 | 8 | 8 |
| 1001 | 11 | 9 | 9 |
| 1010 | 12 | 10 | A |
| 1011 | 13 | 11 | B |
| 1100 | 14 | 12 | C |
| 1101 | 15 | 13 | D |
| 1110 | 16 | 14 | E |
| 1111 | 17 | 15 | F |

## 3.4 INTERCONVERSION OF NUMBER SYSTEMS

The decimal number system is known as **International System** of numbers. This base (base 10) was used initially perhaps for the reason that man has 10 fingers. However, this system is unsuitable for computers because a computer uses electrical and electronic components which can exist only in two states. Hence, for computers the binary number system is required. But, the binary number system at the moment is indispensable for computers as it suffers from the defect of expansion. For example, a number in decimal system requiring only one digit for its representation may require more than one bits in binary form.

To overcome this problem various other number systems such as Octal (base 8) and Hexadecimal (base 16 or H) were developed. A base greater than 10 is preferred because it will require even lesser number of digits. The choices of bases 8 and 16 are useful because of their being multiple of two.

### 3.4.1 Binary to Decimal

A binary number can be converted to its decimal equivalent by adding the weights of the various positions in it which have a 1.

**Example 1:** *Find the decimal equivalent of the following binary numbers:*
(i) 10110 (ii) 101011 (iii) 11011100.

**Solution.**

*(i)* $(10110)_2 = 1 \times 2^4 + 0 \times 2^3 + 1 \times 2^2 + 1 \times 2^1 + 0 \times 2^0$

$= 16 + 0 + 4 + 2 + 0$

$= (22)_{10}.$

It must be noted that the binary number 10110 has five digits in all. The most significant digit (MSD) has the fifth position (starting from rightmost digit) so it is multiplied by $2^4$ and each digit on its right will be half of it in its positional value, so these are multiplied by $2^3$, $2^2$, $2^1$, $2^0$ respectively and the products so obtained are added to get the required decimal equivalent.

*(ii)* $(101011)_2 = 1 \times 2^5 + 0 \times 2^4 + 1 \times 2^3 + 0 \times 2^2 + 1 \times 2^1 + 1 \times 2^0$

$= 32 + 0 + 8 + 0 + 2 + 1$

$= (43)_{10}$

$= 43.$

*(iii)* $(11011100)_2 = 1 \times 2^7 + 1 \times 2^6 + 0 \times 2^5 + 1 \times 2^4 + 1 \times 2^3 + 1 \times 2^2 + 0 \times 2^1 + 0 \times 2^0$

$= 128 + 64 + 0 + 16 + 8 + 4 + 0 + 0$

$= (220)_{10}$

$= 220.$

**Example 2:** *Convert the following binary fractions to their decimal equivalents:*
(i) $(0.111)_2$ (ii) $(0.1010111)_2$ (iii) $(0.1011)_2$.

**Solution**

(*i*) $(0.111)_2 = 1 \times 2^{-1} + 1 \times 2^{-2} + 1 \times 2^{-3}$

$= 1/2 + 1/4 + 1/8$

$= 0.5 + 0.25 + 0.125$

$= (0.875)_{10}$

$= (0.875$

$\therefore \quad (0.111)_2 = (0.875)_{10}$

(*ii*) $(0.1010111)_2 = 1\times2^{-1}+0\times2^{-2}+1\times2^{-3}+0\times2^{-4}+1\times2^{-5}+1\times2^{-6}+1\times2^{-7}$

$= 1/2 + 0 + 1/8 + 0 + 1/32 + 1/64 + 1/128$

$= 0.5 + .125 + 0.03125 + 0.015625 + 0.0078125$

$= (0.6796875)_{10}$

$= (0.6796875$

$\therefore \quad (0.1010111)_2 = (0.6796875)_{10}$

(*iii*) $(0.1011)_2 = 1 \times 2^{-1} + 0 \times 2^{-2} + 1 \times 2^{-3} + 1 \times 2^{-4}$

$= 1/2 + 0 + 1/8 + 1/16$

$= 0.5 + 0.125 + 0.0625$

$= (0.6875)_{10}$

$= (0.6875$

$\therefore \quad (0.1011)_2 = (0.6875)_{10}$

**Example 3:** *Find the decimal equivalent of the following binary numbers:*
(i) $(110010.1011)_2$ (ii) $(1110.1001)_2$.

**Solution**

(*i*) $(110010.1011)_2 = (1 \times 2^5) + (1 \times 2^4) + (0 \times 2^3) + (0 \times 2^2) + (1 \times 2^1) + (0 \times 2^0)$

$+ (1 \times 2^{-1}) + (0 \times 2^{-2}) + (1 \times 2^{-3}) + (1 \times 2^{-4})$

$= 32 + 16 + 0 + 0 + 2 + 0 + 0.5 + 0 + 0.125 + 0.0625$

$= (50.6875)_{10}$

$= (50.6875$

$\therefore \quad (110010.1011)_2 = (50.6875)_{10}$.

(*ii*) $(1110.1001)_2 = 1 \times 2^3 + 1 \times 2^2 + 1 \times 2^1 + 0 \times 2^0 + 1 \times 2^{-1} + 0 \times 2^{-2}$

$+ 0 \times 2^{-3} + 1 \times 2^{-4}$

$= 8 + 4 + 2 + 0 + 1/2 + 0 + 0 + 1/16$

$= 14 + 0.5 + 0.0625$

$= 14.5625.$

**Example 4:** *Provide the missing number* $(11001.1101)_2 = (\ldots\ldots\ldots)_{10}$.

**Solution**

Let us find the decimal equivalent of the binary number.

$(11001.1101)_2 = 1 \times 2^4 + 1 \times 2^3 + 0 \times 2^2 + 0 \times 2^1 + 1 \times 2^0 + 1 \times 2^{-1}$

$+ 1 \times 2^{-2} + 0 \times 2^{-3} + 1 \times 2^{-4}$

$= 16 + 8 + 0 + 0 + 1 + 1/2 + 1/4 + 0 + 1/16$

$= 25 + 0.5 + 0.25 + 0.0625$

$= (25.8125)_{10}$

$= 25.8125$

Hence, the missing number is 25.8125.

### 3.4.2 Decimal to Binary

A positive decimal integer can be converted to binary form by successive division by 2. The procedure is given below:

Divide the given number N by 2 and let the quotient be $q_1$ and the remainder be $R_1$. Again divide the quotient $q_1$ by 2 and let the remainder be $R_2$. Continue the procedure of division till the quotient becomes 0 and in this case let the remainder be $R_n$.

Then, the binary representation by N is given as

$$N = R_n R_{n-1} \ldots\ldots R_3 R_2 R_1,$$

where each of the R's is either 0 or 1.

**Example:** *Convert the following decimal integers into their binary equivalents:*
(i) 25 (ii) 283 (iii) 5280.

**Solution**

*i.* Start dividing 25 by 2 and continue the procedure till the quotient is 0. The procedure is shown below:

| 2 | 25 | |
|---|---|---|
| 2 | 12–1 | (=$R_1$) ↑ |
| 2 | 6–0 | (=$R_2$) |
| 2 | 3–0 | (=$R_3$) |
| 2 | 1–1 | (=$R_4$) |
| | 0–1 | (=$R_5$) |

The required number in the binary number system

$$= R_5\, R_4\, R_3\, R_2\, R_1$$

$$= 11001$$

Thus, $(25)_{10} = (11001)_2$

ii. Start dividing 283 by 2 and continue the procedure till the quotient becomes 0.

| 2 | 283 | |
|---|---|---|
| 2 | 141–1 | (=$R_1$) ↑ |
| 2 | 70–1 | (=$R_2$) |
| 2 | 35–0 | (=$R_3$) |
| 2 | 17–1 | (=$R_4$) |
| 2 | 8–1 | (=$R_5$) |
| 2 | 4–0 | (=$R_6$) |
| 2 | 2–0 | (=$R_7$) |
| 2 | 1–0 | (=$R_8$) |
| | 0–1 | (=$R_9$) |

The required binary equivalent of 283

$$= R_9\, R_8\, R_7\, R_6\, R_5\, R_4\, R_3\, R_2\, R_1$$

$$= (100011011)_2$$

Thus, $(283)_{10} = (100011011)_2$

iii. Start dividing 5280 by 2 and continue the procedure till the quotient becomes 0.

| 2 | 5280 | |
|---|---|---|
| 2 | 2640–0 | (=$R_1$) ↑ |
| 2 | 1320–0 | (=$R_2$) |
| 2 | 660–0 | (=$R_3$) |
| 2 | 330–0 | (=$R_4$) |
| 2 | 165–0 | (=$R_5$) |
| 2 | 82–1 | (=$R_6$) |
| 2 | 41–0 | (=$R_7$) |
| 2 | 20–1 | (=$R_8$) |
| 2 | 10–0 | (=$R_9$) |
| 2 | 5–0 | (=$R_{10}$) |
| 2 | 2–1 | (=$R_{11}$) |
| 2 | 1–0 | (=$R_{12}$) |
| | 0–1 | (=$R_{13}$) |

The required binary equivalent of 5280

$$= R_{13} R_{12} R_{11} R_{10} R_9 R_8 R_7 R_6 R_5 R_4 R_3 R_2 R_1$$

$$= (1010010100000)_2$$

Thus, $(5280)_{10} = (1010010100000)_2$

The decimal digits and their binary equivalents are given below:

| Decimal Digit | | Binary Equivalent |
|---|---|---|
| 0 | 0 | $(0 \times 2^0)$ |
| 1 | 1 | $(1 \times 2^0)$ |
| 2 | 10 | $(1 \times 2^1 + 0 \times 2^0)$ |
| 3 | 11 | $(1 \times 2^1 + 1 \times 2^0)$ |
| 4 | 100 | $(1 \times 2^2 + 0 \times 2^1 + 0 \times 2^0)$ |
| 5 | 101 | $(1 \times 2^2 + 0 \times 2^1 + 1 \times 2^0)$ |
| 6 | 110 | $(1 \times 2^2 + 1 \times 2^1 + 0 \times 2^0)$ |
| 7 | 111 | $(1 \times 2^2 + 1 \times 2^1 + 1 \times 2^0)$ |
| 8 | 1000 | $(1 \times 2^3 + 0 \times 2^2 + 0 \times 2^1 + 0 \times 2^0)$ |
| 9 | 1001 | $(1 \times 2^3 + 0 \times 2^2 + 0 \times 2^1 + 1 \times 2^0)$ |

### 3.4.3 Decimal Fractions to Binary Fractions

While converting decimal fractions to binary fractions, instead of dividing by 2, multiply successively by 2 and instead of noting the remainders as in case of integers, keep track of the overflow. If overflow digits are $f_1, f_2, f_3, ..., f_n$ then the equivalent binary fraction is

$$0 . f_1 f_2 f_3 ..... f_n$$

while multiplying by 2, it must be noted that every time only fractional part is to be multiplied and not the integral part. The following examples illustrate the procedure.

**Example 1.** *Convert the decimal fractional number 0.8125 into its binary equivalent.*

**Solution.**

$$
\begin{array}{lr}
 & 0.8125 \\
 & \times 2 \\
\hline
f_1 & \leftarrow \boxed{1}.6250 \\
 & \times 2 \\
\hline
f_2 & \leftarrow \boxed{1}.2500 \\
 & \times 2 \\
\hline
f_3 & \leftarrow \boxed{0}.5000 \\
 & \times 2 \\
\hline
f_4 & \leftarrow \boxed{1}.0000
\end{array}
$$

(Multiply only the fraction part)

Further multiplication gives only zero digits as overflow.

Thus, $(0.8125)_{10} = 0.f_1 f_2 f_3 f_4$

$= (0.1101)_2$

**Example 2.** *Convert 0.33 into its binary equivalent.*

**Solution.**

| | | |
|---|---|---|
| | 0.33 | |
| | ×2 | |
| $f_1$ | ← [0].66 | |
| | ×2 | |
| $f_2$ | ← [1].32 | |
| | ×2 | (Multiply only the fraction part) |
| $f_3$ | ← [0].64 | |
| | ×2 | |
| $f_4$ | ← [1].28 | |
| | ×2 | |
| $f_5$ | ← [0].56 | |
| | ×2 | |
| $f_6$ | ← [1].12 | and so on. |

Thus, $(0.33)_{10} = 0.f_1 f_2 f_3 f_4 f_5 f_6......$

$= (0.010101...)_2$

### 3.4.4 Mixed Decimal Numbers to Binary

A mixed number consists of an integral part as well as a fractional part. For example, 38.625 is a mixed number. A mixed number in decimal system can be converted to its binary equivalent by converting the integral and fractional parts separately into their binary equivalent.

The following example illustrates this concept:

**Example.** *Convert the decimal number 38.625 into its binary equivalent.*

**Solution.**

The given decimal number has two parts, namely an integral part 38 and a fractional part 0.625. These are to be converted into their binary equivalents separately, as given below:

| | | |
|---|---|---|
| 2 | 38 | |
| 2 | 19–0 | (=$R_1$) |
| 2 | 9–1 | (=$R_2$) |
| 2 | 4–1 | (=$R_3$) |
| 2 | 2–0 | (=$R_4$) |
| 2 | 1–0 | (=$R_5$) |
| | 0–1 | (=$R_6$) |

Thus, the binary equivalent of $(38)_{10} = R_6 R_5 R_4 R_3 R_2 R_1$

$$= (100110)_2$$

Also

$$\begin{array}{lr} & 0.625 \\ & \times 2 \\ \hline f_1 & \leftarrow \boxed{1}.250 \\ & \times 2 \\ \hline f_2 & \leftarrow \boxed{1}.500 \\ & \times 2 \\ \hline f_3 & \leftarrow \boxed{1}.000 \end{array}$$

(Multiply only the fraction part)

Further multiplication gives only zero digits as overflow.

Thus, $(0.625)_{10} = 0.f_1 f_2 f_3$

$= (0.101)_2$

Hence, $(38.625)_{10} = (100110.101)_2$

### 3.4.5 Decimal Numbers to Octal Numbers

For converting integer decimal numbers into their equivalent octal numbers, divide the given number repeatedly by 8 till the quotient obtained is zero. The following example illustrates this concept:

**Example 1.** *Convert the following Decimal numbers into their Octal equivalents:*
(i) 759 (ii) 1598.

**Solution.**

i. Start dividing 759 by 8 and continue the procedure till the quotient is 0. The procedure is shown below:

| 8 | 759 | |
|---|---|---|
| 8 | 94—7 | ↑ LSD |
| 8 | 11—6 | |
| 8 | 1—3 | |
| | 0—1 | MSD |

Thus, $(759)_{10} = (1367)_8$

*(ii)*

| 8 | 1598 | |
|---|---|---|
| 8 | 199—6 | ↑ LSD |
| 8 | 24—7 | |
| 8 | 3—0 | |
| | 0—3 | MSD |

Thus, $(1598)_{10} = (3076)_8$

For converting decimal fractions into their equivalent octal fractions, multiply the fractional part repeatedly by 8 and keep track of the overflow. The process of multiplication continues till the fractional part becomes zero or upto required number of digits.

The following example illustrates this concept:

**Example 2.** *Convert the following decimal fractions to their equivalent octal fractions:*
(i) $(0.125)_{10}$ (ii) $(0.175)_{10}$.

**Solution.** (*i*)

Thus, $(0.125)_{10} = (0.1)_8$

$$\begin{array}{r} 0.125 \\ \times 8 \\ \hline \boxed{1}.000 \end{array}$$

(*ii*)

$$\begin{array}{lr} & 0.175 \\ & \times 8 \\ \hline f_1 & \leftarrow \boxed{1}.400 \\ & \times 8 \\ \hline f_2 & \leftarrow \boxed{3}.200 \\ & \times 8 \\ \hline f_3 & \leftarrow \boxed{1}.600 \\ & \times 8 \\ \hline f_4 & \leftarrow \boxed{4}.800 \\ & \times 8 \\ \hline f_5 & \leftarrow \boxed{6}.400 \\ & \times 8 \\ \hline f_6 & \leftarrow \boxed{3}.200 \\ & \times 8 \\ \hline f_7 & \leftarrow \boxed{1}.600 \\ & \times 8 \\ \hline f_8 & \leftarrow \boxed{4}.800 \\ & \times 8 \\ \hline f_9 & \leftarrow \boxed{6}.400 \end{array}$$

(Multiply only the fraction part)

and so on.

Thus, $(0.175)_{10} = (0.1\ )_8$ recurrence

Here, the bar shows that these digits will be repeated infinitely.

For converting the decimal mixed numbers into their equivalent octal, integral and fractional parts are treated separately. Each part is converted to octal separately.

The following example illustrates this concept:

**Example 3.** *Convert the following mixed decimal numbers to their equivalent Octal:*
(i) 22.21875 (ii) 79.4375.

**Solution.**

i. $(22.21875)_{10}$

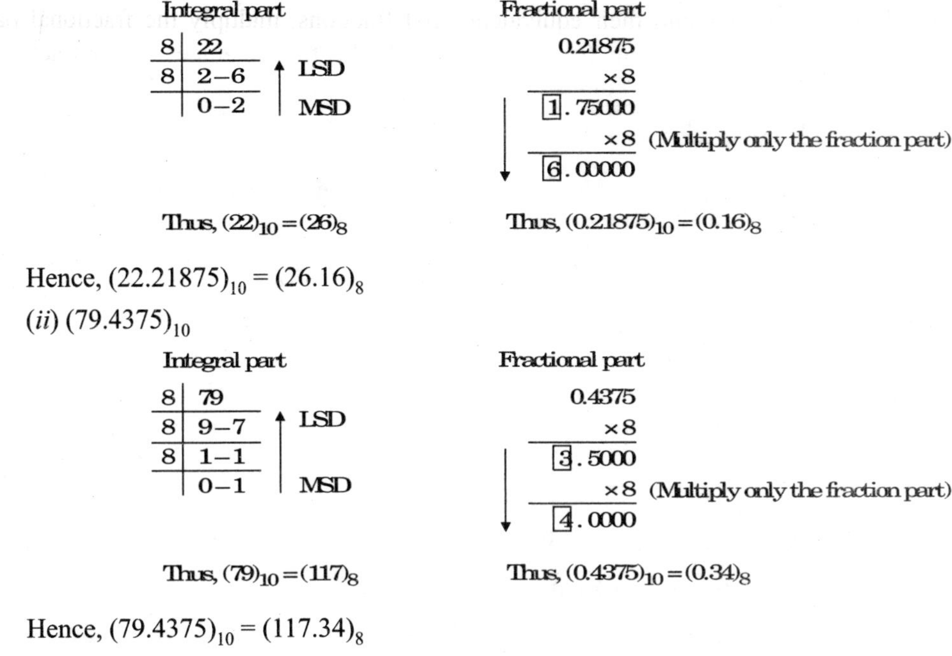


Hence, $(22.21875)_{10} = (26.16)_8$

(*ii*) $(79.4375)_{10}$



Hence, $(79.4375)_{10} = (117.34)_8$

---

**NOTE.** It may be noticed that when a decimal number is converted to its binary equivalent, a long string of binary digits, namely 0 and 1 is obtained. On the other hand, if the same decimal number is converted to its octal equivalent, the number so obtained contains less number of digits compared to binary. In fact, this was the reason for the development of Octal Number System. It must be remembered that computers still work in binary and all these number systems (except binary) are for users' convenience.

---

### 3.4.6 Octal Numbers to Decimal Numbers

A mixed octal number can be converted to decimal number by the formula given below:

$$M = d_{n+1}8^n + d_n8^{n-1} + d_{n-1}8^{n-2} + \ldots\ldots\ d_38^2 + d_28^1 + d_18^0 + d\_{-1}8^{-1} + d_{-2}8^{-2} + d_{-3}8^{-3} + \ldots + d_{-n}8^{-n}$$

Here, M is the mixed number

$d_{n+1}$ is the digit in the $(n + 1)$th position of the integral part

$d_{-1}$ is the digit immediately after the octal point.

The following examples illustrate this concept:

**Example 1.** *Convert the following octal numbers into their decimal equivalents:*
(i) $(47)_8$ (ii) $(564)_8$.

**Solution.**

(*i*) $(47)_8 = 4 \times 8^1 + 7 \times 8^0$

$= 32 + 7 = 39$

Thus, $(47)_8 = (39)_{10}$

(*ii*) $(564)_8 = 5 \times 8^2 + 6 \times 8^1 + 4 \times 8^0$

$= 5 \times 64 + 6 \times 8 + 4 \times 1$

$= 320 + 48 + 4$

$= 372$

Thus, $(564)_8 = (372)_{10}$

**Example 2.** *Convert the following octal fractions to their decimal equivalents:* (i) $(0.34)_8$ (ii) $(0.542)_8$.

**Solution.**

(*i*) $(0.34)_8 = 3 \times 8^{-1} + 4 \times 8^{-2}$

$= 3 \times 1/8 + 4 \times 1/64$

$= 3 \times 0.125 + 4 \times 0.015625$

$= 0.375 + .062500$

$= (0.4375)_{10}$

(*ii*) $(0.542)_8 = 5 \times 8^{-1} + 4 \times 8^{-2} + 2 \times 8^{-3}$

$= 5 \times 0.125 + 4 \times .015625 + 2 \times .001953125$

$= 0.625 + 0.062500 + .003906250$

$= (0.691406250)_{10}$

### 3.4.7 Octal to Binary

The Octal number system is widely used as a shorthand way of expressing binary values. The octal number system groups three binary bits together into one digit (0 to 7) as given below:

| Octal Equivalent | Binary |
|---|---|
| 0 | 000 |
| 1 | 001 |
| 2 | 010 |
| 3 | 011 |
| 4 | 100 |
| 5 | 101 |
| 6 | 110 |
| 7 | 111 |

To convert an octal number to its binary equivalent, each digit of the octal number is converted to its 3 bits binary equivalent.

The following examples illustrate this concept:

**Example 1.** *Convert the following octal numbers into their binary equivalent:*
(i) $(746)_8$ (ii) $(5043)_8$.

**Solution.**

(*i*) $(746)_8 = \underset{7}{\underline{111}}\ \underset{4}{\underline{100}}\ \underset{6}{\underline{110}}$

Replace each octal digit by its 3 bits binary equivalent)

$= (111100110)_2$

Thus, $(746)_8 = (111100110)_2$

(*ii*) $(5043)_8 = \underset{5}{\underline{101}}\ \underset{0}{\underline{000}}\ \underset{4}{\underline{100}}\ \underset{3}{\underline{011}}$

$= (101000100011)_2$

Thus, $(5043)_8 = (101000100011)_2$

**Example 2.** *Convert the following octal numbers into their binary equivalents:*
(i) $(35.216)_8$ (ii) $(417.25)_8$.

**Solution.**

(*i*) $(35.216)_8 = \underset{3}{\underline{011}}\ \underset{5}{\underline{101}}\ .\ \underset{2}{\underline{010}}\ \underset{1}{\underline{001}}\ \underset{6}{\underline{110}}$

$= (11101.01000111)_2$

(Discarding the leftmost and right most zero)

Thus, $(35.216)_8 = (11101.01000111)_2$

(*ii*) $(417.25)_8 = \underset{4}{\underline{100}}\ \underset{1}{\underline{001}}\ \underset{7}{\underline{111}}\ .\ \underset{2}{\underline{010}}\ \underset{5}{\underline{101}}$

$= (100001111.010101)_2$

Thus, $(417.25)_8 = (100001111.010101)_2$

## 3.4.8 Binary to Octal

For converting a binary number into its octal equivalent the following steps are followed:

i. Divide the given binary number before the binary point into groups of three bits each (from right to left) and after the binary point into groups of three bits each (from left to right) by adding 0 bits for completing the groups (if needed).
ii. Replace each group by its octal equivalent.

The following examples illustrate this concept:

**Example 1.** *Convert the following Binary numbers into their Octal equivalents:*
(i) $(11101)_2$ (ii) $(101010011011.10100011)_2$.

**Solution.**

(*i*) $(11101)_2 = \underset{3}{\underline{011}}\ \underset{5}{\underline{101}}$

(Replacing each group by its octal equivalent, 0 added on leftmost position for completing the group)

Thus, $(11101)_2 = 35)_8$

(*ii*)

$(101010011011.10100011)_2 = \underset{5}{\underline{101}}\ \underset{2}{\underline{010}}\ \underset{3}{\underline{011}}\ \underset{3}{\underline{011}} . \underset{5}{\underline{101}}\ \underset{0}{\underline{000}}\ \underset{6}{\underline{110}}$

Replacing each group by its octal equivalent, 0 added on rightmost position for completing the group).

Thus,

$(101010011011.10100011)_2 = (5233.506)_8$

**Example 2.** *Convert the following Binary numbers into their Octal equivalents:*
(i) $(10110101.11001)_2$ (ii) $(11110011.0001)_2$.

**Solution.**

(i) $(10110101.11001)_2 = \underset{2}{\underline{010}}\ \underset{6}{\underline{110}}\ \underset{5}{\underline{101}} . \underset{6}{\underline{110}}\ \underset{2}{\underline{010}}$

Replacing each group by its equivalent, 0 added on leftmost and rightmost position for completing the group).

Thus, $(10110101.11001)_2 = (265.62)_8$

(ii) $(11110011.0001)_2 = \underset{3}{\underline{011}}\ \underset{6}{\underline{110}}\ \underset{3}{\underline{011}} . \underset{0}{\underline{000}}\ \underset{4}{\underline{100}}$

Replacing each group by its equivalent, 0 added on leftmost and two 0's added on rightmost position for completing the group).

Thus, $(11110011.0001)_2 = (363.04)_8$

### 3.4.9 Decimal Numbers to Hexadecimal Numbers

For converting integer decimal numbers into their equivalent hexadecimal numbers, divide the given number repeatedly by 16 (if the remainder is greater than or equal to 10 then write its symbol, that is, A to F, otherwise the digit 0 to 9) till the quotient obtained is zero.

The following example illustrates this concept:

**Example 1.** *Convert the following Decimal numbers into their Hexadecimal equivalents:*
(i) $(28)_{10}$ (ii) $(1795)_{10}$.

**Solution.**

*i.* Start dividing 28 by 16 and continue the procedure till the quotient is 0. The procedure is given below:

| 16 | 28 |
|---|---|
| 16 | 1–C |
| | 0–1 |

Thus, $(28)_{10} = (1C)_{16}$

*ii.*

| 16 | 1795 |
|---|---|
| 16 | 112–3 |
| 16 | 7–0 |
| | 0–7 |

Thus, $(1795)_{10} = (703)_{16}$

For converting decimal fractions into their equivalent hexadecimal fractions, multiply the fractional part repeatedly by 16 and keep track of the overflow. If the overflow is greater than equal to 10 then write its symbol, that is, A to F, otherwise the digit 0 to 9. The process of multiplication continues till the fractional part becomes zero or upto required number of digits.

The following example illustrates this concept:

**Example 2.** *Convert the following decimal functions to their equivalent hexadecimal fractions:* (i) $(0.875)_{10}$ (ii) $(0.28125)_{10}$.

**Solution.**

(*i*)

$$\begin{array}{r} 0.875 \\ \times 16 \\ \hline \boxed{14}.000 \\ =E \end{array}$$

Thus, $(0.875)_{10} = (0.E)_{16}$

(*ii*)

$$\begin{array}{r} 0.28125 \\ \times 16 \\ \hline \boxed{4}.50000 \\ \times 16 \\ \hline \boxed{8}.00000 \end{array}$$

(Multiply only the fractional part)

Thus, $(0.28125)_{10} = (0.48)_{16}$

For converting a mixed decimal number to its hexadecimal equivalent, the integral and fractional parts are converted separately into their hexadecimal equivalents.

The following example illustrates this concept:

**Example 3.** *Convert the following mixed decimal numbers to their equivalent hexadecimals:* (i) $(47.375)_{10}$ (ii) $(835.390625)_{10}$.

**Solution.**

(*i*) $(47.375)_{10}$

**Integral part**

| 16 | 47 | |
|---|---|---|
| 16 | 2–15 | = F ↑ |
| | 0–2 | |

Thus, $(47)_{10} = (2F)_{16}$

**Fractional part**

$$\begin{array}{r} 0.375 \\ \times 16 \\ \hline \boxed{6}.000 \end{array}$$

Thus, $(0.375)_{10} = (0.6)_{16}$

Hence, $(47.375)_{10} = (2F.6)_{16}$

(*ii*) $(835.390625)_{10}$

**Integral part**

| 16 | 835 | |
|---|---|---|
| 16 | 52–3 | ↑ |
| 16 | 3–4 | |
| | 0–3 | |

Thus, $(835)_{10} = (343)_{16}$

**Fractional part**

$$\begin{array}{r} 0.390625 \\ \times 16 \\ \hline \boxed{6}.250000 \\ \times 16 \\ \hline \boxed{4}.000000 \end{array}$$

Thus, $(0.390625)_{10} = (0.64)_{16}$

Hence, $(835.390625)_{10} = (343.64)_{10}$

### 3.4.10 Hexadecimal Numbers to their Decimal Equivalents

The conversion of hexadecimal numbers to their decimal equivalents is performed by using the concept of the positional value of each digit in the number, whether it is an integer, a fraction or a mixed number. The following examples illustrate this concept:

**Example 1.** *Convert the following hexadecimal numbers to their decimal equivalents:* (i) $(9D)_{16}$ (ii) $(517)_{16}$.

**Solution.**

(*i*) $(9D)_{16} = 9 \times 16^1 + D \times 16^0$

$= 144 + 13 \times 1$ (D = 13)

$= 144 + 13$

$= 157$

Hence, $(9D)_{16} = (157)_{10}$

(*ii*) $(517)_{16} = 5 \times 16^2 + 1 \times 16^1 + 7 \times 16^0$

$= 5 \times 256 + 1 \times 16 + 7 \times 1$

$= 1280 + 16 + 7$

$= 1303$

Hence, $(517)_{16} = (1303)_{10}$

**Example 2.** *Convert the following hexadecimal fractions into their decimal equivalents:*
(i) $(0.48)_{16}$ (ii) $(0.125)_{16}$.

**Solution.**

(*i*) $(0.48)_{16} = 4 \times 16^{-1} + 8 \times 16^{-2}$

$= 4 \times 1/16 + 8 \times 1/16^2$

$= 4 \times .0625 + 8 \times 0.00390625$

$= 0.2500 + .03125000$

$= 0.28125000$

Hence, $(0.48)_{16} = (0.28125)_{10}$

(*ii*) $(0.125)_{16} = 1 \times 16^{-1} + 2 \times 16^{-2} + 5 \times 16^{-3}$

$= 1 \times 0.0625 + 2 \times 0.00390625 + 5 \times 0.00024414$

$= 0.0625 + 0.00781250 + 0.00122070$

$= 0.07153320$

Hence, $(0.125)_{16} = (0.0715332)_{10}$

### 3.4.11 Hexadecimal to Binary

For converting a hexadecimal number to its binary equivalent, each digit of the hexadecimal number is converted to its 4-bits binary equivalent. For reading convenience, usually each nibble (4-bit binary equivalent) is written with a little space in between. The following examples illustrate this concept:

**Example 1.** *Convert the following hexadecimal numbers into their binary equivalents:*
(i) $(B9F)_{16}$ (ii) $(8796)_{16}$.

**Solution.**

(*i*) $(59F)_{16} = \underset{5}{\underline{0101}}\ \underset{9}{\underline{1001}}\ \underset{F}{\underline{1111}}$

Replace each hexadecimal digit by its 4 bits binary equivalent)

$= (0101\ 1001\ 1111)_2$

Thus $(59F)_{16} = (0101\ 1001\ 1111)_2$

(*ii*) $(8796)_{16} = \underset{F}{\underline{1111}}\ \underset{3}{\underline{0011}}\ \underset{A}{\underline{1010}} . \underset{C}{\underline{1100}}\ \underset{B}{\underline{1011}}$

Replace each hexadecimal digit by its 4 bits binary equivalent)

$= (1000\ 0111\ 1001\ 0110)_2$

Thus, $(8796)_{16} = (1000\ 0111\ 1001\ 0110)_2$

**Example 2.** *Convert the following hexadecimal numbers into their binary equivalents:* (i) $(F3A.CB)_{16}$ (ii) $(5D.8F)_{16}$.

**Solution.**

(*i*) $F3A.CB)_{16} = \underset{F}{\underline{1111}}\ \underset{3}{\underline{0011}}\ \underset{A}{\underline{1010}} . \underset{C}{\underline{1100}}\ \underset{B}{\underline{1011}}$

(Replace each hexadecimal digit by its 4 bits binary equivalent)

$= (1111\ 0011\ 1010 . 1100\ 1011)_2$

Thus, $(F3A.CB)_{16} = (1111\ 0011\ 1010 . 1100\ 1011)_2$

(*ii*) $(5D.8F)_{16} = \underset{5}{\underline{0101}}\ \underset{D}{\underline{1101}} . \underset{8}{\underline{1000}}\ \underset{F}{\underline{1111}}$

(Replace each hexadecimal digit by its 4 bits binary equivalent)

$= (0101\ 1101 . 1000\ 1111)_2$

Thus, $(5D.8F)_{16} = (0101\ 1101 . 1000\ 1111)_2$

**NOTE:** It must be remembered that whatever number system one may use, the information stored in the computer memory is always in terms of binary digits. It is only for our convenience that we use octal or hexadecimal numbers.

## POINTS TO REMEMBER

- Numbers are represented by a string of digit symbols.
- The binary number system has the base or radix 2, the octal 8 and hexadecimal 16.
- Division remainder method is the most commonly used method for converting from decimal system to other systems. The following steps are carried out for integral part.
  i. Divide the given number of decimal system by the base or radix R of the desired system. By doing so, we get a quotient $Q_1$ and a remainder $R_1$.
  ii. Divided the quotient $Q_1$ by the radix R again to get quotient $R_2$ and a remainder $R_2$.
  iii. Repeat the above process till the quotient is 0 (zero) and a remainder $R_n$ (say).
  iv. Write the converted number as $R_n\ R_{n-1} \ldots R_2\ R_1$ for the integral part.

  For converting decimal fractions to other fractions, instead of dividing by the radix R, multiply successively by R and instead of noting the remainde~s as in case of integers, keep track of the overflow. Stop when fractional part becomes zero or recurrence takes place. If overflow digits are $f_1, f_2, f_3, \ldots f_n$ then he equivalent binary fraction is $0.f_1f_2 \ldots f_n$. (Remember that while multiplying by R, every time fractional part is to be multiplied and not the integral part.)

## EXERCISE

1. What is a Number System? State the utility of Number Systems.
2. Why do digital computers use binary numbers for their operation?
3. Convert the following binary numbers to equivalent decimal numbers:

i. 11011 ii. 10011010

4. Convert the following decimal numbers to equivalent binary numbers:

   i. 44 ii. 155

5. Convert the following real binary numbers to equivalent decimal numbers:

   i. 1101.11 ii. 101001.1101

6. Convert the following decimal numbers to equivalent binary numbers:

   i. 18.71875 ii. 75.6875

7. Convert the following octal numbers to equivalent binary numbers:

   i. 534 ii. 647

8. Convert the following binary numbers to equivalent octal numbers:

   i. 1100110 ii. 10111101

9. Convert the following hexadecimal numbers to equivalent binary numbers:

   i. 6BC ii. 4C3F

10. Convert the following binary numbers to equivalent hexadecimal numbers:

    i. 10110110111 ii. 1101001100

11. Convert the binary number 101101.101101 into octal and hexadecimal number system.

12. The roots of the quadratic equation $x^2 - 12x + 37 = 0$ are 5 and 8. Find the base in which this equation is written.

13. Fill in the blanks:

    i. $(94.00625)_{10} = (\ldots\ldots\ldots\ldots\ldots\ldots)_2$

    ii. $(11011.0101)_2 = (\ldots\ldots\ldots\ldots\ldots\ldots)_{10} = (\ldots\ldots\ldots\ldots\ldots\ldots)_8$

    iii. ASCII stands for .................................. .

14. What is the advantage of using hexadecimal numbers?

## ANSWERS

### Review Questions and Exercises

3. (i) 27 (ii) 154
4. (i) 101100 (ii) 10011011
5. (i) 13.75 (ii) 41.8125
6. (i) 10010.10111 (ii) 1001011.1011
7. (i) 101011100 (ii) 110100111
8. (i) 146 (ii) 275
9. (i) 11010111100 (ii) 100110000111111
10. (i) 5B7 (ii) 34C
11. $(55.55)_8$, $(2D.B4)_{16}$
12. 11

CHAPTER

4

# Computer Codes and Their Types

## 4.1 INTRODUCTION

Digital systems are built using binary devices. Coding is a technique by which a set of objects is represented in a machine by a set of binary numbers called codes. Computers and other digital circuits process data in binary format. To achieve this, a process of coding is required where each alphabet, special character or numeral is coded in a unique combination of 0 s and 1 s using a coding scheme known as *code*. Various binary codes are used to represent data which may be numeric, alphabets or special characters. Codes are also used for error detection and error correction in digital systems. Although, in digital systems in every code used, the information is represented in binary form, but the interpretation of the data is only possible if the code in which the data is being represented is known.

The full form of BCD is 'Binary-Coded Decimal'. Since this is coding scheme relating decimal and binary numbers, hence four bits are required to code each decimal number. For example, (35)10 is represented as 0011 0101 using BCD code, rather than (100011)2. From the example it is clear that it requires more number of bits to code a decimal number using BCD code than using the straight binary code. However, inspite of this disadvantage it is convenient to use BCD code for input and output operations in digital systems. For example, the binary number 1000011 represents 67 (decimal) in straight binary, 43 (decimal) in BCD and alphabet C in ASCII code. Hence while interpreting the data one must be very careful regarding the code used.

## 4.2 CODES

Codes can be broadly classified into following five groups:

*i.* Weighted Binary Codes,

*ii.* Non-weighted Codes,

*iii.* Alphanumeric Codes,

*iv.* Error-detecting Codes and

*v.* Error-correcting Codes.

The commonly used codes are discussed below.

## 4.3 WEIGHTED BINARY CODES

If each position of a number represents a specific weight then the coding scheme is called weighted binary code. In such coding the bits are multiplied by their corresponding individual weight, and then the sum of these weighted bits gives the equivalent decimal digit.

### 4.3.1 NBCD Code

Natural Binary Coded Decimal (NBCD) code is also known as 8-4-2-1 code. It is because 8, 4, 2 and 1 are the weights of the four bits of the BCD code. The weight of the LSB is $2^0$ or 1, that of the next higher order bit is $2^1$ or 2, that of the next higher order bit is $2^2$ or 4, and that of the MSB is $2^3$ or 8. Therefore, this is a *weighted* code and arithmetic operations can be performed using this code which will be discussed later on. The bit assignment 0101, for example, can be interpreted by the weights to represent the decimal digit 5 because $0 \times 8 + 1 \times 4 + 0 \times 2 + 1 \times 1 = 5$. Since four binary bits are used hence the maximum decimal equivalent that may be coded is $15_{10}$ (*i.e.*, $1111_2$). But the maximum decimal digit available is $9_{10}$. Hence the binary codes 1010, 1011, 1100, 1101, 1110, 1111 representing 10, 11, 12, 13, 14 and 15 in decimal are never being used in BCD code. So these six codes are called forbidden codes and the group of these codes is called forbidden group in BCD code. BCD code for decimal digits 0 to 9 is shown in Table 4.1.

**Table 4.1** Illustration of BCD Code of Decimal Digits

| Decimal Digits | BCD Representation |
|---|---|
| 0 | 0000 |
| 1 | 0001 |
| 2 | 0010 |
| 3 | 0011 |
| 4 | 0100 |
| 5 | 0101 |
| 6 | 0110 |
| 7 | 0111 |
| 8 | 1000 |
| 9 | 1001 |

The following examples illustrate the BCD encoding:

**Example 1.** *Give the BCD equivalent for the decimal number 509.*

**Solution.**

The decimal number is 509

BCD code is 0101 0000 1001

Hence, $(509)_{10} = (010100001001)_{BCD}$

**Example 2.** *Give the BCD equivalent for the decimal number 49.27.*

**Solution.**

| The decimal number | 4 | 9 | 2 | 7 |
|---|---|---|---|---|
| BCD code | 0100 | 1001 | 0010 | 0111 |

Hence, $(49.27)_{10} = (01001001.00100111)_{BCD}$

Here, we must distinguish carefully between *encoding* and *conversion*. For example, 14 when converted to binary would be 1 1 1 0. On the other hand, when it is encoded each digit must be represented by a 4-bit code and an encoding is 00010100. As mentioned earlier *encoding requires more bits compared to conversion.* On the average $\log_2 10 = 3.32$ bits are required when decimal numbers are converted to binary; as compared with this 4 bits per digit are needed in encoding. The ratio (4/3.3) = 1.2 is a measure of the extra bits (and consequently extra storage) needed if an *encoding* is used. On the other hand, *conversion of decimal to binary is slower compared to encoding.* It is due to the fact that an algorithm involving successive division is required for conversion whereas encoding is by straightforward table look-up. The slowness of conversion is not a major problem in computations having small volume of input/output. In business computers, where input/output dominates, it is necessary to examine BCD representation. In smaller digital system such as desk calculators, digital clocks, etc., it is uneconomical to incorporate complex electronic circuits to convert decimal to binary and vice versa. Thus BCD representation should be preferred.

### 4.3.2 $84\bar{2}\bar{1}$ Code

It is also possible to assign negative weights to decimal code, as shown by the $84\bar{2}\bar{1}$ code. In this case the bit combination 0101 is interpreted as the decimal digit 3, as obtained from $0 \times 8 + 1 \times 4 + 0 \times (-2) + 1 \times (-1) = 3$. This is a self-complementary code, that is, the 9's complement of the decimal number is obtained just by changing the 1's to 0's and 0's to 1's, or in effect by getting the 1's complement of the corresponding number. For example, if we change the 1's to 0's and 0's to 1's in the previous example we have 1010 which is interpreted as decimal 6, as obtained from $1 \times 8 + 0 \times 4 + 1 \times (-2) + 0 \times (-1) = 6$. And 6 is the 9's complement of 3. This property is useful when arithmetic operations are done internally with decimal numbers (in a binary code) and subtraction is calculated by means of 9's complement.

### 4.3.3 2421 Code

Another weighted code is 2421 code. The weights assigned to the four digits are 2, 4, 2 and 1. The 2421 code is same as that in BCD from 0 to 4; however it varies from 5 to 9. For example, in this case the bit combination 0100 represents decimal 4; whereas the bit combination 1101 is interpreted as the decimal 7, as obtained from $2 \times 1 + 1 \times 4 + 0 \times 2 + 1 \times 1 = 7$. This is also a *self-complementary code,* that is, the 9's complement of the decimal number is obtained by changing the 1's to 0's and 0's to 1's. The 2421 codes for decimal number 0 through 9 are shown in Table 4.2.

**Table 4.2:** Binary Codes for Decimal Digits

| Decimal Digit | (NBCD) 8421 | $84\bar{2}\bar{1}$ | 2421 | Excess-3 |
|---|---|---|---|---|
| 0 | 0000 | 0000 | 0000 | 0011 |
| 1 | 0001 | 0111 | 0001 | 0100 |
| 2 | 0010 | 0110 | 0010 | 0101 |
| 3 | 0011 | 0101 | 0011 | 0110 |
| 4 | 0100 | 0100 | 0100 | 0111 |
| 5 | 0101 | 1011 | 1011 | 1000 |
| 6 | 0110 | 1010 | 1100 | 1001 |
| 7 | 0111 | 1001 | 1101 | 1010 |
| 8 | 1000 | 1000 | 1110 | 1011 |
| 9 | 1001 | 1111 | 1111 | 1100 |

## 4.4 NON-WEIGHTED BINARY CODES

These codes are not positionally weighted. It basically means that each position of the binary number is not assigned a fixed value. Excess-3 codes and Gray codes are such non-weighted codes.

### 4.4.1 Excess-3 Code

A decimal code that has been used in some old computers is excess-3 code. This is an unweighted code. This code assignment is obtained from the corresponding value of 4 bit binary code after adding 3 to the given decimal digit. Here the maximum value may be $1100_2$ since the maximum decimal digit is 9 hence we have to add 3 to 9 and then get the BCD equivalent. Like $84\bar{2}\bar{1}$ and 2421 codes excess-3 is also a self-complementary code, that is, the 9's complement of the decimal number is obtained by changing the 1's to 0's and 0's to 1's. This self-complementary property of the code helps considerably in performing subtraction operation in digital systems.

The following examples illustrate the Excess-3 code encoding:

**Example 1.** *Convert $(359)_{10}$ into its Excess-3 code.*

**Solution.**

| The decimal number is | 3 | 5 | 9 |
|---|---|---|---|
| Add 3 to each bit | +3 | +3 | +3 |
| Sum | 6 | 8 | 12 |

Converting the above each sum into 4 bit binary equivalent, we have

| 4 bit binary equivalent | 0110 | 1000 | 1100 |
|---|---|---|---|

Hence, the Excess-3 code for $(359)_{10}$ = 0110 1000 1100

**Example 2.** *Convert $(58.43)_{10}$ into its Excess-3 code.*

**Solution.**

| The decimal number is | 5 | 8 | 4 | 3 |
|---|---|---|---|---|
| Add 3 to each bit | +3 | +3 | +3 | +3 |
| Sum | 8 | 11 | 7 | 6 |

Converting the above each sum into 4 bit binary equivalent, we have

| 4 bit binary equivalent | 1000 | 1011 | 0111 | 0110 |
|---|---|---|---|---|

Hence, the Excess-3 code for $(58.43)_{10}$ = 10001011.01110110

### 4.4.2 Gray Code

Gray code (or Cyclic Code or Reflected Code) belongs to a class of code known as minimum change code, in which a number changes by only one bit as it proceeds from one number to the next. Hence this code is not useful for arithmetic operations. This code finds extensive use for shaft encoders, in some types of analog-to-digital converters etc. Gray code is **reflected code** and is shown in Table 4.3. The Gray code may contain any number of bits. Here we take the example of four bit Gray Code. The code shown in Table 4.3 is only one of many possible such codes. To obtain a different reflected code, one can start with any bit combination and proceed to obtain the next bit combination by changing only one bit from 0 to 1 or 1 to 0 in any desired random fashion, as long as two numbers do not have identical code assignments. The Gray code is not a weighted code.

**Table 4.3** Four-bit Reflected Code

| Reflected Code | Decimal Equivalent |
|---|---|
| m4 0000 | 0 |
| m3 0001 | 1 |
| 0011 | 2 |
| m2 0010 | 3 |
| 0110 | 4 |
| 0111 | 5 |
| 0101 | 6 |
| m1 0100 | 7 |
| 1100 | 8 |
| 1101 | 9 |
| 1111 | 10 |
| m5 1110 | 11 |
| 1010 | 12 |
| m6 1011 | 13 |
| m7 1001 | 14 |
| 1000 | 15 |

Now we try to analyze the name **"Reflected Code"**. If we look at Table 4.3, we can consider seven virtual mirrors m1, m2, m3, m4, m5, m6 and m7 placed. Now for mirror m1 if we consider the MSB as the refractive index of the input and output medium then leaving out the MSB we can see that all of the eight combinations of three bits each, have its corresponding reflected counterparts. Similarly for mirrors m2 and m5 if we now leave the actual MSB we can consider the combination of three bits where now we consider the third bit as the new MSB. And similar arguments follow as for mirror m1. Similarly we may analyze the cases for mirrors m3, m4, m6 and m7.

**Table 4.4** Binary and Gray Codes

| Decimal Numbers | Binary Code | Gray Code |
|---|---|---|
| 0 | 0000 | 0000 |
| 1 | 0001 | 0001 |
| 2 | 0010 | 0011 |
| 3 | 0011 | 0010 |
| 4 | 0100 | 0110 |
| 5 | 0101 | 0111 |
| 6 | 0110 | 0101 |
| 7 | 0111 | 0100 |

| Decimal Numbers | Binary Code | Gray Code |
|---|---|---|
| 8 | 1000 | 1100 |
| 9 | 1001 | 1101 |
| 10 | 1010 | 1111 |
| 11 | 1011 | 1110 |
| 12 | 1100 | 1010 |
| 13 | 1101 | 1011 |
| 14 | 1110 | 1001 |
| 15 | 1111 | 1000 |
| | | |

The *Hamming distance* (named after its inventor R.W. Hamming) between two equal length binary numbers is the number of positions in which they differ. For example, if A = 0111 and B = 1011, the Hamming distance between A and B is two as they differ in their first and second positions counting from left. The Hamming distance between two successive code groups in a cyclic code is unity, *i.e.*, each code group is adjacent to the next in sequence. Following map (See Fig. 4.1) is coded to ensure that each square is at a unit distance from its adjacent square and each square in this map has four neighbours (adjacent squares).

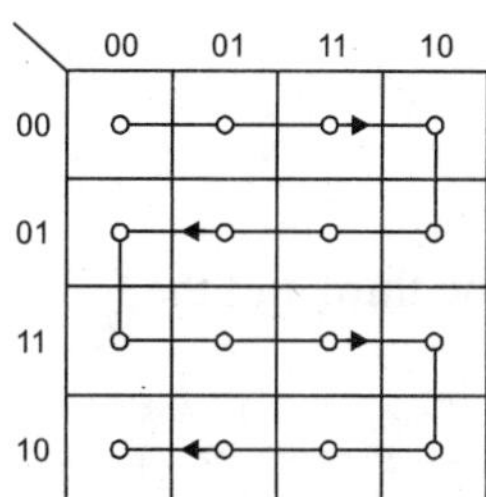


**Fig. 4.1** A chart depicting a cyclic code.

The map shown in Figure 4.1 is called *Karnaugh map* and can be used to construct a large number of cyclic codes. One such code is shown in Table 4.4. Start assigning the code and proceed as shown by the arrow and the mark 'o' in Figure 4.1.

## Conversion of a Binary Number into Gray Code

Any binary number can be converted into equivalent Gray code by following the steps:

i. The MSB of the Gray code is same as the MSB of the binary number;

ii. The second bit next to MSB of the Gray code equals the Ex-OR of the MSB and second bit of the binary number; it will be 0 if there are same binary bits or it will be 1 for different binary bits;

iii. The third bit for Gray code equals the exclusive-OR of the second and third bits of the binary number, and similarly all the next lower order bits follow the same mechanism.

The following examples illustrate the conversion of binary numbers to Gray code:

**Example 1.** *Convert $(101011)_2$ into Gray code.*

**Solution. Step 1.** The MSB of the Gray code is same as the MSB of the binary number.

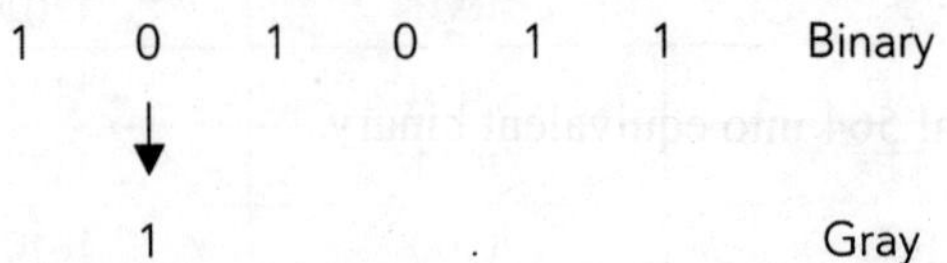


**Step 2.** Perform the Ex-OR between the MSB and the second bits of the binary. The result is 1 which is the second bit of the Gray code.

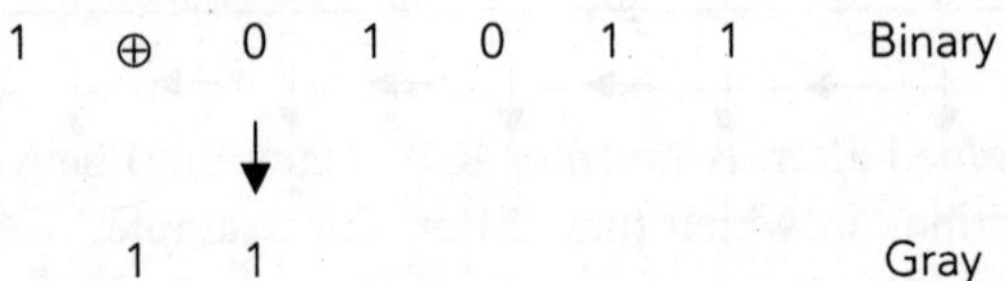


**Step 3.** Perform the Ex-OR between the second and the third bits of the binary. The result is 1 which is the third bit of the Gray code.

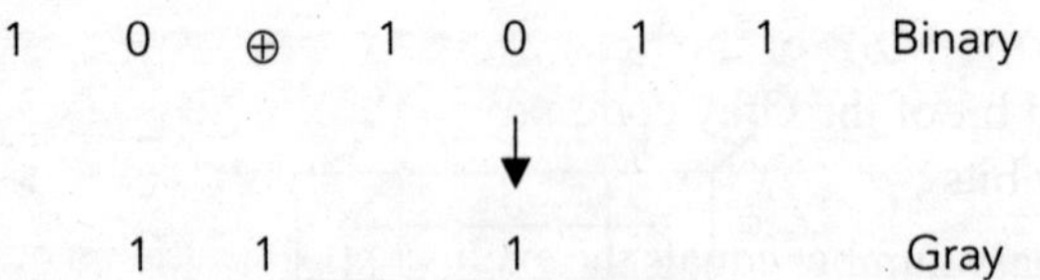


**Step 4.** Perform the Ex-OR between the third and the fourth bits of the binary. The result is 1 which is the fourth bit of the Gray code.

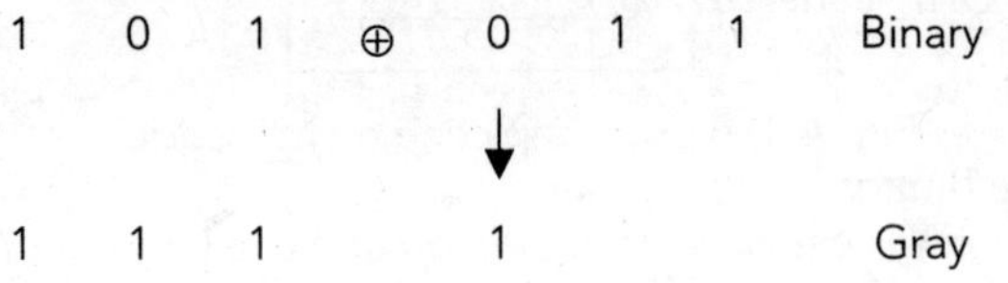


**Step 5.** Perform the Ex-OR between the fourth and the fifth bits of the binary. The result is 1 which is the fifth bit of the Gray code.

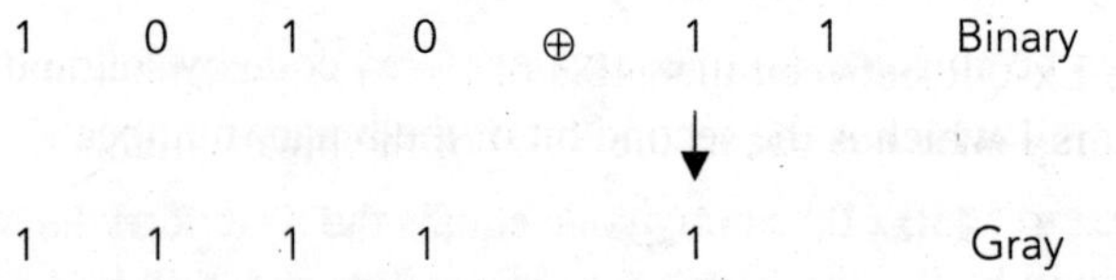


**Step 6.** Perform the Ex-OR between the fifth and the sixth bits of the binary. The result is 0 which is the last bit of the Gray code.

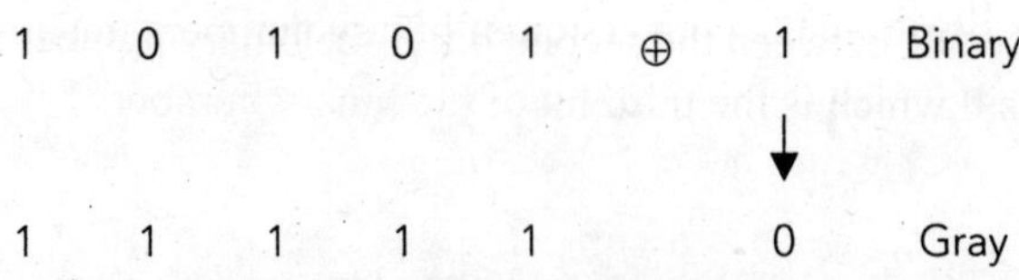

After completing the conversion the Gray code of binary 101011 is 111110.

**Example 2.** *Convert $(564)_{10}$ into Gray code.*

**Solution.**

**Step 1.** Convert the decimal 564 into equivalent binary.

Decimal number 564

Binary number 1000110100

**Step 2.** Convert the binary number into equivalent Gray code

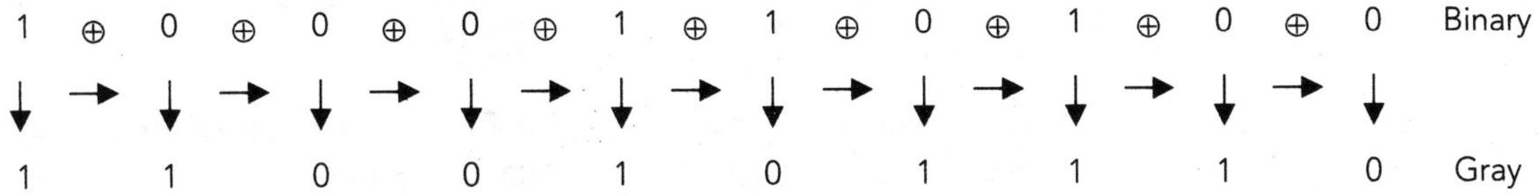


Conversion of Gray Code into a Binary Number

Any Gray code can be converted into equivalent Binary number by following the steps:

*i.* The MSB of the binary number is same as the MSB of the Gray code ;

*ii.* The second bit next to MSB of the binary number equals the Ex-OR of the MSB of the binary number and second bit of the Gray code ; it will be 0 if there are same binary bits or it will be 1 for different binary bits ;

*iii.* The third bit for binary number equals the exclusive-OR of the second bit of the binary number and third bit of the Gray code, and similarly all the next lower order bits follow the same mechanism.

Following example illustrate the conversion of Gray code into binary number:

**Example.** *Convert the Gray code 101101 into a binary number.*

**Solution.**

**Step 1.** The MSB of the binary number is same as the MSB of the Gray code.

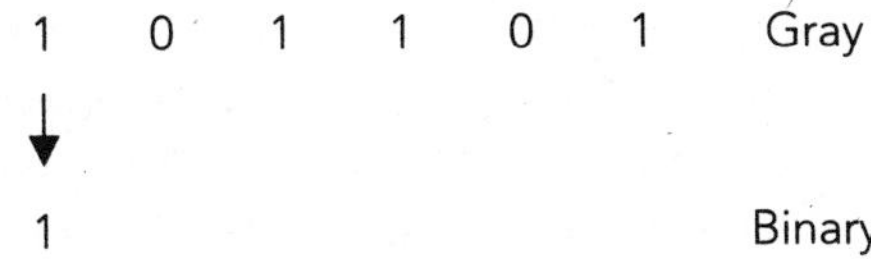


**Step 2.** Perform the Ex-OR between the MSB of the binary number and the second bit of the Gray code. The result is 1 which is the second bit of the binary number.

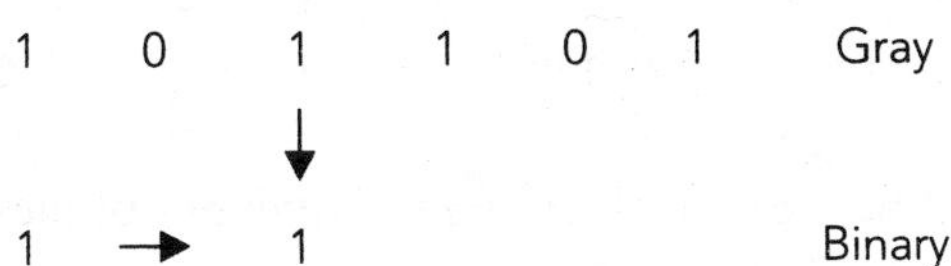


**Step 3.** Perform the Ex-OR between the second bit of the binary number and the third bit of the Gray code. The result is 0 which is the third bit of the binary number.

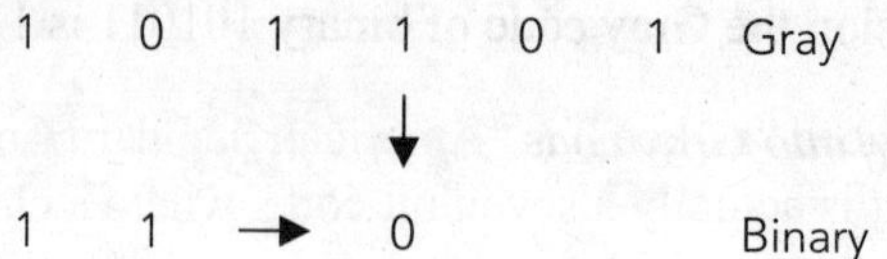


**Step 4.** Perform the Ex-OR between the third bit of the binary number and the fourth bit of the Gray code. The result is 1 which is the fourth bit of the binary number.

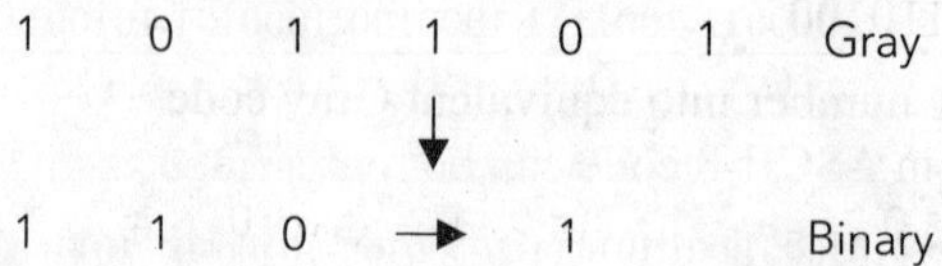


**Step 5.** Perform the Ex-OR between the fourth bit of the binary number and the fifth bit of the Gray code. The result is 1 which is the fifth bit of the binary number.

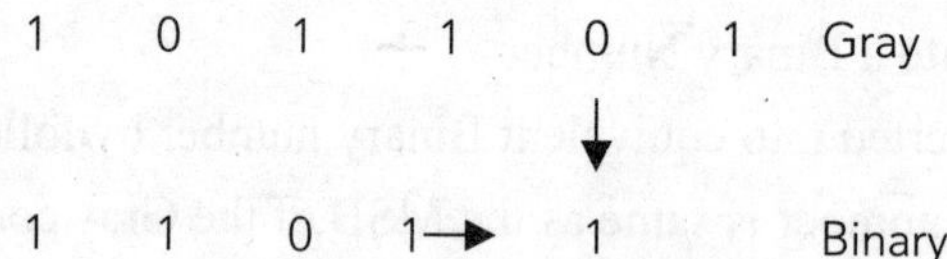


**Step 6.** Perform the Ex-OR between the fifth bit of the binary number and the sixth bit of the Gray code. The result is 0 which is the last bit of the binary number.

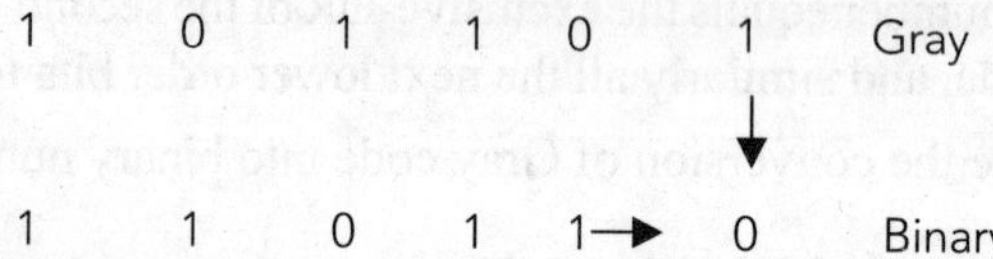


After completing the conversion the binary number of the Gray code 101101 is 110110.

## 4.5 ALPHANUMERIC CODES

Many applications of computer require not only of handling numbers, but also of letters. To represent alphabet it is necessary to have a binary code for the alphabet. In addition the same binary code must represent the decimal numbers and some other special characters. An alphanumeric code is a binary code of a group of elements consisting of ten decimal digits, the 26 letters of the alphabet (both in upper-case and lower-case), and a certain number of special symbols such as #, /, &, %, etc. The total number of elements in an alphanumeric code is greater than 36. Therefore it must be coded with a minimum number of 6 bits ($2^6 = 64$, but $2^5 = 32$ is insufficient). One possible six bit alphanumeric code is given in Table 2.5. It is used in many computers to represent alphanumeric characters and symbols internally and therefore can be called "*internal code*". Frequently there is a need to represent more than 64 characters including the lower case letters and special control characters. For this reason the following two codes are normally used.

### 4.5.1 ASCII

The full form of ASCII (pronounced "as-kee") is "American Standard Code for Information Interchange", used in most microcomputers. It is actually a seven bit code, where a character is represented with seven bits. The character is stored as one byte with one bit remaining unused. But often the extra bit is used to extend the ASCII to represent an additional 128 characters. Some of the codes are shown in Table 4.5.

Now let us represent the word CODES in ASCII-7 code:

| 1000011 | 1001111 | 1000100 | 1000101 | 1010011 |
|---|---|---|---|---|
| C | O | D | E | S |

The same word CODES in ASCII-8 code can be represented as given below:

| 10100011 | 10101111 | 10100100 | 10100101 | 10110011 |
|---|---|---|---|---|
| C | O | D | E | S |

### 4.5.2 EBCDIC

It is pronounced as "ebb-see-dick". It is a 8 bit code and can represent 256 different characters. All of the 256 bit combinations are not meaningful, so the code can still add new characters if required.

The full form of EBCDIC is "Extended Binary Coded Decimal Interchange Code". It is also an alphanumeric code generally used in IBM equipments and in large computers for communicating alphanumeric data. For the different alphanumeric characters the code grouping in this code is different from the ASCII code. It is actually an eight bit code and a ninth bit is added as the parity bit. Out of the 8 bits, the first 4 bits are known as zero bits and the remainder 4 bits represent digit values.

Now let us represent the word CODES in EBCDIC Code:

| 11000011 | 11010110 | 11000100 | 11000101 | 11100010 |
|---|---|---|---|---|
| C | O | D | E | S |

**Table 4.5** Partial List of Alphanumeric Codes

| Character | 6-bit | 7-bit | 8-bit | 12-bit |
|---|---|---|---|---|
| | Internal Code | ASCII Code | EBCDIC Code | Hollerith Code |
| A | 010001 | 1000001 | 11000001 | 12,1 |
| B | 010010 | 1000010 | 11000010 | 12,2 |
| C | 010011 | 1000011 | 11000011 | 12,3 |
| D | 010100 | 1000100 | 11000100 | 12,4 |
| E | 010101 | 1000101 | 11000101 | 12,5 |
| F | 010110 | 1000110 | 11000110 | 12,6 |
| G | 010111 | 1000111 | 11000111 | 12,7 |
| H | 011000 | 1001000 | 11001000 | 12,8 |
| I | 011001 | 1001001 | 11001001 | 12,9 |
| J | 100001 | 1001010 | 11010001 | 11,1 |
| K | 100010 | 1001011 | 11010010 | 11,2 |
| L | 100011 | 1001100 | 11010011 | 11,3 |
| M | 100100 | 1001101 | 11010100 | 11,4 |

| Character | 6-bit Internal Code | 7-bit ASCII Code | 8-bit EBCDIC Code | 12-bit Hollerith Code |
|---|---|---|---|---|
| N | 100101 | 1001110 | 11010101 | 11,5 |
| O | 100110 | 1001111 | 11010110 | 11,6 |
| P | 100111 | 1010000 | 11010111 | 11,7 |
| Q | 101000 | 1010001 | 11011000 | 11,8 |
| R | 101001 | 1010010 | 11011001 | 11,9 |
| S | 110010 | 1010011 | 11100010 | 0,2 |
| T | 110011 | 1010100 | 11100011 | 0,3 |
| U | 110100 | 1010101 | 11100100 | 0,4 |
| V | 110101 | 1010110 | 11100101 | 0,5 |
| W | 110110 | 1010111 | 11100110 | 0,6 |
| X | 110111 | 1011000 | 11100111 | 0,7 |
| Y | 111000 | 1011001 | 11101000 | 0,8 |
| Z | 111001 | 1011010 | 11101001 | 0,9 |
| 0 | 000000 | 0110000 | 11110000 | 0 |
| 1 | 000001 | 0110001 | 11110001 | 1 |
| 2 | 000010 | 0110010 | 11110010 | 2 |
| 3 | 000011 | 0110011 | 11110011 | 3 |
| 4 | 000100 | 0110100 | 11110100 | 4 |
| 5 | 000101 | 0110101 | 11110101 | 5 |
| 6 | 000110 | 0110110 | 11110110 | 6 |
| 7 | 000111 | 0110111 | 11110111 | 7 |
| 8 | 001000 | 0111000 | 11111000 | 8 |
| 9 | 001001 | 0111001 | 11111001 | 9 |
| Blank | 110000 | 0100000 | 01000000 | No punch |
| . | 011011 | 0101110 | 01001011 | 12,3,8 |
| ( | 111100 | 0101000 | 01001101 | 12,5,8 |
| + | 010000 | 0101011 | 01001110 | 12,6,8 |
| * | 101100 | 0101010 | 01011100 | 11,4,8 |
| $ | 101011 | 0100100 | 01011011 | 11,3,8 |
| ) | 011100 | 0101001 | 01011101 | 11,5,8 |
| / | 110001 | 0101111 | 01100001 | 0,1 |
| , | 111011 | 0111100 | 01101011 | 0,3,8 |
| = | 001011 | 0111101 | 01111110 | 6,8 |
| – | 100000 | 0101101 | 01100000 | 11 |

### 4.5.3 Hollerith Code

Generally this code is used in punched cards. A punched card consists of 12 rows and 80 columns. An alphanumeric character is represented by each column of 12 bits each by punching holes in the appropriate rows. The presence of a hole represents a 1 and its absence indicates 0. The 12 rows are marked starting from the top, as 12, 11, 0, 1, 2, 3, 4, 5, 6, 7, 8, and 9. The first three rows are called the zone punch and the last nine are called the numeric punch. The code used here is called the Hollerith code. The alphabets are represented as two holes in a column, one in zone punch and the other in numeric punch; decimal digits are represented as a single hole in a numeric punch. Special characters are represented as one, two, or three holes in a column; while the zone is always used, the other two holes, if used, are in a numeric punch with the 8-th punch being commonly used. The Hollerith code is BCD and hence the transmission from EBCDIC is simple. The Hollerith code is used in the card readers and punches of large computers, while EBCDIC may be used within the computer.

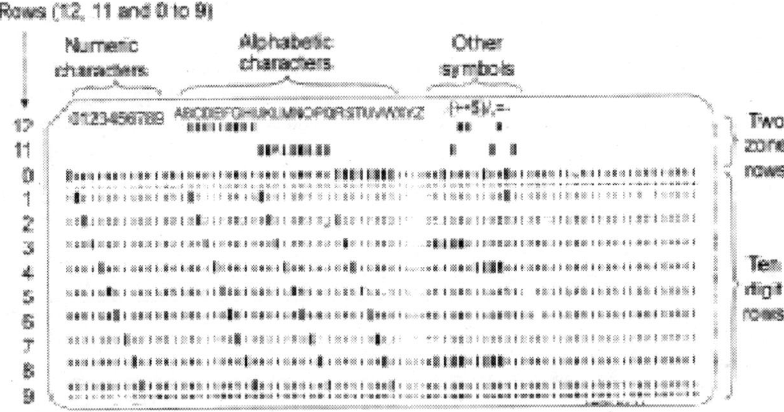


Fig. 4.2

A modern Hollerith card can handle a maximum of 80 alphanumeric characters. As this sample shown, numbers are coded by making a single punch in the appropriate card column; letters and special characters are coded by using double or triple punches. Note that the upper left-hand corner is missing from the card. This helps the machine operators make sure all the cards are turned the same way and that the deck itself has the proper orientation.

### 4.5.4 ISCII

ISCII stands for Indian Standard Code for Information Interchange. There are 18 scheduled languages in India as of today. These are in approximate order of usage: Hindi, Bengali, Telugu, Marathi, Tamil, Urdu, Gujarati, Kannada, Malayalam, Oriya, Punjabi, Assamese, Kashmiri, Sindhi, Konkani, Nepali, Manipuri and Sanskrit.

With the advent of computerization considerable work has been undertaken to facilitate the use of Indian languages on computers. These activities were generally limited to specific languages and were independent exercises of various organizations. Thus making data-interchange impossible. In such a scenario, it was important to have a common standard for coding Indian scripts. GIST (**G**raphics and **I**ntelligence based **S**cript **T**echnology) has played an important role in establishment of Indian standards.

In 1991, the Bureau of Indian Standards (BIS) adopted the Indian Standard Code for Information Interchange (ISCII), the ISCII standard that was evolved by a standardization committee, of which C-DAC was a member, under Department of Electronics during 1986–88. It is an 8 bit code which allows English and Indian Script alphabets to be used simultaneously. It retains the standard ASCII code for English. A common code for all Indian languages is feasible as all Indian scripts have a common origin from the Brahmi script. All GIST products are based on ISCII. Other than this, it has been used by IBM for PC-DOS, Apple for ILK, and several companies are developing products and solutions based on this representation. This has been made mandatory for the data being collected by organizations like the Election Commission, and for projects as Land Records Project etc.

Characters coded in ISCII need 8 bits for each character. This standard does not only apply to the Devnagri script, but also to Gujarati, Bengali, Gurumukhi, Assamese, Telugu, Kannada, Tamil and Malayalam script. Any software which allows ISCII codes, can be used in any Indian script, enhancing its commercial viability. Table 4.6 provides ISCII versions of Devnagri script:

**Table 4.6** Devnagri ISCII Script

| | 0 | 1 | 2 | 3 | 4 | 5 | 6 | 7 | 10 | 11 | 12 | 13 | 14 | 15 | 16 | 17 |
|---|---|---|---|---|---|---|---|---|---|---|---|---|---|---|---|---|
| 240 | | ँ | ं | ः | अ | आ | इ | ई | उ | ऊ | ऋ | | ए | ऐ | ऍ | |
| 260 | ओ | औ | ऑ | क | ख | ग | घ | ङ | च | छ | ज | झ | ञ | ट | ठ | ड |
| 300 | ढ | ण | त | थ | द | ध | न | | प | फ | ब | भ | म | य | | र |
| 320 | र | ल | ळ | | व | श | ष | स | ह | INV | ा | ि | ी | ु | ू | ृ |
| 340 | | ॆ | े | ै | | ो | ौ | ॉ | ् | ़ | । | | | | | ATR |
| 360 | EXT | ० | १ | २ | ३ | ४ | ५ | ६ | ७ | ८ | ९ | | | | | |

## 4.5.5 Unicode

The UNICODE is the new universal coding standard being adopted by all newer platforms. The **Unicode Consortium** is a non-profit organization to develop, extend and promote use of the Unicode Standard, which specifies the representation of text in modern software products and standards. Formally,

**Unicode provides a unique number for every character,**

**no matter what the platform,**

**no matter what the program,**

**no matter what the language.**

Every computer works with numbers. The letters and other characters are stored by assigning a number for each one. Before Unicode was invented, there were hundreds of different encoding systems for assigning these numbers. No single encoding could contain enough characters, for example, the European Union alone requires several encodings to cover all its languages. Even for a single language like English no single encoding was adequate for all the letters, punctuation, and technical symbols in the common use.

These encoding systems also conflict with one another, that is, two encoding can use the same number for two different characters, or use different numbers for the same character. Any system (especially servers) needs to support many different encodings; yet whenever data is passed between different encodings or platforms, that data may be corrupted.

### Utility of UNICODE

The Unicode Standard has been adopted by leading computer companies like Apple, IBM, Microsoft, Oracle and many others. Unicode is required by modern standards like such as JAVA, CORBA 3.0 etc. and is the official way to implement ISO. It is supported in many operating systems, all modern browsers and many other products. The emergence of the Unicode Standard, and the availability of tools supporting it, are among the most significant recent global software technology trends.

Unicode's significance is quite clear from the following points:

*i.* Incorporating Unicode into client-server or multi-tiered applications and websites offers significant cost savings over the use of legacy character sets.

*ii.* Unicode enables a single software product or a single website to be targeted across multiple platforms, languages and countries without re-engineering.

*iii.* It allows data to be transported through many different systems without corruption.

The first version of the Unicode Standard, that is, Unicode 1.0.0 was released in October, 1991. Version numbers for the Unicode Standard consist of three fields: the major version, the minor version and the update version. For historical reasons the numbering within each of these fields is not necessarily consecutive. The latest Unicode Version is Unicode 4.0.0 which is in use from April, 2003. Unicode Version 3.2 represented 95,221 characters, whereas Unicode Version 4.0.0 has added many more characters.

## 4.6 ERROR DETECTING CODES

Binary information may be transmitted through some form of communication medium such as wires or radio waves or fibre optic cables etc. Any external noise introduced into a physical communication medium changes bit values from 0 to 1 or vice versa. *An error detection code can be used to detect errors during transmission. The detected error cannot be corrected, but its presence may be indicated.*

### 4.6.1 Parity Bit Coding Technique

A parity bit is an extra bit included with a message to make the total number of 1's either odd or even. A message of four bits and a parity bit, P, are shown in Table 4.7. In (*a*), P is chosen so that the sum of all 1's is odd (including the parity bit). In (*b*), P is chosen so that the sum of all 1's is even (including the parity bit). In the sending end, the message (in this case the first four bits) is applied to a "parity generation" circuit where the required P bit is generated. The message, including the parity bit, is transferred to its destination. In the receiving end, all the incoming bits (in this case five) are applied to a "parity check" circuit to check the proper parity adopted. An error is detected if the checked parity does not correspond to the adopted one. The parity method detects the presence of one, three, five, or any odd combination of errors. An even combination of errors is undetectable since even number of errors will not change the parity of the bits. The parity bit may be included with the message bits either on the MSB or on the LSB side. Hence in such cases some other coding scheme is to be adopted. Such a coding technique is Check Sums, which is discussed in next section.

**Table 4.7** Parity Bit

| (a) Message | P (Odd) | (b) Message | P (Even) |
|---|---|---|---|
| 0000 | 1 | 0000 | 0 |
| 0001 | 0 | 0001 | 1 |
| 0010 | 0 | 0010 | 1 |
| 0011 | 1 | 0011 | 0 |
| 0100 | 0 | 0100 | 1 |
| 0101 | 1 | 0101 | 0 |
| 0110 | 1 | 0110 | 0 |
| 0111 | 0 | 0111 | 1 |
| 1000 | 0 | 1000 | 1 |
| 1001 | 1 | 1001 | 0 |
| 1010 | 1 | 1010 | 0 |
| 1011 | 0 | 1011 | 1 |
| 1100 | 1 | 1100 | 0 |
| 1101 | 0 | 1101 | 1 |
| 1110 | 0 | 1110 | 1 |
| 1111 | 1 | 1111 | 0 |

### 4.6.2 Check Sums Technique

As we have discussed above the parity bit technique fails for double error, hence we use the Check Sums method in such case. Initially any word A 10010011 is transmitted; next another word B 01110110 is transmitted. The binary digits in the two words are added and the sum obtained is retained in the transmitter. Then any other word C is transmitted and added to the previous sum retained in the transmitter and the new sum is now retained. In the similar manner, each word is added to the previous sum already been retained; after transmitting all the words, the final sum which is called the Check Sum is also transmitted. The same operation is done at the receiving end and the final sum which has been obtained here is being checked against the transmitted Check Sum. There is no error, if the two sums are equal.

## 4.7 ERROR CORRECTING CODES

We have already discussed two coding techniques, which may be used in data transmission to detect errors. But unfortunately the above discussed techniques are not capable of correcting the errors. For correction of errors now we will discuss a code called Hamming code.

### Hamming Code

This coding had been developed by R. W. Hamming where one or more parity bits are added to a data character methodically in order to detect and correct errors. The number of bits changed from one code word to another is known as *Hamming distance.*

Let us consider $A_i$ and $A_j$ to be any two code words in any particular block code. Now the Hamming distance $d_{ij}$ between the two vectors $A_i$ and $A_j$ is defined by the number of components in which they differ. Assuming that $d_{ij}$ is determined for each pair of code words, the minimum value of $d_{ij}$ is called the minimum Hamming distance, $d_{min}$.

For example,

| | | | | | | | |
|---|---|---|---|---|---|---|---|
| $A_i$ | 1 | 0 | 0 | 1 | 0 | 1 | 1 |
| | ↓ | | ↓ | | | ↓ | |
| $A_j$ | 0 | 0 | 1 | 1 | 0 | 0 | 1 |

Here, these code words differ in the MSB and in the third and sixth bit positions from the left. Hence, $d_{ij}$ is 3.

From Hamming's analysis of code distances, some important properties have been derived:

*i.* For detection of single error $d_{min}$ should be at least two.

*ii.* For single error correction, $d_{min}$ should be at least three, since the number of errors, $E \leq (d_{min} - 1)/2$.

*iii.* Greater values of $d_{min}$ will provide detection and/or correction of more number of errors.

The 7-bit Hamming (7, 4) code word $h_1\ h_2\ h_3\ h_4\ h_5\ h_6\ h_7$ associated with a 4-bit binary number $b_3\ b_2\ b_1\ b_0$ is:

$$h_1 = b_3 \oplus b_2 \oplus b_0$$

$$h_2 = b_3 \oplus b_1 \oplus b_0$$

$$h_4 = b_2 \oplus b_1 \oplus b_0$$

$$h_3 = b_3$$

$$h_5 = b_2$$

$$h_6 = b_1$$

$$h_7 = b_0$$

Bits $h_1$, $h_2$ and $h_4$ produce even parity bits for the bit fields $b_3\ b_2\ b_0$, $b_3\ b_1\ b_0$ and $b_2\ b_1\ b_0$ respectively. Generally the parity bits ($h_1, h_2, h_4, h_8, h_{16}\ldots$) are located in the positions corresponding to ascending powers of two (*i.e.*, $2^0, 2^1, 2^2, 2^3, 2^4\ldots = 1, 2, 4, 8, 16\ldots$).

The $h_1$ parity bit has a 1 in the LSB position of its binary representation. Therefore it can check all the bit positions, including it, which have 1's in the LSB position in the binary representation (*i.e.*, $h_1$, $h_3$, $h_5$ and $h_7$). The binary representation of $h_2$ has a 1 in the middle bit position. Therefore it can check all the bit positions, including it, which have 1's in the middle bit position in the binary representation (*i.e.*, $h_2$, $h_3$, $h_6$ and $h_7$). The $h_4$ parity bit has a 1 in the MSB position of its binary representation. Therefore it can check all the bit positions, including it, which have 1's in the MSB position in the binary representation (*i.e.*, $h_4$, $h_5$, $h_6$ and $h_7$).

To decode a Hamming code, checking is to be done for odd parity over the bit fields in which even parity were previously established. For example, a single bit error is indicated by a non-zero parity word $a_4\ a_2\ a_1$, where

$$a_1 = h_1 \oplus h_3 \oplus h_5 \oplus h_7$$

$$a_2 = h_2 \oplus h_3 \oplus h_6 \oplus h_7$$

$$a_4 = h_4 \oplus h_5 \oplus h_6 \oplus h_7$$

If $a_4\ a_2\ a_1 = 000$, we conclude there is no error in Hamming code. On the other hand, if it has a non-zero value, it indicates the bit position in error. For example, if $a_4\ a_2\ a_1 = 110$, then bit 6 is in error. To correct this error, bit 6 has to be complemented.

**Example 1.** *Encode data bits 0110 into a 7-bit even parity Hamming code.*

**Solution.**

Given $b_3\ b_2\ b_1\ b_0 = 0\ 1\ 1\ 0$

Therefore,

$$h_1 = b_3 \oplus b_2 \oplus b_0 = 0 \oplus 1 \oplus 0 = 1$$

$$h_2 = b_3 \oplus b_1 \oplus b_0 = 0 \oplus 1 \oplus 0 = 1$$

$$h_4 = b_2 \oplus b_1 \oplus b_0 = 1 \oplus 1 \oplus 0 = 0$$

$$h_3 = b_3 = 0$$

$$h_5 = b_2 = 1$$

$$h_6 = b_1 = 1$$

$$h_7 = b_0 = 0$$

| $h_1$ | $h_2$ | $h_3$ | $h_4$ | $h_5$ | $h_6$ | $h_7$ |
|---|---|---|---|---|---|---|
| 1 | 1 | 0 | 0 | 1 | 1 | 0 |

**Example 2.** *A 7-bit Hamming code is received as 0110110. What is its correct code ?*

**Solution.**

| $h_1$ | $h_2$ | $h_3$ | $h_4$ | $h_5$ | $h_6$ | $h_7$ |
|---|---|---|---|---|---|---|
| 0 | 1 | 1 | 0 | 1 | 1 | 0 |

Now, to find the error,

Thus, $a_4\ a_2\ a_1 = 010$. Therefore, bit 2 is in error and the corrected code can be obtained by complementing the second bit in the received as 00 10110.

## EXERCISE

1. What are BCD codes?
2. Write a short note on the following:
   i. Character codes
   ii. Error detecting codes
   iii. Error correcting codes
3. Differentiate between ASCII and EBCDIC character codes. Why is EBCDIC code used ?
4. What are the advantages of Grey codes? Discuss their areas of applications.
5. Write a short note on the following:
   i. ISCII
   ii. UNICODE

6. Write the 4-bit BCD code for the following numbers:
   i. $27_{10}$ ii. $135_{10}$
   iii. $86_{10}$ iv. $1034_{10}$
7. Using binary notation, show the BCD coding for the following words:
   i. CODES ii. COMPUTER
   iii. OLYMPICS iv. PROGRAM
8. Why was BCD code extended to EBCDIC?
   i. EARTH ii. LION
   iii. FOX iv. PROCESS

   How many bytes are needed for each of these representations?
9. Using binary notation, write the ASCII-7 and ASCII-8 codes coding for the following words:
   i. LONG ii. SHORT
   iii. MEDAL iv. EXAM

   How many bytes are needed for each of these representations?
10. Perform the following additions using binary number system only.
    i. $1011_2 + 11_2$ ii. $111_2 + 0101_2$
    iii. $1010_2 + 10_2$ iv. $110011_2 + 1100_2$
    v. $11001_2 + 111000_2$ vi. $111111_2 + 110000_2$
    vii. $101.011_2 + 10.110_2$ viii. $1011.1010_2 + 1000.001_2$
    ix. $11001.1011_2 + 10011.0110_2$
11. Evaluate:
    i. $1100_2 - 101_2$ ii. $1101_2 - 1011_2$
    iii. $1010_2 - 111_2$ iv. $11100_2 - 111_2$
    v. $11100_2 - 11011_2$ vi. $1111_2 - 100011_2$
    vii. $101.101_2 - 11.011_2$ viii. $1100.01_2 - 1001.10_2$
    ix. $1001.1_2 - 101.11_2$
12. Find the difference using 1's and 2's complements methods:
    i. $10001_2 - 01010_2$ ii. $10_2 - 10011_2$
    iii. $1101_2 - 1001_2$ iv. $0.11_2 - 0.101_2$
13. Perform the following multiplications:
    i. $1100_2 \times 10_2$ ii. $1110_2 \times 111_2$
    iii. $10101_2 \times 101_2$ iv. $1010.101_2 \times 1.01_2$
    v. $1100.001_2 \times 110.1_2$ vi. $01011_2 \times 1001_2$
    vii. $110111_2 \times 111_2$ viii. $1100_2 \times 1001_2$
14. Divide the following binary numbers:
    i. $1100_2/10_2$ ii. $11000_2/110_2$

iii. $1110011_2/101_2$ iv. $1100010_2/111_2$

v. $11110_2/101_2$ vi. $111011_2/111_2$

15. Why are subtractions using 2's complements used in modern computers? What are the difficulties with BCD or simple binary subtractions?
16. Give the advantages and disadvantages of performing the various arithmetic operations by additive method in the digital computer.
17. Explain Booths multiplication with an example.
18. Subtract $(1010)_2$ from $(1101)_2$ using the 1's and 2's complement methods.
19. ASCII stands for .................................. .
20. Write the Booth coded number for the following binary numbers in 2's complement form:

i. 11101101 ii. 11000110

## Answers

### Review Questions and Exercises

6. i. 00100111 ii. 000100110101 iii. 10000110 iv. 0001000000110100

10. i. 1110 ii. 1100 iii. 1100
iv. 111111 v. 1010001 vi. 1101111
vii. 1000.001 viii. 10011.1100 ix. 101101.0001

11. i. 111 ii. 10 iii. 101
iv. 10101 v. 1 vi. -10100
vii. 10.010 viii. 10.11 ix. 11.11

12. i. 00111 ii. –10001 iii. 0100
iv. 0.001

13. i. 11000 ii. 1100010 iii. 1101001
iv. 1101.01001 v. 1001110.1101 vi. 1100011
vii. 110000001 viii. 1101100

14. i. 110 ii. 100 iii. 10111
iv. 1110 v. 110 vi. Quotient 1000, Remainder 11

# Input and Output Devices

## 5.1 INTRODUCTION

A computer peripheral is any external device that provides input and output for the computer. For example, a keyboard and mouse are input peripherals, while a monitor and printer are output peripherals. Computer peripherals, or peripheral devices, are sometimes called "I/O devices" because they provide input and output for the computer. Some peripherals, such as external hard drives, provide both input and output for the computer.

## 5.2 INPUT CONCEPTS

Input is the process of entering and translating incoming data into machine-readable form so that they can be processed by a computer. The data to be entered are also often referred to as input. But before discussing concepts involving input, let's recall the meanings of some terms. Hardware is all the physical components of a computer system.

Any hardware item that is attached to the main unit of a computer houses the CPU is referred to as a peripheral device. An input device is a peripheral device through which data are entered and transformed into machine-readable form.

Three important things to be concerned with during the input process are:

The method of data preparation (transcriptive or source)

The type of processing to be used (batch or transaction)

The accuracy of the data being entered.

## 5.3 INPUT DEVICES

An input device is any hardware device that sends data to the computer, without any input devices, a computer would only be a display device and not allow users to interact with it, much like a TV. Following continuing research in the field of computer hardware, we have a large number of input devices. Recall that before data can be processed by the computer, they must be translated into machine-readable form and entered into the computer by an input device.

Many input devices can be classified according to:

- Modality of input (e.g. mechanical motion, audio, visual, etc.)
- The input is discrete (e.g. key presses) or continuous (e.g. a mouse's position, though digitized into a discrete quantity, is fast enough to be considered continuous)
- The number of degrees of freedom involved (e.g. two-dimensional traditional mice, or three-dimensional navigators designed for CAD applications)

Pointing devices, which are input devices used to specify a position in space, can further be classified according to:

- Whether the input is direct or indirect. With direct input, the input space coincides with the display space, i.e. pointing is done in the space where visual feedback or the cursor appears. Touch Screens and light pens involve direct input. Examples involving indirect input include the mouse and trackball.
- Whether the positional information is absolute (e.g. on a touch screen) or relative (e.g. with a mouse that can be lifted and repositioned)

Note that direct input is almost necessarily absolute, but indirect input may be either absolute or relative. For example, digitizing Graphics tablets that do not have an embedded screen involve indirect input and sense absolute positions and are often run in an absolute input mode, but they may also be setup to simulate a relative input mode where the stylus or puck can be lifted and repositioned.

Here, we list a variety of input devices:

- Punched Cards and Card Readers
- Keyboards
- Joysticks
- Trackballs
- Mouse
- Touch Screens
- Light Pens
- Touch Pad
- Digitizer
- Voice Recognition
- Key to Magnetic Media
- Financial Transaction Terminals
- Machine Vision Systems
- Source Data Input
- Magnetic-ink Character Recognition (MICR)
- Magnetic Strips
- Optical Recognition
- Point-of-Sale Terminals
- Barcode reader

- Digital camera
- Microphone
- MIDI keyboard
- Mouse (pointing device)
- Remote
- Scanner
- Webcam

### 5.3.1 Punched Cards and Card Readers

"Punched Card" was the one of the most commonly used media for communicating data and instructions to the computer in India before 1980. A punched card is a rigid piece of paper containing rows and columns of numbers. IBM card is called a standardized card which has 80 columns and is of the size 7 ½ inches × 3 ¼ inches × 0.007 inch. The columns are numbered 1-80 from left to right. One of its corner is usually trimmed to help to maintain proper positioning during processing. The top row in a card is called the 12-punch row; next is called 11th row and then next 10 rows are numbered consecutively from '0' to '9'. The top 2 rows are called as Zone Punch Rows and the bottom 10 rows are called as Digit Punch Rows.

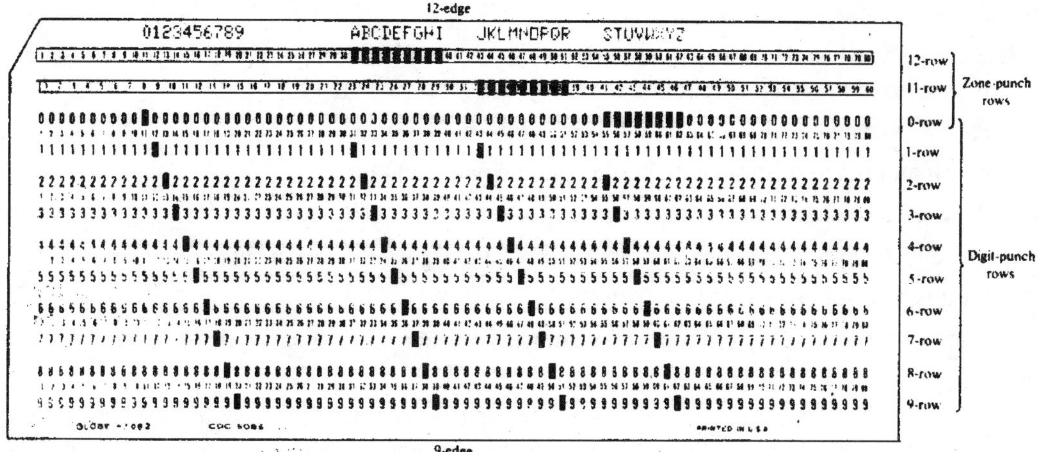


**Fig. 5.1:** Punched Card

These cards are put into a keypunch machine. As the operator keys in the data to be stored, the keypunch machine places holes in the card to represent the data. The pattern of punched holes used to represent characters on the card is called the Hollerith code, named after its inventor, Herman Hollerith.

Each column of the punched card can record a single character as a set of holes punched in the vertical column. Thus a single can hold a maximum of 80 characters. The holes punched in the cards are interpreted by a card reader that translates the punched information into a machine-readable code, then sends it to the CPU for processing.

The punched-card system was one of the first methods used to input data. It has been almost totally replaced by newer, more efficient input devices.

## Key Punching Machine

Punching of data on the card is called Key Punch and key punching is accomplished by means of a key punching machine which looks like a Typewriter. The most common type of key punch machines were IBM 026 and IBM 029. These machines have the following components:

- Keyboard
- Card hopper
- Punching station
- Card stacker
- Column indicator
- Back-space key
- Program control unit
- Program drum
- Reading section
- Switches
- Printing mechanism, etc.

## Card Reader

Card Reader was used as the primary input device in most of the early day computers. A card reader is connected to the computer and is required to initiate the following steps:

- Put the punched cards in the read hopper of the card reader.
- Command is given from computer to read the punched holes.
- Punched holes are read at points for verification of data being read.
- The punched holes are converted into signals and transmitted to the computer for storage.
- Card is then submitted in the output stack.

There are two types of card readers depending upon the mechanism used for sensing the punched holes:

- Photoelectric Card Reader: In photoelectric type card reader, light passing through the punched holes are detected by photoelectric cells. These are faster and accurate in comparison to another type of card reader.
- Wire Brush Card Reader: In brush type card reader, a card is passed between a wire brush and a metal roller. If there exists punch, the brush makes electric contact with the roller and thus sends signals to the computer.

## 5.3.2 Keyboards

A keyboard is one of the today's most common and familiar input device. A keyboard's primary function is to act as an **input device.** The computer **keyboard** is used to enter text information into the computer, as when you type the contents of a report. Using a keyboard, a person can type a document, use keystroke shortcuts, access menus, play games and perform a variety of other tasks. Keyboards can have different keys depending on the manufacturer, the operating system they're designed for, and whether they are attached to a desktop computer or part of a laptop. But for the most part, these keys, also called **keycaps**, are the same size and shape from keyboard to keyboard. They're also placed at a similar distance from one another in a similar pattern, no matter what language or alphabet the keys represent.

**Figure 5.2:** Keyboards

The traditional QWERTY (so called because the first six letters on the top row are Q, W, E, R, T, and Y) typewriter keyboard compromises the basic portion of today's computer keyboard.

A typical computer keyboard contains all the letters, numbers, and symbols of a regular typewriter, plus a variety of other keys. The other keys include:

i. A numeric keypad that looks and functions lime a calculator;
ii. Function keys whose operation can be determined by the user or preprogrammed by the software being used; and
iii. Special keys such as those used to control the movement of the cursor on the computer screen.

**Description:** A keyboard consists of rows of electronic switches ('keys') encased in a plastic surround. Each switch has a graphic on it that describes its function e.g. the switch with the letter 'B' on it will input the 'B' character into the computer. To input data, you need to depress the key. Key strokes are also combined to modify the input e.g. Holding the Shift key at the same time as depressing the 'A' key will cause a capital 'A' to be input rather than a lower case 'a'. Along-side the usual letters and special characters such as:@~()!"$% etc, there are a set if 'F' keys along the top that can be assigned special functions by the software you are running. For example F1 often brings up a help screen (but not always!).

Most keyboards have between 80 and 110 keys, including:

- Alphanumeric keys
- Numeric keypad
- Function keys
- Cursor movement keys

**Alphanumeric keys:** The Alphanumeric **keys** include the letters of the alphabet, generally laid out in the same pattern used for typewriters. According to legend, this layout, known as **QWERTY** for its first six letters, helped keep mechanical typewriters' metal arms from colliding and jamming as people typed. Some people question this story -- whether it's true or not, the QWERTY pattern had long been a standard by the time computer keyboards came around.

Keyboards can also use a variety of other typing key arrangements. The most widely known is **Dvorak**, named for its creator, August Dvorak. The Dvorak layout places all of the vowels on the left side of the keyboard and the most common consonants on the right. The most commonly used letters are all found along the **home row**. The home row is the main row where you place your fingers when you begin typing.

People who prefer the Dvorak layout say it increases their typing speed and reduces fatigue. Other layouts include **ABCDE**, **XPeRT**, **QWERTZ** and **AZERTY**. Each is named for the first keys in the pattern. The QWERTZ and AZERTY arrangements are commonly used in Europe.

**Numeric keys:** To perform mathematical functions, use the numeric keypad as you would a **keypad** calculator. To activate the numeric keypad, press the NUM LOCK key. If you do not press the NUM LOCK key, the numeric keypad will function as cursor control keys.

**Function keys:** Function keys are special-purpose keys, numbered F1 through F10, used to communicate specific fictions to the operating system. These keys simplify tasks that might otherwise require several key strokes. These keys can also be used with other keys to increase the number of functions available. The software program in operation defines the function of these keys. Be sure to read the software owner/user manual to understand the purpose of these keys. These keys are generally located at the top of the keyboard.

**Cursor movement keys:** Cursor control keys move the cursor from one place to another on the display screen. The cursor is the indicator on the display screen that lets the user know where the next entry will be made. Cursor control keys have an arrowhead printed on them pointing in the direction that the key will move. Some keyboards have a separate set of keys for cursor movement; others have the cursor movement keys incorporated into the numeric keyboard. As long as the NUM LOCK key is OFF, the cursor movement keys function. Some software packages use the cursor control keys in combination with each other or with other keys to increase the number of ways and the speed with which you can move the cursor. Another cursor movement key — the SCROLL LOCK/BREAK key – controls screen scrolling. When in the BREAK mode and used in conjunction with the CTRL key, the SCROLL LOCK key will interrupt program execution.

### Advantages

- The most efficient way of entering numbers, text and commands into the computer, as each key has a specific function.
- Inexpensive, as virtually every computer needs one.

### Disadvantages

- You have to learn to type!
- There are 'arrow keys' but they are not as good as a mouse for controlling the screen cursor.
- May cause sore wrists and arms

## 5.3.3 Mouse

Mouse is a pointing device and it has been around us for more than 20 years. Douglas Engelbart of Stanford Research Center developed the mouse in 1963 as an alternative to the keyboard in the 1960s. Mouse was pioneered by Xerox in 1970s. Mouse is one of the biggest breakthroughs in Computer Ergonomics because it frees the user to a large extent from using the keyboard.

The mouse usually contains one to three buttons; as the user rolls it on a flat surface, the mouse controls cursor movement on the screen. When the user presses one of the buttons, the mouse either marks a place on the screen or makes selections from data on the screen.

Different types of mouse are shown in Fig. 5.3.

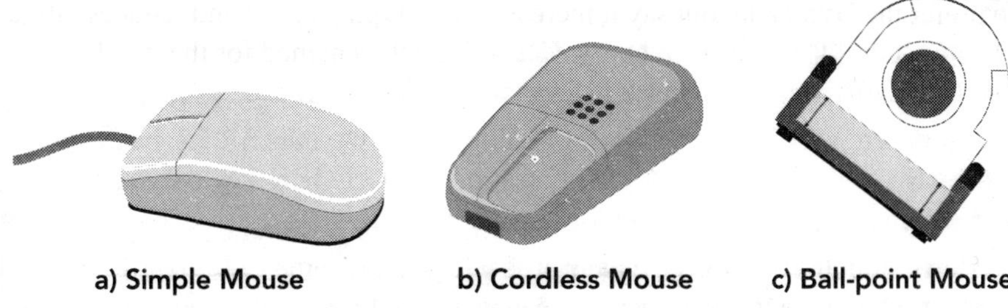

a) Simple Mouse b) Cordless Mouse c) Ball-point Mouse

**Fig. 5.3:** Different Types of Mouse

## Types of Mouse

There are three basic types of Mouse:

- Mechanical Mouse
- Optomechanical Mouse
- Optical Mouse

## Mechanical Mouse

A mechanical mouse has a rubber or metal ball on its underside that can roll in all directions. Mechanical sensors within the mouse detect the direction of the rolling ball and make a movement of the screen pointer accordingly.

## Optomechanical Mouse

Optomechanical mouse is also similar to a mechanical mouse except that it uses optical sensors to detect the movement of the ball on the Mouse Pad.

## Optical Mouse

Optical mouse uses a laser beam to detect the movement of mouse on specially designed Mouse Pad. We must move the mouse along a special mat with a grid so that optical mechanism has a frame of reference. This type of mouse has no mechanical moving parts. Optical mouse respond more quickly and precisely than any other mouse. These are very expensive.

A mouse can be used for many applications ranging from games to designing products with graphics. It provides an alternative for people who are uncomfortable with a keyboard, or it can be used in combination with a keyboard to enhance input operations.

The mouse is also used to draw sketches , diagram etc. on the CRT screen. It is also moved on graphic tablet for drawing work and the same is also used to edit text. For editing text on the screen the cursor is quickly moved to the desired point of the screen by moving the mouse.

## Advantages

- It is simple device and very easy to use.
- It is not that very expensive.
- It moves the cursor faster than the arrow keys of keyboard do.

### Disadvantages

- The movement of the cursor is not very sensitive to movement of mouse.
- If the contact between wheels and mouse pad is lost, the cursor does not move.

## 5.3.4 Joysticks

A joystick is also a pointing device. It is used to move the cursor position on a CRT screen. Its function is similar to a mouse, except that with a mouse the cursor stops moving as soon as you stop moving the mouse. A joystick is a stick which has spherical ball at its lower end as well as at its upper end. A joystick uses a lever to control the position of the cursor. It internally translates the lever position and speed with which the joystick is moved into digital signals that are sent to the computer to control the cursor movement. Most joysticks include two buttons called triggers.

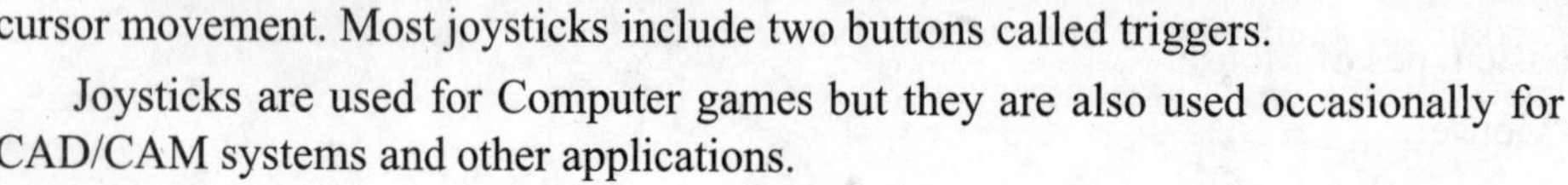

Joysticks are used for Computer games but they are also used occasionally for CAD/CAM systems and other applications.

**Fig. 5.4:** Joystick

## 5.3.5 Trackballs

Trackball is another pointing device. A trackball is a mouse lying on its back. A trackball uses a hard sphere to control cursor movement. The ball can be rotated by hand in any direction. The associated electronic circuitry detects the direction and speed of spin. The trackball translates the sphere's direction and speed of rotation into digital signal used to control the cursor. The information is sent to the CPU for initiating further necessary action.

Different types of Trackball are shown in Fig. 5.5.

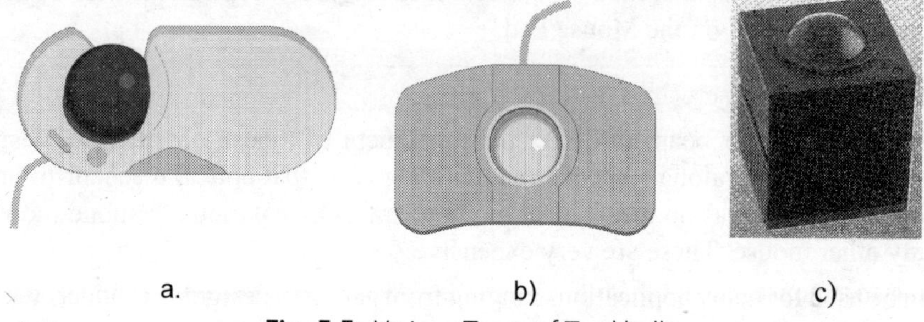

a. b) c)

**Fig. 5.5:** Various Types of Trackballs

### Advantages

- The benefit of using trackball over mouse is that trackball is stationary so it does not require much space to use it.
- We can place a trackball on any type of surface, including our palm or lap.
- Their compact size make them most suitable for portable computers.

### 5.3.6 Touch Screens

A touch screen is basically a display screen which can identify the occurrence and position of a touch inside the display region. The word normally refers to a touch or tap to the display of the gadget by a finger or hand. Touch screens can also identify added inactive objects, such as a stylus. However, if the object identified is active, as with a light pen, the phrase touch screen is normally irrelevant. The facility to interact directly with a display normally specifies the existence of a touch screen.

Such touch screen displays can be connected to computers, laptops, PDAs, cell phones etc. They also project an important function in the blueprint of digital.

**Figure 5.6:** Touch Screen Monitor

Touch screen is a type of display screen that has a touch-sensitive transparent panel covering the screen. A touch screen registers input when a finger or other object comes in contact with the screen. Two touch-screen techniques involve infrared beams and ultrasonic acoustic waves. Infrared beams crisscross the surface of the screen, and when a light beam is broken, that location is recorded.

The other technique involves ultrasonic acoustic waves that pass over the surface of the screen. When the wave signals are interrupted by some contact with the screen, that location is recorded. Because the acoustic waves bend with the curved surface of the screen, they are closer to the screen, thus giving more precision when locating the point of contact.

Touch screens have long been used in military applications. Today, because they have become less expensive, touch screens are found in many other applications. Touch screens have provided information and directions at EPCOT Center at Walt Disney World since 1982.

Visitors simply touch the items on the screen that would like more information about, and the computer displays a screen that supplies them with the details.

Automated lottery machines that use touch screens are becoming popular in supermarkets, carry outs, and retail stores. By touching the screen, selections, such as the type of game and the numbers to play are made. The computer registers the choice, then generates and prints the lottery ticket. Hewlett-Packard is one of the computer company that offers a series of microcomputers that have touch-screen capabilities.

### 5.3.7 Light Pens

A light pen is similar to a mouse, except that with a light pen we can move the pointer and select objects on the display screen by directly pointing to the object with the pen. It is a pen like device which is connected to the machine by a cable. Light pen consists photocells placed in its small tube. When it is brought to the screen, it detects the light emitted from the screen. The photocells are activated and electrical pulses send data to computer which identifies the menu option that activated the photo cell. A light pen can make selections, place objects, or indicate dimensions by simply touching the screen. A light pen does not emit light rather, it reacts to light through a photosensitive detector as its base.

Light pens are shown in Fig. 5.7.

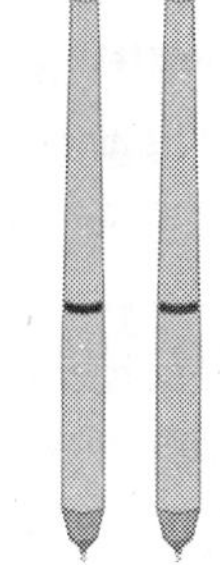

**Fig. 5.7:** Light Pens

A light pen can also be used for graphical work. A user can draw directly on the CRT screen with the light pen if the computer system is provided with CAD package. It can be used to modify the graphs or drawings, identify color or thickness of the objects on the screen.

### 5.3.8 Touch Pad

A small, touch-sensitive pad is used as a pointing device on some portable computers. By moving a finger or other object along the pad, we can move the pointer on the display screen. The touch pad is related to the touch screen, but activated by different means. The touch pad uses pressure-sensitive materials to record data at the point where the pad is touched. Many appliances around the home, such as microwave ovens, use touch pads for programming time or temperature.

**Fig. 5.8:** Touch Pad Using a Point-device

### 5.3.9 Digitizer

A digitizer, or graphics tablet, is similar to a light pen; however, instead of drawing on the screen, a separate tablet is used on which a special stylus is moved. Input tablets or digitizer tablets or graphical tablets are typically found in CAD terminals or engineering workstations, etc. These tablets are work surfaces that contain hundreds of copper wires in the form of a grid, which are connected to the computer. Each copper wire receives electric pulses. A stylus or pen, which is sensitive to these pulses send signals to the computer to form drawings. By selecting commands on the digitizer, objects can be drawn or erased, and coordinates can be marked on the screen. Light pens and digitizers are often used in the mechanical and architectural fields for drawing. The drawings are not made on the tablets directly but normally a sketch of drawing is traced on a paper kept on tablet by this pen, to transmit to the computer.

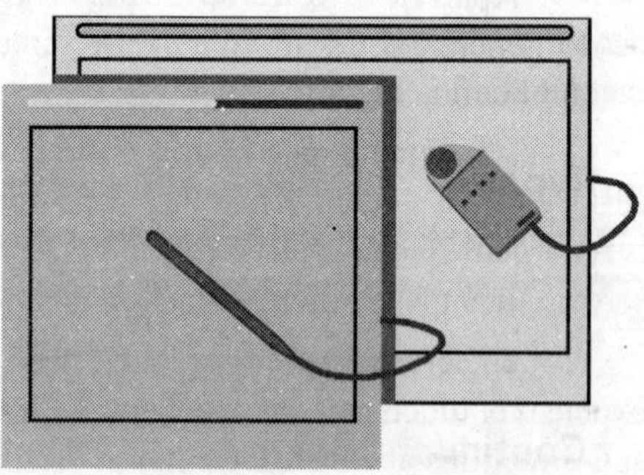

**Fig. 5.9:** Digitizer With Tablet

Digitizers are also called Digitizing Tablets, Graphics Tablets, Touch Tablets, or simply Tablets. Top-view of digitizer along with tablet is shown in Fig. 5.9.

#### Advantages

- The sketches displayed on the screen are neater and more precise than that on paper.
- Digitizers provide a capability of interactive graphics.
- The drawings can easily be changed and their effects can quickly be analyzed, thus saving user time.

#### Disadvantages

- They are costly.
- They are suitable for applications which require high resolution graphics only.

### 5.3.10 Voice Recognition

Audio input provides direct and "user friendly" means of inputting data and instructions to the computer. Recently, a number of Voice Data Entry (VDE) systems have been developed. Voice recognition is one of the newest, most complex input techniques used to interact with the computer. The user inputs data by speaking into a microphone. The simplest form of voice recognition is a one-word command spoken by one person. Each command is isolated with pauses between the words.

With a voice-recognition device, a doctor can ask the computer for information about a patient and not interrupt a surgical operation. Some quality-control inspections can be performed more productively if inspectors can verbally list defects into the microphone of the computer instead of stopping to write them down. Any procedure that requires using both hands and recording data simultaneously can benefit from voice input. Voice recognition also opens up the world of computers to people who are physically challenged and are unable to use traditional types of input devices.

Voice-recognition systems can recognize a few hundred words; however, regional accents and words that sound alike but have different meanings, such as "their" and "there" are difficult to decipher and, thus, cause the system problems. Although research continues in this area, computer voice recognition of continuous speech or normal conversation is not currently available for widespread use.

Apart from Voice Data Entry Systems, some computers and even some calculators have been designed to generate spoken words. Here again the vocabulary is limited thus allowing their use only to limited application areas.

## Types of Voice Systems

There are two types of voice recognition systems:

- Continuous Speech
- Discrete Word

## Continuous Speech

Continuous speech recognition systems are used to control a microcomputer's operations and to issue commands to special application programs. For example, rather than using the keyword to shutdown the system, the user could simply say "Shutdown".

**Examples**

- *Apple Computer's PlainTalk System*
- *IBM's Continuous Speech Series System*

## Discrete Word

A common activity in business is preparing memos and other written documents. Discrete-word recognition systems allow users to dictate directly into a microcomputer using microphone. The microcomputer stores the memo in a word processing file where it can be revised later or directly printed out.

**Example:** *IBM Voice Type Simply Speaking is a popular system*

## Advantages

- Easier to use and much efficient system
- Unwanted inputs or unauthorized speakers can be identified and therefore unwanted access be traced and avoided.
- Computer can be used very effectively by blind or handicapped people.

### Disadvantages

- Computer can have very limited vocabulary i.e., words which can be understood by it.
- The accents or voice of different operators can't be distinguished and the computer will not be able to recognize words which are in its vocabulary.

## 5.3.11 Key to Magnetic Media

In earlier computer systems punched cards were the most common form of input but today the emphasis has switched to magnetic media. In office and business organizations, where traditionally data preparation is a major part of the work, keying information directly to magnetic tape or disk is now standard practice, superseding the use of the traditional punched card. Three methods are distinguishable:

i. Key-to-tape
ii. Key-to-cartridge/cassette
iii. key-to-disk/diskette

### Key-to-tape

A Key-to-tape device, sometimes referred to as a magnetic tape recorder, permits the recording information directly on the magnetic tape. An operator, copying from documents, keys the data electronically using a typewriter like keyboard. The data is stored temporarily by the device and typically displayed on a CRT for visual checking before being transferred to magnetic tape.

### Key-to-cartridge/cassette

Information can also be keyed direct to small magnetic cassette tapes or cartridges and later transferred to standard magnetic tape for processing. A cassette, typically two and half inches by four inches in size, is capable of storing around 200,000 characters of information. A typical cartridge is smaller in capacity, averaging around 30,000 characters. These key input devices are easy to use and compact.

### Key-to-disk/diskette

As with key-to-tape systems, information is entered via a keyboard and a copy displayed on a CRT to allow a visual check. A key-to-disk/diskette system normally comprises a mini computer, a number of key stations and a disk drive. The minicomputer is required to control the input from various stations, enabling the data to be held temporarily for verification and editing before allocation to the disk store. The process of keying to disk or diskette is more efficient and cost effective than punching data on cards for card input.

### Advantages

- The key to magnetic media obviates the need of interposed media such as punched card.
- It is cost effective over a period of time.
- Large amount of data can be stored on the magnetic media which occupies much smaller space than the punched cards.
- The data on magnetic media does not get damaged easily as it does on punched cards.

### Disadvantages

- Main drawback is its high initial cost. But, now-a-days even this cost has reduced substantially.
- This type of system depends on the processor. A breakdown results in all work being stalled.

### 5.3.12 Financial Transaction Terminals

These input devices are mainly for the financial transaction and are used mostly by banks and other finances institutions. Most of you must have seen the Automated Teller Machine (ATM). This machine works on its own. The ATMs are mainly owned by banks. Banks issue cards to the customer. Each card has the account number of the customer and credit limit stored on it magnetically. When the card is inserted in the machine, after checking the account number for validity, the user specific keys of the terminal, instructions can be given. After carrying out specific checks, the machine provides you with the required amount of money and updates your balance.

#### Advantages

- The machine works automatically without any human control
- Customers do not have to travel long distances and stand in long queues to carry out the transaction.

#### Disadvantages

- Fraud cases come across sometimes when people withdraw more money than the credit limit.

### 5.3.13 Machine Vision Systems

Usually robots have cameras fitted in them which act as eyes for them. These cameras grasp the image, scan it and decide the next action. Such machines are said to have vision. Robots with vision are used to identify manufacturing superficial defects in objects, assemble various parts of a system, etc.

Vision-input system is the science and technology of machines that see, where see in this case means that the machine is able to extract information from an image that is necessary to solve some task. As a scientific discipline, computer vision is concerned with the theory behind artificial systems that extract information from images. The image data can take many forms, such as video sequences, views from multiple cameras, or multi-dimensional data from a medical scanner.

**Figure 5.10:** Vision input system

A vision-input system allows a computer to accept by seeing an object. Input data in this case is normally an object's shape and features in the form of an image. The idea is to simulate the capability of a human vision system in a limited sense.

A computer with a vision-input device consists of a digital camera. Digital Camera is an input device used to take pictures and to store directly in computer in digital form. It operates on the same basic principle as a traditional or conventional camera but digital camera sends images directly inside the PC in digital form instead of storing it on a conventional film.

When a picture is taken with digital camera, the electric image of the picture is stored in digital form on the floppy disk or CD-R attached with the camera. The stored picture can be loaded into the computer from the disk for editing. As a technological discipline, vision-input system seeks to apply its theories and models to the construction of computer vision systems.

Examples of applications of Vision-input system include systems for:

- Controlling processes (e.g., an industrial robot or an autonomous vehicle).
- Detecting events (e.g., for visual surveillance or people counting).
- Organizing information (e.g., for indexing databases of images and image sequences).

- Modeling objects or environments (e.g., industrial inspection, medical image analysis or topographical modeling).
- Interaction (e.g., as the input to a device for computer-human interaction).

Vision-input system is closely related to the study of biological vision. The field of biological vision studies and models the physiological processes behind visual perception in humans and other animals. Vision-input system, on the other hand, studies and describes the processes implemented in software and hardware behind artificial vision systems. Interdisciplinary exchange between biological and computer vision has proven fruitful for both fields. Vision-input system is, in some ways, the inverse of computer graphics. While computer graphics produces image data from 3D models, computer vision often produces 3D models from image data. There is also a trend towards a combination of the two disciplines, e.g., as explored in augmented reality. Sub-domains of vision-input system include scene reconstruction, event detection, video tracking, object recognition, learning, indexing, motion estimation, and image restoration.

### Advantages

- Machine vision systems are able to identify objects and carry out required operations on them.
- No human intervention is required.

### Disadvantages

- A slight change in the shape of the object seen by the machine does not allow the specific operation to be carried out.

## 5.3.14 Source Data Input

Recall that data entered directly into a computer system without a transcription process is referred to as source data. Methods of source data input include magnetic-ink character recognition, magnetic strips, and optical recognition.

## 5.3.15 Magnetic-ink Character Recognition (MICR)

MICR is interpretation by a computer of a line of characters written in a special magnetic ink. These characters can be read by humans as well. You may have noticed a line of numbers and some odd-shaped characters on the bottom of your personal cheques. These magnetic ink characters are bank processing symbols representing the cheque number, customer account number, and bank identification number. When the bank receives the cheque, the amount of the cheque is also printed in magnetic ink. The cheques are sent through a MICR reader to interpret the information, update the appropriate accounts and, in some case, sort the cheques afterwards.

Magnetic ink is used on documents such as bank cheques and credit card slips because a MICR device can easily distinguish the appropriate magnetic characters no matter how much a user might have written over them

## 5.3.16 Magnetic Strips

Magnetic strips are thin bands of magnetically encoded data that are found on the backs of many credit cards and automated teller cards. The data stored on the card vary from one application to another, but they include account numbers or special access codes. Magnetic strip cards can also be used to limit access to high security areas. To enter a security area, a person inserts the card into a computerized "read" device; if the card contains the right code, the door automatically opens. Because data cannot be seen or interpreted by simply looking at the card, the stored data can be highly sensitive or personal.

## 5.3.17 Optical Recognition

Optical recognition occurs when a device scans a printed surface and translates the image the scanner sees into a machine-readable format that is understandable by the computer.

The three types of optical recognition described here are:

i. Optical Mark Recognition (OMR)
ii. Optical Bar Recognition (OBR)
iii. Optical Character Recognition (OCR)

**Optical mark recognition (OMR)**: It employs mark sensing, one of the simplest forms of optical recognition, to scan and translate, based on its location, a series of pen or pencil marks into computer-readable form. A computerized optical mark reader scores the tests by identifying the position of the mark, not its shape.

**Optical bar recognition (OBR)**: It is a slightly more sophisticated type of optical recognition. An optical bar reader recognizes and interprets a pattern of lines that form a bar code. Bar codes, also called product codes, appear on products as a series of thick and thin black bars and spaces that are arranged to represent data, such as name of the manufacturer and the type of product. Interpretation of the code is based on the width of the lines rather than the location of the bar code. The bar code does not contain the price of the item. Prices are stored in the computer where the amount can be easily reprogrammed to reflect sale or special offers. The bar code is read by a scanner, and the price and products are then matched by the computer. The price may be displayed at a checkout counter by a point-of-sale (POS) terminal.

**Optical character recognition (OCR)**: It is the most sophisticated type of optical recognition. An optical character reader works in much the same way as the human eye. It does not rely on the magnetic quality of the character such as MICR does; rather, it recognizes specially-shaped alphabetic and numeric characters. Capital and lower case letters, as well as a variety of different optical-character typesets, can be read.

## 5.3.18 Scanners

Scanner is a kind of input device that can read text or printed paper and translates the information in a convenient form to be understood by the computer. A scanner works on the principle of digitizing an image in the form of bit-matrix called 'bit-map'. The bit-map can be stored in a file, displayed on the screen, and can easily be manipulated by relevant packages/programs.

All kinds of scanned documents using an optical scanner gets converted in the form of bit-map and thus it does not distinguish between text or graphics. In order to edit text read by an optical scanner, we need an OCR system to translate the image into ASCII format. Almost all optical scanners sold today come along with OCR packages.

There are six distinct types of scanners:

- handheld
- flatbed

- sheetfed
- photo drum, and
- slide.

Each of these styles has its own practical applications and limitations. Theoretically, you could also include digital cameras as a type of scanner.

Flatbed (or simple) and Hand-held scanners are the most popular scanners in maximum use. These are shown in Fig. 5.11 (a) and (b) respectively.

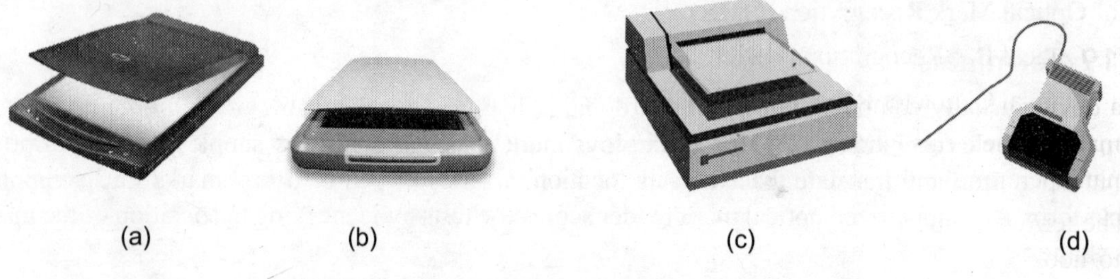


(a) to (c) Flatbed Scanners (d) Hand-held Scanner

**Fig. 5.11:** Types of Scanners

Scanners can be classified on the basis of following:

- Scanning Technology
- Bit-depth
- Resolution
- Size and Shape

Different applications require the use of different types of scanners and each type of scanner has unique features and comes in a different price range.

**Description:** The picture to be input is laid flat, face down on the surface of the scanner and the lid lowered to avoid stray light creeping in.

The scanner sweeps its sensors along the picture. As it does so, an image is built up as a series of 'pixels'. Each pixel represents a tiny part of the picture.

## A scanner can

1. Create a black and white image- handy for line drawings and text.
2. Create a full colour image- excellent for inputting photographs.

The number of pixels can be adjusted to suit the image being taken. For example if a small file is required, then a low-resolution (75 dots per inch) black and white image may be adequate. This will result in an A4 sized image being only a few hundred kilobytes at most.

On the other hand if the highest quality is required then a high resolution (300 dots per inch+) full colour image is taken. This will result in a huge file, easily several Megabytes in size.

### How Scanners Work?

Scanners work a lot like copy machines. But instead of immediately outputting an exact copy of the image, scanners send the information about the original to an electronic storage device connected to a host computer. Most scanners shine a bright light on to an original document or image and then measure the information that is reflected back into the scanner.

These electronic sensors respond to even the slightest variations in light intensity. Some of these sensors are sensitized to various colours; they use filters to block certain colours, which allow other colours to be measured more easily. Or they use prisms to separate the light into colours. Those that use prisms are known as beam splitters and are generally regarded as superior

## 5.3.19 Terminals

It is a device usually equipped with a keyboard and a display device, capable of sending and receiving information. The terms workstation are often changed interchangeably. However, a terminal may not have a human operator. A work station is a terminal at which human operator performs an application.

The terminal typically consists of a Visual Display Unit (VDU), a keyboard, and a communication link to hook the terminal with the main computer system. Terminal is used for inputting data to and retrieving data from remotely located main system.

Monitor (or VDU) and Terminal are shown in Fig. 5.12 (a) and (b) respectively.

**Fig. 5.12:** (a) Monitors (b) Terminal

VDUs are most common form of terminal i.e. a place where the information is displayed on the screen as it is typed.

Terminals fall into the following categories:

- Dumb Terminals
- Smart Terminals
- Intelligent Terminals

### 5.3.19.1 Dumb Terminals

It is a terminal which can do nothing except communicate to and from a CPU. It is also called as a fixed function terminal or non-programmable terminal.

So a dumb terminal can't do any processing of its own and is used only for data input and retrieval. For example, railway reservation clerk might use a dumb terminal at customer counter for booking or canceling tickets.

#### 5.3.19.2 Smart Terminals

These terminals can input and retrieve data and can perform limited processing of its own viz., editing or verifying the data. A smart terminal can not be used for programming. They are designed with a microprocessor chip that contains the circuit needed to perform arithmetic logic and control functions.

#### 5.3.19.3 Intelligent Terminals

There terminals have built-in microprocessors that are user-programmable. They can process small jobs without the need to interact with the mainframe. In addition to keyboard, monitor and communication link, it also includes a processing unit, storage capabilities and software.

### 5.3.20 Voice/Speech Recognition System

Voice recognition technology is prospering with its application being extended to different fields. With most reliable devices fabricated with the help of this technology, you can accomplish the task of installing security effectively.

### 5.3.21 Speech Recognition

Computer technology that enables a device to recognize and understand spoken words, by digitizing the sound and matching its pattern against the stored patterns. Currently available devices are largely speaker-dependent (recognize speech of only one or two persons) and can recognize discrete speech (speech with pauses between words) better than the normal (continuous) speech. Their major applications are in assistive technology for helping people in working around their disabilities. Not to be confused with voice recognition which is used mainly in security devices?

**Figure 5.13:** Voice Systems

Voice recognition or speech recognition is a type of behavioural biometric technology, which is used to identify a user, with the help of pre-stored voice templates in the biometric device. Every individual has a distinct voice structure, which is based upon a number of characteristics. With the help of voice recognition technology, a number of devices have been manufactured to provide security at homes as well as offices. It is impossible for intruders and housebreakers to tamper with this technology and thus, you can rely upon voice recognition systems for maintaining high-level security.

Speech recognition (also known as automatic speech recognition or computer speech recognition) converts spoken words to text. The term "voice recognition" is sometimes used to refer to recognition systems that must be trained to a particular speaker—as is the case for most desktop recognition software. Recognizing the speaker can simplify the task of translating speech.

Speech recognition is a broader solution which refers to technology that can recognize speech without being targeted at single speaker—such as a call center system that can recognize arbitrary voices.

Speech recognition has various applications. It can be used in automated phone systems that allow the users to input choices and browse through menus without pressing any keys. Speech recognition systems are also used in businesses and homes to allow users to dictate to their computers and have their words transcribed into their word processing applications. They are currently being used for legal, medical or other transcription needs.

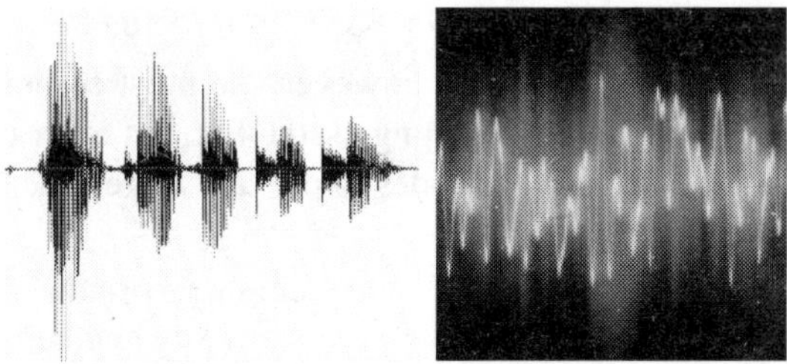

**Figure 5.14:** Speech Recognition

Speech recognition also offers a method for giving computer commands. With voice instructions, users can command their computers to browse through folders, look for a specific file or open and execute a specific program. Speech recognition software is also being used by differently able persons when they make use of their computers.

## Features of Voice Recognition

1. Voice recognition is facilitated by microphones, which record the voice samples and store them for future use.
2. Voice recognition technology is the only form of biometrics, which make use of physical traits (like shape of the vocal trait) as well as behavioural traits (like voice texture, pronunciation and others).
3. Automatic recognition and verification processes are facilitated by this technology.
4. Devices designed using this technology offers voice recorder, voice alerting system and emergency power supports.

## Applications of Voice Recognition

Voice recognition systems (speech recognition systems) are installed on those devices, which have no other alternative of biometric analysis than the voice. Here are few applications of this technology used at various places:

1. Modern cell phones are installed with voice recognition components, to control the access of unfamiliar callers.
2. ATM cards are also making use of this technology to ensure that authorized users use their cards to withdraw money from ATM terminals.
3. Door locks are designed with voice recognition technology to ensure that strangers are not allowed to pose threat to the security of your house and family.
4. Automobile locks and garage locks are also designed with this technology to ensure safety to cars.
5. Computer access is restricted to authorized users with the help pf devices based on this technology.

### 5.3.22 Point-of-Sale Terminal

A point-of-sale (POS) terminal is a device that reads data at the source of a transaction and immediately turns them into usable information. These terminals record data found on bar codes or MICR price tags on each product, calculate cost, and provide the consumer with a detailed receipt of the transaction. Some of these also directly update inventory files.

There are various bar-coding schemes in use; however, the most common is the Universal Product Code (UPC). Department and grocery stores have long used OBR, but other types of stores, factories, and manufacturing operations are starting to use bar codes to provide more efficient, cost-effective control of inventory.

## 5.4 OUTPUT CONCEPTS

The output devices receive results and other information from the computer and provides it to the users. Output is the process of translating data in machine-readable form into a form understandable to humans or readable by other machines. The information that is the result of processing is also often referred to as output. An output device is a peripheral device that allows a computer to communicate information to humans or another machine by accepting data from the computer and transforming them into usable forms.

Output is divided into two general categories:

- Output that can be readily understood and used by humans
- Output to secondary storage devices that hold the data to be used as input for further processing by a computer or for use by another machine.

In today's information society, people require clear, legible and output. Output that can be understood by humans can be categorized as:

- Hard copy
- Soft copy

Hard copy is the output, such as paper, that can be read immediately or stored and read later. It is relatively stable and permanent form of output. Soft copy is usually a screen-displayed output. It is transient form of output and is lost when the computer is turned off. But if the data needed to create the soft copy have been saved on disk or tapes, the soft copy can be reproduced on the screen anytime.

## 5.5 HARD COPY DEVICES

Graphics and text material can be produced with a wide selection of printers and plotters. A printer produces output, usually in the form of text, on paper; however, some printers produce graphics. A plotter produces graphic images on paper. The speed of the devices and the quality of the hard copy are the main features that determine the various prices of printers and plotters.

### Print Quality

The quality available from hard-copy can vary considerably. You may have heard the terms:

- Near-typeset quality
- Letter-quality
- Near-letter quality
- Standard-quality
- Draft-quality

Now, what do these terms mean?

### Near-typeset quality

Near-typeset quality print is similar in quality to what is produced by a typeset machine, such as the print found in a magazine.

### Letter-quality

Letter-quality print is the equivalent of good typewriter print. This print is made using solid-line (fully-formed) characters as opposed to characters made up of dots or lines. Letter-quality print is used traditionally in business letters and in formal correspondence.

### Near-letter quality

Printers that don't produce the fully-formed characters can still print high-quality documents using a near-letter quality print. On some printers this is done when the print head makes multiple passes over the same letters, filling in the spaces between the dots or lines.

### Standard-quality

Standard-quality print is produced when characters composed of dots or lines are formed by a single pass of the print head. Generally, standard quality is suitable for most informal applications.

### Draft-quality

At the low end of the quality scale is draft-quality print, sometimes called compressed print. This print is sometimes used for rough drafts, informal correspondence, or computer program listings. The characters are formed with a minimum number of dots or lines and are smaller than the standard quality characters.

The quality of type that a printer produces is determined by its printing mechanism:

i. Impact and
ii. Non-impact

## 5.6 SOFT-COPY DEVICES

Usually, a user prefers to see what the output looks like before making a permanent copy of it. Viewing the work allows corrections or rearrangement of material to suit specific needs. While most soft-copy output is seen on a display device, voice synthesis devices let us hear it as well.

### Monitors

The most popular and certainly the most viewed form of output is found on the monitor. Monitor is another term for display screen. The term however usually refers to the entire box whereas display screen can mean just the screen. A monitor is a television-like device used to display data or information. Just like other output devices, monitors come in many styles and price ranges. Monitors allow users to view the results of processing, but they can be combined with keyboards so that input data can be viewed and checked as they are entered. This combination of keyboard and monitor is often called a terminal or workstation.

Monitor quality is often judged in terms of resolution, a measure of number of picture elements, or pixels, that a screen contains. A pixel is the smallest increment of a display screen that can be controlled individually - the more pixels, the clearer and sharper the image.

There are two kinds of viewing screens used for monitors:

- Cathode-Ray Tube (CRT)
- Flat-Panel Display

## 5.7 OUTPUT DEVICES

Any peripheral that receives or displays output from a computer. An inkjet printer is a good example of an output device that can make a hard copy of anything on a computer. Below is a listing of all the different computer output devices found on a computer.

- Flat panel
- Monitor
- Printer
- Projector
- Sound card
- Speakers
- Video card

## 5.8 TYPES OF OUTPUT DEVICES

In the world of computers, input/output (I/O) refers to the communication between a computer and the user. Input is the data sent to the system, whereas output is the data sent by the system to the outside world. Computer output devices are computer hardware equipment that is used to communicate the results of data processing carried out by a computer to the user. There are a number of devices, which produce data in different forms, which includes audio, video or hard copy. Output device of computer are types of peripheral hardware connected that is connected to the computer, either using cables or over a wireless network. Immaterial whether you have desktop computers, laptop computers, supercomputers, etc., you will require at least one computer output device.

An output device is any piece of computer hardware equipment used to communicate the results of data processing carried out by an information processing system (such as a computer) to the outside world.

After the computer has processed your data, you often need to produce **output** of the results. This output could be a display on the computer screen, **hardcopy** on printed pages, or even the audio playback of music you composed on the computer.

Examples of output devices:

- Monitors
- Printers
- Plotters
- Speakers
- Headphones
- Voice Response Systems

Most of the computer output devices are common to home as well as office environments. At the same time, there are some devices, which are not as commonly available. Having said that, let's take a look at computer output devices list.

## 5.9 MONITORS

A computer display is also called a display screen or video display terminal (VDT). A monitor is a screen used to display the output. Images are represented on monitors by individual dots called pixels. A pixel is the smallest unit on the screen that can be turned on and off or made different shades. The density of the dots determines the clarity of the images, the resolution.

## 5.10 TYPES OF COMPUTER MONITORS

The computer monitor (also know as a VDU or Visual Display Unit) is the most common computer output device. For desktop computers, cathode ray monitors (CRT) are gradually being replaced by flat-screen monitors such as the Liquid Crystal Displays (LCD) and Thin Film Transistor (TFT) displays used with laptop computers because they use less power and take up less space.

### 5.10.1 CRT Monitor

The traditional output device of a personal computer has been the **CRT** (Cathode Ray Tube) monitor. Just like a television set (an older one, anyway) the CRT monitor contains a large cathode ray tube that uses an electron beam of varying strength to "paint" a picture onto the color phosphorescent dots on the inside of the screen. CRT monitors are heavy and use more electrical power than flat panel displays, but they are preferred by some graphic artists for their accurate color rendition, and preferred by some gamers for faster response to rapidly changing graphics.

**Figure 5.15:** CRT monitor

### 5.10.2 Flat Panel Displays

Portable computers such as a laptop use flat panel displays, because they are more compact and consume less power than CRTs. Portable computers use several kinds of flat panel screens:

### 5.10.2.1 LCD (Liquid Crystal Display) Monitors

Liquid crystal display, also known as liquid crystal diode, is one of the most advanced technologies available at present. Typically, an LCD monitor consists of a layer of color or monochrome pixels arranged schematically between a couple of transparent electrodes and two polarizing filters. Optical effect is achieved by polarizing the light in varied amounts and making it pass through the liquid crystal layer. At present, there are two different types of LCD technology available. These include the active matrix or TFT, and a passive matrix technology. Among these, TFT technology is much secure, reliable and generates better picture quality. On the other hand, passive matrix has a slow response time and is slowly becoming outdated.

Other types of flat panel technology exist (such as **plasma displays**) but LCDs are most commonly used in computers, especially laptops.

Flat panel displays are much lighter and less bulky than CRT monitors, and they consume much less power. They have been more expensive than CRTs in the past, but the price gap is narrowing. You will see many more flat panels in the future.

**Figure 5.16:** Flat panel display (LCD)

### 5.10.2.2 TFT Monitor

A TFT monitor is a LCD display that uses thin-film transistor technology. Flat panel displays are quickly becoming the dominant display of choice and are replacing cathode ray tubes. These days, nearly all of the LCD monitors that are designed and developed use TFT technology to provide the picture. They were developed because, in the past, there was a reliance on the passive matrix LCD display.

**Figure 5.17:** TFT monitor

Since a typical 17-inch TFT monitor has upward of 1.3 million pixels that mean that there would be 1.3 million transistors. However, because the transistors are so small, they don't need very much charge to run. What this guarantees is that the image can be re-drawn very quickly. Therefore, if a mouse is moved across the screen, the pixels would light up as it moved instead of just disappearing.

### 5.10.2.3 Plasma Display Panel

A plasma display panel (PDP) is a type of flat panel display common to large TV displays (80 cm/30 in or larger). They are called "plasma" displays because the technology utilizes small cells containing electrically charged ionized gases, or what are in essence chambers more commonly known as fluorescent lamps.

Plasma Display Panels are flat monitors use the light emitted by ionized gas to display images. The two set of electrodes are arranged on a grid, to which a charge is applied. The display electrode releases the charge to ionize of gas, which in turn, releases the ultraviolet photons that collide with the phosphor coated cell walls and release the light photons. These light photons are then projected on the screen as image.

**Figure 5.17:** A typical modern plasma screen television

## 5.11 CLASSIFICATION OF MONITORS ON THE BASIS OF SIGNALS

On the basis of the type of signal monitors accept, monitors can be classified in the following two categories:

- Digital Monitors
- Analog Monitors

### 5.11.1 Digital Monitors

A digital monitor accepts digital signals rather than analog signals. All monitors except flat-panel displays use CRT technology which is definitely analog. The term digital, therefore, refers only to the type of input received from the video adapter. A digital monitor then translates the digital signals into analog signals that control the actual display.

Although digital monitors are fast and produce clear images, they can't display variable colors continuously. Consequently, only low-quality video standards such as MDA, CGA, and EGA, specify digital signals. On the other hand, VGA and SVGA require an analog monitor. Some monitors are capable of accepting either type of analog or digital signals.

### 5.11.2 Analog Computers

This is the traditional type of color display screen that has been used years in TVs. In reality, all monitors based on CRT technology (except Flat-Panel Displays) are analog. Some monitors are called digital monitors because they accept digital signals from the video adapter.

For example, EGA monitors must be digital because the EGA standard specifies digital signals. Digital monitors must nevertheless translate the signals into an analog form before displaying images. Some monitors can accept both digital and analog signals.

Low-cost digital monitors are often called TTL monitors. Most monitors accept analog signals, which are required by the VGA, SVGA, 8514/A, and other high-resolution color standards.

Some monitors have fixed frequency, which means that they accept input at only one frequency. Another type of monitor, called a multi-scanning monitor, automatically adjusts to the frequency of the signals being sent to it. This means that it can accept input from different types of video adapters. Like fixed-frequency monitors, multi-scanning monitors accept TTL, analog, or both types of input.

## 5.12 FEATURES OF MONITORS

Following are the major features of monitors which characterizes them.

- Size
- Resolution
- Bandwidth
- Refresh Rate
- Interlacing/Non-interlacing
- Phosphor Pitch or Dot Pitch
- Convergence

## Size

Size of the screen is one of the most important features. Like TVs, screen size is measured diagonally i.e. the distance from one corner to the opposite corner diagonally. A typical size for small VGA monitors is 14 inches. Screens of size 16 or more are called full-page monitors. In addition to their size, monitors can be either portrait or landscape.

The screen size is sometimes misleading because there is always an area around the edge of the screen that can't be used. Therefore, monitor manufacturers must now also state the viewable area i.e. the area of screen that is actually used.

## Resolution

The resolution of monitor indicates how densely the pixels are packed. Pixel stands for Picture Element. A pixel is a single point in a graphic image. Graphic monitors display pictures by dividing the display screen into thousand or millions of pixels, arranged in rows and columns. The pixels are so close together that they appear connected. The number of bits used to represent each pixel determines how many colors or shades of gray can be displayed. For example, an 8-bit color monitor uses 8-bits for each pixel making it possible to display 28 (=256) different colors or shades of gray.

In color monitors, each pixel is composed of three dots: red, blue and green. Ideally the three dots should all converge at the same point failing which color pixels appear fuzzy.

In general, the more number of pixels, the sharper the image. Most modern monitors can display 1024 × 768 pixels which is the resolution of SVGA standard. Some high-end models can display 1280 × 1024 or even 1600 × 1200.

## Bandwidth

The amount of data that can be transmitted in a fixed amount of time is called bandwidth. For digital devices, the bandwidth is usually expressed in bits per second (bps). For analog devices, the bandwidth is expressed in cycles per second or Hertz (Hz).

## Refresh Rate

Display monitors must be refreshed many times per second. The refresh rate determines how many times per second the screen is to be refreshed. The refresh rate for a monitor is measured in Hertz (Hz) and is also called the vertical frequency or vertical refresh rate. The old standard for monitor refresh rates was 60 Hz, but a new standard developed by VESA sets the refresh rate at 75 Hz for VGA and SVGA monitors. The faster the refresher rate, the lesser the flickering on monitors.

## Interlacing/Non-interlacing

Interlacing is a display technique that enables a monitor to provide more resolution inexpensively. With interlacing monitors, the electron guns draw only half the horizontal lines with each pass (e.g. all odd lines on one pass and all even lines on the next pass). Because an interlacing monitor refreshes only half the lines at one time, it can display twice as many lines per refresh cycle, giving it greater resolution. Another way of looking at it is that interlacing provides the same resolution as non-interlacing, but less expensively.

A shortcoming of interlacing is that the reaction time is slower, so programs that depend on quick refresh rates (e.g. animation, video, etc.), may experience flickering or streaking. If we are given two monitors that offer the same resolution, the non-interlacing one will generally be better.

### Phosphor Pitch or Dot Pitch

The dot pitch is one of the principal characteristics that determine the quality of display monitors. Another term for dot-pitch is phosphor pitch. It is measurement that indicates the vertical distance between each pixel on a display screen. It is measured in inches. The lower the dot-pitch, the crisper the image. The dot pitch of color monitors for personal computers ranges from about 0.15 mm to 0.30 mm.

### Convergence

Convergence refers to how sharply an individual color pixel on a monitor appears. Each pixel is composed of three dots: red, blue and green. If the dots are badly mis-converged, the pixel will appear blurred one. All monitors have some convergence errors, but they differ in degree.

## 5.13 Video Standards

There are a variety of vide standards that define resolution and colors for displays. Support for a graphics standard is determined by both the monitor and the video adapter. The monitor must be able to show the resolution and colors defined by the standard, and the video adapter must be capable of transmitting the appropriate signals to the monitor.

Following are some popular video standards for PCs:

- Video Graphics Array (VGA)
- Super VGA (SVGA)
- 8514/A
- XGA
- TI 34010

### Video Graphics Array (VGA)

VGA video standard was developed by IBM for personal computers. It has become a de facto standard for PCs. In graphics mode, the resolution is either 640 × 480 or 320 × 200 with 16 colors and 256 colors respectively. In text mode, VGA systems provide a resolution of 720 × 400 pixels. The total palette of colors is 2,62,144.

Unlike earlier graphics standards for PCs - MDA (Monochrome Display Adapter), CGA (Color/ Graphics Adapter) and EGA (Enhanced Graphics Adapter), VGA uses analog signals rather than digital signals. Consequently, a monitor designed for one of the older standards will not be able to use VGA. Since its introduction in 1987, several other standards have been developed that offer greater resolution and more colors, but VGA remains the lowest common denominator. All PCs made today support VGA, and possibly some other more advanced standards.

### Super VGA (SVGA)

SVGA is a set of graphics standard designed to offer greater resolution than VGA. There are several varieties of SVGA, each providing following different resolutions:

- 800 × 600 pixels
- 1024 × 768 pixels
- 1280 × 1024 pixels
- 1600 × 1200 pixels

All SVGA standards support a palette of 16 million colors, but the number of colors that can be displayed simultaneously is limited by the amount of video memory installed in a system. One SVGA system might display only 16 simultaneous colors while another displays the entire palette of 16 million colors. SVGA video standards are developed by a consortium of monitors and graphics manufacturers called Video Electronics Standard Association (VESA).

#### 8514/A

The 8514/A video standard provides a resolution of 1024 × 768 pixels, which gives about 2.5 times resolution of VGA having 640 × 480 pixels. Like VGA, 8514/A provides a palette of 2,62,000 colors, of which 256 can be displayed at one time. On monochrome displays, 8514/A provides 64 shades of gray. Original version of 8514/A relied on interlacing technique that makes it possible provide resolution at low cost. Interlacing, however, carries a performance penalty, so many manufacturers produce non-interlaced 8514/A clones.

#### XGA

XGA stands for extended graphics array. It is a very high resolution graphics standard introduced by IBM in 1990. It was designed to replace the older 8514/A video standards. It provides the same resolutions i.e. 640 × 480 or 1024 × 768 pixels, but supports more simultaneous colors i.e. 65,000 rather than 256 colors. Additionally, XGA allows monitors to be non-interlaced.

#### TI 34010

TI 34010 is a video standard from Texas Instruments that supports a resolution of 1024 × 768. TI 34010 conforms to TI's Graphics Architecture (TIGA). Unlike IBM's 8514/A, which supports the same resolution, TI 34010 is non-interlaced.

## 5.14 Sound Cards and Speakers

An expansion board that enables a computer to manipulate and output sounds. Sound cards are necessary for nearly all CD-ROMs and have become a common place on modern PCs. Sound Cards enable the computer to output sound through speakers connected to the board, to record sound input from a microphone connected to the computer, and manipulate sound stored on a disk.

Nearly all sound cards support MIDI (Musical Instrument Digital Interface) and most sound cards are Sound Blaster compatible. Sound cards use two basic methods to translate digital data into analog sounds.

- Frequency Modulation Synthesis mimics different musical instruments according to built-in formulas.
- Wave-table Synthesis relies on recordings of actual instruments to produce sound. It produces more accurate sound but is a more expensive technique.

## 5.15 PRINTERS

A printer is a peripheral which produces a text and/or graphics of documents stored in electronic form, usually on physical print media such as paper or transparencies. Many printers are primarily used as local peripherals, and are attached by a printer cable or, in most new printers, a USB cable to a computer which serves as a document source. Some printers, commonly known as network printers, have built-in network interfaces, typically wireless and/or Ethernet based, and can serve as a hard copy device for any user on the network. Individual printers are often designed to support both local and network connected users at the same time. There are several printer technologies, the most common of which are:

- the daisy wheel printer
- the dot-matrix printer (also called impact matrix printer)
- the inkjet printer and the bubble jet printer
- the laser printer

Today, daisy wheel printers and matrix printers are hardly ever used.

## 5.16 CATEGORIES OF PRINTERS

A printer is an output device that produces a hard copy of data. The resolution of printer output is expressed as DPI. Printers can be classified into different types in several ways.

First, the printers can be divided into three categories by the way they print.

- Serial Printers: Also called a character printer. Print a single character at a time. They are usually inexpensive and slow.
- Line Printers: Print a line at a time. They are expensive and very fast. Line printers use a band, a chain, etc.
- Page Printers: Also called a laser printer. Print a page at a time. They usually use a laser to produce page images. Quality is best. This is a little bit expensive, but the price of the personal laser printer is decreasing. The price range of the personal laser printer is around $400, today.

Second, printers can be classified into two forms according to the use of a hammer.

- Impact Printers: Hammer hits ribbons, papers or print head. Dot-matrix and daisy-wheel printers are the example. Noisy.
- Nonimpact Printers: They do not have the hammer and do not hit. An example is an ink-jet and laser printer.

**So, let's take a closer look at the various types of printers.**

### 5.16.1 Character Printers

They are used to print only one character at a time. A typewriter is an example of a character printer. Some of character printers are described below.

#### 5.16.1.1 Daisy-Wheel Printer

Daisy-Wheel is a printer mechanism that uses any kind of hub (wheel) having a set of spokes at the margin of the hub. The wheel can be removed to use a different character set. The end of each spoke is a raised image of a type character. When the wheel is turned and the required character is aligned to the print hammer, the character is then struck into a ribbon and onto a paper with the hammer. Daisy-Wheel Printer prints typewriter-like very high quality characters. However, they are slower and less reliable than dot-matrix printers. Microcomputer users seldom use this printer, because the better dot-matrix printers and inexpensive laser printers are available today. The speeds of daisy-wheel printers range from 30 to 60 characters per second (cps).

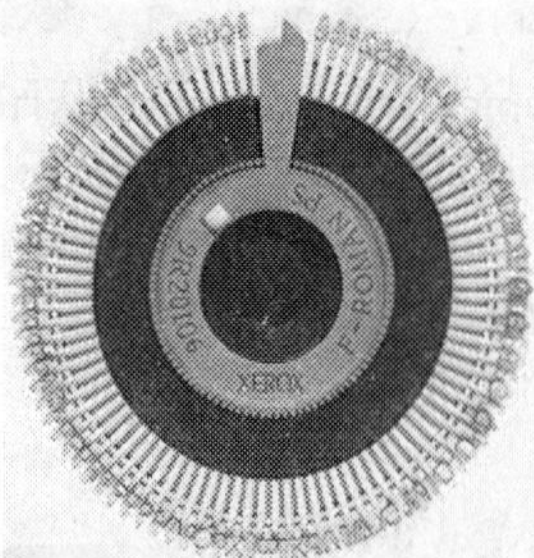

Figure 5.18: A daisy-wheel print wheel

Figure 5.19: Plastic Daisy Wheel

## 5.16.1.2 Dot-Matrix Printer

The dot-matrix printer allows you to print documents on paper thanks to the "back and forth" motion of a carriage housing a print head.

It has a print head containing a rectangular array of protruding wire pins,with the number of pins depending in the quality of the printer. Individual characters or graphics patterns are obtained by retracting certain pins so that the remaining pins form the pattern to the printed.

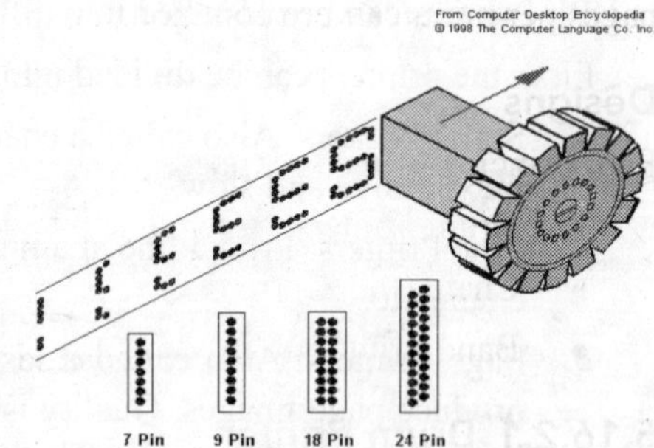


Figure 5.20: Dot Matrix Printer

Dot-matrix printers are printers that write characters and form graphic images using one or two columns of tiny dots on a print head. The dot hammer moving serially across the paper strikes an inked-ribbon and creates images on paper.

- The print head travels from side to side across the paper and is made up of numerous pins which are pushed out to form the shape of each character.
- The pins hit an ink ribbon against the paper so the characters are printed out.
- The paper is usually continuous with holes down each side and perforations so the pages can be easily separated by tearing.

Because the pins make an impact against the paper the characters can be printed through several layers of self-carbonating paper to produce duplicate copies.

Figure 5.21: Dot Matrix Pins

An animation showing how head of a 21 pin dot-matrix printer moves across the paper, firing the pins that strike the ink against the paper.

#### 5.16.1.3 Character Matrix Printer

Character matrix printers are a category of computer printers (typically impact printers) that place characters from a fixed character set anywhere onto a fixed grid of possible locations on the page. Examples of these are daisy wheel printers, golf ball printers, chain printers, and band printers. A character printer prints one character at a time.

### 5.16.2 Line Printers

Line printers, as the name implies, print an entire line of text at a time. The line printer is a form of high speed impact printer in which one line of type is printed at a time. They are mostly associated with the early days of computing, but the technology is still in use. Print speeds of 600 to 1200 lines-per-minuté (approximately 10 to 20 pages per minute) were common.

**Figure 5.22:** IBM 1403 line printer

**Designs**

Four principal designs existed:

- Drum printers
- Chain (train) printers
- Band Printers

#### 5.16.2.1 Drum Printer

In a typical drum printer design, a fixed font character set is engraved onto the periphery of a number of print wheels, the number matching the number of columns (letters in a line) the printer could print. The wheels, joined to form a large drum (cylinder), spin at high speed and paper and an inked ribbon is stepped (moved) past the print position. As the desired character for each column passes the print position, a hammer strikes the paper from the rear and presses the paper against the ribbon and the drum, causing the desired character to be recorded on the continuous paper. Because the drum carrying the letterforms (characters) remains in constant motion, the strike-and-retreat action of the hammers had to be very fast. Typically, they were driven by voice coils mounted on the moving part of the hammer.

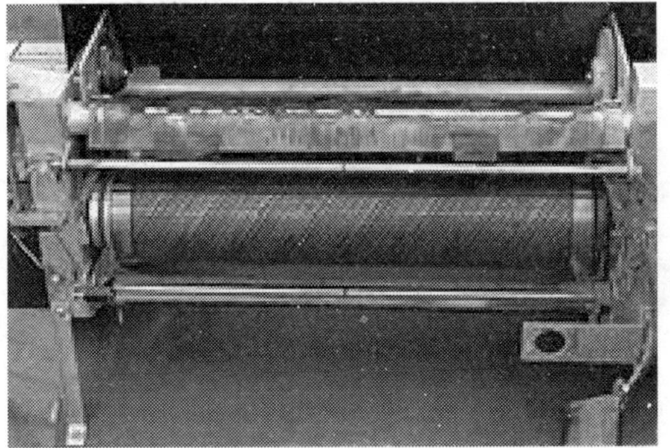

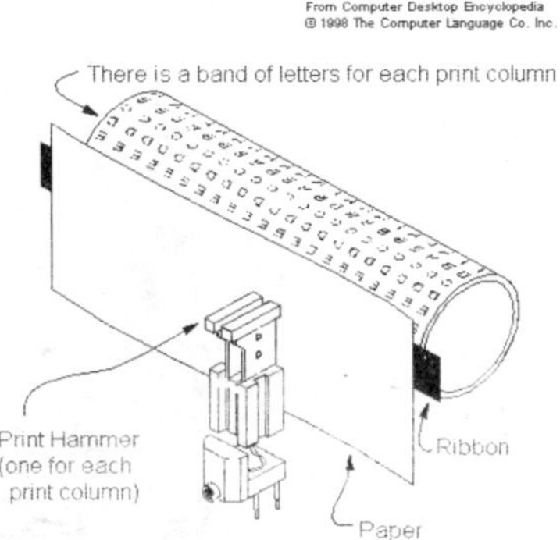


**Figure 5.23:** Drum printer

### 5.16.2.2 Chain Printer

A chain printer (also known as train printers) uses a printing mechanism that uses character typefaces linked together in a chain. The chain spins horizontally around a set of hammers aligned with each position. When the required character is in front of the selected print position, hammer in that position hits the paper into the ribbon against the character in the chain.

This printer is not commonly found around microcomputers, because it is a very expensive, high-speed machine designed originally for mainframes and minicomputers. Chain printers are very reliable and can speed up to 3000 lines per minute.

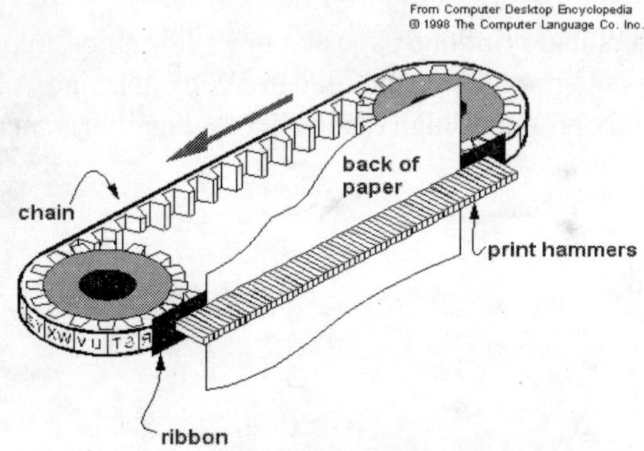


**Figure 5.24:** Chain printer

Character printers and line printers are called impact printers because they use electro-mechanical mechanism, which causes the character shape to strike against the paper and leave an image of the character on the paper.

### 5.16.2.3 Band Printer

A band printer operates in a similar way except it uses a band instead of a chain and has fewer hammers. The hammers on a band printer are mounted on a carriage that moves across the paper to the appropriate print positions. Characters are rotated into place and struck by the hammers. Font styles can easily be changed by replacing a band or chain.

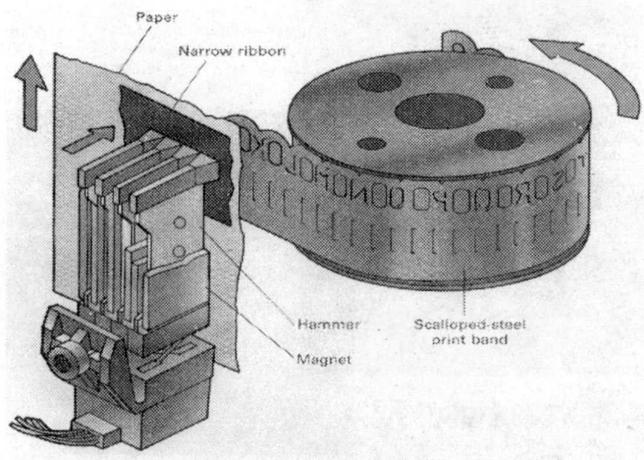


**Fig. 5.25:** Band Printer

(Paper sandwiched between Steel Band and Bank of Hammers)

### 5.16.3 Page Printers

These are the very high speed non impact printers. They can produce documents at speeds of over 20,000 lines per minute. Electronics, xerography, lasers, and other technologies have made these high-volume systems possible. These techniques called electro-photographic techniques have developed from the paper copier technology. Page printers can produce pages of output at a rate equal to a photo copier.

#### 5.16.3.1 Laser Printer

Laser printers are page printers that print one page at a time. It is a non-impact printer. A laser printer is a printer that uses the electro-photographic method used in a copy machine. A laser printer is a common type of computer printer that rapidly produces high quality text and graphics on plain paper.

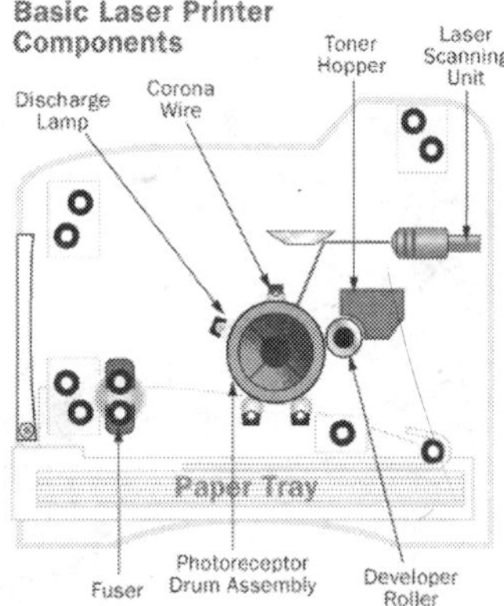


**Figure 5.26 (a):** The basic components of a laser printer

The laser printers produce quality print-outs inexpensively at a high print speed. However, these printers are mostly used in professional and semi-professional settings because of their high cost.

Laser printers use a technology that is close to that used by photocopiers. A laser printer is mainly made up of an elecrostatically charge photosensitive drum that attracts the ink in order to make a shape that will be deposited on the sheet of paper.

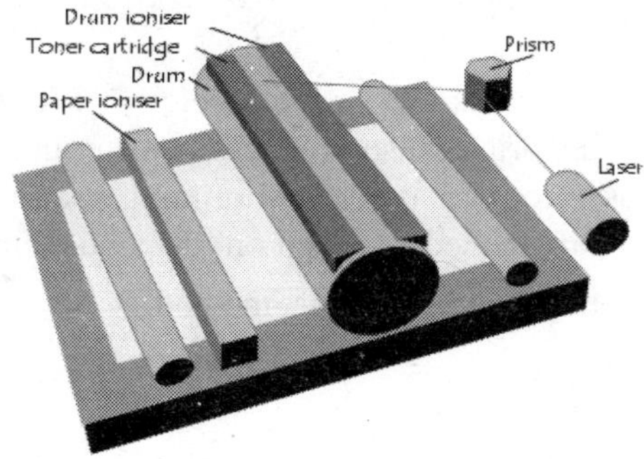


**Figure 5.26 (b):** Drum deposits the ink on the paper.

By turning, the drum deposits the ink on the paper. A heating wire (called a *corona wire*) finally attaches the ink to the paper. Because laser printers do not have mechanical heads, they are quick and quiet. Laser printers are faster than ink jet printers. Their speed is rated in **pages per minute (ppm)**. Laser printers are more expensive than ink jets, but they are cheaper to run in the long term if you just need good quality black and white pages.

### 5.16.3.2 LED Printer

Another printer technology competes with laser printers: LED (Light Emitting Diode) technology. With this technology, an electroluminescent diode printhead polarises the drum with a very fine light ray, making very small dots. This technology is particularly well adapted for obtaining high resolutions (600, 1,200 or 2,400 dpi).

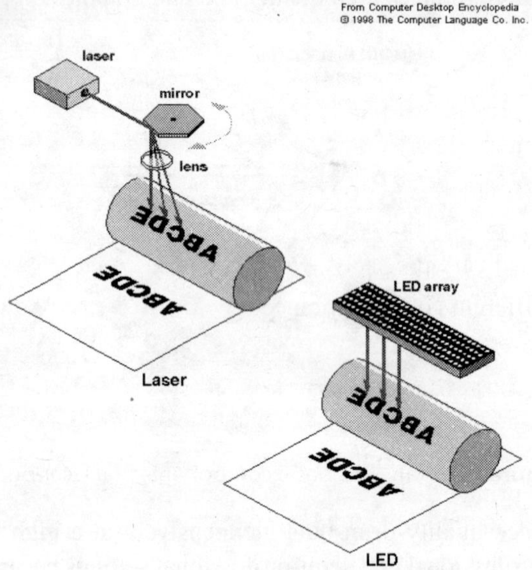


Figure 5.27: LED printer

Given that each diode is makes one point, print speed hardly affects resolution. Moreover, this technology lacks moving parts, which translates into less-expensive and more solid and reliable printers.

### 5.16.3.3 Inkjet Printer

Ink-jet is a printer mechanism that sprays one or more color of ink at high speed onto the paper and produces high-quality printing. This printer also produces color printing as well as high-quality image. That is, ink-jet printers can be used for variety of color printing at a relatively low cost. Ink-jet printing has two methods: Continuous stream method and drop-on- demand method.

Inkjet printing, like laser printing, is a non-impact method.

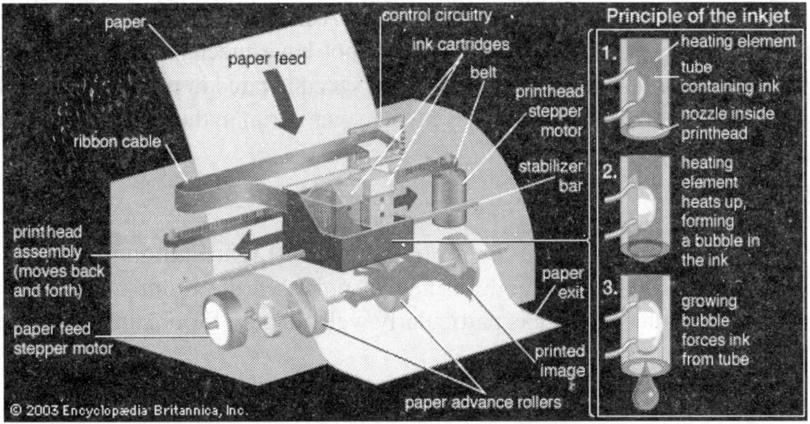


**Figure 5.28:** Ink Jet Printer

An **inkjet** printer is any printer that places extremely small droplets of ink onto paper to create an image. If you ever look at a piece of paper that has come out of an inkjet printer, you know that:

- The dots are extremely small (usually between 50 and 60 microns in diameter), so small that they are tinier than the diameter of a human hair (70 microns)!
- The dots are positioned very precisely, with resolutions of up to 1440x720 dots per inch (dpi).
- The dots can have different colors combined together to create photo-quality images.

## 5.17 PLOTTER

A plotter is a special output device used to produce hardcopies of graphs and designs on the paper. A plotter is typically used to print large-format graphs or maps such as construction maps, engineering drawings and big posters. A plotter is a printer that interprets commands from a computer to make line drawings on paper with one or more automated pens. Unlike a regular printer, the plotter can draw continuous point-to-point lines directly from vector graphics files or commands. There are a number of different types of plotters: a drum plotter draws on paper wrapped around a drum which turns to produce one direction of the plot, while the pens move to provide the other direction; a flatbed plotter draws on paper placed on a flat surface; and an electrostatic plotter draws on negatively charged paper with positively charged toner.

Plotters were the first type of printer that could print with color and render graphics and full-size engineering drawings. As a rule, plotters are much more expensive than printers. They are most frequently used for CAE (computer-aided engineering) applications, such as CAD (computer-aided design) and CAM (computer-aided manufacturing). Hewlett-Packard is the leading vendor of plotters worldwide.

Plotters are divided into four types:

1. Drum plotters
2. Flatbed plotters
3. Inkjet plotters
4. LED plotters

### 5.17.1 Drum Plotter

A drum plotter is pen plotter that wraps the paper around a drum with a pin feed attachment. The drum then rotates the paper as pens move across it and draw the image. It was the first output device used to print graphics and large engineering drawings.

Figure 5.29: A drum plotter

A drum plotter is also known as Roller Plotter. It consists of a drum or roller on which a paper is placed and the drum rotates back and forth to produce the graph on the paper. It also consists of mechanical device known as Robotic Drawing Arm that holds a set of colored ink pens or pencils. The Robotic Drawing Arm moves side to side as the paper are rolled back and forth through the roller. In this way, a perfect graph or map is created on the paper. This work is done under the control of computer. Drum Plotters are used to produce continuous output, such as plotting earthquake activity.

### 5.17.2 Flatbed Plotter

A flat-bed plotter is a mechanical drafting device used with many CAD programs for designers. The paper remains stationary on a flat surface while a pen moves across it horizontally and vertically. A flatbed plotter is also known as Table Plotter. It plots on paper that is spread and fixed over a rectangular flatbed table. The flatbed plotter uses two robotic drawing arms, each of which holds a set of colored ink pens or pencils. The drawing arms move over the stationary paper and draw the graph on the paper. Typically, the plot size is equal to the area of a bed. The plot size may be 20- by-50 feet. It is used in the design of cars, ships, aircrafts, buildings, highways etc. Flatbed plotter is very slow in drawing or printing graphs. The large and complicated drawing can take several hours to print. The main reason of the slow printing is due to the movement mechanical devices.

Figure 5.30: Flatbed Plotter

### 5.17.3 The Inkjet Plotter

This is the third kind of Plotter which is called as the Inkjet plotter. The inkjet plotter creates an image by spraying small droplets of ink onto a piece of paper. A popular choice for advertising agencies and graphic designers, inkjet plotters are used generally for large outputs, such as banners and billboards and large signs often seen on roadsides. They are available in thermal or piezoelectric models. Thermal inkjet plotters use heat to apply droplets of ink, while piezoelectric plotters use charged crystals to apply the ink. Inkjet plotters tend to produce better quality graphics than other types of plotters.

**Figure 5.31:** Inkjet plotter

In Today's world, virtually all inkjets create color. Low-end inkjets make the most of the three ink colors (cyan, magenta and yellow), but finally create a complex black that is often mud-spattered. Four-color inkjets make use of the black ink created for pure black printing alone.

### 5.17.4 LED Plotter

LED plotters are also called as Electrostatic plotters. It works similar to Laser Printers except that it uses LED as the heat source instead of Laser.

**Figure 5.32:** LED plotter

## 5.18 Projector

Projectors are display devices that project a computer created image. The computer sends the image data to the video card which then sends the video image to the projector. They are typically used for presentations or for viewing videos.

An output device that can take the display of a computer screen and project a large version of it onto a flat surface. Projectors are often used in meetings and presentations so that everyone in the room can view the presentation. In the picture to the right, are a ViewSonic projector and an example of what a projector may look like. Projectors used with computers are small devices that are rarely much larger than a toaster and typically weigh a few pounds.

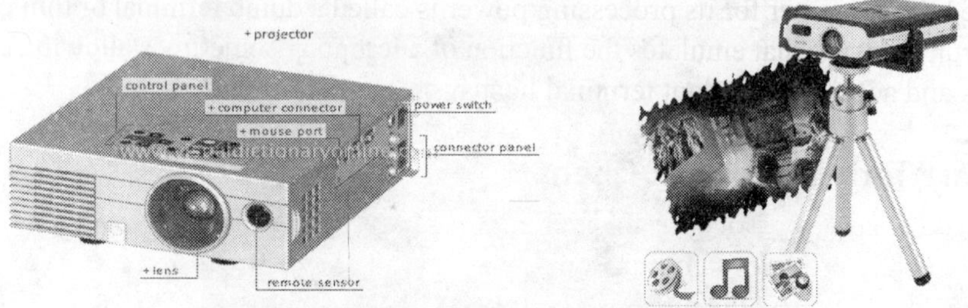


Figure 5.33: Projector

### 5.18.1 Multimedia Projector

Multimedia Projector is a hardware device, with which an image, such as the computer screen, is projected onto a flat screen. Image data is sent to the video card, by computer, which is then translated into a video image and sent to the projector. A projector is often used in meetings or to make presentations, because they allow for a large image to be shown, with which the display is available for a large audience.

You may not have all kinds of output devices, but one multimedia projector is certainly necessary for you. For instance, the multimedia projector is really necessary for office. All computers might not have all the computer output devices, but it certainly does have one of the visual output devices, namely either a monitor or projector.

Figure 5.34: Multimedia Projector

### 5.18.2 Handheld Projector

A Handheld projector (also known as a pocket projector or mobile projector or pico projector) is an emerging technology that applies the use of an image projector in a handheld device. It is a response to the emergence of compact portable devices such as mobile phones, personal digital assistants, and digital cameras, which have sufficient storage capacity to handle presentation materials but little space to accommodate an attached display screen. An important design characteristic of a handheld projector is the ability to project a clear image, regardless of the physical characteristics of the viewing surface.

## 5.19 Terminals

A computer terminal is an electronic or electromechanical hardware device that is used for entering data into, and displaying data from, a computer or a computing system. Early terminals were inexpensive devices but very slow compared to punched cards or paper tape for input, but as the technology improved and video displays were introduced, terminals pushed these older forms of interaction from the industry. A related development was timesharing systems, which evolved in parallel and made up for any inefficiencies of the user's typing ability with the ability to support multiple users on the same machine, each at their own terminal.

The function of a terminal is confined to display and input of data; a device with significant local programmable data processing capability may be called a "smart terminal" or fat client. A terminal that depends on the host computer for its processing power is called a dumb terminal or thin client. A personal computer can run software that emulates the function of a terminal, sometimes allowing concurrent use of local programs and access to a distant terminal host system.

### 5.19.1 Smart Terminal or Fat Client

A fat client (also called heavy, rich, or thick client) is a computer (client) in client–server architecture or networks that typically provides rich functionality independent of the central server. Originally known as just a 'client' or 'thick client', the name is contrasted to thin client, which describes a computer heavily dependent on a server's applications.

A fat client still requires at least periodic connection to a network or central server, but is often characterised by the ability to perform many functions without that connection. In contrast, a thin client generally does as little processing as possible and relies on accessing the server each time input data needs to be processed or validated.

### 5.19.2 Dumb Terminal or Thin Client

A thin client (sometimes also called a lean or slim client) is a computer or a computer program which depends heavily on some other computer (its server) to fulfill its traditional computational roles. This stands in contrast to the traditional fat client, a computer designed to take on these roles by itself. The exact roles assumed by the server may vary, from providing data persistence (for example, for diskless nodes) to actual information processing on the client's behalf.

Thin clients occur as components of a broader computer infrastructure, where many clients share their computations with the same server. As such, thin client infrastructures can be viewed as the amortization of some computing service across several user-interfaces. This is desirable in contexts where individual fat clients have much more functionality or power than the infrastructure either requires or uses.

The most common type of modern thin client is a low-end computer terminal which concentrates solely on providing a graphical user interface to the end-user. The remaining functionality, in particular the operating system, is provided by the server.

## 5.20 AUDIO

3D audio is a technique for giving more depth to traditional stereo sound. Typically, 3D sound or 3D audio is produced by placing a device in a room with Stereo Speakers. The device dynamically analyses the sound coming from the speakers and sends feedback to the sound system so that it can readjust the sound to give the impression that the speakers are further apart.

3D audio devices are particularly popular for improving computer audio where the speakers tend to be small and close together. There are a number of 3D audio devices that attach to a computer's sound card.

## 5.21 VOICE SYNTHESIS

Another emerging technology is voice synthesis and the computers that produce it. Voice synthesis is the process of electronically reproducing the human voice in recognizable patterns. Producing these patterns is an easy task. The English language and its rules of syntax are enough to confuse many humans. The voice response system usually is considered for applications requiring low-speed human-machine interaction. Audio response system is inexpensive. Such systems can be used with PCs. The TI (Texas Instruments Company) has developed a "Speak and Spell" system to teach children to spell and pronounce over 200 elementary words.

## EXERCISE

1. What do you mean by digital camera?
2. Explain the working of scanners?
3. What do you mean by output devices?
4. What are printers? Explain the various types of printers in detail?
5. Explain the various types of plotters?
6. What do you mean by monitor?
7. Explain the various types of monitors?
8. What do you mean by projector?
9. What are input devices?
10. Explain the concept of mouse?
11. Explain the speech recognition system in detail?
12. What are the reasons for the visual display unit to be more popular than punched card reader?
13. What is a Keyboard? How does a simple keyboard differ from an ergonomically designed keyboard.
14. How does VDU act as input as well as output device?
15. Differentiate between 'hardcopy' and 'softcopy' devices.
16. Name any two devices that can be used to output graphs and pictures.
17. What are the most extensively used input devices?
18. Why punched card devices are not used extensively nowadays?
19. Compare the advantages and limitations of a mouse and a keyboard as data input devices?
20. In what circumstances line printers are preferred over dot matrix printers?
21. What is meant by OMR? Explain its functioning.

22. What are the most extensively used output devices?
23. How do sound cards and speakers work as output devices?
24. What are the advantages and disadvantages of MICR technology?
25. How computer accept input from the keyboard? Explain.
26. What is a plotter? State their types and explain the functioning of each.
27. What are two pointing devices used for data input, and how do they work?
28. How does analog monitor differ from digital monitors?
29. What are the two types of printers that are popularly used?
30. What is the relationship between a joystick and a graphic cursor?
31. How do point-of-sale (POS) terminals work?
32. What are the different types of printers?
33. Describe an application for voice-recognizer.
34. What is the criteria for classification of printers?
35. What is a plotter and how does it work?
36. How can the quality of a DMP be controlled?
37. How do Financial Transaction Terminals work? Also state their merits and demerits.
38. What are voice-synthesizers? State their importance.
39. Discuss relative merits and demerits of DMP, Daisywheel printer and Line printers.
40. What are thermal printers and how do they work?
41. What is the difference between a laser printer and a LED printer?
42. What is COM? Also give its advantages and disadvantages.
43. Distinguish among character, line and page printers.
44. What do you understand by 3D audio?
45. What is the difference between an impact and an non-impact printer?
46. What does MICR stand for? State the functioning of MICR input devices.
47. What is a monitor and how does it work?
48. What is a mouse? How does it point on to the screen? Explain its working.
49. Which devices can provide us with graphical output?
50. What are RGB monitors? Explain their working.
51. What are the major characteristics of monitors?
52. What is a joystick? Where is it used? Explain.
53. What is meant interlacing? How does it affect the quality of display systems?
54. What is an output device? What are the major output devices for a computer?
55. Is video camera an input device? Justify your answer.
56. What are the effects of folding or stapling a MICR cheque? How does it effect the data stored?
57. What is refresh rate? What will happen if the refresh rate is not uniformly controlled?

58. What are the different video standards?
59. What do you mean by imaging? Where is it beneficial?
60. Identify the different types of printers and give a brief description of each.
61. What are scanners? Where are they used? Describe different types of scanners.
62. What does VESA stand for? State its contribution in developing video standards.
63. What do you mean by VGA, SVGA, 5814/A, XGA and TI 34010?
64. What are the similarities and dissimilarities between a light pen and touch screen?
65. What are the two most common output devices used with computers? For what is each of them used?
66. What do the bars on a data carrier represent?
67. Name a device that other than monitor that produces soft-copy output?
68. Which kind of printer can produce near-typeset quality output?
69. What are Touch Screens? How do they differ from Touch Pads?
70. What characterizes printer?
71. List some relative advantages and disadvantages of CRT and flat panel monitors.
72. What are Vision Systems? State their importance.
73. Explain how MICR cheques are useful in banks?
74. What is the purpose of a point-of-sale terminals and financial-transaction terminals?
75. What is the difference between a Chain and band line-printers?
76. What is a laser printer? Explain its working.
77. What are bar codes? Give two applications of bar codes.
78. Name an impact printer that prints fully formed characters.
79. List the following in order of their increasing resolution: SVGA, CGA, EGA, VGA.
80. How can you control the quality of a laser printer? Explain.
81. What is OCR? Explain its working.
82. Which output device generates graphs with the greatest precision, a pen plotter or a dot-matrix printer?
83. How does a touch-screen works, and where could it be used?
84. What are the pros and cons of using a plotter for output?
85. What is a digitizer? State its types.

CHAPTER

6

# Memory and Mass Storage Devices

## 6.1 INTRODUCTION

Memory is that portion of a computer system that is used for the storage and subsequent retrieval of data and instructions. Memory is a quite essential component of digital computer. Computer memory exhibits perhaps the widest range of type, technology, organization, performance, and cost of any feature of a computer system.

## 6.2 CHARACTERISTICS OF MEMORY SYSTEMS

The complex subject of computer memory is made more manageable if we classify memory systems according to their key characteristics. The most important of these are listed in Table 6.1

**Table 6.1:** Key Characteristics of Computer Memory Systems

| | | |
|---|---|---|
| a | Location | - CPU<br>- Internal (main)<br>- External (secondary) |
| b | Capacity | - Word size<br>- Number of words |
| c | Unit of transfer | - Word<br>- Block |
| d | Access Method | - Sequential access<br>- Direct access<br>- Random access<br>- Associative access |
| e | Performance | - Access time<br>- Cycle time<br>- Transfer rate |
| f | Physical type | - Semiconductor<br>- Magnetic |
| g | Physical Characteristics | - Volatile/Nonvolatile<br>- Erasable/Non-erasable |
| h | Organization | |

## Location

Let us begin with the location of the memory. There is memory both internal and external to the computer. Internal memory is often its main memory. But there are other forms of internal memory. The CPU requires its own local memory, in the form registers. External memory consists of peripheral storage devices, such as disk and tape, that are accessible to the CPU via I/O controllers.

## Capacity

Next characteristic of memory is its capacity. For internal memory, this is typically expressed in terms of bytes or words. External memory capacity is typically expressed in terms of bytes or Kbytes (KB) or Mbytes (MB). The storage capacity can be expressed in terms of Bytes. Few higher storage units are given below:

| | | |
|---|---|---|
| 1 KB (Kilo Byte) | = 1024 Bytes | = $2^{10}$ Bytes |
| 1 MB (Mega Byte) | = 1024 KB | = $2^{20}$ Bytes |
| 1 GB (Giga Byte) | = 1024 MB | = $2^{30}$ Bytes |
| 1 TB (Tera Byte) | = 1024 GB | = $2^{40}$ Bytes |
| 1 PB (Peta Byte) | = 1024 TB | = $2^{50}$ Bytes |
| 1 EB (Exa Byte) | = 1024 PB | = $2^{60}$ Bytes |
| 1 ZB (Zetta Byte) | = 1024 EB | = $2^{70}$ Bytes |
| 1 YB (Yetta Byte) | = 1024 ZB | = $2^{80}$ Bytes |

## Unit of Transfer

A related concept is the unit of transfer. For internal memory, the unit of transfer is equal to the number of data lines into and out of the memory module. This is often equal to the word length, but sometimes may not be. For main memory, this is the number of bits read out into memory at a time. For external memory, data are often transferred in much larger units than a word, and these are referred to as blocks.

## Access Method

One of the sharpest distinctions among memory types is method of accessing units of data. Four types may be distinguished:

- **Sequential Access:** Memory is organized into units of data, called records. access must be made in a specific linear sequence. Stored addressing information is used to separate records and assist in the retrieval process. A shared read/write mechanism is used, and this must be moved from its current location to the desired location, passing and rejecting each intermediate record.

  Thus the time to access an arbitrary record is highly variable. Tape units are sequential access.
- **Direct Access:** As with sequential access, direct access involves a shared read/write mechanism. however, individual blocks or records have a unique address based on physical location. access is accomplished by direct access to reach a general vicinity plus sequential searching, counting, or waiting to reach the final location. Again, access time is variable. Disk units are direct access.
- **Random Access:** Each addressable location in memory has a unique, physically wired-in addressing mechanism. the time to access a given location is independent of the sequence of prior accesses and is constant. Thus any location can be selected at random and directly addressed and accessed. Main memory systems are random access.

- **Associative:** This is a random-access type of memory that enables one to make a comparison of desired bit locations within a word for a specified match, and to do this for all words simultaneously. Thus a word is retrieved based on a portion of its contents rather than its address. As with ordinary random-access memory, each location has its own addressing mechanism, and retrieval time is constant independent of location or prior access patterns. Cache memories may employ associative access.

## Performance

From user's point of view, the two most important characteristics of memory are capacity and performance. Three performance parameters are used:

- **Access Time:** For random-access memory, this is the time it takes to perform a read or write operation, i.e., the time from the instant that an address is presented to the memory to the instant that data have been stored or make available for use. For non-random-access memory, access time is the time it takes to position the read-write mechanism at desired location.
- **Memory Cycle Time:** This concept is primarily applied to random-access memory and consists of the access time plus any additional time required before a second access can commence. This additional time may be required for transients to die out on signal lines or to regenerate data if they are read destructively.
- **Transfer Rate:** This is the rate at which data can be transferred into or out of a memory unit. For random access memory, it is equal to 1/(Cycle Time). For a non-random-access memory, the following relationship holds:

$$T_N = T_A + N/R$$

where

$T_N$ = Average time to read or write N bits

$T_A$ = Average access time

N = Number of bits

R = Transfer rate in bits per second (bps)

## Physical Type

A variety of physical types of memory have been employed. The two most common types today are semiconductor memory and magnetic memory.

## Physical Characteristic

Several physical characteristics of data storage are important. In a volatile memory, information decays naturally or is lost when electrical power is switched off. In a non-volatile memory, information once recorded remains without deterioration until deliberately changed; no electrical power is needed to retain information. Magnetic memories are non-volatile whereas semiconductor memory may either be volatile or non-volatile.

Non-erasable memory can not be altered, except by destroying the storage unit. Semiconductor memory of this type is known as read-only memory (ROM). A practical non-erasable memory must also be non-volatile.

### Organization

For random-access memory, the organization is a key design issue. By organization is meant the physical arrangement of bits to form words. The obvious arrangement is not always used.

## 6.3 MEMORY HIERARCHY

The design constraints on a computer's memory can be summed up by three questions:

- How Much?
- How Fast?
- How Expensive?

### How Much?

The question of how much is open-ended. If the capacity is there, applications will likely be developed to use it.

### How Fast?

The question of how fast is, in a sense, easier to answer. To achieve greatest performance, the memory must be able to keep up with the CPU. That is, as the CPU is executing instructions, we would not want it to have to pause waiting for instructions or operands.

### How Expensive?

The final question must also be considered. For a practical system, the cost of memory must be reasonable in relationship to other components.

As might be expected, there is trade-off among the three key characteristics of memory, namely, cost, capacity, and access time. At any given time, a variety of technologies are used to implement memory systems. Across this spectrum of technologies, the following relationship holds:

- Smaller access time, greater cost per bit
- Greater capacity, smaller cost per bit
- Greater capacity, greater access time

The dilemma facing the designer is clear. The designer would like to use memory technologies that provide for large-capacity memory, both because the capacity is needed and because the cost per bit is low. However, to meet performance requirements, the designer needs to use expensive, relatively lower-capacity memories with fast access time.

The way out of this dilemma is not to rely on a single memory component or technology, but to employ a memory hierarchy. A typical memory hierarchy is illustrated in Fig. 6.1.

As one goes down the hierarchy, the following occur:

a. Decreasing cost per bit

b. Increasing capacity

c. Increasing access time

d. Decreasing frequency of access of the memory by the CPU

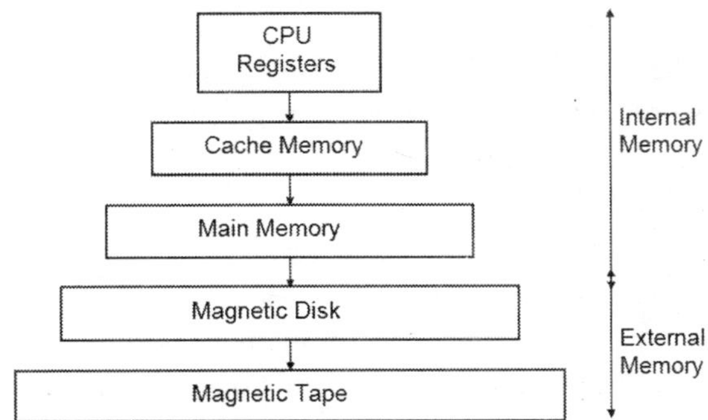


**Fig 6.1:** The Memory Hierarchy

Thus smaller, more expensive, faster memories are supplemented by larger, cheaper, slower memories. The key to success of this organization is the decreasing frequency of access.

Main memory is the principal internal memory system of the computer. Each location in the main memory has a unique address and most instructions refer to a main memory address. Main memory is sometimes extended with a higher speed, smaller cache which is not visible to the programmer or to the CPU. The main memory and its extensions are typically volatile.

Data are stored more permanently on external mass storage devices. These are used to storage program and data files and are usually visible to the programmer only in terms of files and records rather than individual bytes or words. Magnetic disk and tape are the most commonly used external mass storage devices. Magnetic disk is also used to provide an extension to main memory known as virtual storage or virtual memory.

## 6.4 DESIRABLE CHARACTERISTICS OF MEMORY UNIT

The structure of the memory unit is perhaps the most important characteristic of a computer system. Some desirable features of the smallest constituent of the memory unit, i.e., binary cell are as:

- It must be very fast.
- It must be very compact in size.
- It must have two stable states.
- It must be capable of switching infinite number of times between these stable states.
- Cost should be very low.
- Time taken for reading and writing onto the binary cell should be very less.
- Power consumption must be as small as possible.

## 6.5 TYPES OF MEMORY

At present the following three kinds of memory are commonly used in modern computers:

**a.** Primary Memory
- ♦ Core Memory
- ♦ Semiconductor memory

b. Secondary Memory
   - Magnetic Memory
   - Optical Memory

c. Backup Memory

### Primary Memory

All computers except very small systems contain all types of memory, namely, primary, secondary and backup memories. The core memory or semiconductor memory is employed as the primary memory (or main memory) of the computer. It stores programs and data which are currently needed by the CPU.

### Secondary Memory

The magnetic memory is used as secondary (or auxiliary) memory. The information which is not being currently processed resides in the secondary memory. The information which is needed by the CPU for current processing is transferred from the secondary to main memory. The size of the main memory is comparatively much smaller than that of the secondary memory because of its high cost. The CPU communicates directly with the memory. As the CPU employs semiconductor technology and has very high speed, its matching memory must be very fast. Only semiconductor devices can provide the matching speed. Thus the main memory also must employ semiconductor technology. RAM and ROM ICs are used as the main memory of the computer. RAMs are volatile, i.e., their contents are erased when power goes off.

The auxiliary memory is employed for mass storage of programs, data and other information. Auxiliary memory has much larger capacity than main memory and is used to store system software, assemblers, compilers, useful packages, large data files etc. Auxiliary memory should not be of volatile nature but rather must be capable of storing information permanently. Magnetic memory has this property and thus retains the information once it is stored onto it. The magnetic memories such as hard disks and floppy disks are the most common secondary memories used in computers.

### Backup Memory

Backup memory is used to store the copy of the important programs such as operating system, compilers etc. Floppy disks and magnetic tapes can be employed as backup storage. These programs are generally available in the secondary memory but their copies are also kept in the backup memory so that they can be reloaded into the secondary memory in case the programs stored in the secondary memory are lost accidentally or due to any other reason.

## 6.6 CORE MEMORY

This type of memory was introduced in the year 1955. It consists of tiny cores of doughnut-shaped objects called cores. The cores are made of ferromagnetic material. The individual cores are strung on wires to form a core plane. Several core planes are stacked one over the other to form a core stack.

The number of planes upon will depend upon the number of bits in a word. Thus, a 16-bit word will have a series of 17 planes including one plane for parity-checking. The actual number of elements in each plane will depend upon the memory size of the computer.

A basic principle of physics states that if a core is threaded by a wire carrying an electric current, the core will be magnetized in a certain direction, called its polarity, which depends upon the direction of the current through the wire.

The core can be put into one of two states. Furthermore, once the core is magnetized, it will keep its polarity even when the current is removed. It will change its polarity only when a current is sent through the wire in the opposite direction.

Now, one wants to be able to magnetize one core at a time; but it would be extremely inefficient to have one wire for each core. Therefore, cores are threaded by a grid of wires such that each core is threaded by two of the wires which are perpendicular to each other. Then, if currents of half the required strength are sent through the two wires threading a certain core, only that core is magnetized.

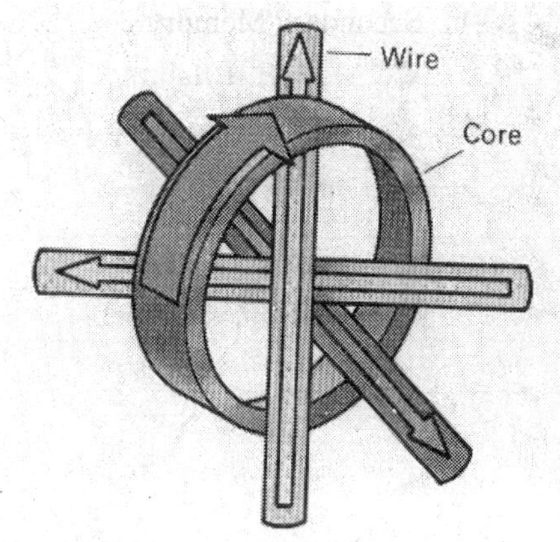


**Fig. 6.2:** Core Memory (One Core Cell)

Reading the polarity of a given bit requires two additional wires, a sense wire and an inhibit wire, passing through the core. First, the computer will polarize the core in some given direction, say 0; then the computer will polarize the core in the opposite direction, 1. If initially the core was 0, then no change in the polarity of the core takes place in the first step; in particular, no current flows through the sense wire, which informs the computer that that core is 0. In the second step, in this case, the computer will simultaneously put a current through the inhibit wire while it attempts to write a 1. This will prevent a change in polarity of the core, so that it remains 0 after it is read. On the other hand, if the core was initially was initially 1, the first step will change the polarity of the core to 0. This will send a current through the sense wire, informing the computer that the core initially contained a 1. The second step restores the core to 1. The magnetic cores are stacked in parallel planes for the actual storage of data.

## 6.7 SEMICONDUCTOR MEMORY

The complete memory unit may be constructed from either bipolar or field-effect transistors on a single silicon chip, which may be referred to as Semi-conductor Memory. These were introduced by IBM in 1971. The semiconductor storage operates on the principle of a flip-flop in which the switch is set to a 0 and 1 position by a Write command which sets or restores the flip-flop.

The semiconductor memory is:

- Faster
- Compact
- Lighter
- Consumes less power
- Static device
- Having no rotating part in it

### Core Memory Vs Semiconductor Memory

The main difference between Core memories and Semiconductor Memories are enumerated in Table 6.2:

**Table 6.2:** Difference Between Core and Semiconductor Memories

| S. No | Core Memory | Semiconductor Memory |
|---|---|---|
| 1. | Non-volatile | Generally Volatile |
| 2. | Destructive readout | Non-destructive readout |
| 3. | Limited range of read & write cycle times | Wide range of read & write cycle times |
| 4. | Moderately priced | Low to moderately priced |
| 5. | High power consumption | Low power consumption |
| 6. | Best for large memories | Best for small or medium-sized memories |
| 7. | Relatively large access time | Short access time |
| 8. | Available only in large blocks | Available in wide variety of sizes |
| 9. | Relatively large and heavy | Relatively small and light |

## 6.8 TYPES OF SEMICONDUCTOR MEMORIES

Semiconductor memories are of two types:

i. RAM (random access memory) and
ii. ROM (read only memory)

### 6.8.1 Random Access Memory (RAM)

It is a type of computer memory that can be accessed randomly; that is, any byte of memory can be accessed without touching the preceding bytes. RAM is the most common type of memory found in computers and other devices, such as printers.

This type of memory is pronounced as 'ramm' and can be used both for reading as well as writing and that is why RAM is also known as Read/Write memory. It is accessible to users. The user enters his program and data into RAM. It possesses random access property. The access time is same for each memory location. RAM is a volatile memory. The information stored into it is retained in it as long as the power supply is on. As soon as the power supply goes off (or interrupted) its stored information is lost. The programmer has to load his program and data into the RAM when the power is resumed.

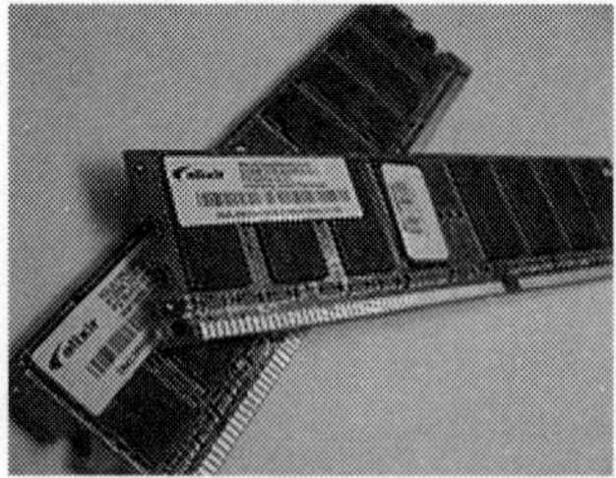

**Figure 6.3:** Random-Access Memory

It is the same as the main memory of computer system. RAM is not the correct name of R/W memory because both RAM and ROM possess random access property. But R/W memory has been called RAM since long and in practice it has become an established name. Thus R/W memory is commonly called RAM.

There are two basic types of RAM:

a. Static RAM (SRAM) and

b. Dynamic RAM (DRAM)

#### 6.8.1.1 Static RAM (SRAM) Vs Dynamic RAM (DRAM)

Static RAMs retain stored information only as long as the power supply is on whereas a dynamic RAM loses its stored information in a very short time (in milli seconds) even though the power supply is on. In a dynamic RAM a binary state is stored on the gate to source to stray capacitor of a transistor of the MOS memory circuit. The presence of charge on the stray capacitor represents 1, and the absence of charge on the stray capacitor represents 0. The charge on these capacitors leak away as a result of normal leakage in a few milliseconds (msec). Therefore, dynamic RAMs have to be refreshed periodically, generally every 2 msec. The dynamic RAMs are cheaper and have high packing density and moderate speed. They consume less power. They are used where large capacity of memory is needed. Static RAMs are costlier and consume more power. They do not need refreshing circuitry. They have higher speed than dynamic RAMs.

In the table below we summarize the main differences between dynamic RAM (DRAM) and static RAM (SRAM).

**Table 6.3:** SRAM Vs DRAM

| **Feature** | **Dynamic RAM (DRAM)** | **Static RAM (SRAM)** |
|---|---|---|
| Storage circuit | Capacitor | Flip-flop |
| Transfer speed | Slower than CPU | Same as CPU |
| Latency | High | Low |
| Density | High | Low |
| Power Consumption | Low | High |
| Cost | Cheap | Expensive |

Even though static RAM is faster than dynamic RAM, its disadvantages prevent it from being used as the main RAM circuit.

Examples of SRAMs are:

- Hitachi HM 6116, 2 K × 8
- HM 6264, 8 K × 8
- HM 6287, 64 K × 1;
- NEC mPD43256, 32 k × 8; etc.

The refreshing and control circuitry for a dynamic RAM may be either on the chip itself or on a separate IC called dynamic RAM controller. If the DRAM and its refresh and control circuitry are on the same IC, it is called iRAM (integrated RAM). In other words the iRAM integrates a dynamic RAM and its control and refreshing circuitry into a single IC. iRAM is also known as quasi-static RAM or pseudo-static RAM.

Static and dynamic RAMs use MOS technology. Semiconductor memories (RAMs and ROMs) are implemented with NMOS. Semiconductor memories using CMOS technology are produced nowadays. They consume very low power. They are at present costly.

SRAMs hold information in a flip-flop circuit consisting of two cross-coupled inverters. In a RAM the memory cell must be associated with read and write facility. Six transistors are needed per memory cell in a static RAM.

DRAMs require less number of transistors per memory cells because information is stored on stray capacitors. Only one transistor is needed to form a memory cell of the DRAM. This results in high packing density of the DRAM compared to SRAM. The capacity of memory chips are given in the form of m × n bits.

For example, the capacity of Hitachi SRAM, HM 6287 is 64 K × 1 bits. The capacity of NEC SRAM μPD43256 is 32 K × 8 bits. A memory chip may be bit-, nibble-, or byte-oriented. The capacity written in the form 64 K × 1 bit means that one bit at a time can be read from or written into the memory. Such memories are bit-oriented. If the capacity is written as 32 K × 8, it means that 8 bits can be read from or written into the memory at a time. This type of memories are byte-oriented.

Examples of DRAMs are:

- Toshiba DRAM TC 51100 of 1 M × 1 bits
- TC 514256 of 256 K × 4 bits, etc.

Intel 21019 is a 1 MB × 9 bit DRAM. 4 MB × 9 bit DRAMs are also available. The ninth bit is for parity checking.

### Advantages of RAMs

- These are available in larger sizes than ROMs
- They serve as temporary data storage
- They can be updated and corrected
- No special programming mechanism like ROMs are required
- These do not require lead time like ROM

## 6.8.2 Read Only Memory (ROM)

Read Only Memory, commonly known as ROM, is a memory which is permanently programmed and can only be read. It also possesses random access property. RAMs are much cheaper compared to RAMs when produced in large volumes to defray the cost of making the mask. The stored information can only be read from ROMs at the time of operation. Information can not be written into a ROM by the users. In other words ROMs are not accessible to users. The contents of ROMs are decided by the manufacturers. The contents are permanently stored in a ROM at the time of manufacturer. From programming mode point of view the ROMs are placed in broad categories:

**Figure 6.4:** Read Only Memory

- Masked-programmed ROMs and
- User-programmed ROMs.

ROMs in which contents are written at the time of IC manufacturing are called mask-programmed RAMs. The following are user-programmable ROMs:

- PROM

- EPROM (or UVPROM)
- E2PROM
- Non-volatile Flash memory

ROMs store information which is not subject to change. They store fixed programs. In microprocessor-based system which are used for industrial controls, ROMs store monitor, assembler, debugging package, function tables such as sine, cosine, square root and code-conversion tables, etc. An example of a ROM is Toshiba Mask ROM, TCS 534000, 512 k × 8 bits.

#### 6.8.2.1 PROM

A version of ROM that can not be changed during normal operation but can be programmed under special conditions is Programmable Read Only Memory (PROM). Its contents are decided by the user. The user can store permanent programs, data or any other kind of information in a PROM. A special equipment called PROM programmer is available for the programming of PROMs. With the help of PROM programmer the user stores his programs in a PROM. PROMs are once programmable, i.e., the user can write his information in a PROM only once. PROMs are more cost effective if small number of chips are to be produced to store certain fixed programs. An example of PROM is 74S287.

#### 6.8.2.2 EPROM or UVEPROM

Many MOS PROMs can be programmed more than once. One variety of such a PROM is the Erasable PROM or EPROM. The stored data in EPROMs can be erased by exposing it to high intensity short wave ultraviolet light for about 18-22 minutes. That's why it may also be called Ultra Violet Erasable PROM. An UV source of 2537 AO wavelength can be used for the purpose. The technique of erasing contents is not easy and convenient because the EPROM IC has to be removed from the computer for the exposure to the UV light. When an EPROM is exposed to UV light the entire data is erased.

The user can not erase the contents of certain selected memory locations. EPROMs are cheap, reliable and hence they are widely used. These are used to store programs which are permanent but requires updation. Permanent programs which are at the research and development stage also need to be stored in EPROM because they are modified several times.

Wherever updation or modification in the programs at the development stages are required, EPROMs are more economical than PROMs because of their reusability. EPROM employ MOS technology and thus store 1 or 0 as the charge or no charge on the insulated floating-gate of the transistor. The UV light causes the stored charge to leak off. Thus the data are erased and it allows the user to reprogram the EPROM. For programming it requires high voltage, 30 V or more. But its operating voltage, i.e, the voltage for read operation is only 5V.

Examples of EPROMs are:

i. Intel's 87C257, 256K (32K × 8) CHMOS EPROM

ii. Intel's 27C040, 4M (512K × 8) CHMOS EPROM

iii. Intel's 27C240, 4M (256K × 16) CHMOS EPROM

iv. Intel's 27C010, 1M (128K × 8) Byte-wide high speed CHMOS EPROM

v. Toshiba, TC571000, 1M (128K × 8) EPROM

#### 6.8.2.3 EEPROM ( or $E^2$PROM or EAPROM)

Another variety in which we can change a particular location, without removing the memory from circuit board is called Electrically Alterable PROM (EAPROM) or Electrically Erasable PROM (EEPROM). The chip can be erased and reprogrammed on the board easily on a byte by byte basis. Either a single byte or the entire chip can be erased in one operation. It requires much shorter time, a few milli-seconds for erasing as compared to 10-20 minutes for EPROM. There is a limit on the number of times the EEPROMs can be reprogrammed, usually 10,000 times. It need not be removed from the computer's board for erasing. Compared to RAMs, EEPROM take much longer time for both writing and erasing a byte. But the access time for reading RAMs, ROMs, PROMs and EEPROMs are comparable, a few hundred nanoseconds.

Intel 2816 is a 16K (2K × 8) EEPROM. The access time for its various versions lies in the range of 220 ns - 400 ns. Any byte can be erased in 9 milliseconds without affecting the data in any other byte. The Intel's 2817A is also an 16K (2K × 8) EEPROM. It possesses automatic byte-erasing facility before write operation. It takes 20 ms for a combined erase/write operation.

**Advantages of ROMs**

- They are non-volatile in nature
- ROMs are easier to interface than RAMs
- ROMs can not be accidentally changed
- ROMs are cheaper than ROMs
- ROMs are easy to test
- These are more reliable than RAMs due to their reduced complexity
- These are static and do not require refreshing
- Its contents are always known and can be verified

#### 6.8.2.4 Non-Volatile Flash Memory

Flash memory is a special type of EEPROM that can be erased and reprogrammed Non-volatile flash memories are also electrically erasable and re-programmable nonvolatile memories. They possess the feature of quick-pulse programming, a typical time is 100 μs for byte-program and 4 sec for chip-program.

EEPROM is similar to flash memory i.e. flash EEPROM. The main difference between EEPROM and flash EEPROM is that the first requires data to be written or erased one byte at a time whereas flash EEPROM chip allows data to be written or erased in blocks and the same makes it faster. The chip is flash erasable and programmable. The whole device is erased in one operation. A typical electrical flash erase time for the chip is 1 second. The access time for read-operation is 150-170 ns. It can be used in place of EPROM.

These are suitable for firmware storage whereas conventional E2PROMs are suitable for parameter storage. When codes are to be updated the entire codes are written to avoid errors. For updation of firmware codes, flash memories are very fast and economical as compared to EPROMs. In case of parameter updation, they need to be rewritten individually byte by byte while system is on-line, in normal operation. Hence, EEPROM are best suited for such applications.

This type of memory is very costly and also they have the limit on the number of times they can be reprogrammed usually 10,000 erase/write operations. But the failure rate is less compared to EEPROMs.

Examples of flash-memories are:

i. Intel 28F512, 512K (64K × 8) bit CMOS Flash Memory

ii. Intel 28F020, 2048K (256 × 8) bit CMOS Flash Memory

### 6.8.3 Applications of ROMs

1. Code Converter: This application is the most obvious use of a ROM. In general a ROM with an N-bit Memory Address Register (MAR) and M-bit Memory Buffer Register (MBR) can realise any N-input M-output combinational circuit.
2. Character Generator: Character displays in dot matrix form use ROMs for decoding and activating the display.
3. Function Generators: Tables for commonly used functions such as Cosine, Sine, Tangent etc may be stored in ROMs. The arguments are entered in MAR and the function values appear in the output register.
4. Control Unit Design: ROMs are used in the design of control units of present day computers.

### 6.8.4 Non-volatile RAM (NVRAM)

A Non-volatile RAM is nothing but a very high speed static RAM and EEPROM packed into a single IC. This type of RAM operates quite similar to RAM and in case of power failure the entire contents of the RAM are transferred automatically in parallel in the EEPROM.

Xicor Inc. has developed a nonvolatile RAM X2201 of 1K capacity. It contains a 1KB RAM and 1KB EEPROM. The entire contents of the RAM are transferred to the EEPROM in 4 ms. Intel 2004 is also a nonvolatile RAM of 512 × 8 bits capacity. It takes 10 ms to transfer the data from RAM to EEPROM. The data from EEPROM are transferred back into RAM when power is resumed. A STORE signal is used to save the contents of the RAM. A signal known as RECALL is used to get the contents back into the RAM from EEPROM.

#### Advantages of NVRAM

- The advantage of the NVRAM is that a battery backup is not needed to save the working data in the event of the power failure. A typical example is the buffer storage for a communication system.
- The NVRAM can be employed for buffer storage for data being transmitted or received over a communication line.
- In the event of power failure, a single microprocessor instruction causes NVRAM to save all the buffered data.

### 6.8.5 Thin Film Memory

Thin-film memory consists of spots of a nickel-iron alloy deposited on a very thin plate of glass or plastic. The spots are connected by very thin copper wires etched into the plate. Each spot operates like a core, and the plate of spots is like a plane of cores. Thin-film memory is much more compact than core memory; each plane of spots is smaller than a single core. It is also faster and is just as stable. Although production costs were at first rather high, new production methods have brought thin-film units within a practical price range. In this type of memory, reading is non-destructive.

### 6.8.6 Magnetic Bubble Memory

This technology of magnetic bubble memory is based on tiny magnetic domains or "bubbles" that appear in certain kinds of crystalline materials under the control of magnetic and electrical fields. The presence of a bubble signifies a 1-bit and the absence a 0-bit. A train of bubbles can be shifted from cell to cell in a shift register to read the storage. Storage density is very high. The bubbles are similar to magnetic cores in that they retain their magnetism indefinitely. High cost and difficulty of production limited wide industry and user acceptance of bubble memories.

### 6.8.7 Holographic Memory

Two forms of holographic storage are available:

- Mechanical and
- Optical.

In the mechanical type of storage, data bits are stored by a laser beam which permanently records the information by "burning" the coating on tape or film. By this way 13 million bits can be stored per square inch. These spots can be read by a laser beam of lesser power.

In the optical holographic memory, a laser beam is passed through an array of light valves to produce binary pattern of darkness and light. This is stored on light sensitive material such as thermoplastics. The data thus stored is read by another laser beam.

## 6.9 MAGNETIC DISKS

A disk is a circular platter constructed of metal or of plastic coated with a magnetizable material. Data are recorded on and later retrieved from the disk via a conducting coil named the head. During a read or write operation, the head is stationary while the platter rotates beneath it.

The write mechanism is based on the fact that electricity flowing through a coil produces a magnetic field. Pulses are sent to the head, and magnetic patterns are recorded on the surface below, with different patterns for positive and negative currents. The read mechanism is based on the fact that a magnetic field moving relative to a coil produces an electrical current in the coil. When the surface of the disk passes under the head, it generates a current of the same polarity as the one recorded.

### 6.9.1 Disk Organization and Formatting

A disk must be prepared for use before data or programs can be stored on it. Each disk, regardless of size, is divided into concentric circles called tracks where data are stored. The disk is also divided into pie-shaped wedges called sectors, which further specify data storage locations on the disk. The number of tracks and sectors is usually determined by the computer's operating system during a formatting operation. The operating system labels each sector of each track with an address so that the computer can go directly to a specific area.

The head is relatively a small device capable of reading to or writing from a portion of the platter rotating beneath it. This gives rise to the organization of data on the platter in a concentric tracks. Each track has the same width as the head. Adjacent tracks are separated by gaps. This prevents, or at least minimizes, errors due to misalignment of the head or simply interference of magnetic fields. To simplify the electronics, the same number of bits are typically stored on each track. Thus the density, in bits per linear inch, increases as we move from the outermost track to the innermost track.

Data are transferred to and from the disk in terms of blocks. Typically, the block is smaller than the capacity of a track. Accordingly, data are stored in block-size regions called sectors. There are typically between 10 and 100 sectors per track, and these may be either fixed or variable length. To avoid imposing unreasonable precision requirements on the system, adjacent sectors are separated by intra-track (or inter-record) gaps.

***How are sector positions within a track identified?***

Clearly, there must be some starting point on the track and a way of identifying the start and end of each sector. These requirements are handled by means of control data recorded on the disk. Thus, the disk is formatted with some extra data used only by the disk drive and not accessible to the user.

### Data Storage on Disks

Data is stored on disks using either of the following two methods:

i. Sector Method
ii. Cylinder Method

## 6.9.2 Sector Method

The diskette is divided into at least eight equal portions called sectors. In other words, each track has partitions called sectors. When the data is stored on the disk using sector method, the address of the data has three parts:

- Surface number
- Track number
- Sector number

For example, the address 015603 means that the required resides on the first surface. The track number is 56 and the sector number is 03. When the address is read by the computer, the read/write head is positioned on the particular track of the specified surface. Then the disk is rotated. R/W head reads the data of the track starting from sector 1. When the required data passes under it, it gets transmitted to the processor. The index hole of the disk indicates the first sector.

## 6.9.3 Cylinder Method

When we have a pack of disks, we prefer to use cylinder method. The number of access arms is equal to the number of disks. each arm has got its own read/write head. The address of the record consists of the cylinder number, surface number and record number. A cylinder is made up of the tracks with the same track number from all the surfaces.

The advantage of using cylinder method is that the read/write heads are all positioned together on the same cylinder but on different surfaces.

## 6.9.4 Characteristics of Magnetic Disk Systems

A magnetic disk system is a mylar or metallic platter on which electronic data can be stored. Although disk resemble phonograph records, they do not have the characteristic spiraling groove, however, data is accessed in much the same was as an individual song is selected on a record. Data files on the disk can be read sequentially or directly.

Table 6.4 lists the major characteristics that differentiate among the various types of disk systems.

**Table 6.4:** Characteristics of Disk Systems

| | | |
|---|---|---|
| 1. | Head Motion | - Fixed-Head<br>- Movable-Head |
| 2. | Disk Portability | - Non-removable Disk<br>- Removable Disk |
| 3. | Sides | - Single-sided<br>- Double-sided |
| 4. | Platters | - Single-platter<br>- Multiple-platter |
| 5. | Head Mechanism | - Contact (floppy)<br>- Fixed gap<br>- Aerodynamic gap (Winchester) |
| 6. | Disk Access Time | |

## Head Motion

First, the head may either be fixed or movable with respect to the radial direction of the platter. In a fixed-head disk, there is one read/write head per track. all the heads are mounted on a rigid arm that extends across all tracks. In a movable-head disk, there is one read/write head. As before, the head is mounted on an arm. since the head must be able to be positioned above any track, the arm can be extended or retracted for this purpose.

The disk itself is mounted in a disk drive, which consists of the arm, a shaft rotates the disk, and the electronics needed for input and output of binary data.

## Disk Portability

A non-removable disk is permanently mounted in the disk drive. The removable disk can be removed and replaced with another disk. The advantage of the second type is that unlimited amounts of data are available with a limited number of disk systems. Furthermore, a disk may be moved from one computer system to another.

## Sides

For most disks, the magnetizable coating is both applied both sides of the platter, which is then referred to as double-sided. Some less expensive disk systems use single-sided disks.

## Platters

Some disk drives accommodates multiple platters stacked vertically about an inch apart. Multiple arms are provided. The platters come as a unit known as disk pack.

## Head Mechanism

Finally, the head mechanism provides a clear classification of disks into three types. Traditionally, the read/write head has been positioned a fixed distance above the platter, allowing an air gap. At the other extreme is a head mechanism that actually comes into physical contact with the medium during a read or write operation. This mechanism is used with the floppy disk, which is a small, flexible platter and the least expensive type of disk.

To understand the third type of disk, we need to comment on the relationship between data density and the size of the air gap. The head must generate or sense an electromagnetic field of sufficient magnitude to write and read properly. The narrower the head is, the closer it must be to the platter surface to function. Since a narrower head means narrower tracks and therefore greater data density, this is desirable. However, the closer the head is to the disk, the greater the risk of error from impurities or imperfections. To push the technology further, the Winchester disk was developed. Winchester heads are used in sealed drive assemblies that are almost free of contaminants. They are designed to operate closer to the disks surface than conventional rigid disk heads, thus allowing greater data density. The head is in the shape of an aerodynamic foil which rests lightly on the platter's surface when the disk is motionless. The air pressure generated by the spinning disk is enough to make the foil rise above surface. The resulting no-contact system can be engineered to use narrower heads that operate closer to the platter surface than conventional rigid disk heads.

As a matter of historical interest, the term Winchester was originally used by IBM as a code name for their 3340 disk model prior to announcement. The 3340 was a removable disk pack with the heads sealed within the pack. The term is now applied to any sealed-unit disk drive with aerodynamic head design.

### Disk Access Time

When the disk drive is operating, the disk is rotating at a constant speed. To read or write, the head must be positioned at the desired track and the beginning of the desired sector on that track. Track selection involves moving the head in a movable-head system or electronically selecting one head on a fixed-head system.

### Seek Time

On a movable-head system, the time it takes to position the head on the track is known as seek-time. In either case, once the track is selected, the system waits until the appropriate sector rotates to line up with the head.

### Latency Time

The time required by a sector to reach below the head is known as latency time. On an average it is half of the time taken for a rotation by the disk.

### Access Time

The time taken to read or write from/into a desired location on the disk is called Access Time of the disk. In other words, access time is the sum of the seek time, if any, and the latency time. Once the head is in position, the read or write operation is then performed as the sector moves under the head.

Mathematically it is written as:

Access time = Average Seek Time + Rotational Latency + Transfer Time

## 6.9.5 Classification of Magnetic Disks

Depending upon the aforesaid characteristics, magnetic disks can be classified in the following manner:

- Floppy Disk
  - 8 inch
  - 5.25 inch
  - 3.5 inch
- Hard Disk
  - Fixed Disk
  - Removable Cartridge
  - Disk Pack
- Magnetic Drum
- Magnetic Cards and Strips
- Zip Disk
- Jaz Disk
- SuperDisk

## Floppy Disks

A floppy diskette, also called simply a diskette or disk, is a small flexible disk. Floppy disks are commonly used as secondary and backup memory in personal computers. These disks are very thin and flexible and hence, they are called floppy. It has been around since the early 1970s.

Floppy disks are made of Mylar with a coating of magnetic material (iron oxide) on it. They are small, convenient and inexpensive. They are removable disks. A floppy disk is inserted into the computer when needed. If the same disk is to be used again and again, it can be kept inserted in the system. It is kept in a square protective cover made of thin plastic. The disk rotates freely in the protective jacket.

Disk surface and its organisation is shown in Fig. 6.5.

The different sizes of floppy disk are:

- 8 inch
- 5 ¼ inch
- 3 ½ inch

Floppy disk has been around us since early 1970s and was originally 8 inches in diameter. Today, the most popular sizes are: 5 ¼ inches square and 3 ½ inches square. Size of 8 inches square is not that popular. 5¼ was the common size and was very popular before 1987. This type of floppy is generally capable of storing between 100 KB and 1.2 MB of data. The most common storage capacities of this size is 360 KB and 1.2MB.

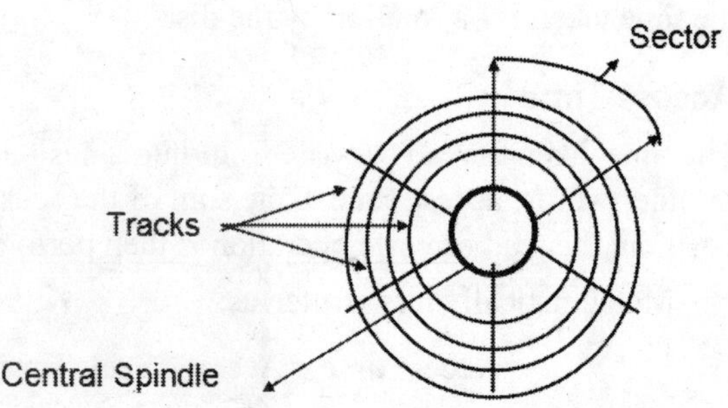

**Fig. 6.5:** Disk Surface and Its Organization

5 ¼ inch and 3 ½ inch floppies are shown in Fig. 6.6 and Fig 6.7 respectively.

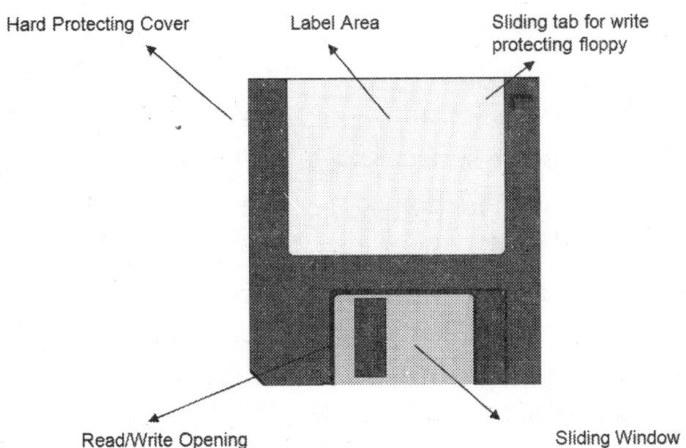


**Fig. 6.6:** 3 ½ Inch (1.44 MB) Floppy

The protective cover of a 3.5 inch disk is hard plastic whereas that of a 5.25 inch disk is thin vinyl. A 5.25 inch disk is also called mini-floppy whereas a 3.5 inch disk is called microfloppy. A disk has semi-random property. Track to track movement of the read/write head is random. The movement on the track while reading or writing data is serial. The most common sizes for PCs are 720 KB (Double Density) and 1.44 MB (High Density). Macintosh supports such disks of 400KB, 800 KB and 1.2 MB.

The average access time is 150-250 ms. It is about a million time slower than semiconductor memory. The access time for the data stored on the disk depends on the following:

i. The seek-time
ii. The search or latency time

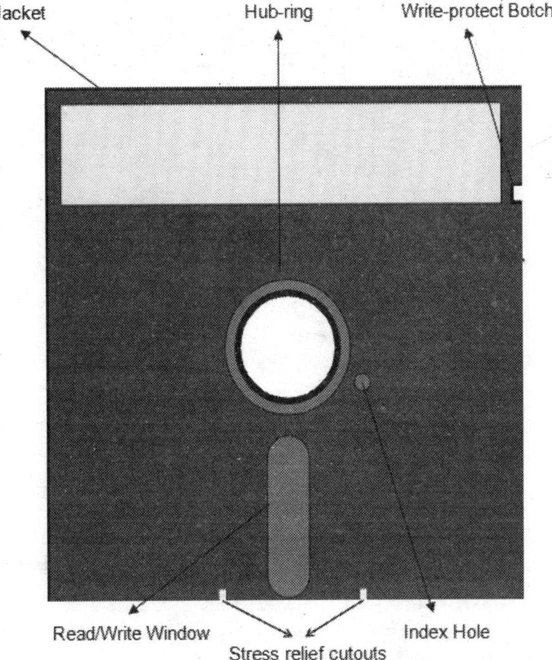


**Fig. 6.7:** 5 ¼ Inch Floppy

## Cautions in Handling Floppy Disks

a. A floppy disk should always be kept in a plastic box when it is not in use. It should be kept in vertical position.

b. Its exposed area of the recording surface should not be touched with fingers.

c. A felt-tipped pen should be used for writing the label. sharp and hard point such as dot pen or any other hard point pen should not be used.

d. Floppy disks should be kept away from magnetic fields such as those generated by electric motors, radios, TVs, tape recorders, telephones and other electric devices.

e. The disk may also be damaged by heat, moisture and dirt. So it should be kept away from excessive heat such as that produced from radiation or direct sun. It should be kept in dust and moisture free environment.

f. The disk should not be removed while drive is running.

g. The disk should not be bent.

## Hard Disk

A hard disk is just that - hard and inflexible. The hard disk is made from materials such as aluminium instead of mylar. The I/O device used to transfer data to and from a hard disk is called a hard-disk drive. The read/write head of a hard-disk drive floats above the surface of the disk at a height of about 50 millionth of an inch (0.00005 inches). In comparison, a human hair is a hundred times larger in diameter.

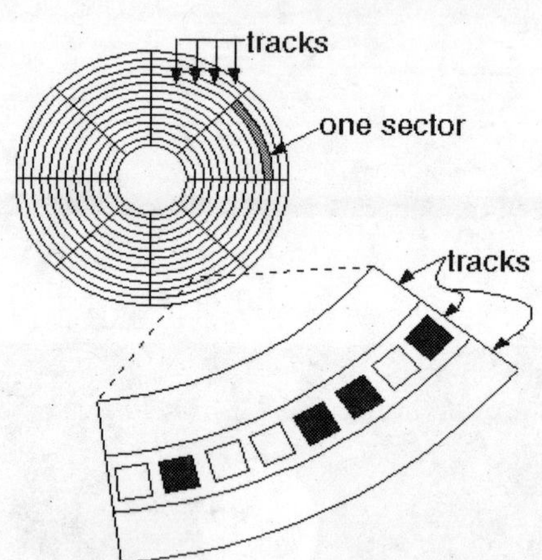


**Figure 6.7:** Tracks and Sectors

## Fixed Disk

A fixed disk is enclosed permanently inside a sealed case for protection from environmental factors. Fixed-disk systems contain one or more hard disks and can be used in all types of computers. Home computer users may be familiar with the 5.25 " fixed-disk systems used with desktops, having typical storage capacities between 10 MB and 2.1 GB. In large computers, the fixed-disk system provides storage capacities in Giga-bytes (GB) or Tera-bytes (TB).

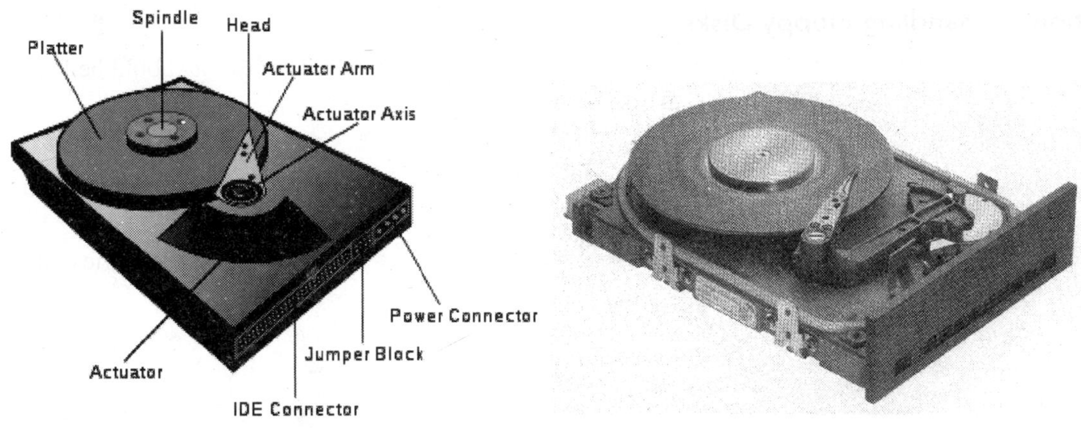


**Fig. 6.8:** Fixed Hard-disk(s) With Removed Outer Jacket

## Winchester Disk

According to one of the authors, the term Winchester comes from an early type of disk drive developed by IBM that stored 30 MB and had 30 ms access time, so its inventor named it a Winchester in honour of the Winchester .30-caliber rifle.

According to another author, in the evolution of hard disk systems, IBM developed smaller rigid disk drives with one fixed and one removable disk pack. Each held about 30 MB of data and hence the model was named as 3030, which soon became "Winchester" (as in 30 caliber Winchester rifles). The dual-drive systems became obsolete, but the name is still used.

The Winchester hard disk, which is used in personal computers, has the following characteristics:

- The head mechanism is enclosed in a sealed environment in which air is continuously filtered and circulated.
- The disk rotates at high speed (about 3600 rpm) and the heads do not touch the surface of the disk
- The disk surface is lubricated so that the heads may rest on the disk without scratches.
- There is a very thin magnetic coating on the disk.

The recent developments in disks include the development of 20 MB-2.1GB storage disks, achieved by vertical recording instead of the present horizontal media surface recording.

## Removable Cartridge

A storage system using Removable Cartridges has the same speed and capacity as a hard disk. These cartridges usually contain only one or two disks. Many hard-disk drives used with small computers are designed to use removable cartridges.

The advantage of this type of disk is that it may be removed at any time and a new or different cartridge may be inserted. For example, a user can have a separate cartridge for each application.

## Disk Pack

A disk pack is another removable storage media in which several hard-disks are packed into a single plastic case. The disk-pack drives are designed for large systems that require larger storage capacities.

Because a disk pack is susceptible to damage by scratching, the top of the first disk and the bottom of the last disk are generally not used.

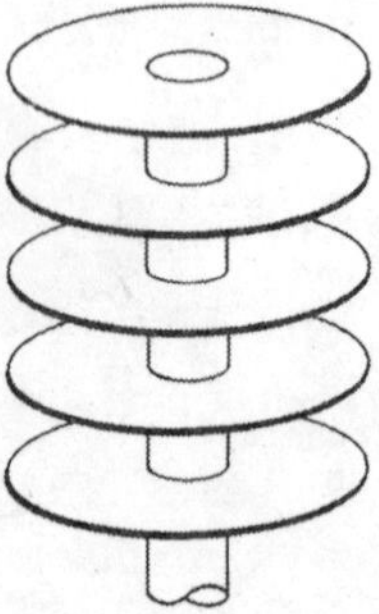

**Fig. 6.9:** Disk Pack Arranged on a Spindle

Disk packs can be interchanged, giving the computer a virtually unlimited amount of secondary storage.

**Fig. 6.10:** Disk Pack

## Advantages of Magnetic Disks

i. The data can be accessed sequentially as well as directly.
ii. The access time is smaller, which results in efficient storage.
iii. When a transaction is made, data can be updated immediately. There is no need to maintain a transaction file.
iv. Software allows files to be altered simultaneously.

v. Disk storage is much more durable and is less likely to be lost because of mishandling or a poor storage environment.

vi. Inquiries can be answered quickly on the spot.

### Disadvantages of Magnetic Disks

i. They are more expensive than magnetic tapes.

ii. Requires complex programming to gain access to files.

iii. These are more heavier (particularly disk packs) and more difficult to replace than a magnetic tape.

iv. Easily transported disks may pose security problems.

v. Requires backup files to be prevent data from being lost during alterations.

vi. When the data in master file is updated in case of a transaction, the old data is lost. Whereas in tapes, a new master-file is formed which has the updated data. The old master file is also retained for the desired time.

## 6.10 MAGNETIC DRUM

A magnetic drum is similar in a concept to a fixed stack magnetic disk, except that the information is stored on the outer surface of a drum, rotating at a high speed as opposed to the surface of a disk. a drum, as the name suggests, is cylindrical in shape, typically about 3 feet in length. The outer surface of the drum is coated in ferro-oxide, enabling the storage of information in coded form as magnetized or non-magnetized spots. The surface is divided into a number of tracks, each having one or more fixed read and record heads.

As in the case of magnetic disk, data are recorded serially along the tracks, from where any particular item can be directly accesses. Magnetic drums are used in places where very fast access and fast transfer speed are required.

A typical drum can store between 100,000 and 10,000,000 characters of information, transfer more than 1.5 million characters per second (CPS) with an appropriate access time of 6 to 29 ms (million seconds). Unlike a disk pack it can not be removed from a unit and replaced and is more expensive than disk. Magnetic drums are not used in our present day computers.

## 6.11 MAGNETIC CARDS AND STRIPS

A magnetic strip is a flexible plastic material of size 2 × 12 inches, on which data are magnetically recorded. Ten such strips put together is called as a sub-cell and twenty sub-cells are placed in a data cell drive. Like disk packs they can be removed. Cards and strips have high storage facility and slow access speed. They are much cheaper than disk packs, can accommodate reasonably large amount of data and the data stored are erasable.

## 6.12 ZIP DISK

These are high-capacity floppy disk drives developed by the Iomega Corporation. Zip disks are slightly larger than the conventional floppy disks, and are about twice as thick. These can store 100 MB of data. As they are relatively inexpensive and durable, so they have become a popular media for backing up hard disks and for transporting large files.

## 6.13 JAZ DISK

These are removable disk drives developed by the Iomega Corporation. The Jaz drive has a 12 ms average seek-time and a transfer rate of 5.5 MB per second. The removable cartridges hold 1 GB of data. The fast data rates and large storage capacity make it a viable alternative for backup storage as well as everyday use.

## 6.14 SUPERDISK

This is a new disk storage technology developed by the Imation Corporation that supports very high-density diskettes. SuperDisk diskettes are etched with a servo pattern at the factory. This pattern then read by the SuperDisk drive to precisely align the read/write head. The result is that a SuperDisk diskette can have 2490 tracks, as opposed to the 135 tracks that conventional 3 ½ inch 1.44 MB diskettes use. This higher density translates into 120 MB capacity per diskette.

Unlike the other removable disk storage solutions, such as the Zip Drive, SuperDisk is backward compatible with older diskettes. This means that you can use the SuperDisk drive to read and write to older 1.44 MB diskettes as well as the new 120 MB SuperDisk diskettes. Imation's current SuperDisk drive is called the LS-120.

## 6.15 OPTICAL DISKS

In 1983, one of the most successful consumer products of all time was introduced: the Compact Disk (CD) digital audio system. The CD is a non-erasable disk that can store more than 60 minutes audio information on one side. The huge commercial success of the CD enabled the development of low-cost Optical Storage Technology that now promise to revolutionize data storage.

Information is written to or read from an optical disk using laser beam. An optical disk has very high storing capacity. Only one surface of an optical disk is used to store data. An optical disk is relatively inexpensive, and has a long life of at least 25 years. Its drives are inherently simple and inexpensive. As the read/write head does not touch the disk surface, there is no disk wear and no problem of head crash. Elaborate error checking codes can be used as there is no problem of space because the disks have very high storage capacity.

The greatest drawback of the optical disk system is its slow average seek time of the drive. In case of a hard disk the read/write head is a tiny magnet whereas in optical system the drive has to move on sizable optical assembly across the disk surface. This increases the seek time. In future it is expected that the access time will be reduced using fibre-optic system.

CD-ROM Drive with Optical Disk is shown in Fig. 6.11.

Portable CD-ROM Drive is shown in Fig. 6.12.

**Fig. 6.11:** CD-ROM Drive With Optical Disk

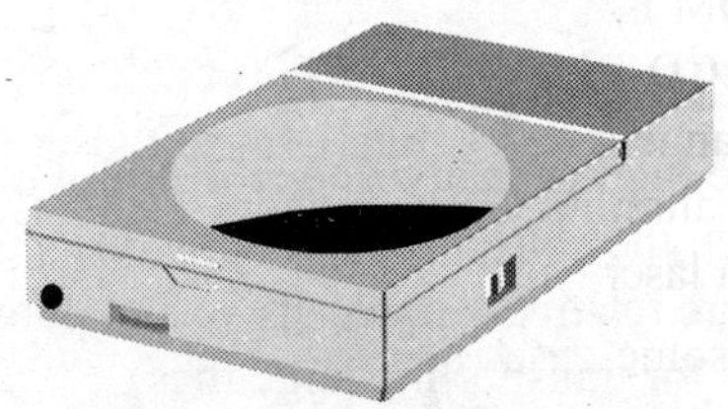

**Fig. 6.12:** Portable CD-ROM Drive

There are mainly following types of optical disk products:

i. Compact Disk (CD)
ii. CD-ROM (Compact Disk Read-Only-Memory)
iii. Compact Disk Interactive (CD-I)
iv. Digital Video Interface (DVI)
v. WORM (Write-Once-Read-Many)
vi. CD-R (Compact Disk-Recordable) Drive
vii. Erasable Optical Disk or CD-RW (ReWritable) Disk
viii. Optical Card
ix. Optical Tape

Optical disk(s) are shown in Fig. 6.13 (a), Fig. 6.13 (b) and Fig. 6.13(c).

a) A CD-ROM Drive

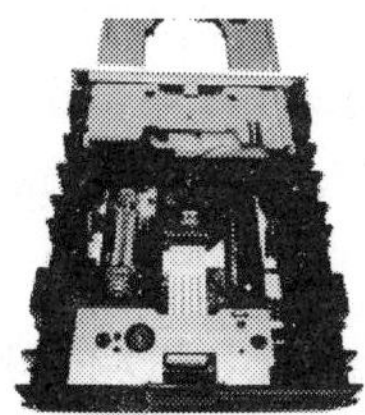

b) A CD-ROM Drive (without case)

(c)The optical lens of a CD Drive

**Figure 6.13**

## Compact Disk (CD)

Compact Disk (CD) is a non-erasable disk that stores digitized audio information. The standard system uses 12 cm disks and can record more than 60 minutes of uninterrupted playing time.

## CD-ROM

CD-ROM is an optical Compact Disk ROM. Prerecorded data can be read out. The manufacturer writes data on CD-ROMs. The disk is made up of resin, such as poly-carbonate. It is coated with a material which will change when a high intensity laser beam is focused on it. The coating material is highly reflective, usually aluminum. The high intensity laser beam forms a tiny pit along a trace to represent 1. For reading the data laser beam of less intensity is employed.

In some cases separate laser beams are employed: one for writing and the other for reading. The reflected laser is sensed by photodiode to read data. The intensity of the reflected light of laser changes as it encounters pit. A pit spreads the light so that the photodiode receives little reflected light. But the surface without pit reflects sufficient light to the photodiode. Thus the change in reflected light is sensed and converted into electrical signals for data reading purpose.

If the coating of the special material on the optical disk is thin film, a hole is formed when the laser beam falls on it. If the layer is a thick film a pit is formed. In some process of thick film, a bubble is formed instead of a pit. The unaltered areas between the pits are known as lands.

First of all, a master disk is prepared. By moulding a special plastic to the master disk, CD-ROMs are produced on mass scale. The plastic copy of the data is then covered with a clear plastic layer and backed with a reflecting coating.

CD-ROMs use long spiral tracks to store data serially. The track is divided into blocks of the same size. A CD-ROM disk rotates at a variable speed so that the pits are read by the laser at a constant linear speed. The speed of the disk is adjusted in such a manner that the track passes under the read/write head at a constant linear velocity (CLV). CD-ROM uses CLV or CAV (constant angular velocity) technology. The reported speeds of players that use CAV are generally not accurate because they refer only to the access speed for outer tracks and inner tracks are accessed more slowly.

CD-ROM is appropriate for the distribution of large amounts of data to a large number of users. Because of the expense of the initial writing process, it is not appropriate for individualized applications.

## Advantages of CD-ROM

- The information-storage capacity is much greater on the optical disk.
- Mass replication of CD-ROMs is inexpensive and very fast.
- These are removable and thus may be used suitably for archival storage.

## Disadvantages of CD-ROM

- It is read-only and can not be updated.
- It has an access time much longer than that of a magnetic disk drive.

## Compact Disk Interactive (CD-I)

Compact Disk Interactive (CDI) optical disk is a specification based on the use of CD-ROM. It describes methods for providing audio, video, graphics, text, and machine-executable code on CD-ROM.

## Digital Video Interface (DVI)

Digital Video Interface (DVI) optical disk is a technology for producing digitized, compressed, representation of video information. The representation can be stored on CD or disk media. Current systems use CDs and can store about 20 minutes of video on one disk.

## WORM (Write Once Read Many)

To accommodate applications in which only one or small number of copies of a set of data is needed, the write-once read many (WORM) type optical disk has been developed. For WORM, a disk has been prepared in such a way that it can be subsequently written once with a laser beam of modest intensity. Thus, with a somewhat more expensive disk controller than for CD-ROM, the customer can write once as well as read the disk. To provide for rapid access, the WORM uses constant angular velocity, at the sacrifice of some capacity.

A typical technique for preparing the disk is to use high-power laser to produce a series of blisters on the disk. when the preformatted medium is placed in a WORM drive, a low-powered laser can produce just enough heat to burst the prerecorded blisters. During a disk-read operation, a laser in the WORM drive illuminates the disk's surface. Since the burst blisters provide higher contrast than the surrounding area, these are easily recognized by simple electronics.

The WORM optical disk is attractive for archival storage of documents and files. It provides a permanent record of large volumes of user data.

## Advantages

i. High capacity
ii. Better reliability
iii. Longer life

## Disadvantages

i. Greater access time as compared to that of hard disk.

## CD-R Drive

It is a special type of disk-drive that can create CD-ROMs and audio CDs. This allows the users to master a CD-ROM or audio CD for publishing. Until recently, CD-R drives were quite expensive, but prices have tremendously come down.

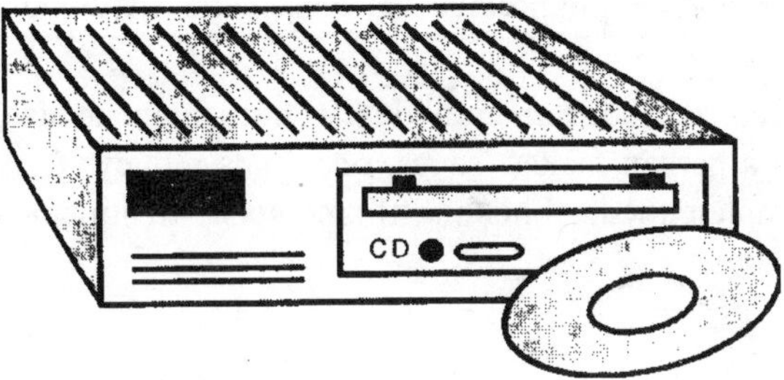


**Fig. 6.14:** CD-R Drive

Multi-session recording feature of many CD-R drives enables us to keep adding data to a CD-ROM over a period of time. This feature is extremely important if we want to use the CD-R drive to prepare backup CD-ROMs. For the purpose of creating CD-ROMs and audio CDs, CD-R software package will also be required besides CD-R drive. These drives can also read CD-ROMs and play audio CDs.

## Erasable Optical Disk or CD-RW Disk

The most recent development in computer optical disks is the erasable optical disk. This disk can be repeatedly written and overwritten, as with any magnetic disk. Although a number of approaches have been tried, the only technology that has proved commercially feasible is the magneto-optical system. In this system, the energy of laser beam is used together with a magnetic field to record and erase information by reversing the magnetic poles in a small area of a disk coated with a magnetic material. The laser beam heats a specific spot while its temperature is elevated. As the polarization process does not cause a physical change in the disk, the process can be repeated many times. For reading, the direction of magnetism can be polarized by laser light. Polarized light reflected from a particular spot will change its degree of rotation depending on the magnetic field's orientation.

The erasable optical disk has the obvious advantages over CD-ROM and WORM that it can rewritten and thus used as true secondary storage. As such, it competes with magnetic disks.

### Advantages of erasable optical disk over magnetic disk

- High capacity: A 5.25-inch optical disk hold about 650 MB of data. The most advanced Winchester disks carry less than half that amount.
- Portability: The optical disk can be removed from drive.
- Semi-random Access: Erasable optical disk also uses format that makes semi-random access feasible.
- Reliability: The engineering tolerance for optical disk are much less than for high-capacity magnetic disks. Thus, they exhibit higher reliability and longer life.

### Drawback

- Access time: The erasable disk has longer access time as compared to that of hard disk.

### Optical Card

The optical or laser card is the of the size as a credit card and has an optical laser-encoded strip that can store approximately 2 MB of data. These cards have many potential uses, most notably for storing credit records or medical histories. Some people predict that these cards may one day lead to a cash-less and cheque-less.

Optical cards have the potential to store an individual's entire financial history, adding to or subtracting from appropriate accounts as a person makes, saves, or spends money. These cards may also supply a hospital with the holder's complete medical history. If emergency treatment is required, this information could expedite care.

### Optical Tape

Continuing developments and refinements in optical technology include Optical Tape. Optical Tape is similar in appearance to magnetic tape, but data are stored by optical-laser techniques. Optical tapes which are in cassette form can store over 8 GB each, and the tape drives can hold 128 cassettes, providing a total storage of about 1 TB (1024 GB). Like other optical methods of data storage, optical is read-only. As optical technology develops, higher densities and expanded uses will result.

### Magneto-Optical Drives

This is a type of disk drive that combines magnetic disk technologies with CD-ROM technologies. Like magnetic disks, these can be read as well written to and like floppy disks, they are also removable. These are faster than floppy and CD-ROM drives but not comparable to hard-disk drives. However, their storage capacity can be more than 200 MBs which is an enormous storage capacity in comparison to floppy disks.

## 6.16 MAGNETIC TAPES

A magnetic tape is usually a 0.5 inch wide plastic tape with a coating of magnetic material on one side. The length is generally 2400 feet. Records are stored on the tape one after the other in the order of the key field.

The records have gaps between them called inter-record gaps (IRG). These gaps are created automatically at the time of writing the data on the tape. A record is read from the tape, then comes the IRG. The tape movement stops. During this time, the record is transferred to the computer. After the transmission the tape movement again starts and next record is read. But if the records are too small then having IRG after each record results in wastage of tape and also slows down the speed of access. So a number of records are grouped together to form a block. Record storage with IRG is shown in Fig. 6.15.

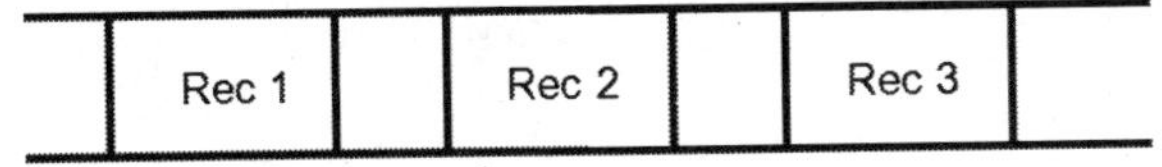


**Fig 6.15:** Record Storage With IRG

There is a gap between two consecutive blocks called the inter-block gap (IBG). The whole block is read by the access mechanism at one time. Storage with IBG is shown in Fig. 6.16.

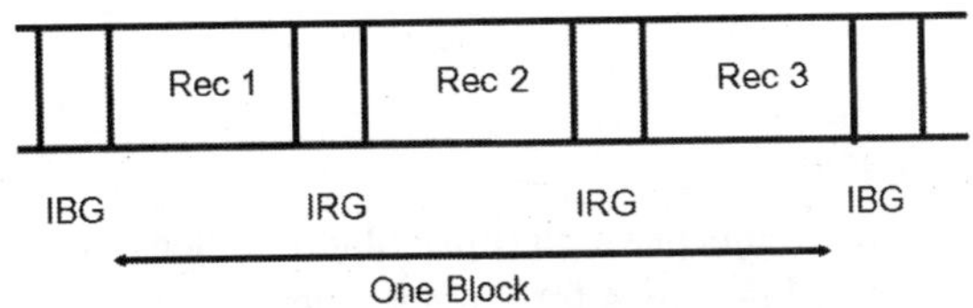


**Fig 6.16:** Storage with IBG

Every tape has a header and trailer label. The header label is at the beginning of the tape and stores the name of file, date of last updation and any other relevant information. The trailer label has the same information as header label. It may be possible that a number of files are stored in a tape.

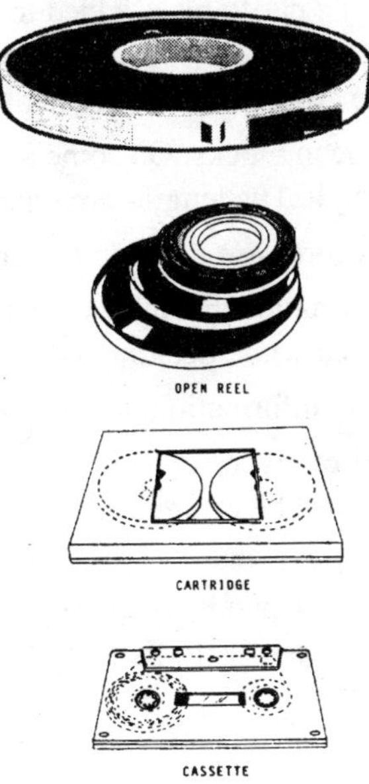


**Fig. 6.17:** Various Types of Magnetic Tapes

## Main Characteristics of Magnetic Tapes

Some major characteristics of magnetic tapes are given as under

- Tape Density
- Character Set Used
- Parity Check
- Blocks: Fixed Length or Variable Length
- Block Size
- Labels
- Mechanical Interlock
- Headers and trailers
- Length of tape
- Drive mechanism
- IRG and IBG
- Blocking/Unblocking Storage
- Tape densities are measured in bits per inch (bpi). Standard densities for 7 track tapes are 200 bpi, 556 bpi and 800 bpi. Standard densities for 9 track tapes are 800, 1600 and 6250 bpi.
- Three character sets are used on magnetic tapes:
    - EBCDIC (8-bit code)
    - ASCII (7-bit code)
    - BCD (6-bit code)
- Parity check is a method in which a parity bit is added to each word during write operation such that total number of bits in each word is either even (even parity) or odd (odd parity). During the read operation a check is made to ensure that the mode of parity is maintained.
- Data is normally stored on the tape in blocks. On some tapes the block is of fixed length whereas on others it may be variable in length. The lengths are separated by a record gap and/or block gap.
- Block size indicates how many records are grouped together, and is usually given in bytes.
- Labels are used to identify the information that follows on the tape and these are system dependent. The following rule may be followed while deciding labels:

  "Label if storing information, no label if transporting".
- Mechanical interlock is provided on every computer tape to prevent accidental overwriting of information. A small plastic ring must be inserted before a tape may be written on. Thus removal of the ring prevents writing.

The amount of the data that can be held depends on the length of the tape, the number of IRGs, and the density of the tape. Density refers to how tightly the data can be packed and stored on a storage media.

Here it is a measure of the number of characters or bytes of data that can be recorded on 1 inch of tape. Data transfer rate - the number of characters or bytes per second that can be transferred from the tape drive to the media or vice-versa - also varies.

## Magnetic Tape Drive And Its Types

A tape drive performs the operation of writing onto the tape and also reading information from the tape. The tape is loaded onto the tape drive in the same way that a movie projector is threaded.

**Fig. 6.18:** Mounting of Magnetic Tape on Drive

There are two types of magnetic tape drive mechanisms. These are:

- Using Vacuum Columns
- Using Tension Arms

## Tape Drive Using Vacuum Columns

In the tape drive using vacuum columns, tape is fed from a supply reel, then passing through a set read/write heads on to a take-up reel. The tape passes through two vacuum chambers, on either side of the read/write heads. This arrangement is required to prevent it from snapping when the tape speed varies. A servo mechanism maintains the correct length of tape between reel and capstan drive. Each track is provided with a read and write head.

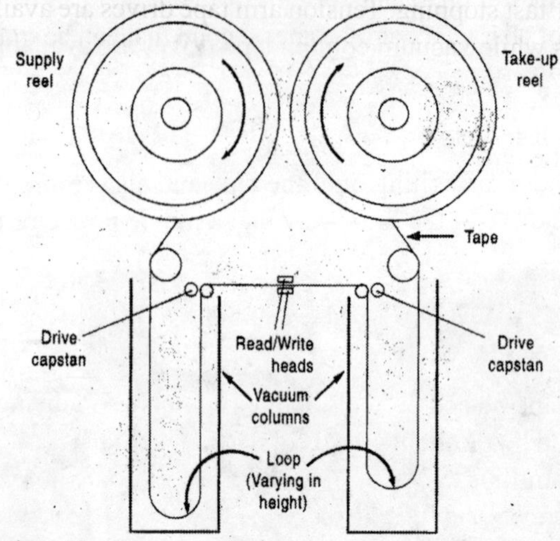


Fig. 6.19: Tape Drive Using Vacuum Columns

### Tape Drive Using Tension Arms

In this type of drive, the tape is laced around a set of tension arms. The upper and lower arms are movable. When the tape is suddenly driven past the heads by the capstan, the mechanism provides a buffering supply of tape. Sufficient tape is maintained between the capstan and the tape reels by a servo mechanism, by driving upper and lower reels.

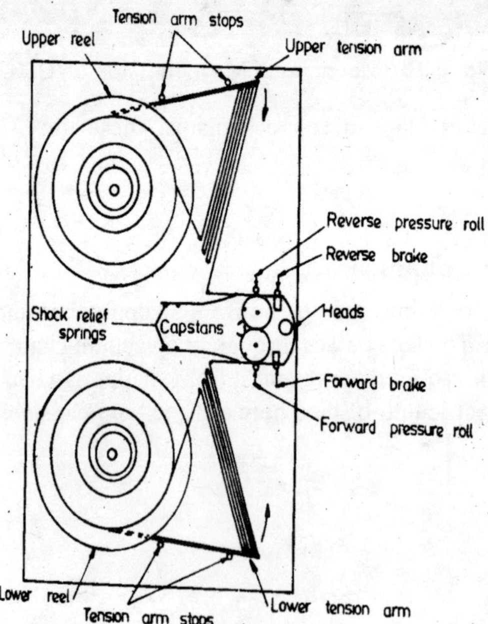


Fig. 6.20: Tape Drive Using Tension Arms

Brakes are also provided for fast stopping. Tension arm tape drives are available in tape speeds of 12.5 ips (inches per second) to 45 ips while vacuum column tape drives are available from 45 ips to 200 ips.

## Types of Magnetic Tapes

There are three forms of magnetic tape:

a. Reel-to-reel Tape
b. Cassette Tape
c. Cartridge Tape

## Reel-to-reel Tape

A reel-to-reel tape is magnetic tape placed on reels about 10.5 inches in diameter. A typical tape is about 2400 feet long, 0.5 inch wide, and holds about 40 MB of data. Data transfer rates vary from approximately 5000 bytes per second to over million bytes per second. The more common tape drives have rates of 60,000 bytes per second. These tapes usually store data at a density of 1600 bytes per inch, but it can range from 800 to 6250 bytes per inch. Reel-to-reel tapes are relatively inexpensive, durable, and can hold a large quantity of data. They are used mainly with large-computer systems.

## Cassette Tape

Cassette tape are similar to those used in audio tape players/recorders. Such types of tape are employed with small computers. The tape is about 0.25 inch wide, enclosed in a plastic case, and that's why suitable for mainly small computers. The major difference between the audio and digital tape cassettes is that the tape cassettes are used for storing data with higher quality and high density digital recording tapes.

They are inexpensive, but can not hold much data, and access to the data stored on them is fairly slow. Cassette tape storage, once very popular with personal computer users, has been largely replaced by the more popular and versatile disk storage systems.

## Cartridge Tape

Cartridge tape is another form of magnetic tape. It is packaged similar to cassette tape but has a much greater data storage density. Cartridge tapes and reel-to-reel systems are very popular as the secondary-storage media for large computer systems.

**Fig. 6.21:** Removable Cartridge Storage (Courtesy Tandy)

Cartridge Tape Drive is shown in Fig. 6.22.

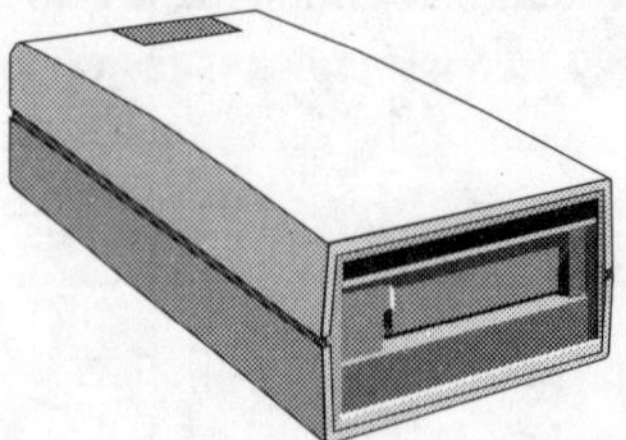

**Fig. 6.22:** Cartridge Tape Drive

### Advantages of Magnetic Tapes

1. It is the cheapest storage medium for sequential access.
2. The storage capacity is very high.
3. A tape is erasable and reusable.
4. It is a low-cost backup
5. They require less space to be stored as compared to other storage devices.
5. Magnetic tapes are less prone to errors
6. Stores large amounts of data in a small space in comparison to punched cards.
6. It is the most suitable backup media for voluminous storage.
7. Transfers data between tape and the CPU rapidly.

### Disadvantages of Magnetic Tapes

1. It is not a very reliable and durable media for storage as when a tape tears, some data is certainly lost.
2. Magnetic tapes require proper labels for content verification.
3. Only sequential access is possible and time required to access depends upon the location of the record on the tape.
4. Tapes are not easily distinguishable superficially.
5. Data can not be inserted in a tape. Each time an updation is to be made, a new copy of tape is made.
6. Environmental factors can distort data stored on magnetic tapes.
7. A tape can be read only by a machine, whereas punched cards can be read visually by an operator.

## 6.17 MAGNETIC TAPE Vs MAGNETIC DISK

Magnetic tape and disk have evolved together since the 1950s, filling different data storage needs for computer users. Tape drives store and archive large amounts of data economically. Disk drives access the data with great speed.

1. **Random Access:** Any data on a disk can be accessed in a few thousandths of a second. This is called random access---you don't need to search every file to find something.

2. **Serial Access:** A magnetic tape drive must search through all the files leading up to the one you want. This is serial access, reading one file after another.
3. **Speed:** For everyday file access, magnetic disk is faster because of its random access feature. For archiving files, tape and disk are about the same speed.
4. **Archiving:** Magnetic tape is less expensive to store large amounts of data for archiving. Data centers also use disks for archiving, though to a lesser extent.
5. **Size:** In 2009, the smallest magnetic disks are the size of a matchbox. The smallest tape drives are about the size of a small book.

## 6.18 VIRTUAL MEMORY

The concept of virtual memory was implemented in 1959 but it was extensively used only after 1970s. Virtual memory is a scheme implemented by hardware or software or both which appears to increase the memory of computer. In this system only that portion of the program and data that are being processed are kept in the primary storage. Information no longer required and needed is swapped between the primary and secondary storage. The swapping is transparent to the user. This process extends memory to the size of secondary storage units plus primary memory storage size and increases processing time and I/O operations.

A virtual memory system offers the following benefits:

- It frees the user from the chore of dividing a large program into modules and managing the transfer of modules between the disk and the main memory.
- It allows efficient sharing of memory space among different users of a timesharing/multiprogramming systems.
- It helps to develop programs that are independent of the configuration and capacity of memory systems

## 6.19 HIGH SPEED MEMORY

We are aware that the access time of main memories is slower than the speed of the processor. Since each instruction require several memory accesses, therefore, faster memories will be of great help in increasing the overall performance of a computer system. The following may be the four serious possibilities to enhance the speed of memory:

- Inserting Cache memory, known as a high speed memory, between the main memory and processor.
- Employing associative addressing in place of random access using which information can be retrieved at a very high speed on the basis of the portion of its contents as an address.
- Employing a faster but expensive technology for main memory having a very smaller access time and the same become available in the time to come due to technological advancement in memories.
- By employing Memory Interleaving using which more words are accessed in a single memory access cycle rather than accessing one word. This is termed as memory interleaving.

## 6.20 CACHE MEMORY

A very high speed small capacity memory introduced as a buffer between the CPU and the main memory is called a Cache Memory. Due to very high cost, small cache memories are intended to provide fast speed of memory retrieval. Only small sizes such as 8KB, 64 K, 128K, 256 KB, 512 KB etc. are normally provided in microcomputers whereas they can have 640 KB to 64 MB RAMs or even more Parts of the current program are copied from the main memory into the high speed cache.

The design of cache memory is such that it is not "visible" to a programmer. The CPU cycle time in a computer is normally much faster than the memory cycle time. Thus every time information is to be read from the memory to be used by CPU, this speed mismatch would make the CPU wait. Employing cache is an attempt to minimize this mismatch.

When the CPU refers to an instruction (or data), it is fetched from the cache if it is already there. This is called a hit. If it is not available, then it is called a miss and in this case the same is read from the main memory.

The hit ratio (h) is defined as follows:

$$h = \frac{\text{Number of times the item is found in cache}}{\text{Total number of addresses referenced}}$$

The hit ratio is a fraction less than unity and is expressed as %age and (1-h) is often called miss ratio. If Tc and Tm are the cycle times of the cache and the main memory respectively, effective memory cycle time is given as:

$$T = h\,Tc + (1 - h)\,Tm$$

**Example 1:** *If hit ratio h = 75 %, cache cycle-time Tc = 200 ns, memory cycle-time Tm = 800 ns, then what will be the effective memory cycle-time?*

**Solution**

Putting value of h= 0.75, Tc = 200 ns and Tm = 800 in the above given expression, we get the effective memory cycle-time,

$$\begin{aligned} T &= 0.75 \times 200 + 0.25 \times 800 \\ &= 150 + 200 \\ &= 350 \text{ ns.} \end{aligned}$$

**Example 2:** *If memory read cycle takes 200 ns and a cache read cycle takes 50 ns, then what will be total time taken to read out the contents in 5 continuous memory references:*

*i. with cache memory and*

*ii. without cache memory*

*whereas first reference brings the main memory contents to cache and next four references from cache memory.*

**Solution**

(i) Time taken with cache $= 200 + 50) + 50 \times 4$

$= 250 + 200$

$= 450$ ns

(ii) Time taken without cache $= 200 \times 5$

$= 1000$ ns

## EXERCISE

1. What are disk systems? Outline their typical characteristics.
2. What is meant by Memory Hierarchy? State its importance.
3. State the function of memory in a computer?
4. What do SRAM and DRAM stand for? Discuss their merits and demerits.
5. What is a hard-disk and how does it work?
6. Differentiate between Core and Semi-conductor memory.
7. What are high speed memories? Explain their usage.
8. What are the advantages and disadvantages of magnetic tapes?
9. What are the different types of memory? Explain their merits and demerits.
10. What is the difference between seek-time and latency-time?
11. Why is magnetic medium more appropriate as a storage medium than a semiconductor medium?
12. Describe the physical characteristics of magnetic tape.
13. What is magnetic strip? Explain its working.
14. How does a random access device differ from a sequential access device?
15. What are various types of semi-conductor memories? State its types and applications.
16. What are the major secondary storage devices?
17. When is magnetic tape storage used?
18. What is a magnetic drum? State its applications.
19. Why is it necessary to have a hierarchy of memory devices in a computer system?
20. What does ROM stand for? Enumerate the applications of ROM.
21. Why do we need secondary storage devices? What are the characteristics of secondary storage?
22. What are the access times of semiconductor memory, hard-disks, and floppy-disks?
23. What is a magnetic tape? State its major characteristics.
24. Explain the working of magnetic media.
25. What are optical disks and how do they work?
26. Why a floppy diskette is named so? How is it different from a hard-disk?

27. Explain the difference between Zip-Disk, Jaz-Disk and SuperDisk.
28. State the applications of ROM and RAM.
29. What are main-, secondary-, and backup-memories? Explain the importance of each.
30. What are the various type of mechanisms used in magnetic tapes?
31. What is virtual memory? State its importance.
32. What does a core-memory mean?
33. What is the role of Cache Memory? Also explain the terms 'hit' and 'miss'.
34. Describe ROM, PROM and EEPROM with their merits and demerits.
35. What are different types of magnetic memory? Outline each of these.
36. What are the traditional approaches to data manipulation and retrieval?
37. What do you mean by buffering? How buffering is helpful in data storage?
38. What would happen if a hard disk drive's read/write head touches the disk while the disk was spinning?
39. Is the distance between a hard disk drive's read/write head and the hard disk smaller than, greater than, or the same as the width of a human hair?
40. State the advantages of magnetic disks over magnetic tapes.
41. What is meant by tape density? How is it measured?
42. Distinguish between the fixed-head and moving-head magnetic disk.
43. Under what circumstances is a new master file created in sequential processing?
44. Outline the advantages of hard-disks over floppy-disks.
45. Which of the file organisation method would you choose and why?
46. How do you protect a fixed hard disk from a head crash?
47. What precautions are to be taken in handling floppy disks?
48. Why don't heads on tape drives experience "crashes"?
49. If a floppy can be used to boot a computer system, what is the need to have a separate ROM for the system?
50. What characteristic of a disk drive determines the worst case latency time?
51. What type of problem does error checking detects?
52. How are physical and logical records related in a magnetic tape?
53. How you can take care of your floppy disks?
54. How data are represented on magnetic tape?
55. Describe the file organisation format on the magnetic tape.
56. What are the two distinguishing features of diskette? Give an example of each feature.
57. What is the purpose of inter-block gap? What information is contained on a magnetic tape header label? What is the purpose of an end-of-file marker?
58. What is magnetic-bubble memory? Explain its working and applications.
59. What is meant by destructive and non-destructive read out?

60. Explain the components as well as working of a floppy-diskette.
61. Compare various types of optical-disks along with their respective areas of application.
62. Why are magnetic disks the most commonly used storage media?
63. How are data represented on disks?
64. What is flash-memory? Explain its usage.
65. What is blocking?
66. Explain data can be accessed on a magnetic disk using index.
67. Discuss seek-time and latency time in relation to fixed-head and moving-head disk systems.
68. What are magnetic cards and where are these used?
69. How are Winchester disks superior to conventional hard disk systems? What is the typical storage capacity of such disks?
70. What is the main difference between the way data is stored in the tape and disk?
71. What types of environmental hazards can damage a magnetic disk or accidentally erase data?
72. What is meant by formatting of a magnetic disk.
73. Differentiate between volatile-memory and non-volatile memory.
74. What factors decide the transfer rate of a disk system?
75. Which are the two basic techniques used for addressing the data records that are stored on a disk?
76. What are the three methods of acccssing files in secondary storage? Explain with an example each of them.
77. Briefly describe the term "sequential access".
78. How does block factor effect on the time required to access the tape?
79. What is meant by magneto-optical disk? Explain its working.
80. Fixed-head disk systems reduce total access time by avoiding either seek time or latency? Which one is neglected and why?
81. What are various types of magnetic-tapes? Compare them with respect to their storage capacities.
82. What do you understand by volatility?
83. The data transfer rate is faster in disk than in a magnetic tape. Why?
84. What do you understand by disk-organisation? Explain.
85. Explain the terms "disk pack" and "cylinder" in a hard-disk.
86. What do you mean by storage?
87. Explain the various primary and secondary storage devices?
88. What do you mean by random access memory? Explain the difference types of random access memory?
89. Difference between dynamic and static RAM.
90. What do you mean by read only memory?
91. What do you mean by essential start-up?
92. Explain the various types of read only memory in detail?

93. What do you mean by magnetic tape?
94. Explain various advantages and disadvantages of magnetic tape?
95. Explain the concept of magnetic disk?
96. Difference between magnetic tape and magnetic disk?
97. What do you mean by hard disk drive? Explain the performance of hard disk drive.
98. What do you mean by optical disk? Explain various optical storage devices.
99. What are the advantages and disadvantages of optical disk?
100. What do you mean by optical disk drive?

CHAPTER

7

# Software and Operating System Concepts

## 7.1 INTRODUCTION

The hardware alone can not perform any particular calculation, computation or manipulation without being instructed exactly what to do, when to do and how to do it. These instructions are very important and are called software.

The software acts as an interface between the user and the computer or a software can be defined as a complete set of instructions written by the programmer which enables the computer to obtain the solution to a problem. These programs give life to the circuitry of computer hardware. It consists of a sequence of instructions and decision rules that direct the computer in performing a given task. The CPU must be told:

- What data is to be processed?
- What manipulation is to be performed on the data?
- What must be the sequence of computation to be performed?
- What must be the format of the output to be produced?

Software may be viewed as a general term that is used to describe any single program or a group of programs.

In its most general form, software is a term used in contrast to hardware to refer to all programs which can be used on a particular computer system i.e. the term software is used to describe program sets needed to operate an information processing system.

## 7.2 SOFTWARE TYPES

Software is the means by which computer systems speak with computer users. Software forms the heart of computer systems.

Software, by definition, is the collection of computer programs, procedures and documentation that performs different tasks on a computer system. The term 'software' was first used by John Tukey in 1958. At the very basic level, computer software consists of a machine language that consists of groups of binary values, which specify processor instructions. The processor instructions change

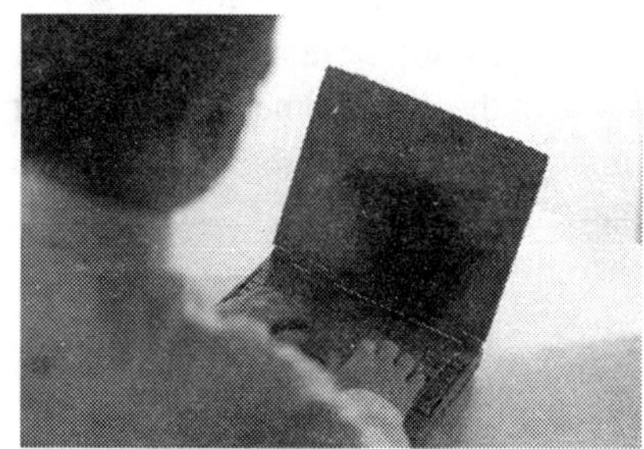

Figure 7.1

the state of computer hardware in a predefined sequence. Briefly, computer software is the language in which a computer speaks. There are different types of computer software.

## 7.2.1 Programming Software

This is one of the most commonly known and popularly used forms of computer software. These software come in forms of tools that assist a programmer in writing computer programs. Computer programs are sets of logical instructions that make a computer system perform certain tasks. The tools that help the programmers in instructing a computer system include text editors, compilers and interpreters.

## 7.2.2 System Software

It helps in running the computer hardware and the computer system. System software is a collection of system programs; device drivers, servers, windowing systems and utilities. System software helps an application programmer in abstracting away from hardware, memory and other internal complexities of a computer.

## 7.2.3 Application Software

It enables the end users to accomplish certain specific tasks. Business software, databases and educational software are some forms of application software. Different word processors, which are dedicated for specialized tasks to be performed by the user, are other examples of application software.

## 7.2.4 Other Software Types

Apart from these three basic types of software, there are some other well-known forms of computer software like inventory management software, ERP, utility software, accounting software and others. Take a look at some of them.

### 7.2.4.1 Inventory Management Software

This type of software helps an organization in tracking its goods and materials on the basis of quality as well as quantity. Warehouse inventory management functions encompass the internal warehouse movements and storage. Inventory software helps a company in organizing inventory and optimizing the flow of goods in the organization, thus leading to an improved customer service.

### 7.2.4.2 Utility Software

Also known as service routine, utility software helps in the management of computer hardware and application software. It performs a small range of tasks.

Utility software may be considered as an application software or system software which is used quite often in the development of a program. In other words, these are the programs that support the operations, management, and users of a computer system by providing a variety of support services. These may include:

- File Conversions
- Data Transfer Utility Software
- Data Compression
- Sort and Merge Utility Software

- Software Guides
- Data Communication within a network
- Disk Optimization
- Calculator utility
- Screen Savers
- Text Editors
- Real time clock utility,
- Disk defragmenters,
- Systems utilities,
- Virus scanners, and so on.

#### 7.2.4.3 Data Backup and Recovery Software

An ideal data backup and recovery software provides functionalities beyond simple copying of data files. This software often supports user needs of specifying what is to be backed up and when. Backup and recovery software preserve the original organization of files and allow an easy retrieval of the backed up data.

### 7.2.5 Miscellaneous Software Types

So far we come across mainly two types of wares, namely, hardware and software. Besides there have been a long list of ware which also requires a brief mention. These are given as under.

**Firmware**

It is a set of micro-programs stored in ROM for the purpose of implementing user's instructions related to their applications. It is named so because these are firmly associated with the hardware by manufacturers.

**Humanware (or Liveware)**

It is nothing but a group of users, end-users, programmers, and other professionals who work with hardware and software of Computer System for an intended application.

**Shareware**

As the programmers want to share the software with us so it gets name shareware. It is a fully functional and will probably include messages called anonymous screens, reminding us that we haven't yet paid for the program we are running. When we make the payment, we will get the latest version of the program.

**Public Domain Software**

It is the most free, most unsupported, and most popular software for people with small budgets. Public domain software is released to anyone to use, copy, include in his or her own programs, or to do whatever seems appropriate. As opposed to freeware, it does not carry a copyright, and there is never any payment expected by the original programmer or author.

**Begware**

It is a type of shareware that uses an extensive number of messages to remind us to pay for our copy.

### Postcardware

Few programmers producing shareware simply ask for a postcard from your local venue. This is their way to travel the world, since many programmers won't do it in person. The better the response the programmer gets, the more inspired the software that will be produced.

### Retail Software

It is a software that we buy from the company or its dealers and pay for it. Nowadays you can purchase retail software through Internet also using the on-line ordering facility.

### Crippleware

It is slightly different from shareware and with crippleware, we receive a program that has one of its major functions absent. Many companies float the idea behind such software that crippled versions of their software make excellent demonstrations. For example, a Word Processor without print feature is crippled.

### Bannerware

It is a software that is released to advertise other software. Bannerware is like the lure to catch us and make us really want other software the authors sell. For example, game programs available through shareware web sites offer additional games when we register.

### Donorware

It is software that if one wants to continue to use company's software, then company make a donation of that software. Some developers ask a certain amount while others don't set any amount.

### Freeware

It is one of the popular ware for which we are normally excited. No charge, no registration, but also no support. Freeware authors release their programs for our use, without expecting or requesting any payment. The authors, however, usually retain their copyright on the software, so we can't start selling it under our name, raking in profit for something we didn't develop.

## 7.3 LANGUAGE TRANSLATORS

These are the programs that help the users in developing programs, procedures and to prepare user programs for computer processing. Language translators translate other programs to machine language. There are mainly three types of language translators:

- Compilers
- Interpreters
- Assemblers

### 7.3.1 Compiler

The compiler is a program that resides on a disk or other mass-storage media. When the compiler is needed, it is called by the computer and loaded into RAM. The user enters his source program on the terminal and too is stored in RAM. The compute then performs the translation. It translates the various statements and expressions into the machine code known as the object program. This is illustrated in *Fig. 7.2.*

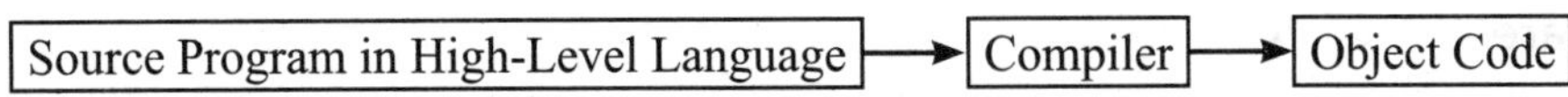


**Fig. 7.2:** Compilation Process

Once the user's program has been translated into object code, the compiler is no longer needed. The object code may also be output to magnetic tape or disk for storage at the same time when it is stored in RAM. The object program can then be executed. It has to be noted that compilers are not needed to run the program and are needed only to translate it. One more point to be remembered is that one compiler is capable of translating source program written in only one high-level language.

The main purpose of high-level languages is to enable the programmer to write programs more easily by being able to concentrate on the problem being solved, rather than on the machine level features of the computer. But, the process of translating high-level language source program into object code will be more lengthy and complex. Hence compiler tend to be longer and more complex programs than assemblers, and hence occupy more central space.

### 7.3.2 Interpreter

An interpreter is a program residing in computer's memory that interprets and executes the high-level language source program. Interpretative higher-level languages use statements, expressions, and commands similar to those used in compiler languages. The user preparing a program writes these expressions line by line using the unique syntax of that language to solve the problem. The problem is usually entered into the computer through a terminal. The interpreter can be stored on some type of external media such as magnetic tape or floppy disk and then brought into RAM when it is needed. In some computers, the interpreter is stored in ROM. In this way, it is always available when needed. The main difference between interpreter and compiler is that the interpreter must reside in memory along with the user's source program.

Unlike a computer, which translates an entire program into object code at one time an interpreter evaluates and translates program statements as the program is executed, one instruction at a time. Thus the interpreter takes one source program instruction, translates it into object code, and executes it. It then takes the next instruction, translates it and so on. Using an interpreter can save space since the interpreter program itself can be quite small, and it eliminates the need to store the program's translated object code in the computer.

On the other hand, it has drawbacks:

i. Program statements that are used multiple times must be translated each time they are executed.
ii. Another big disadvantage is of an interpreter is its slow speed. interpreters execute programs at a speed, 10 to 20 times slower than equivalent machine code generated by an assembler or compiler.

Despite of these disadvantages, interpreter are widely used. They are convenient and easy to use because they are totally interactive. The user can literally sit in front of the computer terminal and converse with the computer and solve problems directly through the interpreter. When a compiler language is used, the source program must first be entered and then compiled. The object code generated by the compiler is then loaded and executed. If a programmer wishes to change something in the program, adding features, correcting errors, or the like, the entire process must be repeated. The program changes are made and then entered. The new source program is then recompiled. Finally the new program is executed. With an interpreter, changes and additions can be made interactively. As soon as we discover that we need to modify or add something, we can do it immediately through the interpreter. When using an interpreter, a programmer gets the feeling that he is directly speaking to a computer and commanding its attention.

In nutshell, the difference between Compiler and Interpreter are listed in ***Table 7.1.***

**Table 7.1:** Compiler Vs. Interpreter

| S.No. | Compiler | Interpreter |
|---|---|---|
| 1. | Entire program is scanned first and then gets translated into machine-code. | The program is translated line by line |
| 2. | Debugging of programs is quite slow in Compilers. | Debugging is ver fast in case of Interpreters. |
| 3. | Only after all the syntax errors are removed from the program, the program is translated in machine-language code. | Each line of program is checked for syntax errors first and is then converted to its equivalent machine code |
| 4. | Changes can't be made due to non-interactive nature of compilers. | Changes can be made quite easily and immediately due to interactive nature of interpreters. |
| 5. | After program is translated into machine code, compilers are no more required for running the program. | Interpreter is required for running the translated machine code equivalent of the program. |
| 6. | Compilers occupy more space in memory during program compilation. | Interpreters occupy lesser space in memory during program translation. |
| 7. | Time for execution is lesser. | Time for execution is larger. |

### 7.3.3 Assemblers

Assembler is that class of language translators which are used to translate an assembly language program into a machine language program. This is illustrated in Fig. 7.3.

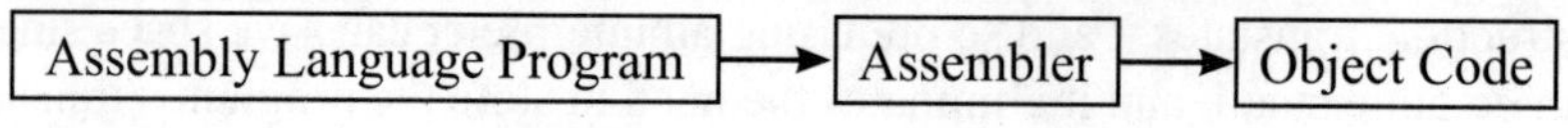


**Fig. 7.3:** Assembly Process

Some good assemblers for Intel 8086/8088 Assembly include MASM (Macro Assembler) 5.0/6.0, TASM (Turbo Assembler), etc.

## 7.4 SYSTEM UTILITY SOFTWARE

System utilities are a wide variety of general purpose programs that greatly speed up and simplify the use of the computer. They are written to enhance man-machine communications and improve programming efficiency. The exact type of systems program used depend greatly upon the specific computer. Typically however, most microcomputers have the following types of system programs:

- Editor
- Loader
- Monitor
- File Manager

- Linker
- BIOS

Besides these, there are also a wide variety of other programs available. We will consider these most commonly used systems programs only.

### 7.4.1 Editor

The most often used systems program is the editor. Editors are interactive programs that are stored in the memory and allow the user to write a program, generate text, or to make a wide variety of changes and additions to either of these. The editor is a systems program that is typically stored on some external mass-storage media. When it is needed, the editor is called into RAM. The programmer then communicates with the editor through the video or hard-copy terminal. Like an interpreter, the editor is interactive. All source programs for assemblers and compilers are typically written with the editor.

Since the editor can be used for creating any type of written material, it is useful for writing letters or preparing manuscripts and reports. It can be used for many other word-processing applications. Once a program or a block of text is created, it can then be edited as required. Lines, words, or single characters can be added, deleted, or otherwise modified. Once the final program or text is complete and error free, and editor stores the final text in a file in RAM. The final text can also be stored on external tape or disk or output to a printer.

### 7.4.2 Loader

Another widely used systems program is the loader. a loader is a short, simple program that is used to load a program into computer's memory. Often, the program resulting from the assembly or compilation process is stored on some external secondary storage media such as floppy diskette. To run that program, it must be loaded into RAM. The loader program is the sequence of instruction that transfers the program from the external media to main memory.

In early minicomputers and some early microcomputers, the loader program actually had to be loaded into RAM manually, an instruction at a time by using the front panel switches. Loading the loader was usually a difficult task since it was time consuming and error prone. Nowadays the loader is permanently stored in ROM and is fixed part of the computer itself. With the loader into ROM, the computer is immediately available to load any external program. closely related to loader is another utility to assist the assembly process called the linkage editor.

The linkage editor allows independently written assembly language programs to share data and variables, by linking them together when they are to be loaded into computer memory and run.

### 7.4.3 Monitor

Another frequently used systems program is the monitor. Almost all microcomputer use some form of monitor. Typically it is stored in ROM and performs all basic functions required in a microcomputer. For example, most monitors perform the same functions typically performed by a hardware front panel. Older microcomputers and many minicomputers used a hardware from panel containing either binary lights and switches or octal or hex keyboards and displays. These hardware front panels were used for entering programs and data and for displaying contents of memory or registers. Using the front panel controls, the user could enter program, execute them, and also perform a variety of editing and debugging functions, all in machine language. The monitor in a microcomputer performs these functions through the video or hard-copy terminal connected to the computer rather than with a hardware front panel.

Some of the functions that can be performed by a monitor are as follows:

1. Enter or load instructions and data
2. Display contents of memory locations or registers
3. Change contents of memory locations or registers
4. Execute programs

All of these functions are usually performed in machine language. Most monitors use either octal or hexadecimal designations when entering or displaying memory or register information. addresses are also expressed in octal or hex notation. Thus the monitor is a program that essentially permits convenient entry, display, debugging and execution of machine language programs.

Monitor programs are widely used for machine language program debugging. The monitor provides a convenient means of sequencing a program, finding the error and then correcting it.

Finally most monitors contain load and store routines that allow programs to be loaded from some external media or stored on external media. In effect, the monitor contains a loader. However, it also allows a machine language program generated under the monitor to be stored on some external media.

### 7.4.4 File Manager

A file manager is a program which permits programmers to create, copy, update or delete files on the disks. A file is a collection of information supplied by the programmer which is stored on the disk as a single entity and is accessible by a name. A directory of files stored on the disk as also maintained by the file manager. The directory itself is also stored on the disk. The directory includes file name, size of the file, date and time, and unused memory capacity of the disk, etc.

### 7.4.5 Locator and Linker

A locator is a program that assigns specific memory addresses for each machine code of a program which is to be loaded into the system memory.

Usually a longer program is divided into a number of smaller subprograms called modules. It is easier to develop, test and debug smaller programs. a linker is a program that links smaller programs to form a single program. While developing a program subroutines are frequently used. The subroutines are stored in a library file. The linker also links subroutines with the main program. The linker links machine codes of the program. Therefore, it accepts user's program after editor has edited the program and compiler has produced machine codes of the program.

### 7.4.6 BIOS

The abbreviation BIOS stands for Basic Input Output System. Some system programs that manage the computer's operations are stored in ROM as firmware. These programs perform the most fundamental types of supervisory and support work. They provide essential services that all programmers need. These service programs (or subroutines) are called Basic Input/Output Services. They are referred to as BIOS or ROM-BIOS. Each program performs one specific task such as writing some characters to the CRT, reading some data from disk memory or reading a character from the keyboard etc. All these are done using software interrupt instruction.

The services provided by ROM-BIOS are:

- Print screen
- Video services
- Disk services
- Serial port (RS-232) services
- Cassette port services
- Keyboard services
- Parallel port (printer) services
- Bootstrap services

and so on.

Other system programs are built on the foundation of ROM-BIOS programs and provide higher-level support services. Operating Systems are examples of higher-level system programs. MS-DOS and UNIX are important operating systems.

There are two important differences between ROM-BIOS and DOS:

1. ROM-BIOS provides system services to users at very low-level, while DOS provides at higher-level.
2. DOS does much services to users directly, which the ROM-BIOS does not.

## 7.5 APPLICATION SOFTWARE

An application package or application program is the software that has been written to process or perform specific job. The term application indicates that the software is applied to the job at hand. application packages are available for all types of tasks. These programs are called Application Packages because they accomplish the processing required for a particular application. They may be for business applications, engineering designs, home applications, teaching aids etc.

An end-user wishing to use an application package has to define his own requirements by means of parameters, which are employed by the programs in the system to produce the specific results required. These are usually written in high-level languages. Of course, the application packages run under the control of the operating system.

Application software is developed to aid in any task that benefits from computation. It is a broad category, and encompasses software of many kinds, including the internet browser being used to display this page. This category includes:

- Business software
- Computer-aided design
- Databases
- Decision making software
- Educational software
- Image editing

- Industrial automation
- Mathematical software
- Medical software
- Molecular modeling software
- Quantum chemistry and solid state physics software
- Simulation software
- Spreadsheets
- Telecommunications (i.e., the Internet and everything that flows on it)
- Video editing software
- Video games
- Word processing

and so on.

Application packages can be classified as:

- General-purpose Application Packages
- Application-specific Packages
- Customised Application Packages

### 7.5.1 General-purpose Application Packages

It is that class of application packages that perform quite commonly used day-to-day tasks and also increase the productivity very significantly and that's why these are also known as productivity packages.

Some important examples of this category include:

- Word processing packages for processing and manipulating text
- Spreadsheet packages for calculating finances and data analysis
- CAD for designing or drafting
- Database packages for management of files, database, storage and retrieval of information
- Engineering design packages
- Communication packages
- Integrated packages, etc.

Some integrated packages have been developed which combine the functions of word processing, spreadsheets, graphics, database management and communication into a single software. MS-Office, Framework and Symphony are good examples of Integrated Packages.

### 7.5.2 Application-specific Packages

It is the type of application packages specifically meant for accomplishing a uncommon application. Few important examples include:

- General Application Packages
  - Payroll

- Personnel Management
- Attendance Management

and so on.

- Business Application Packages
  - Inventory Control
  - Finance and Accounting
  - Marketing Analysis
  - MRP (Material Requirements Planning)
  - Human-resource Management

  and so on
- Scientific Application Packages
  - Computer-Aided Designing and Drafting (CADD)
  - SPSS (Statistical Package For Social Sciences)
  - Computer-Aided Manufacturing (CAM)
  - Statistical Analysis Software (SAS)

  and so on.
- Miscellaneous Application Packages
  - Computer-Based Learning (CBL)
  - MIDI (Musical Instrument Digital Interface) Package
  - Computer-Based Training (CBT)

  and so on

### 7.5.3 Customised Application Packages

It is a kind of application packages developed by the professional programmers. It has become the trend of the present day Software Industry to develop such kind of packages. Natural Language Processing (NLP) is getting world-wide attention because these are non-procedural and are more closer to human conversation. This is trend has been geared up probably due to the development of the non-procedural 4GLs (4th Generation Languages). This trend will continue to grow as the development in multimedia, graphics, artificial intelligence, networking solutions enhance.

## 7.6 OPERATING SYSTEM

"Operating System (OS) is a collection of software written to provide the fundamental instructions that a computer needs to manage resources, such as memory, the file system, and processes".

In other words, OS is a master program that controls a computer's basic functions and allows other programs to access the computer's resources such as disk drive, printer, keyboard, and screen.

There are several definitions of operating system. Few of these are:

"Operating system is a set of system programs which controls all the computer's resources and provides the base upon which application programs can be written".

OR

"An operating system may be viewed as an organised collection of software extensions of hardware, consisting of control routines for operating a computer and for providing an environment for execution of programs".

OR

"An operating system is a set of procedures (manual and/or automatic) that enables people or group of people to share a computer installation efficiently".

OR

"An operating system is a program that act as an intermediary between a user of a computer and the computer hardware. The primary goals of an operating system are:

- To make the computer system convenient to use and
- To use the computer hardware in an efficient manner"

OR

"An operating system is an integrated collection of subsystems and further each subsystem consists of programs that perform specific duties. Just as the processor is the nucleus of the computer system, the operating system is the nucleus of all types software activities".

Examples of operating systems: Linux, MS Windows 95, MS Windows NT, Windows XP, UNIX, DOS and OS/2.

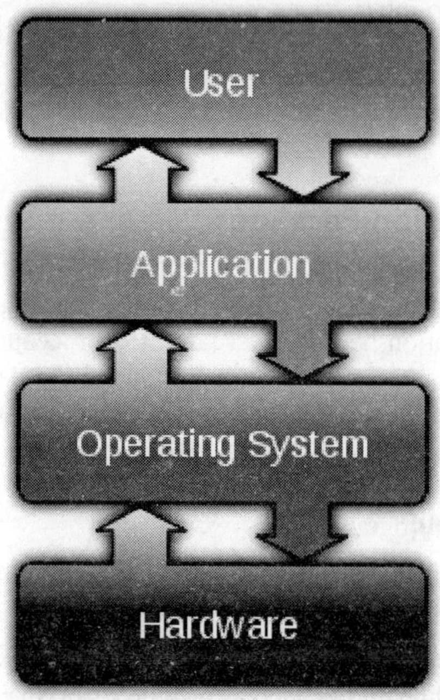


**Fig. 7.4:** Layers of Computer System

It co-ordinates all the hardware and software components of a computer

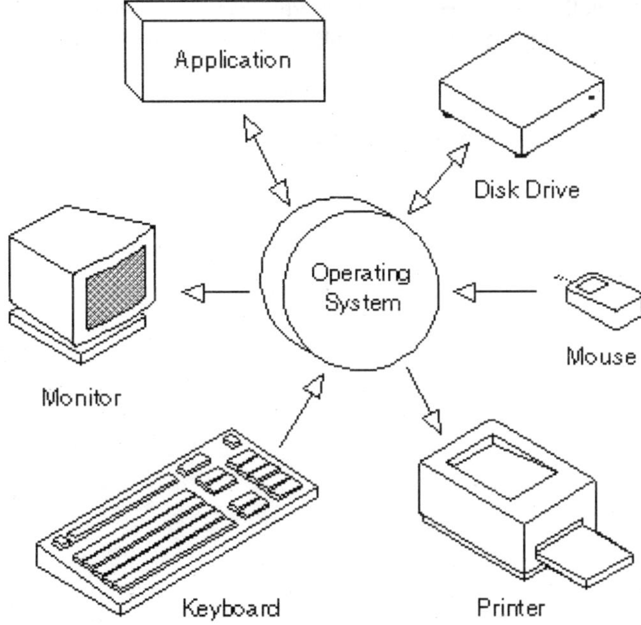


**Fig. 7.5:** OS as Co-ordinator

The following two types of programs make up the operating system:

i. Control programs and
ii. Processing programs

## 7.6.1 Control Programs

These programs oversee system operations and performs tasks such as input/output, scheduling, handling interrupts, and communication with computer operator or programmer. The control programs consist of the following:

a. Supervisor Programs
b. Job Control Programs
c. Input/Output Management Program

## 7.6.2 Processing Programs

These are executed under the supervision of control programs and are used by the programmer to simplify program operation for the computer system. They include language translator programs, link editors, library programs and a set of utility programs. These programs collectively automate the management of all the computing resources available in a computer system including CPU, all peripherals, and software. This integrated collection of programs provides more efficient computer operation. Improved operating convenience is another benefit of an operating system.

Typically, operating systems (OSs) are used in microcomputer systems. They require mass storage media such as magnetic tape or floppy disk. most microcomputers systems use operating systems only with floppy disk mass storage. For this reason, these operating systems are referred to as disk operating systems (DOS). The most commonly used operating systems on personal computers are MS-DOS and PC-DOS.

### 7.6.3 Characteristics of Operating System

- Sharing
- Concurrency
- Long-term Storage
- Non-determinacy

### 7.6.4 Desirable Features of Operating System

- Efficiency
- Reliability
- Small-Size
- Maintainability

Thus the operating system is responsible for directing a given computer into a batch mono-programming system, a multi-programmed system, a time-sharing system or a real-time system. Many operating systems can handle both batch and real-time applications simultaneously.

### 7.6.5 Booting (or Bootstrapping)

The process of loading the operating system into memory is known as booting. When a computer is turned on the operating system must be brought into the memory of computer from the hard-disk storage. The process is normally started by a small program called bootstrap loader. This program resides in a ROM as a firmware. A computer is designed to fetch its very first instruction from the ROM when power is turned on. The first instruction is bootstrap loader. It is very simple program sufficient only to direct the CPU to look for specific file on the disk memory, and executes the instructions stored in the file. The file contains machine codes to direct the CPU to continue loading the rest of the operating system into the memory. When the operating system is fully loaded into the memory, the computer is ready to accept user's commands.

### 7.6.6 Family of operating systems

The family of operating systems have evolved over the years:

a. Windows family of OS:

Windows 1.0

Windows 2.0

Windows 3.0 (the first version to make substantial commercial impact)

Windows 3.1x

Windows 95 (aka Windows 4.0)
Windows 98 (aka Windows 4.1)
Windows Me (aka Windows 4.2)
OS/ 2 (developed jointly with IBM)
Windows NT
Windows 2000 (aka Windows NT 5.0)
Windows XP (aka Windows NT 5.1)
Windows Server 2003 (aka Windows NT 5.2)
Windows Vista (to be released August 2006)
Windows Longhorn Server (to be released shortly after Windows Vista)
Microsoft Codename Blackcomb (to follow Vista)

b. Apple/Macintosh
Apple DOS
ProDOS
GS/OS
Lisa OS
A/UX
Mac OS
System 6
System 7 (code-named "Big Bang")
Mac OS 8
Mac OS 9
Mac OS X
Mac OS X v10.0 (aka Mac OS X 10.0 "Cheetah")
Mac OS X v10.1 (aka Mac OS X 10.1 "Puma")
Mac OS X v10.2 (aka Mac OS X 10.2 "Jaguar")
Mac OS X v10.3 (aka Mac OS X 10.3 "Panther")
Mac OS X v10.4 (aka Mac OS X 10.4 "Tiger")
Mac OS X v10.5 (aka Mac OS X 10.5 "Leopard")
Mac OS X Server
Darwin

c. Unix
d. Linux
e. Solaris.

## 7.7 FUNCTIONS OF OPERATING SYSTEM

The main functions of OS are:

1. It manages the hardware and software resources of the system. In a desktop computer, these resources include such things as the processor, memory, disk, etc.
2. It provides a stable, consistent way for applications to deal with the hardware without having to know all the details of the hardware.

### 7.7.1 Main Functions

OS acts as an interface between hardware and users. It controls overall operations of computers. It is mainly used for job management, data management, virtual memory management, input/output management, process management, security etc.

a. Job Management: OS manages the job waiting to be processed. It recognizes the jobs, identifies their priorities, allocates the memory for the job, schedules and finally runs each job at the appropriate moment.

b. Data Management: Data management keeps track of the data on disk, tape and optical storage devices. The operating system's file system knows where that data are physically stored.

c. Virtual Storage Management: OS is used for virtual memory management. OS makes possible to increase the capacity of main memory with out actually increasing its size.

d. Input/output Management: OS manages the input and output operation of computer. This applies to the flow of data among the different devices of computer and application programs.

e. Process Management: The main activities of process management are job queuing, job scheduling, keeping track of the status of each process etc.

f. Protection and Security: OS job is to secure data inside the memory of computer. Operating systems provide password protection to keep unauthorized users out of the system.

g. User Interface: OS acts as an interface between a user of a computer and the computer hardware.

### 7.7.2 Basic Roles of Operating System

a. Easy interaction between human and computer.
b. Starting computer operation automatically.
c. Loading and scheduling users' programs/processes.
d. Controlling I/O devices
e. Managing various types of memories such as primary, secondary, cache etc.
f. Providing security to users' jobs and files.
g. Accounting hardware resources and handling network communication.
h. Allowing users to share data and software among themselves.
i. Preventing the system from unauthorized user, programs etc.

### 7.7.3 OS as an Extended Machine

The OS effectively isolates the hardware from the user. The user communicates only with the OS and it links the various languages and the systems and applications programs available. The OS fields all requests for services and totally eliminates the need for the user to deal with the hardware or related problems. Thus the operating system allows the user to concentrate on his application and prevents him for having to spend a lot of time determining how things are to be specifically accomplished by the hardware.

In this view, the function of an operating system is to prevent the user with the equivalent of an Extended Machine or Virtual Machine that is easier to program than the underlying hardware.

### 7.7.4 OS as a Resource Manager

An operating system's major function is to manage the resources of the computer system. It allocates the resources on the basis of the user need and system capability. The four major functions of an operating system are:

i. File and Software Management
ii. Input/Output and Peripheral Management
ii. Memory Management
iii. Processor (or CPU) Management

As a Resource Manager, the operating system must perform the following functions for each resource viz. processor, memory, I/O, files:

a. Keep track of status of each resource
b. Decide which job should get the resource and for how much time, according to some policy
c. Allocate the resource to the job decided
d. After the resource is used by the job for the allocated time, make the resource free

## 7.8 OS RELATED COMMON GLOSSARY

### Buffering

A buffer is a region of memory used to temporarily hold data while it is being moved from one place to another. Typically, the data is stored in a buffer as it is retrieved from an input device (such as a keyboard) or just before it is sent to an output device (such as a printer). However, a buffer may be used when moving data between processes within a computer. So, buffering is a process of placing the data in a buffer in order to increase the processing capability of a device.

### Spooling (Simultaneous Peripheral Operations On-Line)

In computer science, spooling refers to a process of transferring data by placing it in a temporary working area where another program may access it for processing at a later point in time. The term 'spool' is an acronym of 'Simultaneous Peripheral Operations On-Line'. This temporary working area could be a file or storage device, but probably not a buffer.

For example: By using a process spooling, multiple users can send jobs to a printer simultaneously. When users send documents (known as print jobs) to a networked printer, each job is stored temporarily on the file server. As the printer finishes printing the current job, the file server sends the next job to the printer so that it can be printed).

## Virtual Memory

Virtual memory is the use of secondary storage devices as an extension of the primary storage of the computer, thus giving the appearance of a larger main memory than actually exists.

### *Paging:*

In paging system, each process is divided into a number of fixed length blocks called 'pages', typically 4K bytes in length. Memory space is viewed as a series of 'page-frames' of the same size. When a process is to be executed, only the pages that are immediately required are loaded into memory.

### *Swapping:*

In a virtual memory system, Swapping is a technique in which high priority process is swap in main memory and low priority process from main memory is swap out. When high priority process is completed, low priority process is swap in again.

## Multiprogramming

It is a form of processing in which a computer holds more than one program in memory and works on them in round-robin fashion that is, by sharing out the processor's time so that each program receives some attention some of the time. This way of working is in contrast to using the processor to run one program at a time.

## Multitasking

Multitasking, in an operating system, is allowing a user to perform more than one computer task (such as the operation of an application program) at a time. Microsoft Windows 2000, IBM's OS/390, and Linux are examples of operating systems that can do multitasking (almost all of today's operating systems can). When you open your Web browser and then open word at the same time, you are causing the operating system to do multitasking.

## Multi-threading

Multi-threading is the ability of an operating system to execute different parts of a program, called threads, simultaneously. The programmer must carefully design the program in such a way that all the threads can run at the same time without interfering with each other.

## Job Scheduling

Job scheduling not only assigns priority to jobs but also admits new jobs for processing at appropriate times. When a user job is submitted, the system takes note of its time of arrival, processing requirement etc. Considering all these factors, the scheduling techniques are chosen. There are two types of scheduling

a. Non-Preemptive Scheduling: In non-preemptive scheduling, a scheduled job always completes before another scheduling decision is made.

b. Preemptive Scheduling: In preemptive scheduling, a scheduling decision can be made even while the job is executing.

Some scheduling algorithms are:

a. FCFS (First Come, First Serve

b. SJF (Shortest Job First)

c. Priority Scheduling
d. Round Robin Scheduling
e. Multilevel Feedback Queue Scheduling
f. Multilevel queue Scheduling

### Interrupt Handling

An interrupt is a signal generated by an event that alters the sequence in which a processor executes instructions. To handle interrupt Operating System has one special routine called ISR (Interrupt Service Routine).

Hardware interrupt: A signal created and sent to the CPU that is caused by some action taken by a hardware device is called hardware interrupt. For example, keystroke depressions and mouse movements cause hardware interrupts.

Software interrupt: A software interrupt, also called an exception, is an interrupt that is caused by software, usually by a program in user mode. Examples of events that cause them are requests by an application program for certain services from the operating system or the termination of such programs.

## 7.9 CLASSIFICATION OF OPERATING SYSTEMS

Within the broad family of operating systems, these may be categorized based on the types of computers they control and the sort of applications they support. These may be classified in the following categories:

- Single-user, Single-task Operating System
- Single-user, Multi-task Operating System
- Multi-user Operating System
- Multi-access Operating System
- Multi-processing Operating System
- Multi-tasking and Multi-threading Operating System
- Real-time Operating System
- Distributed Operating System
- Embedded Operating System

### 7.9.1 Single-user, single task Operating System

As the name implies, this operating system is designed to manage the computer so that one user can effectively do one thing at a time. The Palm OS for Palm handheld computers is a good example of a modern single-user, single-task operating system. Other examples of such operating systems include MS-DOS, PC-DOS, etc.

### 7.9.2 Single-user, multi tasking Operating System

This operating system allows a computer to perform more than one task at a time. Microsoft's Windows and Apple's Mac OS (Leopard) platforms are both examples of operating systems that will let a single user have several programs in operation at the same time.

### 7.9.3 Multi-user Operating System

A multi-user operating system allows many different users to take advantage of the computer's resources simultaneously. UNIX, VMS and mainframe operating systems, such as MVS, are examples of multi-user operating systems.

These operating systems allow two or more users to run their respective programs at the same time by making all these programs resident in the memory of computer. Such operating systems are normally made to work on minicomputers and mainframe computers.

The concept of allowing more than one programs in the memory of computer is called multi-programming. All time-sharing systems need to be multi-programmed but not necessarily all the multi-programmed systems to be time-shared.

In these types of systems, all the resources are shared among different users' programs. The processor (or CPU) is made to switch among these users' programs after a fixed quantum of time called time-slice. The time-slice needs to be very small so that the user should need have feeling that processor is not attending well to them.

**Examples:** *VMS (on DEC Mainframes), UNIX, XENIX, MVS, etc.*

It's important to differentiate here between multi-user operating systems and single-user operating systems that support networking. Windows 2000 and Novell Netware can each support hundreds or thousands of networked users, but the operating systems themselves aren't true multi-user operating systems. The system administrator is the only "user" for Windows 2000 or Netware. The network support and the entire remote user logins the network enables are, in the overall plan of the operating system, a program being run by the administrative user.

### 7.9.4 Multi-access Operating System

In a multi-access operating system, a user may submit a job by typing on a terminal and may use the terminal to monitor and control the job as it runs. These operating systems allow simultaneous access of a single application onto a computer system through two or more terminals.

The operating system shares the computing resources among the different jobs so that it appears to each user that he has entire machine to himself.

An example is provided by some dedicated transaction-processing systems, such as Airline Ticket Reservation Systems, that supports hundreds of active terminals under control of a single program.

### 7.9.5 Multiprocessing Operating System

It is that class of operating systems that have the ability to support more than one process at the same time i.e. allowing more than one programs to run concurrently on the multiple CPUs in a single computer system. These operating systems differ from the time-sharing (or multi-user) operating systems in the manner that these refer to utilisation of multiple CPUs.

In such operating system, the resources are allocated comfortably to the competing processes in a reasonable manner which results in a high throughput.

**Examples:** *OS/2 for high-end PCs, UNIX, MVS, etc.*

### 7.9.6 Multitasking and Multithreading Operating System

These operating systems have the capability to execute more than one task concurrently on a computer system having a single CPU. In these operating systems, CPU switches from one task to another so quickly that it gives the illusion to the user of executing all the programs (or tasks) at the same time.

Multithreading permits different portions of a single program to run concurrently and this it is having the ability of an operating system to execute different parts of a program (called threads) simultaneously. It requires the programmer to design the program so carefully that all the threads can run at the same time without interfering with each other.

**Examples:** *Windows 95/98, Windows NT, OS/2, etc.*

### 7.9.7 Real-time Operating Systems (RTOS)

Real-time operating systems are used to control machinery, scientific instruments and industrial systems.

Real-time operating systems are used in environments where a large number of events, most external to the computer, must be accepted and processed in a short-time or within certain deadlines.

These operating systems have the following peculiar characteristics:

- Fast response time
- Feedback mechanism
- Reliability

A primary objective of real-time operating systems is to provide quick response-times, and thus meet the scheduling deadlines. In the design of these operating systems, user-convenience and resource utilisation are of secondary concern.

These operating systems must be designed in such a manner that response-time to the external-stimulus is very immediate as the same are designed for the purpose of controlling and monitoring of external activities with timing constraints.

Such applications include:

- Industrial Control
- Telephone Switching Equipments
- Flight-Control
- Real-time Simulators
- Few Military Applications

etc.

The traditional operating systems like MS-DOS and UNIX are very different from real-time operating systems because memory management and file-management are of least importance in comparison to processor and input/output management.

**Examples:** *Some examples of real time operating systems are:*

- *BLMX (Board-Level Multitasking eXecutive)*
- *BSO/RTOS (Boston Systems Office/ Real-time Operating System)*
- *CCP (Communication Control Program) Operating System for IBM System/3*

- *iRMX (Intel's 8086 family Real-time Multitasking Executive) Operating System*
- *DMERT (Duplex Multiple Environment Real-time) Operating System*

*etc.*

### 7.9.8 Distributed Operating Systems

A distributed operating system governs the operation of a distributed computer system and provides a virtual machine abstraction to its users. The key objective of a distributed operating system is transparency. Ideally, component and resource distribution should be hidden from users and application programs unless they explicitly demand otherwise.

These operating systems usually provide the means for system-wide sharing of resources, such as computational capacity, files and I/O devices. In addition to typical operating system services provides at each node for the benefit of local clients, a distributed operating system may facilitate access to remote resources, communication with remote processes, and distribution of computations.

The added services necessary for pooling of shared system resources include:

- Global naming
- Distributed file system, and
- Facilities for distribution of computations, such as inter-node process communication and remote procedure calls.

### 7.9.9 Embedded Operating System

Embedded operating systems are mainly executed on computers that control devices. These devices are mobile phones, TV sets etc. These systems consist of circuits and 32-bit microprocessors that control the functioning of various operations.

Apart from the above main criterion for classification of operating systems, there will be other criterion as well, like basing on whether it is open code or not and whether it is available for free and similar.

Fig. 7.6 shows widely used operating systems in the market.

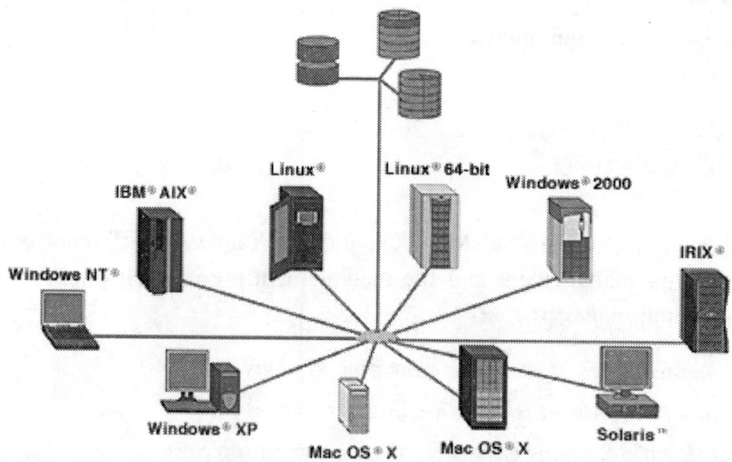


**Fig. 7.6:** Widely used OS

## 7.10 FORMS OF DATA PROCESSING

Data processing is any computer process that converts data into information or knowledge. There are many types of data processing techniques. Some of these are:

### 7.10.1 Batch Processing

It is also called deferred Processing or off-line processing in which tasks are stored in the form of batches and processed each batches as requirement. It is a slow process of data processing. The purpose of batches is to give full control over the data as it is easier to handle a batch at a time.

Due to turnaround delays and offline debugging, batch is not very convenient for program development. Programs that do not require interaction and programs with long execution times may be served well by a batch operating system. Examples of such programs include:

- Payroll
- Forecasting
- Statistical Analysis, and
- Large Scientific Number-crunching Programs.

Serial processing combined with batch-like command files is also found on many PCs.

### 7.10.2 On-line Processing

The on-line processing is a fast processing in which input device is directly connected to computer. It is also called direct access or random access processing. In this processing result of data processing transaction is available immediately. E.g. ATM (Automated Teller Machine).

### 7.10.3 Real-time Processing

Real time means immediate response from computer. The essential feature is that the input data must be processed quickly enough so that further action can be promptly taken on the result.

### 7.10.4 Distributed Data Processing

A data processing system in which processing is decentralized with the computers and storage devices at different geographical locations.

## 7.11 OPERATING SYSTEM CHOICES

There are more than a dozen of operating systems commonly used by users. Few of these are discussed below:

### 7.11.1 DOS

DOS is an acronym for "Disk Operating System". DOS is a 16-bit, single-user operating system that does not support multi-tasking. It is far easier to administer than UNIX, but less powerful. Compared to graphical interfaces such as Windows and Mac OS X, it's also not particularly user-friendly.

### 7.11.2 Microsoft Windows Operating System

The Windows operating system is developed and maintained by Microsoft, the company founded by Bill

Gates. The first version was released in 1985. Since then, it has grown significantly, and it now dominates the market. Windows uses a graphical user interface to make it easier for people to use their computers. The primary ways that people navigate are through icons on the desktop and the Start menu.

The Windows operating system, like the Macintosh and Linux, allows people to manage files and run software programs on desktop and laptop computers.

Windows is the most popular PC operating system in the world. A brief outline of few of the popular Windows operating systems is provided below.

### 7.11.2.1 Windows XP

Windows XP was released in October 2001 and was designed to replace all previous versions of Windows. It is offered in two versions:

- Home and
- Professional.

Both Home and Professional can be upgraded from Windows 98, Windows 98SE, and Windows ME. Windows NT 4.0, Windows 2000 and Windows XP Home can all be upgraded to Windows XP Professional. Windows 95 and earlier versions of Windows are up gradable to either version. Main Features

- Less crashes than Windows 98 - virtually gone is the infamous 'blue screen of death' that signalled a crashed system.
- Error messages are less impersonal and end with 'We are sorry for the inconvenience.'
- Installation of peripheral hardware such as printers, scanner and digital cameras is virtually automatic.
- Many users can share the same PC. Each can have their own password and individualized desktop, my documents folder and web favourites for example. With 'Fast User Switching' a user can turn the PC over to another user without logging off. The first user's program continue running and can be resumed when the second user is done.
- New look to the desktop with bold greens and blues in places, beige in others. The classic Windows 98 style can be restored without functional loss.
- Home networks are automatically recognized and configured. Broadband access can be setup with a few simple steps.
- Folders are smarter and have related Task Panes that contains tasks that match the type of files found it. For example, a folder with photos would have a Task Pane containing an instant viewing capability such as a thumbnail viewer.
- Files can be dragged and dropped on a CD-RW drive icon. Once you have placed all the files you want on the icon, you tell it burn them an it does it. No special CD writing software is required.
- A smarter Start menu lets you keep your favourite programs permanently near the top. A second column contains access to key features like the control Panel and Search.

### 7.11.2.2 Windows ME

Windows ME is successor to Window 98 appeared late in 2000. It is very similar in look and feel to Windows 98 with a few added features. Main Features

- A more reliable streamlined process that reduces the start up time for the PC.

- Automatic restoration of backup version of a file in the event of file corruption.
- Protection of files from modification from other software programs.
- Windows Media Player 7 was included.

### 7.11.2.3 Windows 2000

Windows 2000 arrived early in 2000. It is based on the NT operating kernel and targeted toward business users. It is sometimes referred to as Windows NT 5.0 and contains over 29 million lines of code. It is offered in four versions: Professional, Server, Advanced Server and Datacenter Server New features of Professional

- Support for FAT16, FAT32 and NTFS file systems. Each file is encrypted with a randomly generated key.
- A better application installation tracker.
- Memory protection for individual applications and processes so that a single application can not lock up the system.
- A file encryption system and secure VPN allows a private LAN over the Internet.
- Native support is provided for ATM and cable modems.

### 7.11.2.4 Windows 98

Windows 98 was released in 1998. It retained and refined the desktop look of Windows 95. A second edition called Windows 98SE was released in 1999 and offered some fixes and improvements to the first edition. Main Features

- The biggest advance was the introduction of Internet Explorer, which is a web browser allowing you to view and download web pages from remote servers across the Internet.
- An improved File System, FAT32 (File Allocation Table) was introduced. It enabled hard drives bigger than 2G bytes to be used with the OS. By default Windows 98 uses FAT16, which is the file system used on all previous Windows versions and DOS.
- In Windows 98 you have the option of using FAT32 when first setting up a hard drive.
- Windows 98 is backward compatible with Windows 3.1, Windows 95, and the MS-DOS® operating systems.

### 7.11.2.5 Windows 95

It was released in 1995 and had the first desktop appearance that has pretty much been retained in all versions of Windows since. Main Features

- The desktop with icons on it first debuted.
- A taskbar was added to the bottom of the desktop. Program Manager was replaced with a 'Start' button on the taskbar. It is used to start programs, open documents, customize the system and get help. Toolbars such as quick launch, desktop, address and links can be placed on the taskbar. Running applications that have been minimized also appear on the taskbar.
- Windows Explorer replaced File Manager as the tool to manage folders and files.
- Long Filenames (up to 256 characters) were supported which was a tremendous improvement over 8 characters in all earlier versions of Windows as well as DOS.

- Plug and Play compatibility was added which meant you could plug in new hardware (expansion cards) which Windows would recognize and set it up for you. This feature wasn't quite there but was a start in the right direction. Prior to this when you installed new hardware you had to manually insure there were no Interrupts (IRQ) or I/O address conflicts with existing hardware. Failure to do so could produce very strange results or even worse yet, no operation at all.
- The Registry appeared, combining what had been multiple configuration files, into two files.
- The right mouse click arrived allowing rapid access and text manipulation.

#### 7.11.2.6 Windows NT

It was released in 1994 this was the first Windows OS to support 32 bit programming model of the 386, 486 and Pentium processors. Support for long filenames also appeared for the fist time.

It provided advanced security features, advanced network support and user administration which made it a first choice for many in the business environment.

#### 7.11.2.7 Windows 3.1.1

In 1993 Microsoft released 3.1.1. It was dubbed 'Windows for Workgroups' and provided network support so that multiple PCs could share files and printers.

#### 7.11.2.8 Windows 3.1

In 1992 V3.1 brought True Type fonts, multimedia support, OLE and common dialog boxes. It ran only in protected mode and required a 80286 or better processor.

#### 7.11.2.9 Windows 3.0

Released in 1990 this OS became widespread in both home and office PCs. It supported the protected mode of the 80x86 processors available at the time. A menu bar ran across the top much like the menu bar in all Windows based applications programs.

Main Features

- Program Manager provided access to program icons which were kept inside a number of different 'group windows'. A simple mouse click on any icon would start the program it represented.
- File Manager allowed easy access and control to all the files on one's hard drive.
- Print Manager and the Control Panel appeared.

#### 7.11.2.10 Windows 2.0

Released in April 1987, it had improved windows that could overlap one another. It also included enhancements to the keyboard and mouse interface.

The release of the 80386 processor enabled multitasking of many DOS programs. Windows 2.0 competed with IBM presentation manager of the OS/2 operating system.

#### 7.11.2.11 Windows 1.0

Released November 1985. It ran on DOS and used fixed tiled windows.

#### 7.11.2.12 Windows

The first Microsoft offering was released in the November 1983.

### 7.11.3 UNIX

UNIX (pronounced as YOO-niks) is a computer operating system originally developed in 1969 by a group of AT&T employees at Bell Labs. UNIX runs on many types of computers, including supercomputers, notebook PCs, mainframes and minicomputers. Its main ability is that it works with so many kinds of hardware.

### 7.11.4 LINUX

Linux is a generic term that commonly refers to Unix-like computer operating systems that use the Linux kernel. Linux is one of the most prominent examples of free software and open source development; typically all the underlying source code can be used, freely modified, and redistributed by anyone.

Ubuntu, NepaLinux, UserLinux etc are few examples of Linux distributions.

## 7.12 MOBILE OPERATING SYSTEMS

Like computer operating system a mobile operating system is a software platform on top of which other programs run. When you purchase a mobile device, the manufacturer will have chosen the operating system for that specific device. The operating system is responsible for determining the functions and features available on your device, such as thumb wheel, keyboards, WAP, e-mail, text messaging and more.

Some of the more common and well-known Mobile operating systems include the following:

### 7.12.1 Symbian OS

Symbian OS has become a standard operating system for smartphones, and is licensed by more than 85 percent of the world's handset manufacturers. The Symbian OS is designed for the specific requirements of 2.5G and 3G mobile phones.

Symbian features pre-emptive multitasking and memory protection, like other operating systems (especially those created for use on desktop computers). EPOC's approach to multitasking was inspired by VMS and is based on asynchronous server-based events.

**Fig. 7.7:** Symbian OS

Symbian OS was created with three systems design principles in mind:

- the integrity and security of user data is paramount
- user time must not be wasted
- all resources are scarce

To best follow these principles, Symbian uses a microkernel, has a request-and-callback approach to services, and maintains separation between user interface and engine. The OS is optimised for low-power battery-based devices and for ROM-based systems (e.g. features like XIP and re-entrancy in shared libraries). Applications, and the OS itself, follow an object-oriented design: Model view Controller.

### 7.12.2 Windows Mobile OS

The Windows Mobile platform is available on a variety of devices from a variety of wireless operators.

You will find Windows Mobile software on Dell, HP, Motorola, Palm and i-mate products. Windows Mobile powered devices are available on GSM or CDMA networks

Windows Mobile 6.5 is based on the Windows CE 5.2 kernel, and features a suite of basic applications developed with the Microsoft Windows API. It is designed to be somewhat similar to desktop versions of Windows, feature-wise and aesthetically. Additionally, third-party software development is available for Windows Mobile, and software applications can be purchased via the Windows Market Place for Mobile.

**Fig. 7.8:** Windows Mobile 6.5 OS

### 7.12.3 Palm OS

Since the introduction of the first Palm Pilot in 1996, the Palm OS platform has provided mobile devices with essential business tools, as well as capability to access the Internet or a central corporate database via a wireless connection.

Palm OS Garnet applications are primarily coded in C/C++. Two officially supported compilers exist: a commercial product, Code warrior Development Studio for Palm OS, and an open source tool chain called prc-tools., based on an old version of gcc. CodeWarrior is criticized for being expensive and is no longer being developed, whereas PRC-Tools lacks several of CodeWarrior's features. A version of PRC-Tools is included in a free Palm OS Developer Suite (PODS).

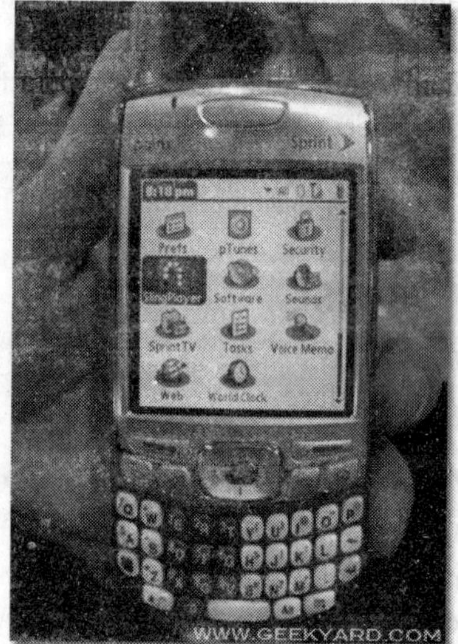


**Fig. 7.9:** Palm OS

### 7.12.4 Mobile Linux

The first company to launch phones with Linux as its OS was Motorola in 2003. Linux is seen as a suitable option for higher-end phones with powerful processors and larger amounts of memory. While not originally designed to be portable,Linux is now one of the most widely ported operating system kernels, running on a diverse range of systems from the iPAO (a handheld computer) to the IBM Z/Architecture (a massive mainframe server that can run hundreds to thousands of concurrent Linux instances). Linux runs as the main operating system on IBM's Blue Gene supercomputers. As of November 2010, Linux is the OS on 91.8% of systems on the Top 500 supercomputers list. Linux has also been ported to various handheld devices such as Tuxphone, Apple's ipod and i phone .Some operating systems developed for mobile phones use modified versions of the Linux kernel including Google Android, Hp webOs and Nokia Maemo.

### 7.12.5 MXI

MXI is a universal mobile operating system that allows existing full-fledged desktop and mobile applications written for Windows, Linux, Java, Palm be enabled immediately on mobile devices without any redevelopment. MXI allows for interoperability between various platforms, networks, software and hardware components.

### 7.12.6 Android

**Android** is a software stack for mobile devices that includes an operating system, middle ware and key applications. Google Inc purchased the initial developer of the software, Android Inc., in 2005. Android's mobile operating system is based on the Linux Kernel. Google and other members of the Open Handset Alliance collaborated on Android's development and release. The Android Open Source Project (AOSP) is tasked with the maintenance and further development of Android. The Android operating system is the world's best-selling Smartphone platform.

In May 2011, researchers at University of Ulm publicized a security flaw, present in all Android devices running AndroidOS 2.3.3 and earlier versions (more than 99% of all Android devices worldwide), that affects all Google services using the ClientLogin authentication protocol (such as authentication tokens widely used by eBAY and other online services) and allows hackers access any personal data available through Android's application programming interfaces (APIs), thus stealing the user's digital credentials over open wireless networks. In response, Google announced a fix that would be rolled out transparently to the use.

**Fig. 7.10:** Android

## 7.13 USER INTERFACE

Interface is a common boundary between the user and the computer system. OS provides two types of User interface.

### 7.13.1 CUI (Command User Interface)

A CUI (command user interface) is a user interface to a computer's operating system or an application in which the user responds to a visual prompt by typing in a command on a specified line, receives a response back from the system, and then enters another command, and so forth. MS-DOS and UNIX are CUI operating systems.

### 7.13.2 GUI (Graphical User Interface)

GUI is graphical user interface. It is user friendly and easy to understand and use. A GUI uses windows, icons, and menus to carry out commands such as opening files, deleting files, moving files, etc. and although many GUI Operating Systems are operated by using a mouse, the keyboard can also be used by using keyboard shortcuts or arrow keys.

A few examples of a GUI Operating Systems: Microsoft Windows 95, Apple Mac OS etc.

A few examples of a GUI interfaces are: GNOME, KDE etc.

Desktop view of GUI of Windows 7 Home Premium is shown in Fig. 7.11.

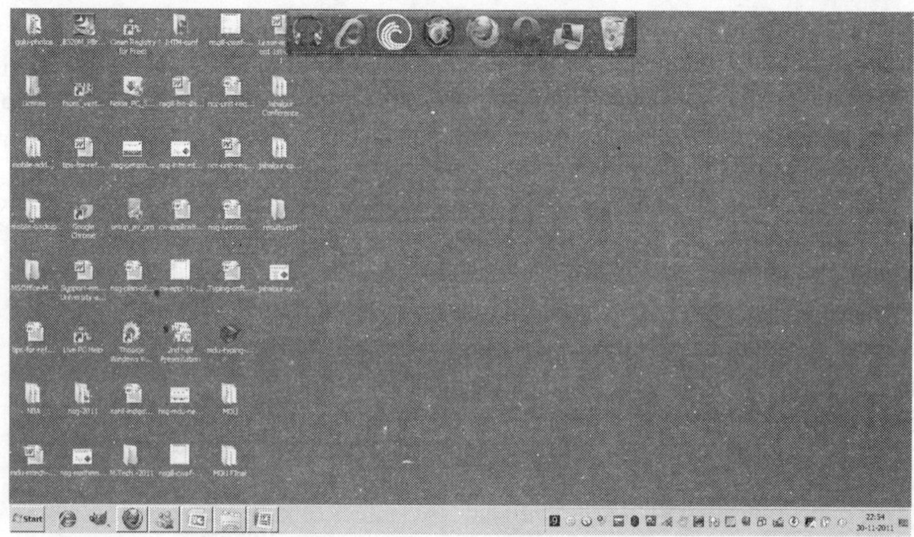

Fig. 7.11: Desktop View of Windows 7 Home Premium

### 7.13.3 Common Features of GUI

A present day GUI has the following common features:

- Pointing device(s): These allow users to point at different parts of the screen as well as can be used to initiate a command. Besides, these can also be used to manipulate objects on the screen by:
  - selecting objects on the screen
  - moving objects around the screen, or
  - merging several objects into another object

**Examples:** *Mouse, light pen, joystick, touch sensitive screen, touch pad and so on.*

- Windows: It graphically display the progress of the action initiated. When a screen is divided into several independent regions, each one of these is called a window. Each window can highlight results related to the action fired in the respective window.
- Switching capability: Windows system offers the switching capability from one application to another or for sharing of data among various applications.
- Resizing and Movement: Windows system also support resizing as well as moving around feature of windows.
- Graphical Bit-mapped Displays: Bit-mapped display are made up of small pixels and offer a very high resolution. Bit-mapped displays have almost replaced character-based displays. Bit-mapped displays wonderful support graphic manipulation. This feature of these displays is also called WYSIWYG i.e. What You See Is What You Get.
- Functionality to support graphics along with height-parameters, color attributes, video-attributes, etc.

- Icon: Icons provide a symbolic representation of any system-entity or user-defined object, etc. such as file, folder, address, table, book, applications and so on. A folder icon consists a group of files or other folder icons. Double clicking on the folder icon causes a window to be opened displaying a list of icons and folder icons representing the folder's contents.
- Dialog box: Dialog box is used to capture user information or to present information to the user. Normally, a dialog box is displayed to get additional information. Dialog boxes are also used to indicate error messages in the form of alert boxes. Dialog boxes also use a wide range of screen control elements to communicate with the user.
- Check box: Such a box is used to capture the information intending confirmation pertaining to any kind of actions desired by the end-user.
- Sliders: These are used to show the relative position of the contents or to move to a different position.
- Desktop Metaphors: In desktop graphical metaphor, users are not aware of applications and they deal with files, folder, drawers, clipboard and an out-box. For example, merely clicking the mouse on an icon representing the Report cause word processor to get started and to load the report file automatically.
- Menus: The functionality on a GUI system must be arranged in the form of structured menus such as horizontal menus, pull-down menus, etc. From the menu, the end-user can select any operation of his choice such as File, Edit, Search, Tool and so on. Rather than remembering commands at each stage, a menu can be used to provide a list of items. Each menu element can be either a word or an icon representing a command or a function. Menu item can be invoked by moving the cursor on the menu item and selecting the item by clicking the mouse.

## 7.13.4 Components of GUI

GUIs consists of four major components:

- Windowing System: It allows to display multiple applications at the same time and it includes programming tools for designing movable and resizable windows, menus, dialog boxes, check boxes, and other items on the display.

  **Example:** *Macintosh, X Window, etc.*
- Imaging Model: It describes how fonts and graphics are designed on the screen and such a model is capable of handling typeface, color, shading, dimension and size of graphical primitives such as simple or complex lines, curves, etc. Some GUIs support more than one imaging model.
- API (Application Program Interface): API is a set of programming language functions that allow the programmer to specify how the actual application will control the menus, scroll bars and icons that appear on the screen.
- Set of Interface Development Tools: GUI development environments may incorporate toolkits and frameworks. Most of these toolkits are based on object-oriented approach.

### 7.13.5 CUI Vs GUI Operating Systems

**Table 7.2:** CUI Vs GUI OS

| GUI | CUI |
|---|---|
| It is based on graphical user interface mode. | It is based on command user interface mode. |
| It is graphical and user friendly. | It is more textual and less user friendly. |
| It is very common. | It is less common. |
| It uses keyboard and mouse. | It uses only keyboard. |
| It consists of different components such as text box, icon, desktop, pointing device etc. | It does not consist such components. |
| E.g. MS-Windows OS | E.g. MS-DOS OS |

## EXERCISE

1. Differentiate between assemblers, compilers and interpreters.
2. How is system software different from system utilities? Explain.
3. What do you understand by an Integrated Software?
4. Describe two commonly used utility programs.
5. What kind of a program is used to backup from one data storage to another?
6. What is postcadware? How is different from bannerware?
7. Differentiate between application and system software.
8. What is meant by GUI?
9. What are the important features of GUI? Explain.
10. Differentiate between shareware and freeware.
11. What do you understand by GUI standards? Explain.
12. What are various components of GUI? Explain.
13. What is crippleware? Give an example.
14. How is freeware different from donorware? Explain.
15. What is a public domain ware?
16. What is a computer software?
17. Is word-processing package a system software? Justify your answer.
18. What are the functions of an assembler?
19. What are different types software? Explain.
20. What are different types of application packages? Illustrate through suitable examples.
21. What is input to the compiler?
22. Is Oracle an Application Package? Justify your answer.
23. Discuss the features of an integrated package.

24. What are advantages of Windows environment?
24. Enumerate functions of a monitor program.
25. What is the difference between Loader and Linker?
26. What is the output of the compilers?
27. What are monitors? State their significance.
28. What is BIOS?
29. What do you understand by application-specific package?
31. What is a bootstrap program?
30. What is an Editor? What are the capabilities of an Editor?
31. What is a firmware?
32. What is a File Manager? Outline its responsibilities.
33. What is the purpose of the Loader and Locator?
34. What is an operating system?
35. Discuss the important functions of an operating system.
36. Is Windows 95/98 an operating system? Justify your answer.
37. What are the services provided by ROM-BIOS?
38. What is a begware?
39. What is meant by a programming language?
40. If each new generation of language enhances interaction between programmers and the computer, why not write programs using the most recent generation of languages?
41. What are the differences between high-level and low-level languages?
42. Associate each of language with a particular generation of languages.
43. What are various generations of computer programming languages?
44. What are problem-oriented languages?
45. What is the difference between machine- and assembly-language?
46. What are non-procedural languages? Give few examples.
47. Why are low-level and high-level languages are named so?
48. What are Application Generators? Give few examples.
49. What are procedural languages? Give few examples.
50. What are various types of high-level languages?
51. State the capabilities of Query Languages?
52. What are DSSs (Decision Support Systems)? How are they helpful?
53. What do you understand by Specialised Languages? Give few examples.
54. What are Object-Oriented Programming Languages? Give few examples.
55. What are multi-purpose programming languages? Name three such languages.
56. What do you understand by Fifth Generation Languages (5GLs)?

57. What are Report Generators?
58. What are the differences between 3GLs and 4GLs?
59. Name a procedure-oriented programming language in each of the three classifications, namely, scientific, business, and specialised.
60. What are query languages? Give few examples.
61. What are Natural Languages?
62. What do you understand by Character Codes?
63. What is a Number System? State their utility.
64. Why Binary Number System is followed in computer systems?
65. Differentiate between Octal and Hexa-decimal Number System?
66. What are BCD Codes?
67. Differentiate between ASCII and EBCDIC Character Codes.
68. What is the utility of Hexa-decimal Number System?

CHAPTER 8

# Programming Languages and Program Development

## 8.1 INTRODUCTION

A language is a vehicle for communication. In order to communicate with each other, humans need languages like English, Hindi, etc. In the same manner, for communicating with the computer, we use computer language called programming language. A programming language consists of all the symbols, characters and usage rules that permit people to communicate with computers. Learning to program requires learning all these symbols and rules.

There are many programming languages available and each one has its symbols, character set and syntax but each language has an instruction set that permits those familiar operations to be performed.

We know that the computer can neither think nor can make any decision on its own. It needs instructions to understand what to do. A program is a set of logically related instructions that are arranged in a sequence that guides the computer to solve a problem.

The process of writing a program is called programming. If a system is not correctly programmed; it delivers incorrect results.

## 8.2 HISTORY OF PROGRAMMING LANGUAGES

The first programming languages predate the modern computer. From the first, the languages were codes. Herman Hollerith realized that he could encode information on punch cards when he observed that railroad train conductors would encode the appearance of the ticket holders on the train tickets using the position of punched holes on the tickets. Hollerith then proceeded to encode the 1890 census data on punch cards which he made the same size as the boxes for holding US currency.

The first computer codes were specialized for the applications. In the first decades of the twentieth century, numerical calculations were based on decimal numbers. Eventually it was realized that logic could be represented with numbers, as well as with words. For example, Alonzo Church was able to express the lambda calculus in a formulaic way. The Turing machine was an abstraction of the operation of a tape-marking machine, for example, in use at the telephone companies. However, unlike the lambda calculus, Turing's code does not serve well as a basis for higher-level languages - its principal use is in rigorous analyses of algorithmic complexity.

Like many "firsts" in history, the first modern programming language is hard to identify. From the start, the restrictions of the hardware defined the language. Punch cards allowed 80 columns, but some of the columns had to be used for a sorting number on each card. Fortran included some keywords which were the same as English words, such as "IF", "GOTO" (go to) and "CONTINUE". The use of a magnetic drum for memory meant that computer programs also had to be interleaved with the rotations of the drum. Thus the programs were more hardware dependent than today.

To some people the answer depends on how much power and human-readability is required before the status of "programming language" is granted. Jacquard looms and Charles Babbage's Difference Engine both had simple, extremely limited languages for describing the actions that these machines should perform. One can even regard the punch holes on a player piano scroll as a limited domain-specific programming language, albeit not designed for human consumption.

### 8.2.1 1940s

In the 1940s the first recognizably modern, electrically powered computers were created. The limited speed and memory capacity forced programmers to write hand tuned assembly language programs. It was soon discovered that programming in assembly language required a great deal of intellectual effort and was error-prone.

In 1945, Konrad Zuse published details of his programming language Plankalkül. However, it was not implemented in his time and his original contributions were isolated from other developments because Germany was isolated during the war.

Some important languages that were developed in this time period include:

- 1943 - Plankalkül (Konrad Zuse)
- 1943 - ENIAC coding system
- 1949 - C-10

### 8.2.2 1950s and 1960s

In the 1950s the first three modern programming languages whose descendants are still in widespread use today were designed:

- FORTRAN, the "FORmula TRANslator", invented by John W. Backus et al.;
- LISP, the "LISt Processor", invented by John McCarthy et al.;
- COBOL, the COmmon Business Oriented Language, created by the Short Range Committee, heavily influenced by Grace Hopper.

Another milestone in the late 1950s was the publication, by a committee of American and European computer scientists, of "a new language for algorithms"; the Algol 60 Report (the "ALGOrithmic Language"). This report consolidated many ideas circulating at the time and featured two key innovations:

- The use of Backus-Naur Form (BNF) for describing the language's syntax. Nearly all subsequent programming languages have used a variant of BNF to describe the context-free portion of their syntax.
- The introduction of lexical scoping for names in arbitrarily nested scopes.

Algol 60 was particularly influential in the design of later languages, some of which soon became more popular. The Burroughs B5000 was designed to be programmed in an extended subset of Algol.

Some important languages that were developed in this time period include:

- 1951 - Regional Assembly Language
- 1952 - Autocode
- 1954 - FORTRAN
- 1958 - LISP
- 1958 - ALGOL
- 1959 - COBOL
- 1962 - APL
- 1962 - Simula
- 1964 - BASIC
- 1964 - PL/I

### 8.2.3 1967-1978

The period from the late 1960s to the late 1970s brought a major flowering of programming languages. Most of the major language paradigms now in use were invented in this period:

- Simula, invented in the late 1960s by Nygaard and Dahl as a superset of Algol 60, was the first language designed to support object-oriented programming. Smalltalk (mid 1970s) provided a complete ground-up design of an object-oriented language.
- C, an early systems programming language, was developed by Dennis Ritchie and Ken Thompson at Bell Labs between 1969 and 1973.
- Prolog, designed in 1972 by Colmerauer, Roussel, and Kowalski, was the first logic programming language.
- ML built a polymorphic type system (invented by Robin Milner in 1978) on top of Lisp, pioneering statically typed functional programming languages.

Each of these languages spawned an entire family of descendants, and most modern languages count at least one of them in their ancestry.

The 1960s and 1970s also saw considerable debate over the merits of "structured programming", which essentially meant programming without the use of GOTO. This debate was closely related to language design: some languages did not include GOTO, which forced structured programming on the programmer.

Some important languages that were developed in this time period include:

- 1970 - Pascal
- 1972 - C
- 1972 - Smalltalk
- 1972 - Prolog
- 1973 - ML
- 1978 - SQL

### 8.2.4 1980s

The 1980s were years of relative consolidation. C++ combined object-oriented and systems programming. The United States government standardized Ada, a systems programming language intended for use by defense contractors. In Japan and elsewhere, vast sums were spent investigating so-called "fifth generation" languages that incorporated logic programming constructs. The functional languages community moved to standardize ML and Lisp. Rather than inventing new paradigms, all of these movements elaborated upon the ideas invented in the previous decade.

However, one important new trend in language design was an increased focus on programming for large-scale systems through the use of modules, or large-scale organizational units of code. Modula, Ada, and ML all developed notable module systems in the 1980s. Module systems were often wedded to generic programming constructs.

Although major new paradigms for programming languages did not appear, many researchers expanded on the ideas of prior languages and adapted them to new contexts. For example, the languages of the Argus and Emerald systems adapted object-oriented programming to distributed systems.

The 1980s also brought advances in programming language implementation. The RISC movement in computer architecture postulated that hardware should be designed for compilers rather than for human assembly programmers. Aided by processor speed improvements that enabled increasingly aggressive compilation techniques, the RISC movement sparked greater interest in compilation technology for high-level languages.

Language technology continued along these lines well into the 1990s. However, the adoption of languages has always been driven by the adoption of new computer systems, and in the mid-1990s one of the most important new systems in computer history suddenly exploded in popularity.

Some important languages that were developed in this time period include:

- 1983 - Ada
- 1983 - C++
- 1985 - Eiffel
- 1987 - Perl
- 1989 - FL (Backus)

### 8.2.5 1990-2000

The rapid growth of the Internet in the mid-1990s was the next major historic event in programming languages. By opening up a radically new platform for computer systems, the Internet created an opportunity for new languages to be adopted. In particular, the Java programming language rose to popularity because of its early integration with the Netscape Navigator web browser, and various scripting languages achieved widespread use in developing customized applications for web servers. Neither of these developments represented much fundamental novelty in language design; for example, the design of Java was a more conservative version of ideas explored many years earlier in the Smalltalk community, but the widespread adoption of languages that supported features like garbage collection and strong static typing was a major change in programming practice.

Some important languages that were developed in this time period include:

- 1990 - Haskell

- 1990 - Python
- 1991 - Java
- 1993 - Ruby
- 1994 - PHP
- 2000 - C#

### 8.2.6 Current Trends

Programming language evolution continues, in both industry and research. Some current directions in programming languages include the following:

- Mechanisms for adding security and reliability verification to the language: extended static checking, information flow control, static thread safety.
- Alternative mechanisms for modularity: mixins, delegates, aspects.
- Component-oriented software development.
- Increased emphasis on distribution and mobility.
- Integration with databases, including XML and relational databases.
- Open Source as a developmental philosophy for languages, including recent languages such as Python, Ruby, and Squeak.
- Support for Unicode so that source code (program text) is not restricted to those characters contained in the ASCII character set; allowing, for example, use of non-Latin-based scripts or extended punctuation.

## 8.3 MACHINE LANGUAGE

This is a sequence of instructions written in the form of binary numbers consisting of 1s and 0s to which the computer responds directly. A machine language would have two parts.

The first part is the command or an operation that tells the computer what functions are to be performed. The second part of the instruction is the operand that tells the computer where to find or store the data on which the desired operation is to be performed. The machine language is the only one that computer can understand directly. In the earlier computers programmers had to translate instructions directly into machine language from the computers understood. This task was very difficult and very few programmers could do this job. So, this language was very difficult to understand. But the main advantage of this language is that it is faster in execution as the computer directly starts executing it.

## 8.4 ASSEMBLY LANGUAGE

To ease the burden of the programmer, mnemonic operation codes and symbolic addresses were developed during the early 1950s. The mnemonic refers to a memory aid. One of the first steps for improving the program preparation process was to substitute letter, symbols and mnemonics for the mnemonic machine-language operation codes. Today every computer has a mnemonic code, though the actual symbols vary among makes and models.

Machine language is still used by the computer as it process data but assembly language software first translates the specified operation code symbol into its machine language equivalent. Symbolic addressing is the practice of expressing an address not in terms of its absolute numeric location but in terms of symbols that are convenient for the programmers. Programmers no longer assign actual address numbers to symbolic data items. Now, they merely specify where they want the first location in the program to be and an assembly language program takes it from there, allocating locations for instructions and data.

A program written by a programmer in an assembly language is called a Source Program. After this source program has been converted into machine code by an assembler, it is referred to as an Object Program. The main advantage of assembly language is that the programs written in it are easy to understand as compared to the programs of machine language. And a big drawback is that they are machine-oriented, depending upon the model of processor being used.

Also, the programs written assembly language are slower to execute as compared to those in the machine language. An assembly language program is not as fast as the machine language. It has to be translated first into machine (binary) language code. A machine cannot execute an assembly language program directly as it is not in a binary form. An assembler is needed in order to translate an assembly language program into the object code executable by the machine.

## 8.5 HIGH LEVEL LANGUAGE (HLL)

The development of mnemonic technique and macro-instruction led, to the development of high level languages that are often oriented towards a particular class of problem. Unlike assembly programs, HLL programs may be used with different makes of computers with the little modifications. Thus, re-programming expense may be greatly reduced when new equipment is acquired.

The main advantages of HLL are as follows:

| | | |
|---|---|---|
| Readability | : | Programs written in these languages are more easily readable than those in assembly language and machine language. |
| Portability | : | Programs could be run on different machines with little or no changes. |
| Easy debugging | : | Errors are easy to find and remove. |
| Easy software development | : | Software could easily be developed using the HLL. |

The time and cost of creating machine and assembly languages was quite high. And this was the prime motivation for the development of high level languages.

## 8.6 GENERATION OF PROGRAMMING LANGUAGES

Programming language is a systematic notation by which we describe computational process. Computational process means steps for solving a problem. Programming language consists of symbols, characters and certain rules. There are various programming languages each with a specific purpose. Every language has its own instruction set that permits the operation to be performed.

If we want to make our computer to do something for us, we have to tell the computer what to do in a language that a computer understands called a machine language (language of 0 and 1). Communication with the computer is possible only if we develop a third language that can be understood by both us and the computer. Such a language is called a Programming Language.

Programming languages can be classified broadly in the following four categories:

- Low Level Language

- High Level Language
- Very High Level Language
- Natural Language

The programming languages are said to be low or high or very high or natural, depending on how far from the internal architecture of the machine the user is operating at. If we are operating in close proximity of the internal architecture by means of a machine-language or assembly language, then it is called a low-level language. Thus, low-level languages include machine-language and assembly language.

The languages used depending on the relative convenience of the users (like English or more natural way) is referred to as high-level, very high-level or natural language. Movement from machine language towards natural language puts away a user far away from internal details of the computer, thereby increasing the level of the language.

Another categorisation on the basis of the introduction of the programming languages is as follows:

| | | |
|---|---|---|
| First Generation Language | : | Machine Language |
| Second Generation Language | : | Assembly Language |
| Third Generation Language | : | High Level Languages |
| Fourth Generation Language | : | 4 GLs (4th Generation Languages) or Very High Level Language |
| Fifth Generation Language | : | Natural Language |

### 8.6.1 First-Generation Language: Machine Language

Inside a computer, data and program instructions are represented by a series of on-off signals that carry out a system of binary coding. Numbers, letters and other characters are represented by sequences of binary 1 and 0. This method of coding information is called Binary Notation.

The binary notation system for each individual computer is known as its Machine Language. It is the language understood by a computer because it is formed of binary numbers (0 and 1). 0's and 1's are actually the absence and presence of electric pulses. Instruction in machine language is a sequence of 0's and 1's. A computer's machine language establishes the proper electronic states, either on or off, for the recording and processing of instructions and data items.

In a machine language, each number, letter, or other character is represented by a specific combination of 1 or 0 codes. Each position within a coding system is known as a BIT (for Binary digIT). A series of bits, usually 8-bits called Byte, is used to represent a letter, number, or special character.

Instruction consists of two parts:

1. Operation Code (Op-Code)
2. Address or addresses of one or more memory location containing an operand or operands.

| Op-Code | Operand Addresses |
|---|---|

***Zero Address Instruction***

If there is no operand address field in the instruction specified, then it is called a Zero-address instruction. The following is the format of such an instruction:

| Op-Code |
|---|

**Example:** *A stack-organised computer does not use an address field for instruction like ADD, etc.*

PUSH X
PUSH Y
ADD

### *Single Address Instruction*

If there is only one address operand of a memory location/register in an instruction, then it is called single address instruction. Its format is:

| Op-Code | Addresses |
|---|---|

**Example:** *Instruction requiring an implied accumulator register (AC). For example, ADD instruction in the example given below*

LOAD X
ADD Y

### *Two Address Instruction*

If there are addresses of 2 memory locations after the OP code, it is called two address instruction. These instructions are quite common in commercial computers. Its format is:

| Op-Code | Addresses -1 | Addresses -2 |
|---|---|---|

**Example:** *The ADD & MOV instructions in the following example are 2-address instruction*

MOV R1, Y
ADD R1, X

### *Three Address Instruction*

If the instruction has addresses of 3 processor registers/ memory-locations following the OP code, it is called 3 address instruction. Its format is:

| Op-Code | Addresses -1 | Addresses -2 | Addresses -3 |
|---|---|---|---|

The advantage of 3-address instruction format is that the same results in short programs while evaluating arithmetic expressions.

**Example:** *The following example illustrates use of such 3-address instructions:*

ADD R1, X, Y
ADD R2, U, V
ADD Z, R1, R2

### Advantages of Writing Machine Language Program

1. Computer understands the machine language.
2. Time taken to execute program is less.

### Disadvantages

1. Programmer has to remember the following:
   a. Binary equivalent of the OP codes
   b. Binary equivalent of the addresses of the memory locations being used.
2. Machine language are machine dependent and thus the programs written for one machine are of no use for another machine which differs from the former in its internal architecture.
3. It is very difficult to debug machine language programs.
4. Time taken for developing programs in machine language is very consuming.
5. Size of machine language programs is very lengthy.
6. Programs written in machine language are quite sensitive to a minor change i.e. even to a bit change.

## 8.6.2 Second Generation Language: Assembly Language

To overcome the problems caused by machine language, a major step was the development of 'Symbolic Languages', which permit the use of mnemonic operation codes and symbolic addresses. 'Assembly Language' was developed in the early 1950s and thus it was considered as the second generation language.

Programs used mnemonic operation codes or symbolic address codes just similar to that of operation code and operand in machine language respectively. Mnemonic refers to memory aid which are extracted from various operators e.g. mnemonic code 'A' may be represented for ADD.

The program which converts assembly language instructions into machine codes are known as Assembler. Assembler converts source program into object-code, where a source program refers to the program written in assembly language and object-code refers to the program converted by the assembler into machine language.

### Advantages

i. Assembly Language is much simpler in understanding, learning and developing in comparison to machine language.
ii. Mnemonics are far easier to use than op-codes.
iii. Time taken for developing assembly language programs is comparatively much less than its corresponding machine-language program.
iv. Symbolic names were assigned to actual storage elements in the operand part.
v. Chances of committing mistakes while writing assembly language programs are quite less.
vi. Relieves from remembering all binary op-codes and addresses of memory locations.
vii. Saves time and the machine may be utilized efficiently with less error in program preparation.

## Disadvantages

i. Assembly language is again 'machine-oriented' language and thus differs from machine to machine which makes it peculiar to architecture.

ii. Execution of programs takes more time as it has to be converted into machine language.

iii. Assembly language is still at the machine level and all the rules concerning instructions and input formats have to be scrupulously observed.

### 8.6.3 Third Generation Languages (3GLs):High-Level Languages (HLLs)

With the languages introduced by the third generation of computer programming, words and commands (instead of just symbols and numbers) were being used. These languages therefore, had syntax that was much easier to understand.

Languages in which instructions are given in English-like text rather than in binary digits that computer understands are known as high-level languages. Instructions used are termed as macro instructions which mean that a single instruction may produce several lines of machine language codes. Mnemonic technique further enhances the power of high level languages.

These languages are also referred to as Procedural Languages because these languages require every step of the task to submit to the computer in the form of a procedure.

High level languages may further be classified into following classes according their areas of application:

- Scientific Programming Languages
- Business Programming Languages
- General or Multipurpose Languages
- Specialized Programming Languages
- Interactive Programming Languages
- Object-Oriented Languages

#### 8.6.3.1 Scientific Programming Languages

High-level programming languages used for scientific applications are known as scientific programming languages.

Examples

i. FORTRAN (FORmula TRANslation)

ii. ALGOL (ALOGOrithmic Language)

iii. IAL (International Algebraic Language) [Later named as ALGOL]

iv. PL/I (Programming Language I)

v. COGO (COordinate GeOmetry Language)

vi. APL (A Programming Language)

vii. Pascal (Named after a great scientist Blaise Pascal)

etc.

#### 8.6.3.2 Business Programming Languages

High-level languages used for business applications are known as Business Programming Languages.

Examples:

i. COBOL (COmmon Business Oriented Language)

ii. PL/I (Programming Language I)

etc.

#### 8.6.3.3 General or Multipurpose Languages

General or multipurpose languages are equally effective for business, scientific, graphical and other applications. IBM was very much in the forefront of progress at this time and saw the opportunity in providing a computer system for a wide range of users, and following this IBM 360 emerged. To accommodate the new hardware PL/I was the most popular general purpose language. Later on many such languages came into existence.

Examples:

i. PL/I (Programming Language I)

ii. Pascal

iii. BASIC (Beginner's All-purpose Symbolic Instruction Code)

iv. C

v. JOVIAL (Jules' own version if International Language)

vi. Ada

etc.

#### 8.6.3.4 Specialized Programming Languages

High-level languages used for specialized applications are known as Specialized Programming Languages.

Examples:

i. LISP (LISt Processing)

ii. PROLOG (PROgramming in LOGic)

iii. Ada (Named after a first lady programmer Augusta Ada)

iv. LOGO (for teaching geometry, mathematics and programming to children)

v. RPG (Report Program Generator)

vi. Modula-2

vii. APT (Automatic Programming Tool)

viii. NELIAC (Navy Electronics Laboratory International Algol Compilers)

ix. CORAL (For Real-time Applications)

x. FORTH (Originally developed to be used by astronomers & later used for process control applications)

xi. SIMULA/ SIMULA 67 (Simulation Language)

xii. GPSS (General Purpose Simulation System) Language

xiii. SNOBOL (StriNg-Oriented symBOlic Language)

xiv. SIMSCRIPT (Simulation Script) Language

etc.

#### 8.6.3.5 Interactive Programming Languages

High-level programming languages used for real-time and time-sharing applications are known as Interactive Programming Languages.

Example:

i. BASIC (Beginner's All-purpose Symbolic Instruction Code)

ii. APL (A Programming Language)

iii. Interactive FORTRAN

iv. QUICKTRAN (Subset of FORTRAN and designed for use with multi-access systems)

etc.

#### 8.6.3.6 Object-Oriented Languages

It is another category of languages which are object-oriented and these languages must be capable of supporting:

- Classes and Objects
- Encapsulation of objects
- Polymorphism
- Inheritance between classes

Examples:

i. C++

ii. Smalltalk

iii. Eiffel

iv. Simula

v. Object Pascal

vi. Object C

vii. CLOS, etc.

### 8.6.4 Fourth Generation Languages (4GLs): Very High Level Languages (VHLLs)

The syntax used in 4GL is very close to human language, an improvement from the previous generation of languages. 4GL languages are typically used to access databases and include SQL and ColdFusion, among others.

These languages are also referred to as Non-procedural Languages because these are designed for the end users that matches with application procedure rather than the algorithmic procedure to achieve the desired results. The aim of the 4th generation is to make languages much more problem oriented. The 4GLs are designed to enable users who are not trained programmers to develop applications. Often it is based on a non-procedural language with relational database support.

Moreover, 4GLs are languages that were developed as a result of the dissatisfaction of business users with large conventional languages like COBOL. These users were often not professional programmers who wished to obtain quick results from data stored in a computer.

The term 4GL encompasses:

a. Presentation Language e.g. Report Generator, Query Language.
b. Special Languages e.g. language expressions/phrases used in Databases & Spreadsheets.
c. Application Generator that define, input, update and report data to build applications.
d. Very high level languages are used to generate application code.

Looking analytically into the wide-perspective of 4GLs, these can be classified mainly into three categories:

- Application Generators
- Production-Oriented 4GLs
- End-User-Oriented 4GLs

### 8.6.4.1 Application Generator (or Production-Oriented) 4GLs

These languages generate solutions for routine applications. Typical operations include data entry, ideally with full checking, and updating of files or databases.

These languages are designed primarily for computer professionals which help them in creating Information Systems. An application generator consists of a software system with numbers of program modules, pre-programmed for various functions. These languages are aimed at producing higher productivity in comparison to 3GLs for a specified application.

Examples:

i. AG's Natural 2
ii. FOCUS
iii. NATURAL
iv. PACBASE
v. ADR's (Application Definition Records) Ideal
vi. FUSION
vii. MAPPER System
viii. UFO
ix. LIC II
x. PACBASE, etc.

### 8.6.4.2 End-User-Oriented (or Query Languages) 4GLs

This type of 4GL is End-user Oriented Language which primarily specifies what the desired output should be instead of stressing the details of how the input or intermediate data should be manipulated. Users write down programs in 4GL to query a database and to create databases.

Examples:

i. QBE (Query-by-example)
ii. SQL (Structured Query Language)
iii. DATATRIEVE
iv. HAL
v. EASYTRIEVE PLUS
vi. INQUIRE
vii. Honeywell PDQ
viii. QMF
ix. INTELLECT

#### 8.6.4.3 Decision-Support and Financial Planning 4GLs

These languages were developed to help the user to make informed and thereafter appropriate decisions. These languages provide the user with facilities to build databases and then to perform statistical calculations, such as an analysis of trends on data.

Decision support systems are interactive software designed to help managers make decisions. Financial planning languages are particular kinds of decision support systems that are employed for mathematical, statistical and forecasting procedures among other uses. Decision-support languages are usually business-oriented and are typically used in the planning stage for analysing projected financial investments. These may include graphics facilities to enhance the display of material. These languages range from simple spreadsheets like Lotus 1-2-3, VisiCalc, etc. to languages with sophisticated statistical and operation research features for decision-making. Most of these languages include some important facilities viz. windowing, data scrolling, etc.

Examples:

i. Metaphor
ii. Info Center/1
iii. FCS
iv. IFPS
v. EXPRESS
vi. Command Center
vii. SPSS-X
viii. Application System, etc.

### Advantages of 4GLs

i. These may be easily used by non-programming end-users as well as professional programmers.
ii. Improves productivity due to easier programming, updation, and maintenance.
iii. Default alternatives are built-in and thus the end-user need not specify these alternatives thereby reducing the size of instruction(s)
iv. Hardly requires its staff to undergo a very intensive training.

v. Result-oriented approach is followed which emphasize on what is to be done rather than how the same is to be done.

vi. 4GLs are typically database-oriented and thus relieves the user from knowing most of the programming skills.

**Disadvantages**

i. Less efficient than 3GLs because 4GLs require larger processor speed to perform operations more efficiently.

### 8.6.5 Fifth Generation Languages (5GLs): Natural Languages

These are known as 5th generation language and are often called Natural Languages because of their resemblance to the natural spoken English Language. These languages are still in the development stages. Application of these languages will be quite beneficial in the area of Artificial Intelligence (AI) and Expert Systems (ES).

5GLs are currently being used for neural networks. A neural network is a form of artificial intelligence that attempts to imitate how the human mind works.

Natural languages have the following two characteristics:

i. These are developed to enable the computer to become "intelligent" and "smart".

ii. These are designed to help a computer establish communication with humans in a more natural way.

Natural languages refer to software that enables computer to accept, interpret, and execute instructions in the 'native' language of the end-user i.e. in English language. These languages are also referred to as Knowledge-based Language because natural languages are used to interact with a base of knowledge on some subject. The use of a natural language to access a Knowledge-base is called a Knowledge-based System.

**Example:** *Two popular natural languages are PROLOG and LISP.*

## 8.7 CLASSIFICATION OF PROGRAMMING LANGUAGES

Every computer programming language is not capable for all kinds of tasks or areas of applications. There are limitations, and actually, different languages are used for different tasks. Depending upon the purpose the language is used primarily for, these can be grouped in the following categories:

- Software Languages
- Procedural or Procedure-Oriented Languages
- GUI-based Languages
- Object-Oriented Languages
- Web Languages

### 8.7.1 Software languages

These languages are used for creating executable programs. These can create anything from simple console programs that print some text to the screen to entire operating systems. These vary greatly in terms of power and complexity. Few of these languages are briefly discussed below:

### C

It is a general-purpose structured programming language. C is characterized by the ability to write very concise source programs. The compiler of C is commonly available for the computers of all sizes. The compilers are usually compact and they generate object programs that are small and highly efficient as compared to the programs written in any other language. The programs written in the C language are high portable; the program written for one computer with very few changes can run on another computer. The reason for this is that C relegates most computer-dependent features in its library functions. Thus every version of C is accomplished by its own set to library functions.

Dennis Ritchie developed C in 1970s at Bell Telephone laboratories. It was the modified versions of two earlier languages, called BCPL and B, which were also developed at Bell Laboratories.

Originally designed to be a systems programming language but since then has proven itself to be able to be used for various software applications such as business programs, engineering programs, and even games. The UNIX operating system is written in C.

### C++

Descendant of the C language. The difference between the two languages is that C++ is object-oriented. C++ was developed by Bjarne Stroustrup at Bell Labs and is a very popular language for graphical applications.

### Visual Basic

A language developed by Microsoft based on the BASIC language. Visual Basic is used for creating Windows applications. The VBScript language (also developed by Microsoft) is based on Visual Basic.

### Java

Java was developed by James Gosling the chief programmer of Sun Microsystems. Java is an object-oriented programming language that was developed after C++. Java was designed to be small, simple and portable across platforms. James Gosling started a project on controlling consumer electronics devices with a language C++. After some time he found that C++ was not suitable for the project. They faced many problems with the complicated aspects of C++, program bugs and memory leaks. So, Gosling decided to develop a new language that could overcome these problems.

It is a powerful and flexible language that can be used to create applets (a program that is executed from within another program) that run inside web pages as well as software applications. Things you can do with Java include interacting with the user, creating graphical programs, reading from files, and more. Java is often confused with Javascript, but they are two different languages.

As Gosling liked the object oriented features of C++, he decided to take C++ as the base for the new language. He developed a new language, Oak, which was later, called Java.

## 8.7.2 Procedure-oriented Programming Languages

A type of programming where a structured method of creating programs is used. With procedure-oriented programming, a problem is broken up into parts and each part is then broken up into further parts. All these parts are known as procedures. They are separate but work together when needed. A main program centrally controls them all.

Some of the procedure-oriented languages are discussed below.

## LOGO

LOGO was designed by Seymour Papert who was a teacher in the USA. He designed this language so that the children could learn computers by drawing pictures. Most of its commands enable us to draw pictures. This is one of the reasons why LOGO is called a graphic language. The usage of LOGO is based on a friendly little animal called the TURTLE. It is the name given to the LOGO cursor. It looks like a small triangle. The TURTLE has a head which is the upper tip of the triangle. It can be turned around its center in all direction and it can also move forward and backward.

## FORTRAN

It is the short form for FORmula TRANslation. As the name suggests it is used extensively in numeric data types such as an integer, real, float and complex. It was the only language developed by the IBM in 1957. Since then, it has been modified into many versions and the latest version FORTRAN 99, is currently available in the markets. The original work on FORTRAN was started in 1954. As the result of this effort, FORTRAN was introduced in 1957 for IBM 704 computer. FORTRAN is very useful for carrying out scientific and mathematical computations.

The main feature of FORTRAN is very useful for carrying out scientific and mathematical computations. The main feature of FORTRAN is that it can handle the complex numbers very easily. But the syntax of FORTRAN is very rigid. FORTRAN language is not suitable for a large amount of data. But, it is not suitable for a large amount of data. So, it is not used for business programming applications.

## COBOL

COBOL stands for Common Business Oriented Language and is one of the popular languages used for business applications. The language has provisions that make computerization of business data processing procedures relatively easy. COBOL is suitable for processing large volumes of data and several reports can generate using COBOL based on the stored data. COBOL programs are characterized by their easy readability due to their verbose syntax and good data organizations ad file handling.

COBOL is an English like language with instruction coded using self-documenting English words rather than short abbreviation. Also, the rules of programming in COBOL conform to many of the rules for writing. Due to its similarity with English, COBOL programs are easy to read and write.

Thus people in business, who rely on computer output but have no computer expertise, can understand the programs written in COBOL. That is why COBOL is called a self-documenting language which is self-explanatory. COBOL was initially developed in 1959 by a group called the CODASYL (Conference On DAta SYstems Languages) Committee with the objectives of developing a standard business-oriented language for which all major manufacturers would provide compilers.

The American National Standards Institute (ANSI) then formed an NASO COBOL committee to develop more satisfactory standards for the language. This led to the availability of ANSI COBOL in 1969. This standard was, however, modified and finally, it approved a standard for COBOL in 1985 and is it is also referred to as COBOL 85.

## BASIC

Basic stands for Beginners' All-Purpose Symbolic Instruction Code. It is the most popular computer programming language. He main characteristic of BASIC is to handle both mathematical and business problems; this language was developed specifically for the time-sharing environment but can so be used as a standard programming language in batch-processing environment. This language is easy to understand. But the main problem in BASIC is that most versions of this language do not support indexed files.

### PROLOG

Prolog stands for PROgramming in LOGic. Prolog was developed in France in 1973. Prolog is very popular in Japan where it is adopted as the official programming language for the fifth generation computers.

As the name suggests, PROLOG lays stress on the usage of logic to solve problems. PROLOG is basically known as a theorem-providing system, using a formal logic technique known as predicate calculus to prove the truth of propositions from a set of axioms.

PROLOG is a conventional language. It waits for us to type in facts and rules that are related to the program that we want to solve. Then, if we ask the right type of questions, PROLOG would work out and display it on the screen.

So, we can say that the computer programming in PROLOG consists of the following steps:

- Declaring some facts about objects and their relationship.
- Defining some rules about objects and relationship.
- Assuming questions about objects and their relationship.

### PASCAL

Pascal is a high Level Language that was developed by the Professor Nickalus Wirth at Eidgenossisehe Technisehe Houcheshule (ETH) in Zurich, Switzerland. The first report on the language appeared in the literature in 1971 and revised reports, describing the language with its improvements, appeared in 1972 and 1973. The first Pascal Reference Manual for Pascal programming was produced in 1974.

Pascal is a general-purpose language that can be used for a wide range of numeric and non numeric applications. The primary objectives behind the development of Pascal were as follows:

- The language should be efficient to implement and easy to execute on modern computers.
- The language should be used for teaching the important concept of computer programming.
- The language should be used for the development of well-structured and well organized programs.

The aforementioned features make Pascal a very good introductory programming language.

## 8.7.3 GUI Based Languages

Few of GUI-based languages are discussed below:

### Visual Basic

What is Visual Basic? The "Visual" part refers to the method used to create the graphical user interface (GUI). Rather than writing numerous lines of code to describe the appearance and location of interface elements, you simply add pre-built objects into place on screen. If you've ever used a drawing program such as Paint, you already have most of the skills necessary to create an effective user interface.

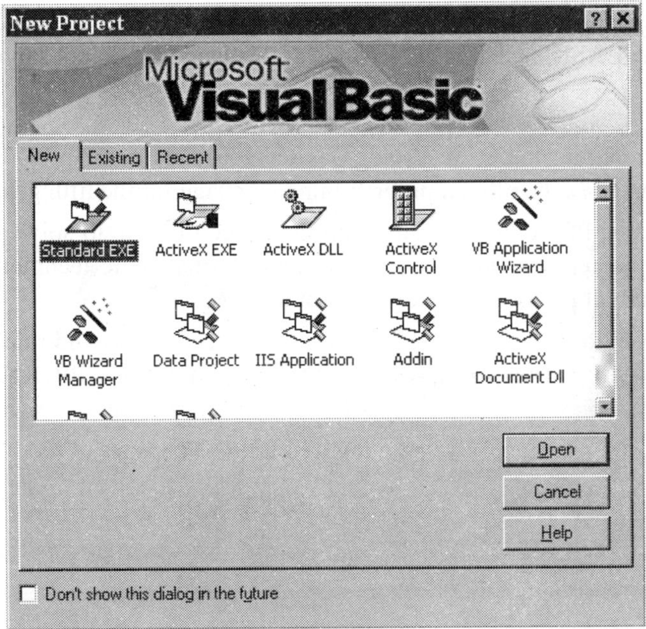


**Figure 8.1:** Visual Basic

The "Basic" part refers to the BASIC (Beginners All-Purpose Symbolic Instruction Code) language, a language used by more programmers than any other language in the history of computing. Visual Basic has evolved from the original BASIC language and now contains several hundred statements, functions, and keywords, many of which relate directly to the Windows GUI. Beginners can create useful applications by learning just a few of the keywords, yet the power of the language allows professionals to accomplish anything that can be accomplished using any other Windows programming language. The Visual Basic programming language is not unique to Visual Basic. The Visual Basic programming system, Applications Edition included in Microsoft Excel, Microsoft Access, and many other Windows applications uses the same language. The Visual Basic Scripting Edition (VBScript) is a widely used scripting language and a subset of the Visual Basic language. The investment you make in learning Visual Basic will carry over to these other areas.

## Visual C++

Since Visual Basic and Visual C++ are similar in nature, you can assume that one is offshoot of Basic and the other is offshoot of C++. If you have graduated from Basic you will use Visual Basic and if you have been using C++, then Visual C++ is for you. However, the similarities end here, both of them are very useful development tools and differ a lot in usage.

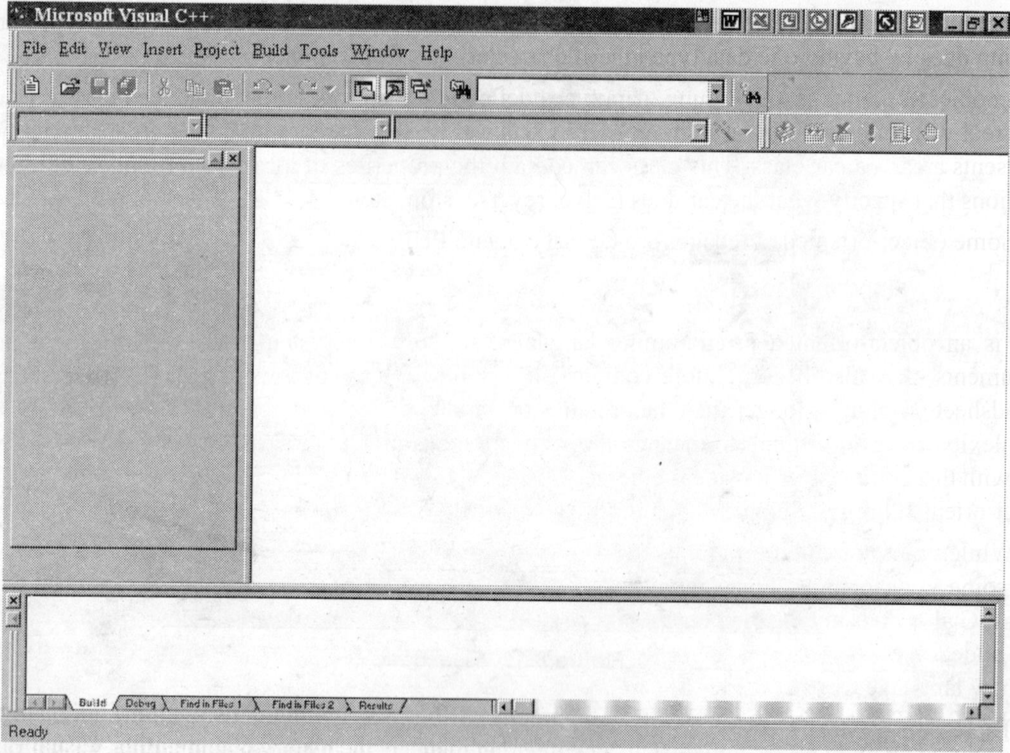


**Figure 8.2:** Visual C++

## C#

It is known as C sharp. Since both C and C++ are DOS based programming languages and do not support Windows and Internet, Microsoft, the producers of C# have decided to produce something which can take care of this problem. So the net result is C#. It enables programmers in quickly building solutions for the Microsoft.net platform. If Visual Basic and Visual C++ were offshoot of Basic and C++, then you can imagine that C# is the offshoot of C.

## VB.NET

It is the latest version of Visual Basic for the Internet. It is quite powerful development tool at par with other developing tools. With this you can create projects for Windows and Internet. Visual Basic .Net is a complete development environment; every tool you will need to create your Visual Basic projects is accessed from within Visual Basic.

The Visual Basic environment is called the IDE, short for Integrated Development Environment, and its design framework in which you build applications. To work with Visual Basic projects, you must use Visual Basic IDE.

## 8.7.4 Object Oriented Programming Languages

A type of programming where data types representing data structures are defined by the programmer as well as their properties and the things that can be done with them. With object-oriented programming, programmers can also create relationships between data structures and create new data types based on existing ones by having one data type inherit characteristics from another one.

In object-oriented programming, data types defined by the programmer are called classes (templates for a real world object to be used in a program). For example, a programmer can create a data type that represents a car - a car class. This class can contain the properties of a car (color, model, year, etc.) and functions that specify what the car does (drive, reverse, stop, etc.)

Some object-oriented languages are C++, Java, and PHP.

### C++

C++ is an object-oriented programming language. As software systems develop into more powerful instruments, they also become more complex. Every new release of a word processor, a database, or a spreadsheet program is longer than the previous one and contains more features. This increasing size and complexity makes it difficult to manage the software development process. As programmers struggle to deal with this complexity, new ideas emerge. One collection of these ideas is based on a philosophy called object-oriented programming.

While object-oriented programs can be written in languages such as C or BASIC, these languages lack some vital features. For example, C provides no mechanism to hide variables from unauthorized access. C also does not enable one class to be declared as a subclass of another. These and other features were added to the C language by Dr. Bjarne Stroustrup at AT &T's Bell Labs in the early 1980s. He called this new language C++.

There is no standard definition for the C++ language. At any given time, it is classified into three states-called traditional C++, contemporary C++ and future C++. Traditional C++ is the language as it had existed in release in AT & T versions and which is supported by all the major compilers. Contemporary C++ consists of traditional C++ with some new features which are approved by e committee but implemented by only a few compilers. Future C++ is the language which is under discussion in the committee with new features that have been approved but not yet implemented.

### Java

Java was developed by James Gosling the chief programmer of Sun Microsystems. Java is an object-oriented programming language that was developed after C++. Java was designed to be small, simple and portable across platforms. James Gosling started a project on controlling consumer electronics devices with a language C++. After some time he found that C++ was not suitable for the project. They faced many problems with the complicated aspects of C++, program bugs and memory leaks. So, Gosling decided to develop a new language that could overcome these problems.

As Gosling liked the object oriented features of C++, he decided to take C++ as the base for the new language. He developed a new language, Oak, which was later, called Java.

### Java Vs C++

Java is most popular because it is used for Internet programming. Previously, only HTML was used for creating web pages. But it is difficult to depend only upon one language for developing the application as a typical diversity exists on Internet in terms of hardware and software. Servers on Internet have to store multiple copies of the same program that has been compiled for different hardware and software environments.

Java is the answer to these problems that exist on the Internet. In java, you can write a single program (called an applet) that is platform-independent. Platform-independent means that the program can be used at any platform with any operating system. The applet can be executed on Internet. Java is an object oriented-language just like C++ but it has some difference as compared to C++. IN Java, the following features are prominent:

- No pointers
- No multiple inheritance
- No goto
- No operator overloading

In C++ we can allocate and deallocate the memory by new and delete. The Java language has an embedded auto garbage collection mechanism. The garbage collector simplifies Java programming by automatically freeing memory area when it is not required.

So, Java is simple as compared to C++. Java code is divided into classes. Java is like any client\server model. Java is reliable. A reliable language is one that allows us to write programs that do not crash when least expected and would also de but-free.

Java is comparable in speed to other languages like C++. Java has sophisticated multitasking features that have been integrated into the language which make it very simple to use and at the same time very robust.

## 8.7.5 Web Languages

These languages are used for creating and editing pages on the web. These are capable of doing anything from putting plain text on a webpage, to accessing and retrieving data from a database. These vary greatly in terms of power and complexity. Few of these languages are briefly discussed below:

### HTML (Hyper Text Markup Language)

HTML is the core language of the world wide web that is used to define the structure and layout of web pages by using various tags and attributes. Although a fundamental language of the web, HTML is static - content created with it does not change. HTML is used to specify the content a webpage will contain, not how the page functions.

### XML (Extensible Markup Language)

XML is a language developed by the W3C (World Wide Web Consortium) which works like HTML, but unlike HTML, allows for custom tags that are defined by programmers. XML allows for the transmission of data between applications and organizations through the use of its custom tags.

### Javascript

Javascript is a language developed by Netscape used to provide dynamic and interactive contents on web pages. With Javascript, it is possible to communicate with HTML, create animations, create calculators, validate forms, and more. Javascript should not be confused with Java languages.

### VBScript

VBScript language a is Scripting Edition of Visual Basic language developed by Microsoft that works only in Microsoft's Internet Explorer web browser and web browsers based on the Internet Explorer engine such as FlashPeak's Slim Browser. VBScript can be used to print dates, make calculations, interact with the user, and more. VBScript is based on Visual Basic, but it is much simpler.

### PHP

PHP is a recursive acronym of Hypertext Preprocessor. PHP is a powerful language used for many tasks such as data encryption, database access, and form validation. PHP was originally created in 1994 By Rasmus Lerdorf.

### Java

Java is a powerful and flexible language created by Sun MicroSystems that can be used to create applets (a program that is executed from within another program) that run inside web pages as well as software applications. Things you can do with Java include interacting with the user, creating graphical programs, reading from files, and more. Java is often confused with Javascript, but they are two different languages.

## 8.8 PROBLEM SOLVING WITH COMPUTERS

Problem solving with computers involves following several steps:

1. Clearly define the problem
2. Analyse the problem and formulate a method to solve it
3. Describe the solution in the form of an algorithm
4. Draw a flowchart of the algorithm
5. Write the computer program
6. Compile and run the program (debugging)
7. Test the program (debugging)
8. Interpretation of results

All the above steps are discussed below.

1. Clearly define the problem: This can be trivial for simple problems but solutions to complex problems can be ineffective if the problem is not clearly defined. A great deal of time can be wasted if the problems are not clearly identified and defined at the beginning of a project.
2. Analyse the problem and formulate a method to solve it: Understanding the problem and choosing a correct method to solve it can be difficult especially for the more complex problem. A poorly understood problem or invalid method can lead to a bad solution. Again this becomes important for more complex problems.
3. Describe the solution in the form of an algorithm: At this stage the solution is stated for the first time in the form of a written algorithm. The algorithm gives a step-by-step description of the solution.
4. Draw a flowchart of the algorithm: This gives the logical flow of the solution in a diagrammatic form, and provides a plan from which the computer program can be best written. The logical flow of the algorithm can be seen by tracing through the flowchart and, if necessary, writing down the evolution of numerical values.

5. Write the computer program: Here you use your knowledge of the programming language to convert the logical flow of the solution in the flowchart/algorithm to a set of instructions (the source code) for the computer.
6. Compile and run the program: Program development always involves a cycle of writing-compiling-running the program until it is complete, free of errors, and works in the way the programmer expects it to work. Debugging (removal of errors from a program) usually involves:
   - correcting compile-time errors
   - correcting link-time errors
   - correcting run-time errors
   - correcting errors that give unexpected or wrong results
7. Test the program: After the initial stage of debugging the program can be tested more rigorously. Various input values can be given and the output checked. If possible, the program should be checked against a problem that has a known solution. Note that the absence of unexpected results does not mean that the program is correct; i.e. the output could still be wrong! For large programs it is usual to check that each section of program does what you intend it to do; this usually involves placing output statements throughout the program, the output statements are removed after each section has been successfully tested.
8. Interpretation of results: If a program simple outputs the mean value of a list of numbers then there is clearly no need for interpretation. However, it is sometimes necessary to make some analysis of the output before you can say you have arrived at the solution. Always think carefully when taking results from a computer - how was the result generated? What assumptions were made? How should the results be applied to solve the problem?

### Verification and Validation

If the program has an important application - for example to calculate student grades or guide a rocket then the program MUST be tested properly to make sure it does what the programmer intends it to do and that it is actually a valid solution to the problem. The tests are commonly divided as follows:

- Verification - verify that program does what you intended it to do; steps 7(8) above attempt to do this.
- Validation - does the program actually solve the original problem i.e. is it valid? This goes back to steps 1 and 2 - if you get these steps wrong then your program is not a valid solution.

## 8.8 CONCEPT OF PROGRAMMING

Computer Programming is the art of making a computer do what you want it to do. At the very simplest level it consists of issuing a sequence of commands to a computer to achieve an objective.

Essentially, a computer (guided by the instructions in programs) performs three basic functions:

1. It receives data (input)
2. It process data by various computations and actions (processing)
3. It emits data (output)

These functions are accomplished by giving the computer a program consisting of a sequence of statements.

The profession or "art" of programming deals with

- analyzing a problem
- developing a plan for solving the problem (algorithm)
- designing and coding a program
- testing and debugging
- implementation and maintenance

A programmer is a person who uses skills in each of these areas to solve problems with computer programs.

There are two aspects to computers. One, you use the computer and the other is to make the computer work for you. This first one is very easy. You run the program which has been designed and created for use. But, it is the second which is very important. This covers the programming part. With programming you design the process where you ask the computer to work according to you. Here the privilege of making any error is not there. Because, you are going to be tested by the computer, which is very accurate.

Programming is one of the step in system development cycle and it starts once the detailed design is over and program specification have been obtained. Flow charts are the first tool developed for design. Flow charts are drawn up as a pictorial guide by programmers for planning the procedure for the solution of a program.

### 8.8.1 Computer Program

A computer program (also software, or just a program) is a sequence of instructions written to perform a specified task with a computer. A computer requires programs to function, typically executing the program's instructions in a central processor. The program has an executable form that the computer can use directly to execute the instructions. The same program in its human-readable source code form, from which executable programs are derived (e.g., compiled), enables a programmer to study and develop its algorithms.

Computer source code is often written by computer programmers. Source code is written in a programming language that usually follows one of two main paradigms: imperative or declarative programming. Source code may be converted into an executable file (sometimes called an executable program or a binary) by a compiler and later executed by a central processing unit. Alternatively, computer programs may be executed with the aid of an interpreter, or may be embedded directly into hardware.

Computer programs may be categorized along functional lines: system software and application software. Two or more computer programs may run simultaneously on one computer, a process known as multitasking.

Systematic notations for these steps are the computation steps referred to as programming languages. A person engaged in the activity of programming is referred to as programmer.

### 8.8.2 Characteristics of a Good Program

A good program has to have the following characteristics:

| | |
|---|---|
| Accuracy | The program must do what it is supposed to do and meet the criteria laid down in its specification. |

| | |
|---|---|
| Reliability | The program must ALWAYS do what it is supposed to do and never crash. |
| Efficiency | The program must use the available store space and resources in such a way that the system's speed is not wasted. |
| Robustness | The program should cope with invalid data without stopping with no indication as to the cause and without creating errors. |
| Usability | The program must be easy to use and well documented. |
| Maintainability | The program must be easy to amend, having good structuring and documentation. |
| Readability | The code in the program must be well laid out and explained with comments. Since it is that you are one who is going to read the program always, there will be others too. |
| Portability | It should be seen that the program is easy to transfer to other machines as well. |

### 8.8.3 Steps in Program Development

The following basic steps are involved in writing computer programs:

1. Problem identification
2. Task analysis and data analysis
3. Output identification
4. Designing the solution
5. Data validation
6. Implementation and debugging
7. Final documentation and maintenance

These steps are mostly performed in sequence mentioned, however, in some cases you can do otherwise too.

## 8.9 PROGRAMMING PARADIGMS

It is not that there are no rules for writing programs, there are a few of them. We must adhere to these rules to write good programs. Some of these are discussed below.

### 8.9.1 Unstructured Programming

This type of programming is straight forward programming. Here, everything is in a sequential manner. It does not involve any decision making. A general model of these linear programs is:

1. Read a data value.
2. Compute an intermediate result.
3. Use the intermediate result to compute the desired answer.
4. Print the answer.
5. Stop.

### 8.9.2 Structured Programming

Structured programs are the ones that are divided into functional modules and arranged in an hierarchical order instead of programs written in a sequence. Structured programming refers to the process in which we break the overall job down into separate piece of modules. These modules, in turn, are broken down into smaller pieces which can also be further subdivided. Modules must be chosen in such a way that we can specify how they have to interact. In effect, there is a contact between each pair of modules.

## Advantages of Structured Programming

1. Decreases the complexity of the program by breaking it down into smaller logical units.
2. Allows several programmers to perform coding simultaneously.
3. Allows common functions to be written once and then used in all the programs needing it.
4. Decreases debugging time, because modules make it easier to isolate errors.
5. Amendments to single modules do not affect the rest of the program.
6. It saves time to use modular structures rather than using self made structure. If a job can be done well by using what is already available and known to be well tried and tested then trying out something new for sake of it, is a waste of effort.
7. Standard method; so, less time is required in writing programs.
8. It is easier to name modules in such a way that they are easy to find in the documentation and consistent.

Various characteristics of Structured Programs can be listed out as:

1. Two-way decision statements are based on IF...THEN, IF...THEN...ELSE and nested IF statements.
2. A rule of thumb is that the modules should not be more than one half page long. If they are longer than this, they should preferably be split into two or more sub-modules.
3. The programs are based on top-down modular design. In other words, the problem at hand is analyzed or broken down into major components, each of which is again broken down it necessary. Therefore, the process involves working from the most general down to the most specific. The design of the modules is reflected in hierarchy charts.
4. Loops and not custom designed with the use of the GO TO statement, but are based on the consistent use of WHILE...WEND and FOR...NEXT. In WHILE...WEND, the loop is based on the truth of a condition and in FOR...NEXT, on a counting process and the number of repetitions that can easily be predicted.
5. Each module has one entry point and one exit point. The GOTO statement is never used to jump from one module in the program to another.

## 8.9.3 Procedural Programming

As the name sounds it is based on certain procedures. A procedure call is used to invoke the procedure. After the execution of statements, flow of control returns to the position from where call was made. Procedures can be further divided into sub procedures. With the help of sub procedures, programs can be written more structured and error free. For example, if the procedure is correct, every time it is used it produces correct results.

### 8.9.4 Modular Programming

One of the key concepts in the application of programming discipline is the design of a program as a set of units referred to as blocks or modules. A program module is defined as the part of a program that perform a separate function, e.g., input, input validation, processing of one type of input. A program module may be quite large, so that it may be further divided into logical sub modules. The process of subdivision continues until all modules are of manageable size in terms of complexity of logic and numbers of instructions.

#### Advantages of Modular Programming

1. Program maintenance becomes easier because the affected modules can be quickly identified and changed.
2. If a programmer leaves the project midway, it is easier for someone else to take over a set of self contained modules.
3. In a very large project, several programmers may be working on a single program. Using a modular approach, each programmer can be given a specific set of modules to work on. This enables the whole program to be finshed sooner.
4. Some modules will be standard procedures used again and again in different programs or parts of the same program.
5. More experienced programmers can be given a more complex module to write and the junior programmers can work on the simpler modules.
6. Since module is small, it is simpler to understand it as a unit of code. It is therefore easier to test and debug, especially if its purpose is clearly defined and documented.
7. A large project becomes easier to monitor and control.
8. Modules can be tested independently, thereby shortening the time taken to get the whole program working.

## 8.10 SYSTEM DESIGN TECHNIQUES

Following are the main designing techniques called Top Down and Bottom Up.

### 8.10.1 Top Down Design

Top down design approach is performed in a special way. The main program is written first. It is tested before sub programs are written. To do this, the actual sub programs are replaced with stubs. The stubs simply test to see if the data is passed correctly. After the main program is written and checked each module is written and tested in turn. This should first be done without the main program in order to isolate a stub if an error occurs.

If the module and the main program run properly then the next module is written and checked and so on. To describe the program at its highest level, we use something called the universal program and then by a process of stepwise refinement work out the details of each part of the program.

#### Advantages of Top Design

1. At each stage, the sub programs are tested by themselves and then the main program is tested. Whenever modules are added, they are tested with the main program so if any error occurs it will

probably be in a module only and this will be easy to debut.

2. It is desirable for modules to be kept small in general. As far as possible a module should be less than 100 statement lines long.

**Top down implementation**

1. Start with a very simple and short statement of what the program does. This is the top level in the design.
2. Go to the next level of details for the whole program, try to describe the program as sequence, selection or repetition of main tasks. Each of these tasks should be complete in itself but will be described in greater detail at the next level of program development. These tasks are called modules. A module should have just one entry point and just one exit point.
3. This process is repeated step by step and at each step all the modules at that levels are refined or developed to the next level of details. This is called step-wise-refinement. The step-wise-refinement stops when there are sufficient details for the procedure to be written in a programming language.
4. At the intermediate steps in the refinement, pseudo code or flowcharts are used to represent the procedure.
5. At every state unnecessary details are left out.
6. It is important that at each state the individual modules are checked to make sure that they perform the correct actions on the appropriate data.

### 8.10.2 Bottom Up Design

A bottom up approach would be to write the most basic subroutines in the hierarchy first and then use them to make more sophisticated subroutines. The pure bottom approach is generally not recommended because it is difficult to anticipate which low level subroutines will be needed for any particular program. It can often be a useful first step to produce a library of basic functions and procedures before embarking on a major project. In the bottom up approach it is usually assumed that the basic routines created will be general enough to be used more than once.

Using the subroutines, to construct a program, save yourself repeating the same lines of code by reusing it. A routine that is used many times has a very difficult status to those higher in the hierarchy. It is more like a basic instruction in the programming language than a large scale program component.

## 8.11 COMPUTER PROGRAM LIFE CYCLE

No computer program is ever lasting. Each program overgrows itself. A program is actually the result of your own logic and thought process. If you think something today then it is not possible that you will think the same way a month onwards. If so then probably your mind has struck and is not developing. So once you read your own program, there is every likelihood that you will think of some improvements. The change in program can also occur owing to expansion or changes in the nature of the business, the economic environment, the need to keep up with the new technology or other factors, a program may become inadequate to meet the future needs.

### 8.11.1 Data Handling and Declaration

Data handling is basically the level of managing data. This can be divided into the following levels.

1. In the first step it is the operating system which handles the data. It manages the physical storage and retrieval of data on floppy disk, CD or other storage device.
2. It refers to the software that allows for the creation, storage, retrieval and manipulation of files interactively at a terminal or personal computer.
3. It is also the management of all data and information within an organization and includes data administration.
4. Lastly it is a function within an organization that manages data. It analyses, classifies and maintains all the data and data relationships. Data handling or administration coordinates the development of data models and data dictionaries which, combined with transaction volume, are the raw materials for database.

### 8.11.2 Types of Data

Let us see the type of data which can be used for running the program.

#### Constants

This is the data which is predetermined before a program is used. Values remain unchanged during the execution of a program. It has a fixed range in computer applications.

#### Variables

Here the data may change or be assigned different values as the program runs. There are limitations imposed by language on maximum number of characters used to form variable names.

### 8.11.3 ALGORITHM

An algorithm is a finite sequence of instructions, logic, an explicit, step-by-step procedure for solving a problem. An algorithm is an effective method expressed as a finite list of well-defined instructions for calculating a function. Algorithms are used for calculation, data processing, and many other fields. An algorithm may be expressed as a pseudo code that is shorthand notation of English sentences.

The computer scientist Niklaus Wirth stated that:

Programs = Algorithms + Data

The algorithm is part of the blueprint or plan for the computer program, an algorithm is:
"An effective procedure for solving a problem in a finite number of steps."

#### Definition:

"An algorithm is a finite set of instructions which, if followed, accomplish a particular task".

Definition of Algorithm (after Al Kho-war-iz-mi a 9th century Persian mathematician) - an ordered sequence of unambiguous and well-defined instructions that performs some task and halts in finite time

Let's examine the four parts of this definition more closely

1. an ordered sequence means that you can number the steps

2. unambiguous and well-defined instructions means that each instruction is clear, do-able, and can be done without difficulty
3. performs some task
4. halts in finite time (algorithms terminate!)

Algorithms can be executed by a computing agent which is not necessarily a computer.

In addition every algorithm must satisfy the following criteria:

| | |
|---|---|
| Step 1: | Input: There are zero or more quantities which are externally supplied. |
| Step 2: | Output: At least one quantity is produced. |
| Step 3: | Definiteness: Each instruction must be clear and unambiguous. |
| Step 4: | Finiteness: If we trace out the instructions of an algorithm, then for all cases the algorithm will terminate after a finite number of steps. |
| Step 5: | Effectiveness: Every instruction must be sufficiently basic that it can in principle be carried out by a person using only pencil and paper. It is not enough that each operation be definite, but it must also be feasible. |

A problem can be solved by using a computer only if an algorithm can be written for it. In addition, the use of algorithm provides many other benefits:-

1. While writing an algorithm, you identify the step-by-step procedure, the major decision points, and the variables necessary to solve the problem. This helps you in the development of the corresponding program.
2. Identification of the procedure and the decision points reduces the problem into a series of smaller problems of more manageable size. Therefore, problems that would be difficult or impossible to solve as a whole can be approached as a series of small solvable sub problems.
3. With the use of an algorithm, decision making becomes a more rational process. This is because algorithms comprise of sub tasks, where each sub task is atomic in nature and is supported by facts.
4. With the use of an algorithm, the same specified steps are used for performing the tasks. This makes the process more consistent and reliable.

Let's follow an example to help get an understanding of the algorithm concept.

Algorithm 1.1: Add Two Numbers
Step 1: Start
Step 2: Enter the value of A and B.
Step 3: A=10, B=5.
Step 4: Perform operation C = A + B.
Step 5: Store the result in C.
Step 6: End

Let us take one more example, to find biggest number between two given numbers. Think the logic, and you'll feel it's very easy to write the steps of an algorithm.

Algorithm 1.2: Find the Greater number among two numbers.
Step 1: Start
Step 2: Read two positive integer numbers 'A' and 'B'
Step 3: If A is greater than B, then go to step 4 else goto step 5.
Step 4: Print "A is greater than B" goto step 6.
Step 5: Print "B is greater than A"
Step 6: End.

Once these steps are performed on data specified in the problem, the desired result or output is obtained. Whenever an algorithm can be specified it makes sense to wonder about its behavior.

This was realized by Charles Babbage, the father of Computers in 1830. An algorithm is a finite set of instructions, which when followed, perform a particular task.

### 8.11.3.1 Characteristics of an Algorithm

Let us try to present the scenario of a man brushing his own teeth (natural denture) step-by-step and say it is an algorithm.

Step 1. Take the brush

Step 2. Apply the paste

Step 3. Start brushing

Step 4. Rinse

Step 5. Wash

Step 6. Stop

If one goes through all these steps without being aware of the statement of the problem, he/she could possibly feel that this is the algorithm for cleaning a toilet. This is because of several ambiguities while comprehending every step. The step 1 may imply toothbrush, paintbrush, toilet brush, etc. Such an ambiguity should not be an instruction (step) of an algorithmic. Thus, every step should be made unambiguous. An unambiguous step is called definite instruction. Even if the step 2 is rewritten as apply the toothpaste, to eliminate ambiguities yet the conflicts such as, where to apply the toothpaste and where the source of the toothpaste is, need to be resolved. Hence, the act of applying the toothpaste is not mentioned. Although unambiguous, such unrealizable steps can not be included as an instruction (step) of an algorithmic as they are not effective.

The definiteness and effectiveness of an instruction implies the successful termination with desire output of that instruction. However the above two may not be sufficient to guarantee the termination of the algorithm. Therefore, while designing an algorithm care should be taken to provide a proper termination for algorithm.

Therefore, an algorithm can be defined as a sequence of definite and effective instructions, which terminates with the production of correct output from the given input.

In other words, viewed little more formally, an algorithm is a step-by-step formalization of a mapping function to map input set onto an output set.

Thus, every algorithm should have the following five characteristic features.

- Input
- Output

- Definiteness
- Effectiveness
- Termination

Algorithm Design and Analysis (ADA) is a branch of Computer Science that consists of designing and analyzing computer algorithms. The "**Design**" pertains to the description of algorithm at an abstract level by means of a pseudo language, and proof of correctness that is, the algorithm solves the given problem in all cases.

### 8.11.3.2 Algorithmic Notations

The pseudo code uses notations used in common languages like PASCAL and C language. For example, if-else structure, for loop structure, while loop structure, do-while loop structure. A conditional statement of an algorithm has the following form.

1) **If-Else Structure:**

```
If (condition) then
Block 1    //     Instruction(s)
Else
Block 2    //     Instruction(s)
           // End of Structure
```

Comments are given with the symbol // for better understanding of the instructions of an algorithm. It is good practice to give comments about the instructions of the algorithm. The above pseudo code executes Block 1 if the condition is true otherwise Block 2 is executed. A block is a set of instructions and it may contain one or more instructions. Sometimes, the If-Else structure is nested and appears as given below.

If (condition) then

```
Block 1   // Instruction(s)
Else If (condition) then
Block 2   //Instruction(s)
Else
Block 3   //Instruction(s)
// End of Structure
```

**(2) For loop Structure**

We use for loop structure to repeat to certain Block (instructions) up to fixed number of times. There is a counter, which keeps track of the number of repetitions. The structure of **for** loop is given below.

```
For Counter = i to j
{Instruction 1, Instruction 2… Instruction n}
```

There are three things hidden in the for loop structure.

a. Counter initialization

b. Condition checking

c. Increment of Counter

**(3) While loop Structure**

When we are not sure about the number of repetitions of a block then we use while loop structure as follows.

```
while (condition)
{Instruction 1, Instruction 2… Instruction n}
```

**(4) Do-while loop Structure**

When we are not sure about the number of repetitions of a block (instructions) and want that the block could execute at least once then we use do-while loop structure as follows.

```
Do
{Instruction 1, Instruction 2… Instruction n} while (condition)
```

**(5) Conditions and Concatenation of Conditions**

We use conditions to make the number of execution of a block finite or infinite, some times as there is need. We use some logical operators like AND, OR, NOT, etc to concatenate the conditions. Conditions are expressions, which give the value TRUE (1) or FALSE (0). When we use the logical operators then we evaluate NOT, AND, and OR in sequence. If conditions are concatenated by AND operator then result is TRUE if and only all conditions are TRUE otherwise FALSE and in case of OR operator, result is TRUE if at least one of the conditions is TRUE and FALSE otherwise.

$C=C_1$ AND $C_2$ AND…AND $C_n$ =TRUE if and only if $C_1=C_2=\ldots=C_n$=TRUE, otherwise FALSE and $C=C_1$ OR $C_2$ OR…OR $C_n$ =TRUE if at least one the $C_1$, $C_2$,…,$C_n$ is TRUE, otherwise FALSE. The NOT operator reverses the value of the condition. If $C_1$ is TRUE then NOT $C_1$ is FALSE.

For example, consider the following conditions and show their values after concatenation.

| Condition | Value |
|---|---|
| $C_1$ | 1 |
| $C_2$ | 1 |
| $C_3$ | 0 |

a. $C_4=C_1$ AND $C_2$

b. $C_5=C_2$ AND $C_3$

c. $C_6=C_1$ AND NOT $C_3$

**Solution**

a) $C_4$= 1 AND 1=1

b) $C_5$=1 AND 0=0

c) $C_6$=1 AND NOT 0= 1 AND 1=1

The fundamental knowledge necessary to solve problems using a computer is the notation of an algorithm. For example, suppose we have an array **DATA** of numerical values with size **N** in memory.

We want to find the location **K** and the value **MAX** of the largest element of **DATA**. An algorithm for this problem can be constructed as illustrated in Figure 8.3.

The execution of an algorithm begins at **Step1** and continues from there in sequential order unless the result of a condition tested or an unconditional transfer specifies otherwise. In the algorithm given in Figure .3, **Step 1** is executed first if the array **DATA** is empty, the algorithm terminates; otherwise **Step 2** is performed. In this step, **MAX** is initialized to the value of **DATA [I].** Firstly **I** is 1 and variable **I** is incremented by 1. **Step 3** leads to termination of this algorithm if we have already tested the last element of the array **DATA**; otherwise **Step 4** is performed. In this step, the value of **MAX** is compared with the value of next element of the array **DATA**. If **MAX** is less than the next element, **MAX** is assigned this new value (by calling Step 2). If the test fails, no reassignment takes place. The completion of **Step 4** is followed by **Step 5** where control returns to the **Step2** when we assign new value to **MAX** and increment the subscript by 1.

It is very much advisable to the readers that before writing a program design an algorithm for a problem. Do not try hit and trial method. Sometimes it may be costly and may result into damaging the system. Keep in mind that C language is middle-level language. So, any bad instruction can damage the system. Designing an algorithm is simple for any problem when we have some solution for that. Derive the solution step by step considering the flow of processing. If some steps are missing or misplaced then result will be undesirable.

```
Step 1: [Initialization]
        I = 1
        K = 1
Step 2: [Increment counter]
        MAX = DATA [I]
        I = I + 1
Step 3: [Test counter]
        If I > N then
        Write K, MAX and Exit
Step 4: [Compare and update]
        If MAX < DATA [I] then
        K = I
Step 5: Go to Step 2:
```

Figure 8.3: Search Algorithm

### 8.11.3.3 Types of Algorithm

An algorithm is defined as "Step by step approach to solve any problem". There are mainly three types of algorithm exist, which are given as below:

1. Sequential Algorithm
2. Conditional Algorithm
3. Iterative Algorithm

**1. Sequential Algorithm:** an algorithm whose steps are executed sequentially i.e. execution of algorithm takes place in the same order in which an algorithm is developed. For example consider following algorithm to add two numbers

```
Read A
Read B
C=A+B
Print "Sum is"
Print C
```

**2. Conditional Algorithm:** An algorithm whose execution depends upon certain conditions are called conditional algorithms. For example consider the following algorithm to check whether a given number is positive or negative.

```
Read A
If A>0 then
Print "A is positive"
Else
Print "A is negative"
End IF
```

**3. Iterative Algorithm:** an algorithm that repeat a statement of group of statement for number of times such an algorithm is called iterative algorithm. For example consider the following algorithm that will find the sum of first 100 Natural numbers:

```
Set S=0
For I=1 to 100
S=S+I
I=I+1
End For
Print "Sum of First 100 Natural numbers is"
Print S
```

An algorithm can be described in several ways. One way is to give it a graphical form of notation which is known as Flow Chart. This form places each processing step in a "box" and uses arrows to indicate the next step. Different shaped boxes stand for different kinds of operations.

### 8.11.3.4 Different ways of stating algorithms

There are several ways of stating an algorithm. The following are four different ways of stating algorithms:

1. Step-Form
2. Flowchart
3. Nassi-Schneiderman
4. IPO Chart
5. Pseudocode
6. Hierarchy Chart

### 8.11.4 Step-Form Algorithms

This form of algorithm is the simplest and consists of a sequence of numbered steps or points. It is the easiest to learn at first since it is rather like a "to-do" list however once you have mastered other ways of stating algorithms you are unlikely to continue using this form.

**Example:** *First of all the problem to solve is:*

Design a program which counts all the vowels on a given page of text.

Remember in the second lesson we came up with a strategy for designing algorithms so use this as a starting point:

Step 1: Investigation step

1. Identify the processes
2. Identify the major decisions
3. Identify the loops
4. Identify the variables

Step 2: Preliminary algorithm step

1. Devise a "high level" algorithm
2. Step through the algorithm. Does this "walk-through" reveal any major problems? If it does then correct the problems.

Step 3: Refining the algorithm step

1. Incorporate any refinements indicated in step 2.
2. Group together processes where appropriate
3. Group together variables where appropriate
4. Test the algorithm again by stepping through it

### 8.11.5 FLOWCHART

A flowchart is a diagrammatic representation that illustrates the sequence of operations to be performed to get the solution of a problem. Flowcharts are generally drawn in the early stages of formulating computer solutions. Flowcharts facilitate communication between programmers and business people. These flowcharts play a vital role in the programming of a problem and are quite helpful in understanding the logic of complicated and lengthy problems. Once the flowchart is drawn, it becomes easy to write the program in any high level language. Often we see how flowcharts are helpful in explaining the program to others. Hence, it is correct to say that a flowchart is a must for the better documentation of a complex program. Flowcharting is a tool for analysing processes. It allows you to break any process down into individual events or activities and to display these in shorthand form showing the logical relationships between them. Constructing flowcharts promotes better understanding of processes, and better understanding of processes is a pre-requisite for improvement.

Flow charts are easy-to-understand diagrams showing how steps in a process fit together. This makes them useful tools for communicating how processes work, and for clearly documenting how a particular job is done. Furthermore, the act of mapping a process out in flow chart format helps you clarify your understanding of the process, and helps you think about where the process can be improved.

A flow chart can therefore be used to:

- Define and analyze processes.
- Build a step-by-step picture of the process for analysis, discussion, or communication.
- Define, standardize or find areas for improvement in a process

Also, by conveying the information or processes in a step-by-step flow, you can then concentrate more intently on each individual step, without feeling overwhelmed by the bigger picture.

### 8.11.5.1 Flowchart Symbols and Their Usage

Now we define in detail the meaning and significance of each of these symbols. Oval is used for two purposes, to define the starting (START or BEGIN) point of flowchart and to define the ending point (END) of flowchart.

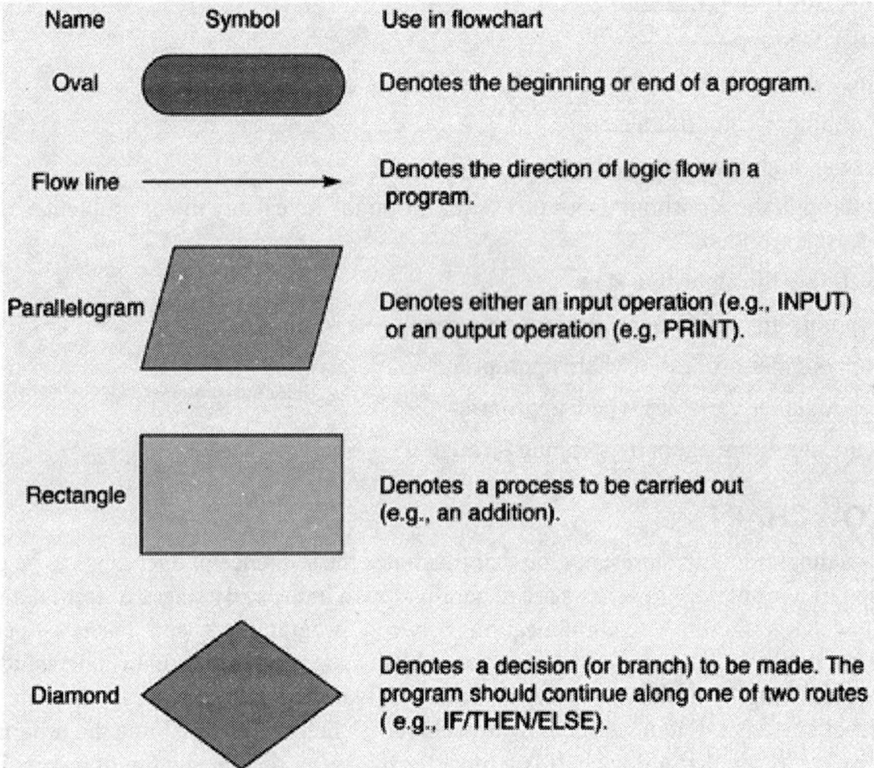


**Figure 8.4:** General Flowchart Symbols

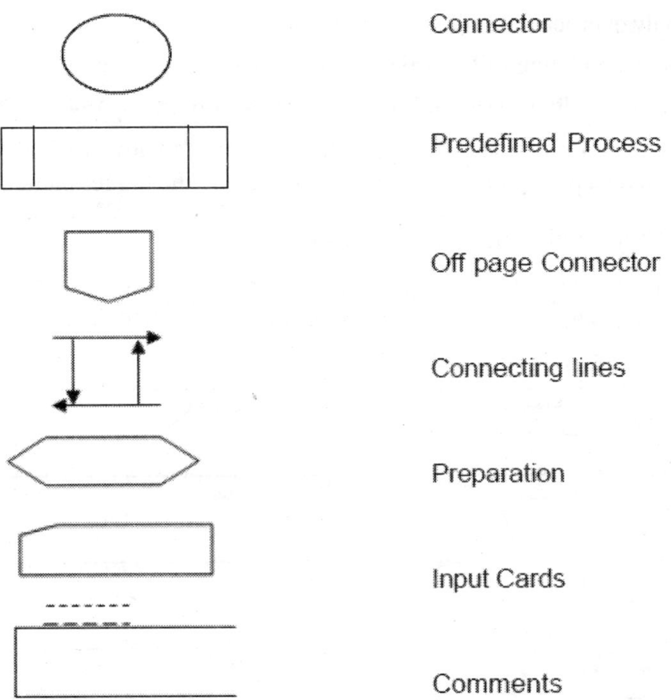


**Figure 8.5:** Special Flowchart Symbols

**PARALLELOGRAM:** Parallelogram is used for input-output. This is the input symbol to indicate the input from standard input or output to standard output device.

**RECTANGLE:** The rectangle is used to indicate the processing. Inside, this processing box statements of processing are specified.

**DIAMOND:** The diamond shaped box is decision box. This has one entry point. There will be at least two exit points depending upon the decision taken inside the symbol. When a condition is tested, if the condition is true, the path for "yes" is followed. If the condition is false, the path for "no" is followed.

**CIRCLE:** If flowchart is discontinued at some point and continued again at another place, the connector symbol is used. It is a circle with a number written inside it. If a flowchart is discontinued at some point, a circle is drawn pointing away from the chart. Another circle with same number inside it is placed where the flowchart is to be continued.

**SMALL PENTAGON:** Sometimes due to spaces limitations or due to some other reasons, it becomes necessary to terminate a flowchart temporarily and continue from the next page. In such situations this off page connector is used. A number is written inside it. Same number is placed in another pentagon on next page where the flowchart is to be continued.

**Comment symbol:** This symbol contains the comment. These comments are included for the documentation purpose to make the understanding of flowcharts easy.

**PENTAGON (rectangle with five corners):** The symbol having five corners is used for indicating the input-output. This symbol indicates the input from or output to punched cards.

**HEXAGON (flat):** This is the preparation box. This box contains the loop setting statement, *i.e.*

**ARROWS** These arrows are to indicate the direction of the flow of control. This means these statements indicate the next statement to be executed.

Figures 8.6 and 8.7 show the flowcharting symbols for special processing and input-output purpose. These symbols are rarely used in flowcharting.

| Symbol | Meaning |
|---|---|
| | Internal Storage |
| | Documents |
| | Multi-document |
| | Manual Input |
| | Manual Operation |
| | Punched tape |
| | Or operation |
| | Sorting of data |
| | Magnetic Disk |
| | Collate |
| | Extract |

**Figure 8.6:** Set of advanced flowchart symbols

| Symbol | Meaning |
|---|---|
|   | Merge two data |
|   | Storage data/ online Storage |
|   | Delay |
|   | Sequential Access Storage/Magnetic Disk |
|   | Summing Junction |
| 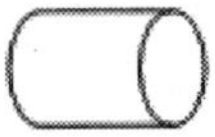  | Direct Access Storage |
| 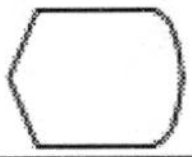  | Display |

**Figure 8.7:** Set of advanced flowchart symbols

### 8.11.5.2 Conventions of flowcharts

1. Each symbol of flowchart denotes a particular type of operation.
2. A note is written inside each symbol to indicate the specific function to be performed.
3. Flowcharts are read from top to bottom and left to right.
4. Sequence of operations is performed until a terminate symbol designates the end of the run.
5. Crossed lines do not imply any logical relationship.
6. Where two incoming lines join one outgoing line, they should not join at the same point.
7. Annotation should be included within the symbol to process decision file and input, output giving an indication of the action decision file or document used.
8. Identification of the symbols on a flowchart is aided by numbering the most left top symbols sequentially from 1, so that each symbol can be referred uniquely. Connectors and terminators need to be numbered.
9. Flowcharts are not case-sensitive, so instructions inside the symbols can be written in any case.

A sample flowchart is given in Fig. 8.8.

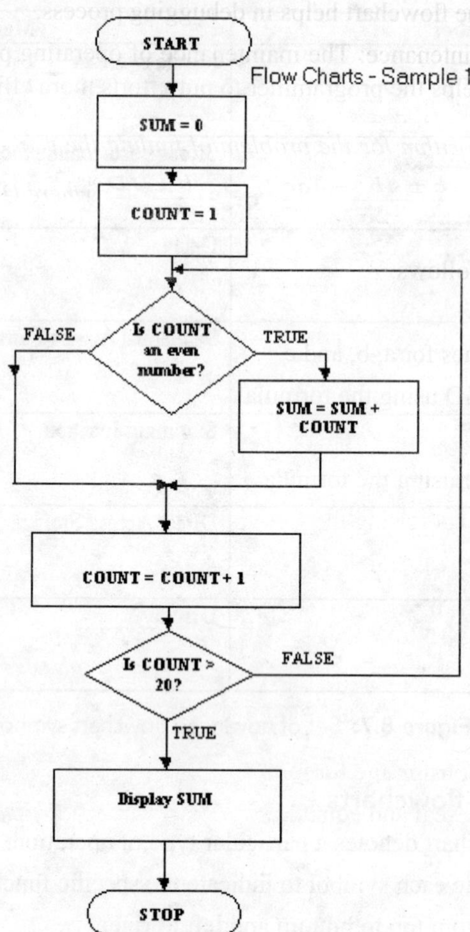


**Figure 8.8:** A Sample Flowchart

### 8.11.5.3 Advantages of Flowcharts

The benefits of flowcharts are as follows:

1. Communication: Flowcharts are better way of communicating the logic of a system to all concerned.
2. Effective analysis: With the help of flowchart, problem can be analyzed in more effective way.
3. Proper documentation: Program flowcharts serve as a good program documentation, which is needed for various purposes.
4. Efficient Coding: The flowcharts act as a guide or blueprint during the systems analysis and program development phase.

5. Proper Debugging: The flowchart helps in debugging process.
6. Efficient Program Maintenance: The maintenance of operating program becomes easy with the help of flowchart. It helps the programmer to put efforts more efficiently on that part.

**Example 1:** *Write an algorithm for the problem of finding the roots of a quadratic equation ax2 + bx + c = 0. Using the formula* $\frac{-b \pm \sqrt{b^2 - 4ac}}{2a}$ or $\frac{-b \pm \sqrt{D}}{2a}$ *where D = b2 - 4ac. Draw flowchart for this algorithm*

**Answer:** Algorithm is as follows:

1. Start
2. Read the numeric values for a, b, and c.
3. Calculate the value of D using the formula .
4. if D> 0
   a. Calculate one root using the formula .
   b. Calculate another root using the formula .
   c. Display "roots are real and distinct".
   d. Display "Root 1 = ", .
   e. Display "Root 2 = ",
   f. Exit
5. If D=0, then
   a. Calculate one root using the formula.
   b. Display "roots are real and equal".
   c. Display "Root 1 = ", .
   d. Display "Root 2 = ",
   e. Exit
6. If D=0, then
   a. Calculate one term using the formula .
   b. Calculate another term using the formula or
   c. Display "roots are imaginary".
   d. Display "Root 1 = ", +i.
   e. Display "Root 2 = ", +i.
   f. Exit
7. Stop

Details of the flowchart are shown in Figure 10.8.

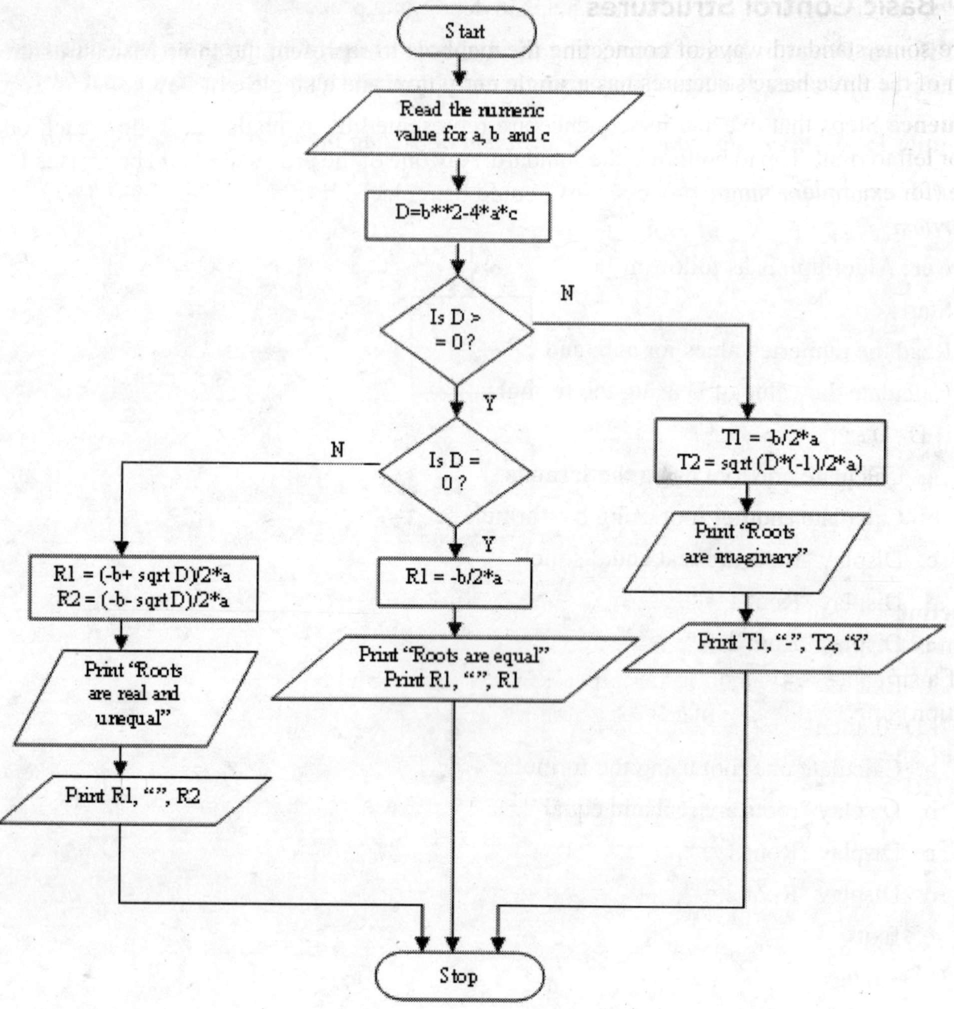


**Figure 8.9:** Flowchart for quadratic equation

Flowcharts are designed to facilitate encoding. Following section expresses the representation of different mathematical and logical expressions in flowcharts.

#### 8.11.5.4 Limitations of Using Flowcharts

1. Complex logic: Sometimes, the program logic is quite complicated. In that case, flowchart becomes complex and clumsy.
2. Alterations and Modifications: If alterations are required the flowchart may require re-drawing completely.
3. Reproduction: As the flowchart symbols cannot be typed, reproduction of flowchart becomes a problem.
4. The essentials of what is done can easily be lost in the technical details of how it is done.

### 8.11.6 Basic Control Structures

There are some standard ways of connecting the symbols to represent the three basic structures. Notice that each of the three basic structures has a single entry flow and a single exit flow.

**Sequence** Steps that execute in sequence are represented by symbols that follow each other top to bottom or left to right. Top to bottom is the standard. Any one of the processes could be replaced by another structure (for example, a single process "box" could be replaced by a sequence of two process "boxes").

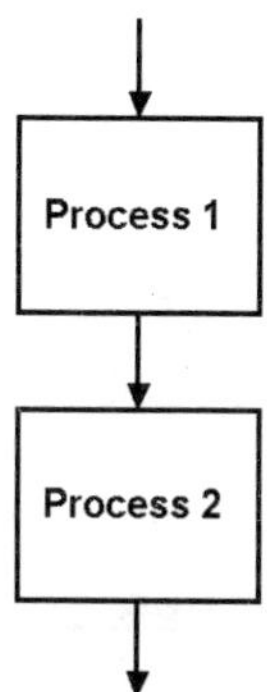


**Selection** Once the condition is evaluated, the control flows into one of two paths. Once the conditional execution is finished, the flows rejoin before leaving the structure. Once again the single entry, single exit nature of a structure is evident. Either process could be replaced with any structure (sequence, selection, or repetition) or it could be omitted (for example the process on the "NO" side might not exist).

As an alternative, the "Question" could be replaced with a Boolean expression and the branches labeled "TRUE" and "FALSE".

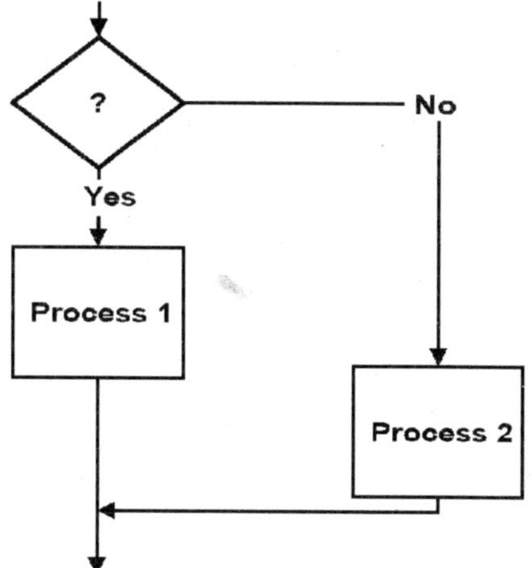


**Repetition or** Iteration or Looping

Either the processing repeats or the control leaves the structure. (Again, the process could be replace another structure).

Notice that the return line joins the entry line before the question. Never try to insert processing in the entry line between the join and the question.

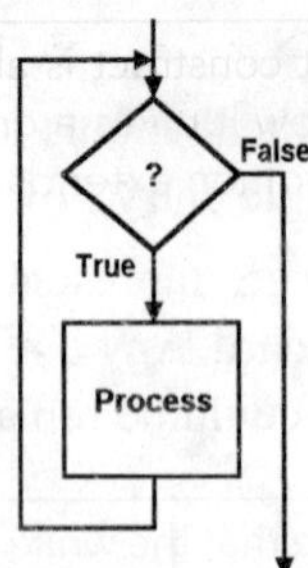


## 8.11.7 Nassi-Schneiderman Diagram

The Nassi-Schneiderman (NS) diagram is a graphical method of stating algorithms. Many people claim that it is very easy to read, especially for beginners. That is probably true but maintaining NS diagrams can be a problem for the program designer. Here is a simple example of a NS diagram:

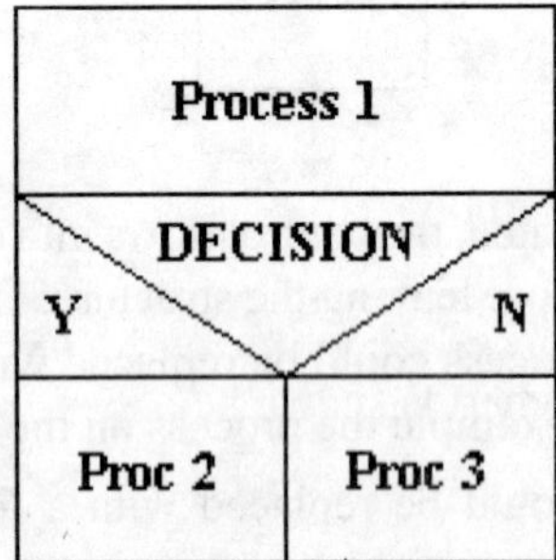


**Figure 8.10:** A Sample NS Diagram

The diagram indicates an algorithm with a process (Process 1) followed by a decision. Each outcome of the decision has a process associated with it. If the decision evaluates as true then Proc 2 is carried out, if false then Proc 3 is carried out. In the table that follows you will see the symbols that are used in NS diagrams. As with flow charts the symbols are few and easily remembered. The different symbols are "fitted" together like pieces in a jigsaw puzzle.

### 8.11.7.1 NS Symbols and Constructs

**Table 8.1:** NS symbols and constructs

| | |
|---|---|
| Process | The process symbol looks much the same as the program flow chart symbol. You'll see soon though that NS diagrams look quite different from the flow charts you have used before. |
| DECISION Y N | The decision symbol is quite different. You will see soon how it is used. |

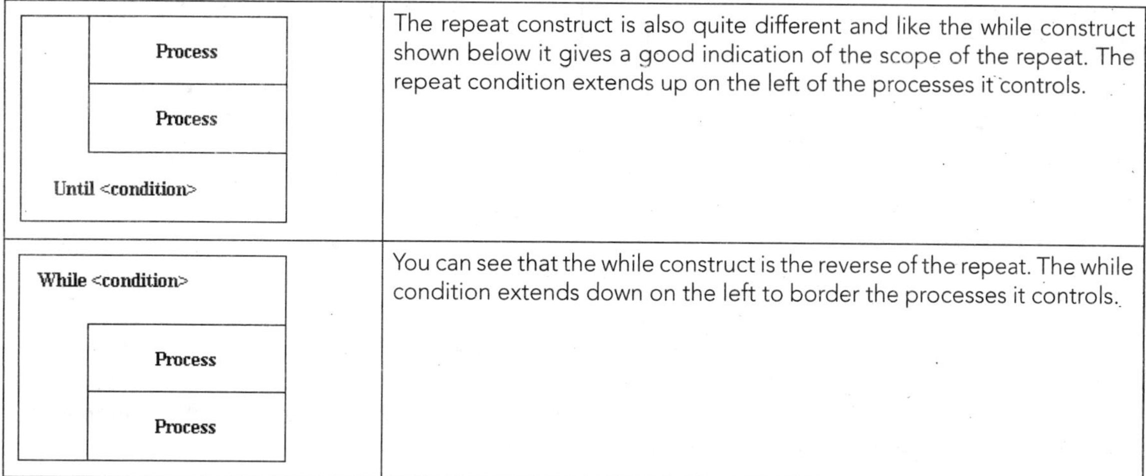

| | |
|---|---|
| Process<br>Process<br>Until <condition> | The repeat construct is also quite different and like the while construct shown below it gives a good indication of the scope of the repeat. The repeat condition extends up on the left of the processes it controls. |
| While <condition><br>Process<br>Process | You can see that the while construct is the reverse of the repeat. The while condition extends down on the left to border the processes it controls. |

### 8.11.7.2 Designing programs with NS diagrams

Drawing program designs with NS diagrams is quite simple but the NS method differs from the program flow chart method. Apart from different symbols NS does not use connectors between the symbols.

### NS Diagram Vs Flowchart

A comparison of an NS chart and a flow chart is shown below:

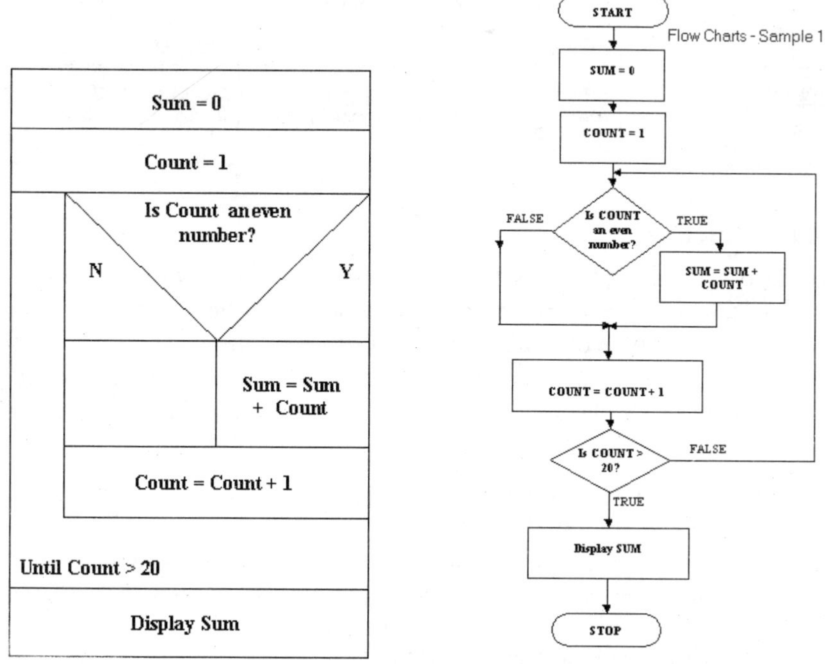


Figure 8.11: Comparison of Sample NS Diagram and Flowchart

As with the flow the direction of sequence in the NS chart is from top to bottom. There are some problems with the NS charts that don't really occur with flow charts:

- It is not as easy to stress the process one entry-one exit point rule as it is in flow charts.
- The null-else is not really obvious.
- Modification of an NS diagram probably requires more work than the equivalent flow chart.

### 8.11.8 IPO Charts

A useful and relatively simple tool to use in the analysis stage to identify inputs, outputs and corresponding process is the IPO table. An IPO (Input/Processing/Output) Table shows the inputs to an object, the required outputs for that object, and the processing that is necessary to convert the inputs into the desired outputs.

**Example:** *CarRental, Inc., leases automobiles for its salespeople and wishes to create an application that will determine the gas mileage for each type of automobile.*

- Input should include: the make of the automobile, the beginning odometer reading, the ending odometer reading, and the gallons of gasoline consumed.
- Output should include the miles per gallon for the car being tested. (note: gas mileage = (ending odometer reading - beginning odometer reading)/gallons used.).
- In addition, the program should classify the car using the following scheme: "gas guzzler" for cars with gas mileage less than 18 mpg, "economy" for cars with gas mileage above 28 mpg, and "average" for cars with gas mileage between 18 and 28 mpg.

An IPO table for this example is given in Table 8.2.

**Table 8.2:** Sample IPO Table

| Input | Process | Output |
|---|---|---|
| - make of automobile - beginning_odometer_reading - ending_odometer_reading - gallons_used | gas_mileage = (ending_odometer_reading - beginning_odometer_reading)/gallons_used | - gas_mileage in miles per gallon (mpg) - classification |

### 8.11.9 PSEUDOCODE

Pseudocode is another programming analysis' took that is used for planning program logic. ''Pseudocode" means imitation or false and ''Code" refers to the instruction written in a programming language. Pseudocode, therefore, is an imitation of actual computer instructions. Instead of using symbols to describe the logic steps of a program, as in flowcharting, Pseudocode uses a structure that resembles computer instructions. Because it emphasis's the design of the program, Pseudocode is also called Program Design Language.

The rules of Pseudocode are reasonably straightforward. All statements showing "dependency" are to be indented. These include while, do, for, if, switch.

No standard for pseudocode syntax exists. However, there are some commonly followed conventions to help make pseudocode written by one programmer easily understood by another programmer.

#### Most of these conventions follow two concepts:

- Use indentation to show the action part of a control structure
- Use an ending *phrase word* to end a control structure

The sequence control structure simply lists the lines of pseudocode. The concern is not with the sequence category but with selection and two of the iteration control structures.

The following are commonly used ending phrase-words:

| Control Structure | Ending Phrase Word |
|---|---|
| If then Else | Endif |
| Case | Endcase |
| While | Endwhile |
| For | Endfor |

The *Do While* and *Repeat Until* iteration control structures don't need an ending phrase-word. We simply use the first word, then the action part, followed by the second word with the test expression. **Here is one of the examples.**

**Example:** *Pseudocode for the CarRental, Inc. problem stated above.*

```
Begin procedure
Input make, beginning_odometer, ending_odometer, and gallons_used
   gas_mileage = (ending_odometer - beginning_odometer)/gallons_used
   Output gas_mileage If gas_mileage < 18 then Output "Gas Guzzler" EndIf If
   gas_mileage > 28 then Output "Economy" EndIf If gas_mileage >= 18 And gas_
   mileage <= 28 then Output "Average" EndIf
End procedure
```

### 8.11.9.1 Types of Pseudocode

Pseudocode is made up of the following basic logic structures that have been proved to be sufficient for writing any computer program.

1. Sequence
2. Selection (IF....THEN....or IF....THEN)
3. Iteration (DO....WHILE or REPEAT.....UNTIL)

### 1. Sequence Logic

It is used for performing instructions one after another in sequence. Thus, for sequence logic, pseudocode instructions are written in the oper, or sequence, in which they are to be performed. The logic flow of pseudocode is from the top to the bottom.

### 2. Selection Logic

It is also known as decision logic, is used for making decisions. It is used for selecting the proper path out of the two or more alternative paths in the program.

Logic Selection Logic is depicted as either an IF....THEN or an IF....THEN....ELSE structure.

### 3. Iteration Logic

It is used to produce loops when one or more instructions may be executed several times depending on some condition. It uses two structures called the DO.....WHILE and the REPEAT....UNTIL. They are illustrated by flowcharts. Their corresponding Pseudocode are also given in DO....WHILE and

REPEAT......UNTIL are used for looping. The differences are that in the DO....WHILE, the looping will continue as long as the condition is true. The looping stops when the condition is not true. On the other hand, in case of REPEAT.....UNTIL, the looping continues until the must contain a statement that will change the condition that controls the loop. If it doesn't the looping will continue without end, which of the case of an infinite loop.

Remember that no program should contain an infinite loop. Also note that the condition is tested at the loop of the loop in the DO....WHILE and at the bottom of the loop in the REPEAT....UNTIL. ENDDO marks the end of a DO....WHILE structure and UNTIL followed by some condition marks the end of the REPEAT.....UNTIL structure.

### 8.11.9.2 Difference between Pseudocode and Flowchart

Pseudocode differs from the flowchart in the following ways:

1. Pseudocode is self-explanatory and does not requires a separate documentation. This is so because it is written in plain English language.
2. Pseudocode has a structure similar to that of a programme written in BASIC or PASCAL language. But flowcharts have a tendency to extend flow lines in all directions and thus their paths of instructions do not parallel the final BASIC code.

### 8.11.9.3 Advantages and Limitations of Pseudocode

Pseudocode has three main advantages:

- Converting a Pseudocode to a programming language is much easier as compared to converting a flowchart or a decision table.
- As compared to a flowchart, it is easier to modify the Pseudocode of program logic when program modifications are necessary.
- Writing of Pseudocode involves much less time and effort than drawing an equivalent flowchart Pseudocode is easier to write than an actual programming language because it has only a few rules to follow, allowing the programmers to concentrate on the logic of the program.

However, Pseudocode suffers from the following limitations:

- In case of Pseudocode, a graphic representation of program logic is not available.
- There are no standard rules to follow in using Pseudocode. Different programmers use their own style of writing Pseudocode and hence a communication problem occurs due to lack of standardization.
- For a beginner, it is more difficult to follow the logic of or write Pseudocode as compared to flowcharting.

## 8.11.10 Hierarchy Charts

A hierarchy chart provides a graphical representation about the overall structure of the program. They describe what each module of the program does and how the modules are related to one another.

**Example:** *Hierarchy Chart for the CarRental, Inc. problem is given in Fig. 8.7*

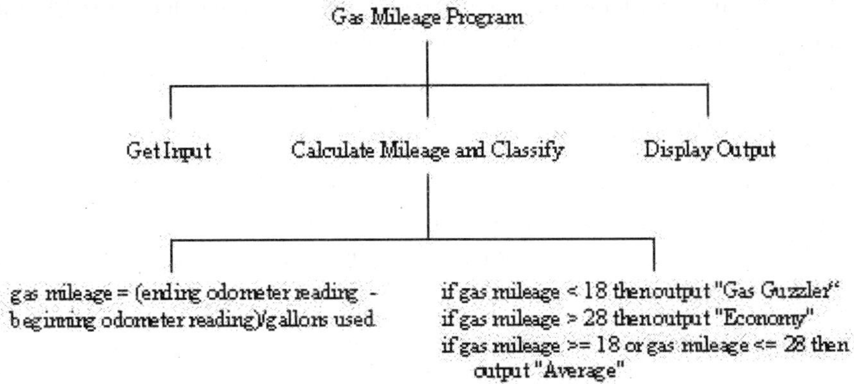


**Figure 8.12:** Hierarchy Chart Example

## 8.11.11 Trace Table

After the flowchart has been drawn for the given problem, it is essential *to* check that the method and plan deployed to solve the problem functions correctly and produces the desired results. There after the flowchart is translated into high level language to be run on the computer. The manual test of the flowchart is called *dry run* or *desk check.*

As the name suggests, the trace table traces the sequence, step by step, which leads to the solution of the problem. In the process of tracing, the result of each step and its effect on the next step becomes clear. The logic involved in solving the problem becomes evident. If any error at any stage is discovered while framing the algorithm, or drawing of flowchart, it shows itself at the time of dry run. In presence of any error, the system designed to solve the problem will not function correctly and will produce the incorrect results during dry run. The trace table helps in locating the stage at which the error has occurred and also the nature of error, so that thereafter the error could be eliminated.

### How to perform the dry run or desk check?

The dry run or desk check is performed to check each stage of the solution developed to solve the problem. The steps involved in it are as follows:

a. Draw the table containing as many columns as the number of activities in the flowchart (i.e., one column for each geometrical figure in the flow chart).

b. Write the activity performed in each vertical columns as the number of activities in the flow chart (i.e:, one column for each geometrical figure in the flow chart).

c. Consider a suitable numerical value, for the variable as required, in the flow chart within the prescribed range.

d. Keep on writing the values in each column in accordance to the activity mentioned above each column.

e. Check that the values generated in each column as per the activity mentioned in it are correct and are as expected (this is done by comparing the values generated according to each activity with the values which should occur).

f. In case of any error locate the stage at which the error was raised and identify the nature of error.
g. Take adequate measures to eliminate the detected errors.
h. Recheck the flowchart till it is error free.

### How a program is executed?

Following are the necessary steps involved in the execution of the program.

a. Since the compilers of different high level languages are different hence the compiler for the high level language, in which the program has been written, is loaded in the memory of the computer.
b. The source program is fed to the computer through some input device. The control unit stores the program in the main memory of computer..
c. The compiler or interpreter used, not only converts source program in machine code but also check each line for syntax error.
d. The syntax error message is conveyed to the user by central processing unit through the output devices. The program shall not be executed unless the program is made completely error-free.
e. Memory locations are allotted to each variable, by the name of each variable itself, in the main memory.
f. The result of the executed program is communicated to the user, in high level language, through the output devices.

## 8.11.12 Decision Table

Though earlier discussed flowcharts give a clear idea of direction of flow of data but it has a disadvantage. This is, the flowcharts become more complicated and difficult to understand if there are several decisions to be taken in a program. Also a flowchart may run for more than one page. So at times following and understanding a flowchart becomes more difficult. Because of these disadvantages, in such complex cases instead of flowcharts there is another algorithm development and documentation aid that is the decision table. A *decision table* depicts in a tabular form the set of conditions to be tested and the sequence of actions to be performed to solve a problem. This aid is useful in solving the problems, which require a large number of decisions.

| STUB | ENTRY |
|---|---|
| CONDITION | RULE NUMBER |
| ACTION | |

**Figure 8.13:** General layout of Decision Table

Decision table is a table defining the problem and the actions to be taken. It is a single representation of conditions and actions. Figure 8.13 shows the general layout of any decision table. A decision table consists of two main partitions- STUB and ENTRY.

The stub part is divided into an upper quadrant called the conditional stub and a lower quadrant called the action stub. The entry part is also divided into two quadrants. The upper quadrant is called the condition entry and a lower quadrant is called the action entry. The *condition stub* contains in the question form, the condition that may exist. The *action stub* contains outlines in the narrative form, the action to be taken to meet each condition. The condition entry provides the answers to the questions that are asked in the condition stub quadrant. The action entry indicates the appropriate action resulting from the answers to the conditions in the condition entry quadrant. We now consider an example to understand the way of writing the entries in a decision table.

**Example 2:** *In a marketing firm, commission is given based on the sales. If sales are less than 5000.00, then there is no commission. If sales is more than or equal to 5000. 00 but less than 10000 then commission is 2%. If sales is greater than or equal to 10000 but less than 50000 then commission is 4%. If sales is greater than 50000. 00 the discount is 6%.*

**Answer:** Now we draw a decision table for it. In this case, the conditions are

If sales are less than 5000.00

If sales are less than 10000.00

If sales is less than 50000.00

If sales is greater then 50000.00

From the Figure 8.9, we note certain things. First of all, we see that the answers have been denoted by Y & N and blank column & row denotes that the corresponding condition has not been tested. The check mark (X) denotes the action. Each column indicates a rule. For example rule 3 is, "IF sale is less than 50000 and greater than 10000/- then allow 4% discount".

| STUB | | ENTRY | | | | | |
|---|---|---|---|---|---|---|---|
| | | 1 | 2 | 3 | 4 | 5 | 6 |
| (Condition) | | | | | | | |
| | Sale >= 50000? | Y | N | N | N | N | N |
| | Sale < 50000? | | Y | Y | Y | Y | Y |
| IF | Sale >= 10000? | | | Y | N | N | N |
| | Sale < 10000? | | | | Y | Y | Y |
| | Sale >= 5000? | | | | | Y | N |
| | Sale < 5000? | | | | | | Y |
| | (Action) | | | | | | |
| | Allow 6% discount | X | | | | | |
| THEN | Allow 4% discount | | X | | | | |
| | Allow 2% discount | | | | X | | |
| | No discount allowed | | | | | | X |

**Figure 8.14:** Decision Table for Example 2

**Example 3:** *Students results are declared using the following rules: There are two subjects in the examination called main and ancillary. If a student gets 50 % or more in the main subject and 40% in the ancillary he/she is passed. If he/she gets less than 50% in the main subject, he/she must get 50% or more in the ancillary to pass. However, the minimum pass marks are 40% in the main subject. If a student gets 60% or more in the main subject, he/she is allowed to repeat ancillary subject if the ancillary subject is less than 40%. However, there are a group of students in the class who are granted special consideration. Their percentage is 40% in main and 40% in ancillary. If they get less than 40% in the ancillary, they are allowed to repeat that subject, if they obtain 40% or more in the main subject.*

**Answer:** The decision table for this problem is shown in Figure 8.10.

| Conditions | Rule1 | Rule2 | Rule3 | Rule4 | Rule5 | Else |
|---|---|---|---|---|---|---|
| Main marks %age | ≥50 | ≥40 | ≥60 | ≥40 | ≥40 | |
| Ancillary marks % age | ≥40 | ≥50 | <40 | ≥40 | <40 | |
| Special status | No | No | No | Yes | Yes | |
| Actions | | | | | | |
| Pass | x | x | - | x | - | - |
| Repeat | - | - | x | - | x | - |
| Fail | - | - | - | - | - | x |

Figure 8.15: Decision Table for Example 3.

### 8.11.12.1 Rules for drawing decision table

The rules that should be following while constructing the decision table are as follows:

1. A decision should have a same.
2. The logic of the table is independent of the sequence in which condition rules are written.
3. Duplication of the terms must be eliminated.

### 8.11.12.2 Advantages of decision table

Decision tables are best suited for dealing with complex branching routines such as complex links of inventory control or calculating purchasing discounts, sales commissions, etc. These tables are easier to construct than flow charts if several conditions are to be tested and decisions to be taken. Also, it is easier to follow the table when a particular condition is met just by coming down the column.

## 8.11.13 Program Testing

Program testing is an investigation conducted to provide stakeholders with information about the quality of the product or service under test. Software testing can also provide an objective, independent view of the software to allow the business to appreciate and understand the risks of software implementation. Test techniques include, but are not limited to, the process of executing a program or application with the intent of finding software bugs (errors or other defects).

Program testing can be stated as the process of validating and verifying that a software program/ application/product:

1. meets the requirements that guided its design and development;

2. works as expected; and
3. can be implemented with the same characteristics.

Program testing, depending on the testing method employed, can be implemented at any time in the development process. However, most of the test effort occurs after the requirements have been defined and the coding process has been completed. As such, the methodology of the test is governed by the software development methodology adopted.

Different software development models will focus the test effort at different points in the development process. Newer development models, such as Agile, often employ test driven development and place an increased portion of the testing in the hands of the developer, before it reaches a formal team of testers. In a more traditional model, most of the test execution occurs after the requirements have been defined and the coding process has been completed.

### 8.11.13.1 Sample Testing Cycle

Although variations exist between organizations, there is a typical cycle for testing. The sample below is common among organizations employing the Waterfall development model.

- Requirements analysis: Testing should begin in the requirements phase of the software development life cycle. During the design phase, testers work with developers in determining what aspects of a design are testable and with what parameters those tests work.
- Test planning: Test strategy, test plan, testbed creation. Since many activities will be carried out during testing, a plan is needed.
- Test development: Test procedures, test scenarios, test cases, test datasets, test scripts to use in testing software.
- Test execution: Testers execute the software based on the plans and test documents then report any errors found to the development team.
- Test reporting: Once testing is completed, testers generate metrics and make final reports on their test effort and whether or not the software tested is ready for release.
- Test result analysis: Or Defect Analysis, is done by the development team usually along with the client, in order to decide what defects should be treated, fixed, rejected (i.e. found software working properly) or deferred to be dealt with later.
- Defect Retesting: Once a defect has been dealt with by the development team, it is retested by the testing team.
- Regression testing: It is common to have a small test program built of a subset of tests, for each integration of new, modified, or fixed software, in order to ensure that the latest delivery has not ruined anything, and that the software product as a whole is still working correctly.
- Test Closure: Once the test meets the exit criteria, the activities such as capturing the key outputs, lessons learned, results, logs, documents related to the project are archived and used as a reference for future projects.

## 8.11.14 Program Debugging

Debugging is a methodical process of finding and reducing the number of bugs, or defects, in a computer program or a piece of electronic hardware, thus making it behave as expected. Debugging tends to be harder when various subsystems are tightly coupled, as changes in one may cause bugs to emerge in another.

As software and electronic systems have become generally more complex, the various common debugging techniques have expanded with more methods to detect anomalies, assess impact, and schedule software patches or full updates to a system. The words "anomaly" and "discrepancy" can be used, as being more neutral terms, to avoid the words "error" and "defect" or "bug" where there might be an implication that all so-called errors, defects or bugs must be fixed (at all costs). Instead, an impact assessment can be made to determine if changes to remove an anomaly (or discrepancy) would be cost-effective for the system, or perhaps a scheduled new release might render the change(s) unnecessary. Not all issues are life-critical or mission-critical in a system. Also, it is important to avoid the situation where a change might be more upsetting to users, long-term, than living with the known problem(s) (where the "cure would be worse than the disease"). Basing decisions of the acceptability of some anomalies can avoid a culture of a "zero-defects" mandate, where people might be tempted to deny the existence of problems so that the result would appear as zero defects. Considering the collateral issues, such as the cost-versus-benefit impact assessment, then broader debugging techniques will expand to determine the frequency of anomalies (how often the same "bugs" occur) to help assess their impact to the overall system.

## 8.11.15 Program Documentation

Program documentation or source code documentation is written text that accompanies computer software. It either explains how it operates or how to use it, or may mean different things to people in different roles.

### Role of documentation in software development

Documentation is an important part of software engineering. Types of documentation include:

1. Requirements: Statements that identify attributes, capabilities, characteristics, or qualities of a system. This is the foundation for what shall be or has been implemented.
2. Architecture/Design: Overview of software. Includes relations to an environment and construction principles to be used in design of software components.
3. Technical: Documentation of code, algorithms, interfaces, and APIs.
4. End User: Manuals for the end-user, system administrators and support staff.
5. Marketing: How to market the product and analysis of the market demand.

### 8.11.15.1 Report Generation

Commercial applications use formatted outputs. These formatted outputs are known as reports. A formatted report may have the following:

1. Report heading
2. Page heading
3. Page numbering
4. Footers
5. Some remarks
6. Date, month and year of printing

Commercial outputs may also extend over multiple pages. In that case, one will have to keep a provision in his program so that certain details get printed on every page. For example, one may have to print page headings on every page. Report may be of

1. Single page
2. Multiple pages

Multiple page reports in general may consist of following parts:

***Report Heading***

It represents the title of the report and appears, only on the first page of the report.

***Report Sub Heading***

It is printed as and when required on each page.

***Page Heading***

It is printed on the top of each page.

***Page Footer***

It is printed at the bottom of each page. It is generally the total number of records on the page, sum of the numeric data, etc.

***Report Detail***

This constitutes the main body of report. The output details or the information of the main consequence are listed in this group.

### 8.11.15.2 Reports with Control Break

The most important objective of a program is reporting. We need summarized information for decision making. For presenting the summarized information one can use the concept of control break. In control break report, one need to group information based on some common criterion, maybe department, cost centre, etc.

A control break report can have the following:

1. Records of a particular region are grouped together and printed at one page.
2. When the control break occurs, certain procedures are followed. Such as total sales of that region.
3. It may be necessary that performance of each region is printed on each page, i.e., when the control break occurs the report is printed on a fresh page.
4. At the end of the report, it may be necessary to calculate and print the grand totals.

### 8.11.15.3 Operation on Files

There are some basic operations which can be performed on the files. They are:

- Writing on the file
- Reading the file for updating or outputting
- Deleting the file

Let us discuss each one of these in detail.

### Writing to a File

This is the process of making the data permanent on the tape or disk. It can be done with the help of data which has been keyed in either by off-line or by on-line method. Here the data is first stored in the memory and then written on the output medium.

### Reading the File for Updating or Outputting

File created in the above step is used here. Once the data from the file comes to the memory, use have the option of making changes or doing calculations based on it or even send the data for printing.

### Deleting the File

It is a process in which you delete the file from the storage media making way for some other data to be stored in.

### 8.11.15.4 File Updation

It is a process in which a data file is processed for changes in the records. These changes can be many to one records or one to many records. You may have to skip various records which do not have any changes or you may have to make several changes in the same record. Updation can be done on both sequential and non-sequential, i.e., random access files.

### Sequential File Updation

This process is mostly used in the case of files being on the magnetic tapes. Because of the possibility of record insertions and/or deletions, during an update run, the computer processing creates new master file records. In many applications, some master file records are also deleted from the file. So you need to have one file having the master record before updation and the second having master records after affecting the changes in the master file.

### Random File Updation

This process is mostly used in the cases where the file is on floppy disk or hard disk where the data is stored in random. Here a record is added, deleted or modified without affecting any other record in the file. Also when the record is to be accessed the same mapping function, key to address transformation, is used to transform the key to obtain its address. Thus while storing or accessing the record the same mapping function is used to find the address of the record.

### Multiple Handling of Updation

Here since you are using more than one file, all the files in use must have the same sequence. Either all of them should be in sequence or all of them in random access mode. The records from all the files are called into the memory and converted into a single stream for updating. Once updated the data is transferred back to the files.

## 8.12 PROGRAM DEVELOPMENT PROCESS

So far we have discussed about programming concepts and other necessary aspects. Here we will discuss about various steps involved in writing and developing software, which are as under:

### 8.12.1 Program Definition

Unless you define it how would you know what is to be done. So this is the first step. Various activities involved in this are:

1. Determine objectives of the current system
2. Study the current system
3. Analyse new objectives
4. Prepare design specifications.
5. Identify user's responsibility of data inputs and outputs to other systems
6. Prepare plan for design and implementation phases
7. Produce a report for the user and systems management.

### 8.12.2 Program Design

We have recently read about the various types of program designs. Choose one of them to design your program. This should envisioned as a step-by-step procedure. The programmer's problem is then to design a process (or algorithm) which, on being given the correct inputs, produced the required outputs. A program specification also includes a description of the constraints which must apply to the solution. This step consists of preparing documents that will guide the actual coding of the program. This step is considered complete when a clean compile walk-through has been held and the program design has been approved.

### 8.12.3 Coding

This step is the process of transforming the program logic design documents into a computer language format. This stage translates the program design into computer instructions. When the coded program is ready in a high level language, it is entered in a source file using any editor or word processor.

### 8.12.4 Debugging

Who does not make error? When you type the program and try to run it, you are bound to get errors. This process of correcting errors is called Debugging. Debugging aids the built in the computer which give diagnostic messages about any error in the program language either during coding or during key-punching. The errors are corrected and the program is debugged again to find out further errors, if any. This process is repeated till the program is error free. Debugging does not point out logical or arithmetic errors. Debugging program is an important part of program preparation and may even take more time than the actual program writing.

#### 8.12.4.1 Types of Errors

Once a program has been typed in, different types of errors may show up. These include:

**Syntax/Semantic errors**

Syntax is a set of rules governing the structure of an relationship between symbols, words and phrases in a language statement. A syntax error occurs when a program cannot understand the command that has been entered. Computer does not have any intelligence. Therefore, it can do what it is made to do provide it known how to do it. For this, a computer has an operating system and the compiler for programming language. These software convert the instructions given to a computer into a machine language equivalent. When we give the same instruction in a high level language, i.e., similar to English, then the computer compiler first translates it into the machine language and then the switches in the microprocessor of the CPU are so set that the computer performs these instructions one by one.

The compiler which translates the high level language instructions will be able to translate into exact machine language instructions, provided it has received the instructions correctly. If not, then the result will be absurd. For example, when we say Mangoes and Man goes, the meaning totally changes in English. Similarly, in computer language also, a little change in the position of comma or semicolon or a gap will make all the differences in the meaning of the entire instruction. This type of error is called **syntax error** and it is very harmful to the working of the computer. The compiler is able to detect such errors and gives the indication about those locations where the instructions are not understandable. A programmer then correct such instructions and then retypes the syntax errors.

## Logic Errors

Logic refers to a sequence of operations performed by a software or hardware. Software logic or program logic is the sequence of instructions in a program. Logic errors are the errors that have been entered in the instructions created because of the mistake made by a program. Suppose you wanted the sum of A and B and put the result in the variable C. This is accomplished by typing:

$$C: \ = A + B$$

But while typing, the programmer has typed the following expression:

$$C: \ = A - B$$

Such a program will run properly but will give erratic result because the value of C will not be the sum of A and B but it will be the difference of A and B which is quite different. Such errors can only be detected with the help of test data that will give the input values of A and B and the resultant value that should come out of the program as a result of the operation performed on A and B. If the result given by the computer an the result calculated manually with the help of a calculator are the same, then you can say that there is no logical error. Otherwise a logic error may be present in the program.

The logical error given above is very simple. However, all logic errors used not be the result of wrong typing. They could also be the result of wrong definition, as for example. When the sales turnover of a company is checked on the printed price instead of the discounted price. Here if sales are defined as Y and the quantity is defined as X. If we by mistake interpret these two quantities differently, i.e. sales as X instead of Y. Then also the error committed is a logical error. In such a case the result will be logical.

## Runtime Error

Runtime errors occur when a program is run on the computer and the results are not achieved due to some misinterpretation of a particular instruction. This could be some thing like dividing a number by zero which results in a very large value of quotient. At the time of executing a program, the runtime error is detected. Because, one of the values for which a program needs to calculate the result may be to divide the quantity by a very small quantity and the resultant value will be so large that it cannot be interpreted by the computer. This will then be shown as a runtime error. For example, the mass of an electron is very small value. If one divides a quantity by the mass of the electron, the result may be so large that it is beyond the capacity of the machine.

To overcome this problem, there is a built-in error detector in the language interpreter or compiler which will give the message and that will reflect the reason for run time error.

### 8.12.5 Program Testing

It is the job of the program to test, as far as possible, that all parts of the program work correctly. It should be realized that complete testing is not possible except in the case of the most trivial program; one can never be completely certain that all errors have been removed, but sufficient tests can be performed to give a reasonable measure of confidence in the program. The situation is analogous of testing children on multiplication tables; once a child has answered a certain number of multiplication table tests correctly, at some point or other the teacher assume that all other tests will be answered correctly and testing ceases.

#### 8.12.5.1 Designing a Test Plan

Since we cannot test everything because there may be many number of if then else decision and all the test data may not be able to test all the loops. Each test must be carefully planned to provide more information about the program. A major benefit of preparing a comprehensive test plan with expected results is that it forces the programmer to think carefully about the program and often errors are spotted even before running the test.

Testing requires the following:

1. A thorough knowledge and understanding of what the program is supposed to do.
2. Plan out in advance what ought to be tested.
3. To work out expected results for each of the test cases.
4. Writing out the test plan.

#### 8.12.5.2 Methods of Testing

The objectives of testing can be stated in two basic questions:

1. Does the logic work properly? This means, answering the following:
   i. Does the program work as intended?
   ii. Can it be made to crash?
2. Is the necessary logic present? This means answering the following:
   i. Are there any functions missing?
   ii. Does the program or module do everything specified?

There are two different ways of testing. These are:

1. Functional testing
2. Logical or structural testing

#### Functional Testing

Functional testing is carried out independently of the code used in the program. It involves looking at the program specification and creating a set of test data that covers all types of inputs and getting outputs and program functions. This type of testing is also known as "black box testing".

### Logical (structural) Testing

Logical testing (white box testing) is dependent on the code logic and derives from the program structure rather than its function. In other words, we study the program code and try to test each possible path in the program at least once. The problem with logical testing is that it will not detect the missing functions. One method of devising a test plan is to start with a set of functional test cases and then add additional tests to exercise each statement in the program at least once, making sure that each decision is tested for all outcomes.

## 8.12.6 Documentation and Program Maintenance

Documentation of a software system involves collecting, organizing, storing and maintaining a complete historical record of programs and other documents used or prepared during different phases of the system development. The documentation of a program is a continuous process. The program specifications, the algorithmic representation and the program itself can all be considered part of the documentation of a program. However, after successfully completing the program, we must ensure that our documentation us complete and it is in a finished, usable form. This includes both technical documentation for the programmers who maybe working with and modifying the completed program and user-level documentation for the users of the program.

One of the mistaken ideas held by too many programmers is that the documentation for a program should be written only after the program is "finished". This is a very dangerous point of view! It will certainly lead to inadequate documentation and might result in an incomplete or incorrect program. Documentation is a continuous process. It starts when we first begin to formulate a clear problem statement and continuous as we device a solution, express the solution algorithmically and code the algorithm as a computer program. The proper point of view is that documentation is an inherent part of a program. It is therefore meaningless to assert that documentation should be written after the program is finished.

Most programs that are written by professional programmers are used in a production environment. This means that once a program is deemed operational it is used on a regular basis, usually by people other than the author(s). For example, programs to process payrolls, maintain inventories, or handles hotel or airline reservations are invariably used by people who did not write them. Moreover, these people are usually not even programmers. In this sort of environment, we can appreciate the need for the following two different kinds of documentation.

### 8.12.6.1 User Documentation

It provides the information that one needs in order to use a program. This information includes a number of different items. These items are:

1. A description of the application area of the program or what will this program do?
2. A description of the input data that the program requires.
3. A description of the output produced by the program.
4. A description of the commands needed to start the program.
5. A description of the kinds of interactions that are possible with the program.
6. An explanation of all the messages that the program can produce.
7. A discussion (in nontechnical terms) of the performance capabilities and limitations of the program.

### 8.12.6.2 Technical Documentation

This kind of documentation is addressed to programmers who might be faced with the task of modifying the program at some time. Perhaps a mistake will become apparent after the program has been placed into use, or a decision may be made to enhance the program by adding a new feature. In either case, good technical documentation is a necessity.

### 8.12.6.3 Uses of Documentation

The uses of documentation are as follows:

1. They facilitate communication about an application between the technical development personnel and the non-technical users.
2. Documents are very helpful in initiating and training not just new employees, but old employees changing jobs or learning to use a computerized version of an old job. Good documentation will provide a self-instructional approach that will allow employees to advance at their own pace.
3. The documents are essential during abnormal maintenance when a new programmer must maintain a system after the original programmer or analyst has left. This is very common and serious problem. There are numerous cases where an application was left undocumented and could not be maintained. When this occurs, the application must be developed all over again.
4. Documents are essential even among technical personnel not only during developing of a system but also during operations and normal maintenance.
5. The provides a package that will contain the information needed to change the system should the environment or management's needs alter.
6. Documentation prevents system dislocation and cost that might otherwise occur if knowledge of the system were centered in a few individuals who resigned, relocated or were subsequently reassigned other duties.

### 8.12.6.4 Limitations of Documentation

Documentation has the limitations inherent in human communication. The difference in the backgrounds of the user and the documenter and the nature of the high technology that is being documented. This makes the test of a sound documentation more difficult.

Everything cannot be conveyed through the documentation only. It may be difficult for an analyst to convey one's assumptions and one's view of how the system could and should be improved given changed circumstances (of technology or user), interaction which would be invaluable to maintenance and redevelopment.

### Multiple Choice Questions

1. Computer understands only one language and that is:

   a. Source Language  b. Machine Language

   c. High Level Language

2. Computer language used for scientific calculations are:
   a. LOGO b. FORTAN
   c. BASIC
3. The language used for development of various games is:
   a. C b. C++
   c. Java
4. C# allows you to develop for Windows and:
   a. DOS b. Internet
   c. Both
5. Visual Basic is a development tool:
   a. Yes b. No
6. A person engaged in programming is called:
   a. Operator b. Programmer
   c. Analyst
7. Data whose value remains the same thoughout the program is called:
   a. Variable b. Constant
   c. Communicator
8. The process of correcting errors is called:
   a. programming b. flow charting
   c. debugging
9. A syntax error occurs when the system cannot understand a:
   a. command b. logic
   c. flow
10. Pseudocode is written in:
    a. machine language b. English language
    c. programming language

## Descriptive Type Questions

1. What is meant by a programming language?
2. If each new generation of language enhances interaction between programmers and the computer, why not write programs using the most recent generation of languages?
3. What are the differences between high-level and low-level languages?
4. Associate each of language with a particular generation of languages.
5. What are various generations of computer programming languages?
6. What are problem-oriented languages?
7. What is the difference between machine- and assembly-language?
8. What are non-procedural languages? Give few examples.

9. Why are low-level and high-level languages are named so?
10. What are Application Generators? Give few examples.
11. What are procedural languages? Give few examples.
12. What do you mean by computer program?
13. What is algorithm?
14. Explain the different types of algorithms in detail?
15. What is flowchart? Explain the types of flowcharts?
16. What do you mean by pseudocode?
17. What do you mean by program testing?
18. Explain the concept of debugging?
19. What do you mean by program documentation?
20. What are various types of high-level languages?
21. State the capabilities of Query Languages?
22. What are DSSs (Decision Support Systems)? How are they helpful?
23. What do you understand by Specialised Languages? Give few examples.
24. What are Object-Oriented Programming Languages? Give few examples.
25. What are multi-purpose programming languages? Name three such languages.
26. What do you understand by Fifth Generation Languages (5GLs)?
27. What are Report Generators?
28. What are the differences between 3GLs and 4GLs?
29. Name a procedure-oriented programming language in each of the three classifications, namely, scientific, business, and specialised.
30. What are query languages? Give few examples.
31. What are Natural Languages?
32. What is programming?
33. What is data handling?
34. What all the steps in program life cycle?
35. What are Pseudocodes?
36. What is the difference between Pseudocode and flow chart?
37. Which are the various parts of reports?
38. What operations you can perform on the files?
39. Which are the different methods of file updation?
40. What do you understand by top down design?
41. How program testing is done?
42. Describe the various type of errors you get when the program is run?
43. What do you understand by documenation of program?

44. What are the usage and limitations of program documentation?

45. Write a short note on the following:

| | |
|---|---|
| LOGO | FORTRAN |
| COBOL | BASIC |
| PROLOG | PASCAL |
| C | C++ |
| Java | Visual Basic |
| Visual C++ | C# |
| VB.NET | |

CHAPTER 9

# Data Communication and Related Concepts

## 9.1 INTRODUCTION

Data communication is the process of electronically sending data from one point to another. Linking one computer to another permits the power and resources of that computer to be tapped. It also makes possible the sharing and updating of data at different locations.

Computers that are physically located close to each other, either in the same room or building, can communicate data through a direct-cable link. Computers located far apart use a special form of data communication - telecommunication.

The process of using communication facilities such as telephone system and microwave relays to send data between computers is a form of data communication sometimes referred to as telecommunication, or teleprocessing.

## 9.2 DATA COMMUNICATION

We all are acquainted with some sorts of communication in our day to day life. For communication of information and messages we use telephone and postal communication systems. Similarly data and information from one computer system can be transmitted to other systems across geographical areas. Thus data transmission is the movement of information using some standard methods. These methods include electrical signals carried along a conductor, optical signals along an optical fibers and electromagnetic areas.

"Data Communications is the transfer of data or information between a source and a receiver. The source transmits the data and the receiver receives it."

Suppose a manager has to write several letters to various clients. First he has to use his PC and Word Processing package to prepare his letter. If the PC is connected to the entire client's PCs through networking, he can send the letters to all the clients within minutes. Thus irrespective of geographical areas, if PCs are connected through communication channel, the data and information, computer files and any other program can be transmitted to other computer systems within seconds. The modern form of communication like e-mail and Internet is possible only because of computer networking.

The effectiveness of data communication depends upon these three fundamental characteristics.

1. Delivery: The system must deliver the data to the correct destination. The data must be received by the device or user to whom it was sent.
2. Accuracy: The system must deliver data accurately. Data that have been altered in transmission and left uncorrected are unusable.
3. Timeliness: The system must deliver data in a timely manner. Data delivered late are useless. In real time transmission data must be delivered without significant delay as in case of audio and video data.

Data communication consists of five basic components:

1. Message: The message is the information or data to be communicated. i can be text, numbers, pictures, sound or video or combination of these.
2. Sender: The sender is the device that sends the message. It can be a computer, work station, camera etc.
3. Receiver: The receiver is the device that receives the message. It can be a computer, work station, television etc.
4. Medium: The transmission medium is the path by which message travels from sender to receiver. It can be a wire, coaxial cable, fibre optics, laser or radio waves etc.
5. Protocol: A protocol is a set of rules that governs the data communication. It represents the agreement of communicating devices. Without a protocol devices can not communicate to each other.

## 9.3 FORMS OF DATA TRANSMISSION

There are two forms of data transmission:

- Analog Data Transmission
- Digital Data Transmission

***Analog data transmission*** is the transmission of data in a continuous waveform. The telephone system is an example of a system designed for analog data transmission.

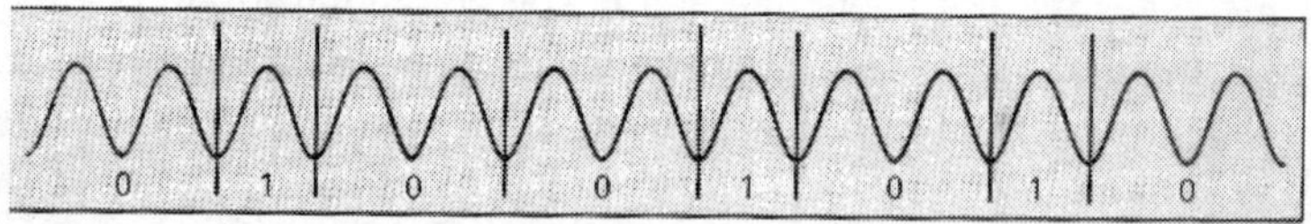


**Fig 9.1:** Analog Signal (Waveform)

***Digital data transmission*** is the transmission of data using distinct on and off electrical states. Recall that data in digital form are represented as either on (1) or off (0). Because the data communication is faster and more efficient than analog, it would seem that all data communication between computers would be in digital form, however, that is not the case. Totally digital is possible; however, the telephone system, an analog system, is used for a great percentage of data communication because it is the largest and most widely used communication system in place. Because of the expense involved in converting to a digital system in place. Because of the expense involved in converting to a digital system or running a duplicate digital system, a method was devised allowing the digital data to be transmitted over telephone lines. The process is called modulation-demodulation.

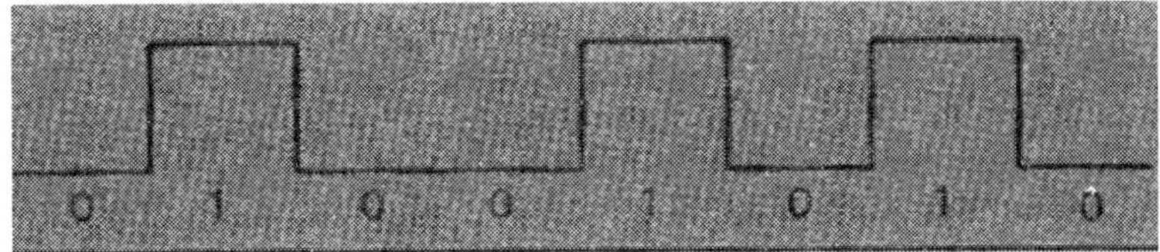


**Fig. 9.2:** Digital Signal

### Benefits of Digital Data Transmission

The following are the benefits gained by transmitting data in digital form:

- Ability to achieve extremely low error rates on digital circuits
- Properly designed digital circuits are less susceptible to distortion and interference
- Regeneration of digital signals to extend length of the link without accumulating additional noise and distortion as would be the case with analog repeaters
- Digital multiplexing is much simpler than frequency division multiplexing on analog lines
- Digital components and circuits are less expensive and more reliable than analog ones.
- Various forms of digital signals can be integrated and transmitted together e.g. data, digitized voice, digitized TV and FAX
- Complicated and complex functions such as statistical multiplexing and digital switching may be implemented on digital systems at low cost because the signals do not require expensive modems for conversion into digital form before they may be processed.

## 9.4 MODEM AND ITS TYPES

The word Modem stands for **Mo**dulator-**Dem**odulator. Data in computer is formatted as digital signals. However, because telephone lines were designed to transmit the human voice, they format data as analog signals. For communication between computers to take place over a telephone line, the digital signal must be converted to an analog signal before it is transmitted. After its journey over the telephone lines, the analog signal must then be reconverted back to a digital signal so that it can be used by the receiving computer.

The process of converting a digital signal to an analog signal is called modulation. Demodulation is the process of reconverting the analog signal back to a digital signal. The device that accomplishes both of these processes is called a modem.

When all the telephone lines become digital carrier, the modem will no longer be required. Till then you need a modem to connect tó Internet, dial-into the bulletin board systems (BBSs) and other commercial on-line services and to send/receive E-Mail and Fax messages. Most modems today are capable of sending and receiving faxes. These modems are called Fax-Modems. Most manufacturers supply the software for their modems. Microsoft Windows 95 has its own modem utilities including utilities for sending and receiving faxes.

The speed at which modems can transfer data is measured in bits per second (bps). The modems that usually uses for connecting to the Internet have transfer rates in the range of 14,4 Kbps. But modems with transfer rates of 28.8 Kbps, 33.6 Kbps and 56 Kbps are now available in the market. If we intend to use a modem to explore the WWW and download a lot of files we should buy a faster modem of 28.8 Kbps or 33.6 Kbps.

Different types are Modems are shown in ***Fig. 9.3.***

**Fig. 9.3:** Modems

The three basic types of modems used in microcomputers are:

a. Acoustic Modem
b. External Direct-connect Modem
c. Internal Direct-connect Modem

### 9.4.1 Acoustic Modem

The acoustic modem, or acoustic coupler as it is sometimes called, has two cups into which the handset of your telephone is placed. The acoustic modem sends data through the mouthpiece and receives data through the ear-piece of the handset. This type of modem is not used very often today because:

i. The signal is much more susceptible to distortion than with other types of modems; and
ii. The carbon microphones used in a telephone handset limit the rate of data transmission.

### 9.4.2 External Direct-connect Modem

An external direct-connect modem is external to the computer and connects directly to the telephone line with a modular phone jack. The direct connection greatly reduces the signal's distortion and permits faster data transfer rates. A popular external direct-connect modems have a variety of features not found on acoustic modems, including the ability to:

- Check the operating status using status lights and speakers
- Change the speed at which data are transmitted
- Dial and answer the phone automatically
- Respond to commands from a communication program
- Self-test to verify the modem's ability to correctly transmit data

Because the specialised circuitry in these modems allows them to perform these and other functions, they often called ***smart or intelligent*** devices.

### 9.4.3 Internal Direct-connect Modem

An internal direct-connect modem has all the needed communication circuitry on a plug-in board that fits into one of the expansion slots inside the computer. A separate communication board or serial port with

RS-232 interface is not needed. Internal direct-connect modems also link directly to the telephone line with a modular phone jack. These modems have many of the same special features as the external direct-connect modems. In addition, they take no desk space and are ideal for use in portable computers.

***Internal Direct-connect Modem vs. External Direct-connect Modem*** Both of these can be compared in Table 9.1.

**Table 9.1**

| S. No. | Internal Direct-connect Modem | External Direct-connect Modem |
|---|---|---|
| 1. | Very difficult to install and configure | Easy to install and configure |
| 2. | Has its own built-in serial port and is thus unaffected by the UART chip problem. | It may require a new serial port if machine is old and the modem is faster. |
| 3. | It doesn't require a serial cable or additional power socket. | It requires an additional electrical socket and cable |
| 4. | It doesn't require additional desk space | It will need desk space. |
| 5. | When modem gets stuck, we need to turn off the machine and then turn it on, which results in wastage of time | When it gets stuck, getting it back to work is as easy as flipping a switch |
| 6. | It may require changes in hardware settings. | It hardly requires any change in hardware settings |

## 9.5 COMMUNICATION CHANNELS

A communication channel is a medium through which data is transmitted among devices. It provides a way for data to be exchanged between remote sites and a computer or among multiple computer. The main providers of communication channels for computer users are the telephone companies and long distance carriers. It is also possible for an organisation to set up its own wires, cables, or electronic links to establish a private a communication capability. With either of these approaches, the primary types of channels available for transmission of data include the following:

- Wire cable
- Microwave
- Fibre optics
- Communication Satellites
- Laser beams
- RADAR

### 9.5.1 Wire Cable

Wire cable it is the most common type of data communication channel in use. It includes telegraph lines, telephone lines, and coaxial cables. These are the most popular channels. It can be classified in the following two categories:

- Telegraph Cable
- Telephone Cables
- Twisted-pair Cable
- Co-axial Cable

## Telegraph Cable

A telegraph line usually consists of a single strand of wire connecting two points. The name telegraph ties this kind of channel to the days when transmissions took place on strands of wire that usually ran beside railroad tracks. Signals were initiated at telegraph keys that served as switches to make or break connections. Communication occurred when trained operators decoded the series of clicks that made up Morse Code.

This type of channel is simple and inexpensive. On telegraph lines, communication takes place in one direction at a time. Services available on telegraph lines are Simplex and Half-duplex transmissions.

## Telephone Cables

One-way-at-a-time transmission would not work foe telephone calls. People want to be able to talk whenever they feel they have something to say. Therefore, telephone lines use two carriers, or a pair of wires to make it possible to send and receive signals at the same time. This kind of transmission is called full-duplex service. Under full-duplex transmission, two people can talk at once or two data transmission points can be sending and receiving at the same time.

Telephone Lines are shown in Fig. 9.4

**Fig. 9.4:** Telephone Lines

Telephone lines also make possible one-way transmission of greater information volumes than telegraph lines. This is because two wires have a far greater transmission capacity, or bandwidth, than one. Thus, while single telegraph lines carry about 60 words per minute, a single pair of wires that make up a telephone line can carry 1200 or more words per minute, depending on the line quality and signal generation methods.

## Twisted-pair Cable

It is the oldest and still most common transmission line. It consists of copper wires twisted into pairs. These lines are used in established communication networks throughout the world for both voice as well as data transmission.

### Co-axial Cable

It consists of a sturdy copper or aluminium wire wrapped with spacers to insulate and protect it. The insulation minimises the interference and distortion of the signals the cable carries. Groups of coaxial cables may be bundled together in a big cable for ease of installation. High-quality co-axial cables can be placed underground and laid on the floors of lakes and oceans. They allow high-speed data transmission.

Coaxial cables are used on mainframe computers to link the processor to secondary storage units and other high-speed peripherals. These are also used to transmit TV signals from cameras to broadcast transmitters or across the country for broadcast into different regions. Data transmission capabilities of coaxial cable channels run into the millions of bits per second tom provide broadband service.

#### Advantages

- Easier to use
- Cheaper to use the extensive wire-cable networks that already exists.
- Reduced compatibility problems due to standardised technology used to transmit data over wire cables

#### Disadvantages

- As data is transmitted in analog form while using wire cable, so digital data must be converted to an analog signal before they reach the wire cable.
- Conversion from digital data to analog signal requires special hardware
- Digital to analog form and then back to digital form conversion slows down the transmission of data.
- Wire cable is subject to electrical interference making it less reliable than other types of communication channels.
- Difficult to create physical links needed where users are separated by large distances or natural barriers such as mountains or seas.

## 9.5.2 Microwave

Another type of analog communication channel is microwave. Microwave signals are transmitted through the atmosphere as radio and television signals are transmitted rather than through wire cables. A microwave system consists of towers located at intervals of 25 to 30 miles on which dish-like antennas are mounted. Microwave signals must be transmitted in a straight line as they do not bend around corners or around the curve of the earth. Transmitter stations redirect and boost the signals. Satellites are also used to direct microwaves over geographically dispersed large areas.

Microwave systems have the capacity to carry large quantities of data i.e. both digital and analog at high rates of speed. They are used for the transmission of TV and telephonic signals.

Microwave tower and Radio Tower are shown in ***Fig. 9.5.***

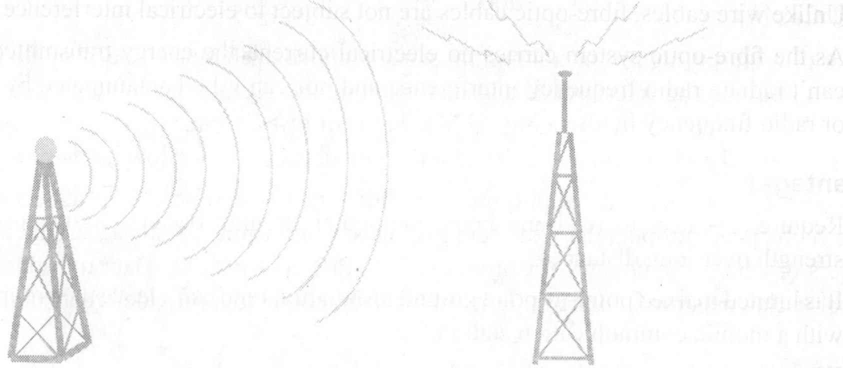

Fig. 9.5: (a) Microwave Tower (b) Radio Tower

### Advantages

- Microwave has a much lower error rate thus making it more reliable as compared to wire-cable.
- Communication links can be made over large distances and rough terrains as there are no physical links between the sending and receiving systems.

### Disadvantages

- Very high cost of ground stations and satellites to support a microwave communication channels.

## 9.5.3 Fiber Optics

Third type of communication channel is fibre optics. Unlike wire cable and microwave, a fibre-optic channel transmits data in digital form. It uses light impulses that travel through clear flexible tubing. The tubing is thinner than a human hair and hundreds of them can fit in the same amount of space required for one wire cable. Technical developments continue to drive down the costs of installing, using and manufacturing fibre optics which will help to make it competitive with traditional cabling.

The 'core' of a fibre-optic cable is a very thin strand of highly refined cylindrical glass. The glass core of the cable may have a diameter as small as 4.5 mm or as large as 400 mm. A second layer of glass is called the clad which surrounds the core. The clad is fused directly to the core so that it is very difficult to see the boundary between the two with naked eyes.

### Advantages

- Transmission losses of fibre-optic cables are much lower than that of wire cables.
- Fibre optics are very reliable communication channels.
- Photons of light rather than an electrical signal move through the optical fibre and thus there are no chances of any sparking, which results into a safer system.
- Provide substantial size and weight reduction as well as increased speed and greater carrying capacity.
- Data can be transmitted at very high speeds with few or no errors.
- Glass is immune to corrosive and oxide degradation and thus will stand up well in hostile environments.

- Unlike wire cables, fibre-optic cables are not subject to electrical interference.
- As the fibre-optic system carries no electrical current, the energy transmitted through the fibre can't radiate radio frequency interference and nor can it be contaminated by any external noise or radio frequency fields.

### Disadvantages

- Require repeaters to read and boost the signal strength because light pulses will lose signal strength over long distances.
- It is limited to fixed point-to-point ground installations and can't leave the ground nor be associated with a mobile communication station.
- Ways in which the light source can be modulated are limited.
- Higher-power devices required as light-emitting sources are very costly.

## 9.5.4 Communication Satellites

The availability of communication satellites has made it possible to transmit microwave signals over thousands of miles. Satellites have now become an integral part of the world-wide communication system. Communication satellites in space orbiting 22,000 miles above the earth, are also used as microwave relay stations because they rotate at the precise point and speed above the equator that makes them appear stationary to microwave transmitters on the ground. The satellite is nothing more than a radio-relay station but they have one potential i.e. the capability of a direct line-of-sight path to 98 % of the earth's surface.

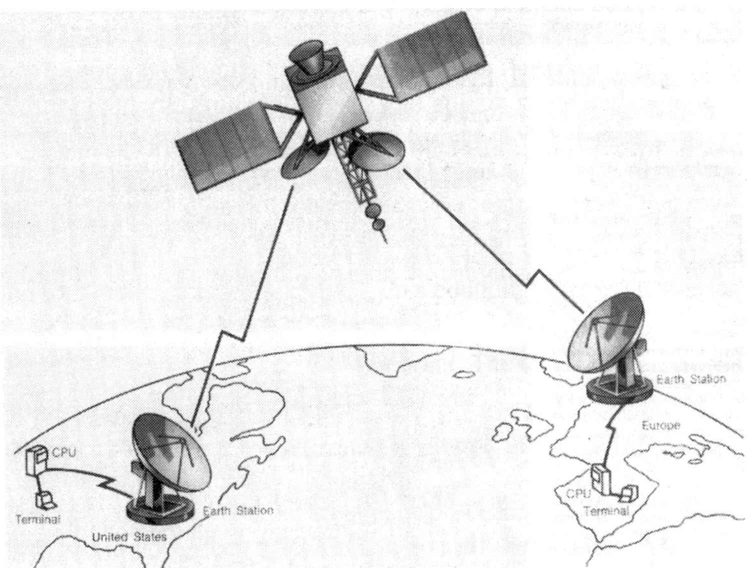


**Fig. 9.6:** Communication over geographical locations using Communication Satellites

Among the dozens of satellites now orbiting the earth and handling voice, video and data communications are those launched by INTELSAT (International Telecommunication Satellite Consortium). INTELSAT began with the Early Bird satellite in 1965 and now forms a world-wide communication system for over 100 countries. It accounts for most long-distance international communications.

Parts of communication satellite are shown in Fig. 9.7.

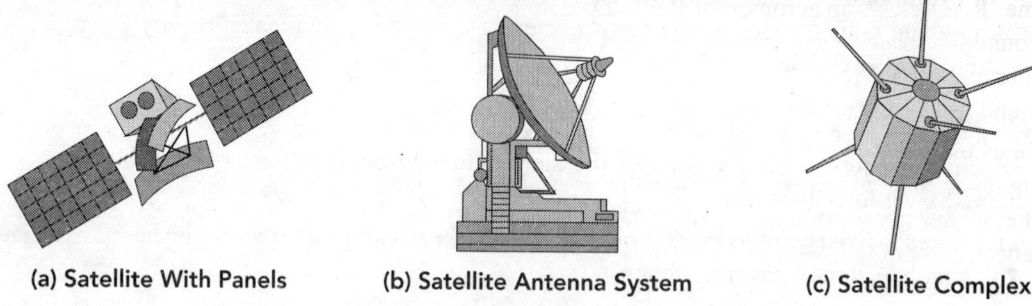

(a) Satellite With Panels (b) Satellite Antenna System (c) Satellite Complex

**Fig. 9.7:** Parts of Communication Satellite

## Satellite Components

The following are five major components in a satellite:

- Transponder: It is a high frequency radio receiver, a frequency down-converter and a power amplifier, which is used to transmit the down-link signal.
- Antenna System: The antenna system contains the antennas and mechanisms to position them correctly. Once properly in place, they will generally function trouble-free for the life of the satellite.
- Power Package: Power package is nothing but the power supply to the satellite. The satellite must be powered either from a battery or solar energy system. In the case of communication satellites in the Clarke orbit, a combination of battery power and solar energy is used. A solar cell system supplies the power to run the electronics and charge the batteries during the sunlight cycle and the battery furnishes the energy during eclipse.
- Control and Information System: It is called the Station Keeping system. The function of the Station Keeping system is to keep the satellite in the correct orbit with the antennas pointed in the exact direction desired.

Rocket Thruster System: It is also called the Station Keeping system

## 9.5.5 Laser Beams

Laser beams can also be directed over distances and can serve as communication channels. As is true for microwave links, laser beams travel in straight lines and require line-of-sight relay points. Most applications of laser beams for data transmission are over short distances. Examples include links between office buildings that are across the street from one another.

## Advantages

- Great potential for use of light as a broadband and high-quality data communication carrier.
- Limitations
- Infrared radiation of laser beams may be dangerous to health.
- Controlled environment is required for laser beam systems.

### 9.5.6 RADAR

The name 'RADAR' is an acronym of Radio Detecting And Ranging. It denotes the method of scanning the surrounding space by means of high frequency radio waves, which are sent out from a powerful transmitter and are reflected by any objects, which they encounter. The reflected beam is picked up by a receiver and its strength and direction gives information on the size, distance, altitude, etc. of the object.

If for example, an observer in an aircraft wishes to survey by radar the terrain over which he is flying, a rotating radar beam is directed downward from the aircraft. The beam scans a circular area in the form of a sector, which sweeps round and round. Depending on the nature of the reflecting objects, the intensity of the reflected beam will vary. The transmission and reception of the high frequency waves are effected in the radar apparatus.

**Fig. 9.8:** RADAR System

The radar waves are generated in the transmitter, which is equipped with radio tubes of special designs. The transmitting antenna usually also functions as the receiving antenna. The process is called 'periodic changeover'. The receiver picks up the reflected beam and the corresponding electronic circuits are used to deflect an electron beam in a CRT (cathode ray tube). The beam is so deflected that it scans the luminescent screen from the center to the edge while it rotates at the same speed as the antenna.

RADAR Screen is shown in Fig. 9.9.

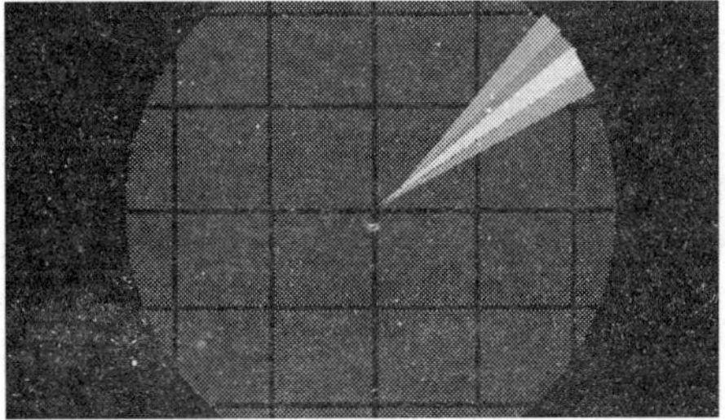

**Fig. 9.9:** RADAR Screen

Most radar sets employ pulse radar. This is so called because the transmitter sends out short intense bursts or pulses of energy with a relatively long interval between the pulses. The receiver is active during this interval. When sufficient time has elapsed to permit the reception of echoes from the most distant objects of interest, the transmitter sends another short pulse and the cycle is repeated.

## 9.6 DATA TRANSMISSION MODES

There are three ways for transmitting data from one point to another

1. **Simplex:** In simplex mode the communication can take place in one direction. The receiver receives the signal from the transmitting device. In this mode the flow of information is Uni.-directional. Hence it is rarely used for data communication.
2. **Half-duplex:** In half-duplex mode the communication channel is used in both directions, but only in one direction at a time. Thus a half-duplex line can alternately send and receive data.
3. **Full-duplex:** In full duplex the communication channel is used in both directions at the same time. Use of full-duplex line improves the efficiency as the line turn-around time required in half-duplex arrangement is eliminated. Example of this mode of transmission is the telephone line.

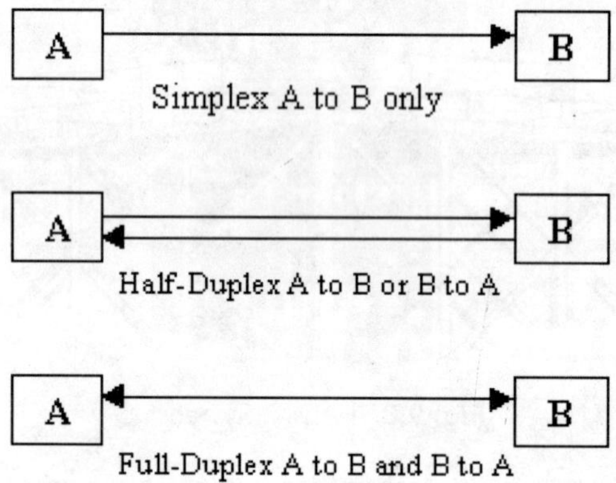


**Figure 9.10:** Data Transmission modes

## 9.7 COMMUNICATION CHANNEL CONFIGURATIONS

The following two are the principal communication channel configurations:

- Point-to-point
- Multi-point

### 9.7.1 Point-to-point Configuration

In a point-to-point channel configuration, a device (e.g., a terminal or computer) is connected directly to another device by a dedicated communication channel, giving those devices sole use of that channel. Point-to-point channel can be an inefficient and costly configuration if a terminal is not active enough to keep the line busy.

### 9.7.2 Multi-point Configuration

Another configuration is multi-point channel configuration in which three or more devices are connected to the same line. The multi-point configuration uses the communication channel more efficiently and reduces the amount of inter-cabling needed, which ultimately lower its cost.

Two methods are used to determine which device gets access to a channel:

- Polling and
- Contention.

#### Polling

In polling, the computer checks each device, one at a time, to see if the device has a message to send. If the device has a message ready, transmission begins; if not, the computer moves on to the next device to poll it. After all devices have been individually polled, the process begins again.

#### Limitation

A disadvantage to polling is that if there are no messages to be sent by the device being polled, the computer's processor will be idle, wasting expensive processor time.

#### Contention

Contention method puts the devices in control, i.e., each device monitors the communication channel to see if the channel is free. If the channel is free, the device will send its message. If the communication channel is being used, the device will wait for a pre-determined amount of time and will try again. This process is repeated until the channel is free.

#### Limitation

A problem with this approach is that although the processor is not idle, one device can tie up the communication channel for long periods of time.

## 9.8 CHANNEL SHARING

The purpose of channel sharing is to increase the efficiency of use of a communication channel. The following are three methods used to regulate the flow of data from communication channels into a computer:

- Multiplexing
- Concentration
- Controlling

### 9.8.1 Multiplexing

Multiplexing is a form of data transmission in which one communication channel carries several transmissions at the same time. The telephone lines that carry our daily conversations can carry thousands or even more of conversations at a time using multiplexing concept. The exact number of simultaneous transmission depends on the type of communication channel and the data transmission rate. Accordingly, the communication channel is shared in such a way as to maximum the utilization of the channel capacity.

Thus the method of dividing a single channel into many channels so that a number of independent signals may be transmitted on it is known as Multiplexing.

### Multiplexing schemes can be divided into three basic categories:

1. Frequency Division Multiplexing (FDM)
2. Time Division Multiplexing (TDM)
3. Wave Division Multiplexing (FDM)

## 9.8.1.1 Frequency Division Multiplexing (FDM)

FDM is the technique used to divide the bandwidth available in a physical medium into a number of smaller independent logical channels with each channel having a small bandwidth. The method of using a number of carrier frequencies each of which is modulated by an independent speech signal is in fact frequency division multiplexing.

Three voice-grade telephone channels are multiplexing using FDM. When many channels are multiplexed together, 400Hz is allocated to each channel to keep them well separated. First the voice channels are raised in frequency, each by a different amount. Then they can be combined, because no two channels how occupy the same portion of the spectrum. Notice that even though there are gaps (guard bands) between the channels, there is some overlap between adjacent channels, because the filters do not have sharp edges. This overlap means that a strong spike at the edge of one channel will be felt in the adjacent one as non-thermal noise.

Frequency-division multiplexing works best with low-speed devices. The frequency division multiplexing schemes used around the world is to some degree standardized. A wide spread standard is 12 400-Hz each voice channels (300Hz for user, plus two guard bands of 500Hz each) multiplexed into the 60 to 108 KHz band. Many carriers offer a 48 to 56 kbps leased line service to customers, based on the group. Other standards upto 230000 voice channels also exist.

**Example:** *The allocated spectrum is about 1 MHz, roughly 500 to 1500 KHz. Different (stations, each operating in a portion of the spectrum. With the interchannel separation great enough to prevent interference. This system is an example of frequency division multiplexing.*

### Advantages of FDM

1. Here user can be added to the system by simply adding another pair of transmitter modulator and receiver demodulators.
2. FDM system support full duplex information flow which is required by most of application.
3. Noise problem for analog communication has lesser effect.

### Disadvantages of FDM

1. In FDM system, the initial cost is high. This may include the cable between the two ends and the associated connectors for the cable.
2. In FDM system, a problem for one user can sometimes affect others.
3. In FDM system, each user requires a precise carrier frequency.

### 9.8.1.2 Time Division Multiplexing (TDM)

TDM is another popular method of utilizing the capacity of a physical channel effectively. Each user of the channel is allotted a small time interval during which is may transmit a message. Thus the total time available in the channel is divided and each user is allocated a time slice. In TDM, user send message sequentially one after another. Each user can, however, use the full channel bandwidth during the period he has control over the channel. The channel capacity is fully utilized in TDM by interleaving a number of messages belonging to different users into one long message. This message sent through the physical channel must be separated at the receiving end. Individual chunks of message sent by each user should be reassembled into a full message.

Unfortunately, TDM can only be used for digital data multiplexing. Since local loops produce analog signals, a conversion is needed from analog to digital in the end office. Where all the individual local loops come together to be combined onto outgoing trucks.

**Example:** *In some countries, the individual stations have two logical sub channels: music and advertising. These two alternate in time on the same frequency first a burst of music, then a burst of advertising, then more music and so on. This situation is time division multiplexing.*

#### Advantages of TDM

1. It uses a single links.
2. It does not require precise carrier matching at both end of the links.
3. Use of capacity is high.
4. Each to expand the number of users on a system at a low cost.
5. There is no need to include identification of the traffic stream on each packet.

#### Disadvantages of TDM

1. The sensitivity to other user problem is high.
2. Initial cost is high.
3. Technical complexity is more.
4. The noise problem for analog communication has greater effect.

### 9.8.1.3 Wave Division Multiplexing (WDM)

Wave or **Wavelength Division Multiplexing (WDM)** is used with fibre optic cables. WDM is a technology that closely resembles frequency division multiplexing, but is specifically used to combine lots of Optical Carrier signals into a single optical fibre.

The WDM technique relies on a laser that is designed to emit single colours of light. Each of the signals that are to be transmitted is then attached to a laser that will emit a different coloured light beam. All these individual light beams are then sent at the same time. At the receiving end, a device splits the combined colours back into the original individual colours again.

### 9.8.2 Concentration

Frequently, it is necessary to connect more devices to a computer than the communication channel can handle at once. Concentration is the process of connecting and serving these devices. A concentrator, often a minicomputer, is the hardware that provides concentration. When the number of devices transmitting exceeds the capability of the communication channel, the data are stored in a buffer for later transmission. Many multiplexers also provide concentration.

### 9.8.3 Controlling

Controllers or cluster controllers, link groups of terminals or other devices to a communication channels. The controller polls the status of each terminal and transfers data from a terminal to the host computer when necessary.

## 9.9 FRONT-END PROCESSORS

A front-end processor is a processor that handles all the data-communication control functions. While the CPU in the front-end processor handles all the communication tasks, the CPU of the main computer is free to work on other tasks. The two processors interact only when data need to be passed between them. A typical front-end processor might control scores of communication channels of varying types and speeds coming from a number of diverse remote terminals.

Indeed, front-end processors are computers i.e. they have some identical circuitry and perform many of the operations that a data processing equipment performs. These can be programmed to perform a variety of functions such as concentration, error control, code conversion, buffering, and other functions related to data and message control.

## 9.10 DATA TRANSMISSION

In the present Information Technology (IT) scenario, speed of data transmission has a significant role to play. Every information enthusiast wants to be able to make the data transmission speeds even more faster. Information that once took days to receive now seems to be available on the very next moment of pressing the key.

#### What is Baud Rate?

The rate at which data is transferred is called the baud rate. In fact, baud rate is the number of times per second the signal being transmitted modulates or demodulates. Baud rate is measured in terms of bits per second (bps). Although higher speeds are possible, typical data transmission speeds are 300, 1200, 2400, 4800, 9600, 14,400 bps. There are two factors that determine the rate at which data can be transmitted over communication channels:

- Channel bandwidth
- Method of data transmission

### 9.10.1 Channel Bandwidths

The bandwidth, or grade, of a communication channel determines the rate, or speed, at which data can be transmitted over a channel. The term ***"bandwidth"*** is often shortened to ***"band"***. There are three bands for communication channels:

- Narrow-band
- Voice-band
- Broad-band

The slowest of these is ***the narrow-band channel***, which transmits data at rates between 40 and 100 bps. A telegraph line is a narrow-band channel.

***Voice-band channel*** can transmit data at rates between 110 and 9,600 bps. Telephone lines are voice-band channels.

The fastest of these is the ***broad-band channel***, which can transmit data at rates up to several mega-bits per second (mbps). Advancement in technology continues to improve to allow data to be transmitted on some types of broad-band channels in the range of billions-of-bits-per-second (bbps). Microwaves, coaxial cables, and fibre optics are all broad-band channels.

### 9.10.2 Methods of Data Transmission

There are two methods of transmission:

- Asynchronous Transmission
- Synchronous Transmissions

#### 9.10.2.1 Asynchronous Transmission

It is a transmission method in which one character is sent at a time and the transfer of data is controlled by start bits and stop bits. Each character is surrounded by bits that signal the beginning and end of the character. These characters allow the receiving terminal to synchronise itself with the receipt of data on a character-by-character basis.

Asynchronous transmission is the least expensive of the two methods. It is often used in low-speed transmission of data in conjunction with narrow-band and some lower speed voice-band channels where the transmitting device operates manually or at irregular intervals.

#### 9.10.2.2 Synchronous Transmission

In this type of transmission method, blocks of characters are transmitted in timed sequences. Rather than using start and stop bits around each character, each block of characters is marked with synchronisation characters. The receiving device accepts data until it detects a special ending character or a predetermined number of characters at which time the device knows the message has come to an end.

#### Protocols

A set of traffic rules and procedures framed for data transmission are called data-transmission protocols. The same protocols must be followed by all devices participating in the communication session. These rules may vary from one device to another.

#### Handshaking

Prearranged signals defining the protocol to be followed when transmitting and receiving data are sent between computers in an exchange called handshaking.

## EXERCISE

1. What do you understand by data communication?
2. What is data communication media? What are various types of communication media?
3. What is a communication package?
4. Enumerate the functions performed by a communication package.
5. What is a modem? How does it work? Explain.
6. What do you understand by analog and digital signals?
7. What are microwave systems?
8. What is a RADAR? How does it work?
9. What are communication satellites and how do they function?
10. What is fibre-optics? State the importance if fibre-optics in communication systems.
11. What are the advantages and disadvantages of fibre-optic cables?
12. What is an Electronic Mail/Message System (EMMS)? Enumerate the services rendered by an EMMS.
13. What is a Voice Mail System? How does it function?
14. What is message distribution system? What are its functions.
15. What is microwave and how it can be used for computer communication? What are their advantages and disadvantages?
16. What is a FAX system? Explain its working.
17. What do you means by Information Retrieval Systems? State their importance.
18. What components are typically found in a simple data communication system?
19. Enumerate the facilities offered by Bank-at-home and On-line-brokerage information services.
20. Illustrate a microwave communication link used for point-to-point data transfer.
21. What are commercial database services? Explain any two important commercial database services of your choice.
22. Which type of communication channel can transmit data in digital form?
23. Why are computing and communication technologies merging?
24. What is a front-end-processor? State its function.
25. What is a multiplexer? What is the purpose of a multiplexer?
26. Describe and sketch how a point-to-point configuration works.
27. What is polling? State its usage.
28. Illustrate the difference between bit-rate and baud-rate?
29. "Coaxial cable has smaller bandwidth than optical fibre". Explain it.
30. What is twisted-pair cable? In what situations are they suitable for use in data communication?
31. Describe the process of concentration.
32. What are the benefits of internal and external modems?

33. Differentiate between narrow-band, voice-band and broad-band communication channels.
34. List and describe the various types of modem.
35. What do you understand by modulation and demodulation? Why is modulation used in signal transmission?
36. What purpose do modems serve in data communication systems?
37. What is the normal speed of transmission of digital signals on a telephone line?
38. Give a brief description of the transmission characteristics of coaxial cable and optical fibre.
39. Describe the various modes in which the transfer of data can occur.
40. When are public telephone lines used to connect a terminal to a computer?
41. How are data transmission speeds measured? What are some typical speeds?
42. What facts must be known in order to communicate with a large computer system?
43. What is an intelligent modem?
44. What are the advantages of using fibre-optic as compared to copper wires for data communication?
45. Explain the various types of communication channels.
46. What is meant by file-transfer protocols? Explain.
47. What are serial and parallel data transmission? When are they used in data communication?
48. Why is earth to satellite transmission frequency different from satellite to earth transmission frequency?
49. What is channel-sharing? How can it be accomplished?
50. When is RS2332-C standard interconnection used? Explain the characteristics of the RS232-C interface.
51. What are the various methods of data transmission?
52. What do you understand by Gateway Services?
53. How does Videotext Service differ from Teletext Service?
54. What is video-conferencing? What is the infrastructure required for video-conferencing?
55. How does laser beam work as a communication media?
56. What are the common media used in data transmission? Also give their advantages and disadvantages.
57. Outline the application of laser beam communication media.
58. What is teleconferencing? Outline its benefits and limitations.
59. What are the components required for a communication package?
60. What is the difference between analog and digital transmission? Give their relative advantages and disadvantages?
61. What is a microwave media? Explain its utility in data transmission.
62. What is a communication protocol? Why are they required in creating networks?
63. What is packet switching? Why is this method used for digital communication between computers?
64. What do you understand by multiplexing?

65. What is meant by computerised conferencing?
66. What is meant by bandwidth of a channel? State its importance.
67. Why are channels multiplexed for signal processing?
68. What is an E-Mail service? What are various E-Mail types?
69. What is a acoustic-coupler? How is it different from normal modem?
70. Explain the terms Simplex, Half-duplex and Full-duplex.
71. What is the capacity of coax for digital transmission? What is its typical bandwidth?
72. What do you understand by the term broadband and baseband? How do they differ?
73. What is the purpose Xmodem and Kermit Protocols?
74. What are the main advantages of satellite communications?
75. What is a Bulletin Board System (BBS)? State its types.
76. Differentiate between synchronous and asynchronous data transmission modes.
77. Why is modulation used in signal transmission?

CHAPTER 10

# Computer Networks and Internet

## 10.1 INTRODUCTION

Computers that are physically located close to each other, either in the same room or building, can communicate data through a direct-cable link. Computers located far apart use a special form of data communication - telecommunication.

The process of using communication facilities such as telephone system and microwave relays to send data between computers is a form of data communication sometimes referred to as telecommunication, or teleprocessing.

## 10.2 COMPUTER NETWORK

A computer network is an interconnection of various computer systems located at different places. In computer network two or more computers are linked together with a medium and data communication devices for the purpose of communicating data and sharing resources. The computer that provides resources to other computers on a network is known as server. In the network the individual computers, which access shared network resources, are known as workstations or nodes.

### 10.2.1 Need of Computer Network

The need of a computer network arose due to:

- Limited resources
- Desire to share the resources
- Cost Reduction

Today, that's a limiting view, because the most important resource is information. Network lets us share information and the same is achieved by Resource Sharing.

**Fig. 10.1:** Computer Network

#### Resource Sharing

The purpose of many computer networks is to permit a far-flung community of users to share computer resources. Many such users now have their own microcomputers, so the shared resources have to be interesting enough to warrant access via a network. The facilities accessible by networks are in fact becoming more interesting at a rapid rate.

The remote computer may contain software which a user needs to employ. It may be proprietary software kept at one location. It may require a larger machine than any at the user's location. The distant computer may provide access to data which is stored and maintained at its location. Sometimes the remote machine controls a large or special printing facility. Sometimes the remote machine compiles programs which are used on smaller peripheral machines.

The resource sharing will automatically result in Cost Reduction.

### Cost Reduction

There are various aspects of technology which are likely to force the price of terminal usage drastically lower. This is important because almost all aspects of telecommunications are characterised by high price elasticity. In other words, when the price comes down, the usage goes up.

## 10.2.2 Key Issues in a Computer Network

The following are the major key issues to be thrashed out very carefully before we go for a computer network:

- Nature of Nodes: Whether participating nodes are homogeneous or heterogeneous in nature?
- Topology: Which of the computer topology has to be followed? Computer topology accounts for the physical arrangement of participating computers in the network.
- Interconnection Type: Whether interconnection type is point-to-point, multi-point, or broadcast type?
- Reliability: How reliable our network is? Reliability aspect includes error rate, redundancy and recovery procedures.
- Channel Capacity Allocation: Whether allocation of channel capacity is time-division or frequency division?
- Routing Techniques: Whether message between nodes are to be routed through: Deterministic, Stochastic, and Distributed routing techniques?
- Models: Which of the models i.e. Analytical models, Queuing models, Simulation models, Measurement and Validation models are applicable?
- Channel Capacity: What are the channel capacities of the communication lines connecting nodes?
- Access: Whether computer access in the network is direct-access or through a sub-network?
- Protocols: What levels, standards and formats are to be followed while establishing communication between participating nodes?
- Performance: How is higher performance of computer network achieved? Response time, time to connect, resource utilisation, etc. contribute towards performance of computer network.
- Control: Whether centralised control, distributed control or hierarchical control of participating nodes of computer network is suitable?

## 10.3 TYPES OF COMPUTER NETWORK

The following are different types of networks:

1. Local Area Network (LAN)
2. Wireless Local Area Network (WLAN)
3. Wide Area Network (WAN)
4. Metropolitan Area Network (MAN)
5. Storage Area Network (SAN)
6. Campus Area Network (CAN)
7. Personal Area Network (PAN)
8. Desk Area Network (DAN)

### Criteria for Classification of Computer Networks

The following are the characteristics used to classify different types of computer networks:

- Topology: Topology is nothing but the geometric arrangement of positioning computer systems to involve them in the form of a network. For example, Star topology, Bus topology, etc.
- Protocol: The protocols are nothing but the set of rules and signals that are used for communication in the network. For example, 'Ethernet' is one of the most popular protocols for LANs.
- Architecture: Networks can usually be classified in the following two types:

i. Peer-to-peer architecture

ii. Client-Server architecture

All of the above have been described next in this chapter.

### 10.3.1 Local Area Network (LAN)

A local area network (LAN) is two or more computers directly linked within a small well-defined area such as a room, building, or group of closely placed buildings. A LAN may be made up of only microcomputers or any combination of microcomputers and large systems.

LANs is shown in Fig. 10.2.

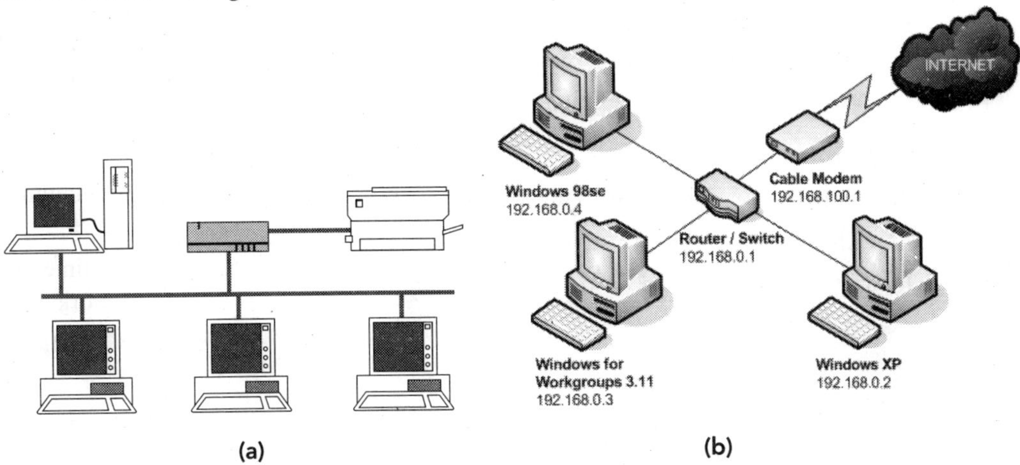


**Fig. 10.2:** Local Area Network(s)

The computer network which connect the computers in the different parts of the same big city like metropolitan city may be referred to as Metropolitan Area Network (MAN).

Interest in local area networks is constantly growing due to following two developments:

- Development of powerful and user-friendly micro-computers
- Developments in communication technology

The difference between a LAN and a multi-user system is that a LAN is made up of stand-alone computers whereas a multi-user system typically has one computer that is shared among two or more terminals.

A LAN usually consists of the following:

i. Two or more computers
ii. Peripheral devices such as printers and hard-disk drives
iii. Software to control the operation of the computers or other devices connected to the LAN
iv. Special cables, usually coaxial or fibre optic, to connect the computers and other devices
v. A plug-in board to handle the data transmissions.

A benefit of a LAN is the reduction of hardware costs because several computers and users can share peripheral devices such as laser printers, hard-disk drives, color plotters, and modems. Another advantage is the users can share data.

Ensuring the security and privacy of data are two concerns of LAN users. The LAN must get the data to its destination, transmit the data correctly, and prevent unauthorised users from gaining access to that data. These tasks are accomplished through both the hardware and LAN software.

They vary in the type and number of computers that can be connected, the speed at which data can be transferred, and the type of the software used to control the network. Some LANs require that all the computers be of a certain brand, while others allow a variety of brands to be connected. The number of computers in a LAN varies widely from smaller LANs that typically connect 2 to 25 computers, to large LANs that can connect as many as 10,000 computers.

The length of the cable connecting a computer to a LAN also varies depending on the LAN. Most LANs allow cables of about 1000 feet, but some allow cables of several miles to be used. The data transfer speeds range from several thousand bits per second to around 10 million bits per second. The programs that control the LANs also vary in the features they offer. Some programs allow the use of more than one operating system; others allow only one. On some LANs, file access is limited to one user at a time; on others, more than one user can access a file simultaneously.

## Hardware Requirements for LAN

The following are major hardware components/devices required for establishing LAN:

- Transmission Channel
- Network Interface Unit (NIU)
- Servers
- Workstations

## Transmission Channel for LAN

Generally four types of channels are used for data transmission in a LAN. These are:

- Twisted Pair Cable
- Coaxial Cable
- Fibre-Optic Cables
- Radio Waves

## Network Interface Unit

Network interface units connect each devices in the LAN network to shared transmission device. It contain the rules or logic to access the LAN. NIU is also used to implement LAN protocols and for device attachments. Its function depends on the type of topology used in LAN.

## Servers & Workstations

One of the major benefits of implementation of LAN is sharing expensive resources such as storage devices, printers etc. This is achieved through providing servers on the LAN. It is dedicated computer that controls one or more resources. This contains both hardware and software interface for LAN. Three major categories of services used in LANs are:

- File Server
- Printer Server
- Modem Server

In networking, file server is used to share storage space for files. Besides providing storage space for files in a LAN environment, it is used for taking periodical backup, and also to provide gateway to other servers within and between LANs.

Similarly printer server is used to handle printing works of all workstation connected in the network.

In LAN environment also modem is required to get connected to other network or simply to use a telephone. A modem server is used to share this expensive resource by all connected workstations in a network ring.

## LAN Software

LAN operating system is required to operate on the LAN system. It has basically two aspects:

- Server Software
- Workstation Software

LAN operating system facilitates:

- Sharing of expensive resources e.g. printer, storage space etc.
- Security for data
- Connection to other network.

There are various types of LAN operating system. Some popular LAN operating systems are:

- Novel Netware
- Ethernet

- Corvus
- ArcNet
- LAN Server
- Omni Net
- PC Net
- IBM PC LAN
- Etherlik Plus, etc.

## 10.3.2 Wireless LAN (WLAN)

WLANs provide wireless network communication over short distances using radio or infrared signals instead of traditional network cabling.

A WLAN typically extends an existing wired local area network. WLANs are built by attaching a device called the access point (AP) to the edge of the wired network. Clients communicate with the AP using a wireless network adapter similar in function to a traditional Ethernet adapter.

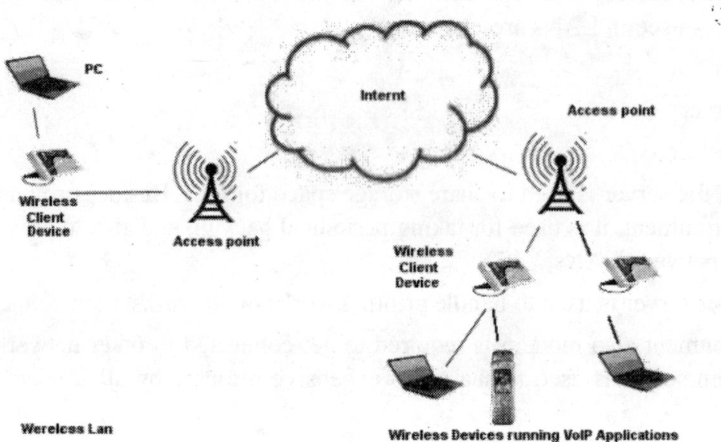


**Fig. 10.3:** Wireless Local Area Network (WLAN)

Network security remains an important issue for WLANs. Random wireless clients must usually be prohibited from joining the WLAN. Technologies like WEP raise the level of security on wireless networks to rival that of traditional wired networks.

## 10.3.3 Wide Area Networks (WAN)

A wide area network (WAN) is two or more computers that are geographically dispersed, linked by communication facilities such as telephone system or microwave relays. This type of network is usually limited to use by large corporations and government agencies because of the high costs involved in building and maintaining them.

A WAN is a network that links separate geographical locations and this network can be a public system or any of the various packet switched services provided by the public telecommunication agencies.

The main difference between a WAN and LAN is that, the LAN is under the complete control of the owner, whereas the WAN needs the involvement of another authority like telecom department. LANs are successful and capable of handling very high data transfer rates at low cost because of the small area covered. Besides LANs have a lower error rate than WANs.

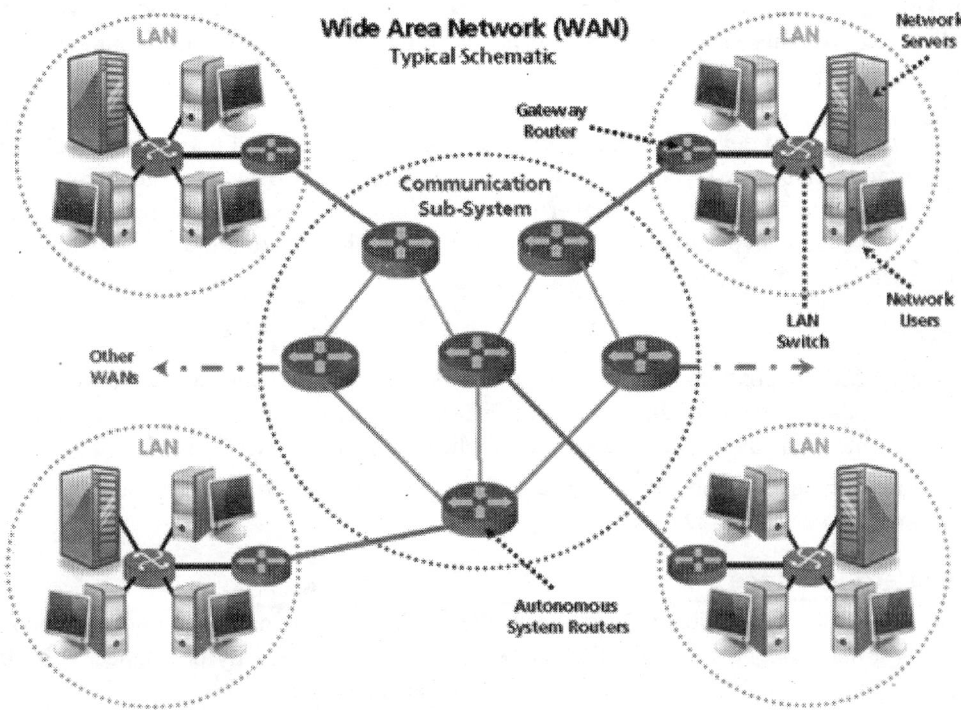


**Fig. 10.4:** Wide Area Network (WAN)

### Transmission Channel for WAN

Generally three types of channels are used for data transmission in a WAN. These are:

- Radio Waves
- Microwaves
- Communication Satellites

### Hardware Requirements for WAN

There are mainly four hardware devices which are required to establish linkage between geographically separated computers. These are:

- Bridges
- Routers
- Gateways
- X.25 Standard Interface

### Bridges

Bridges are used to connect two LANs that use the identical LAN protocols over a wide area. The bridge acts as an address filter which picks up packets from one LAN that are intended for a destination on another LAN and passes these packets on the network. The amount of processing required at the bridge is minimal because all the devices use the same protocols. In case the distance between two LANs is very large then the user is required to employ two identical bridges at either end of the communication link.

### Routers

Router is a special type of device that can be used to connect networks that may not be similar. Such type of devices provide connectivity between two LANs or two WANs over large geographical distances. These devices operate at the Network Layer of the OSI model. These devices participate in a routing protocol to access the network topology, and on the basis of this information routers compute the best route from a sender to the receiver.

### Gateways

Gateways are used to connect two dissimilar LANs. The terms Gateways and Routers are used interchangeably, though there is discriminating difference between the two. A router operates at the network layer whereas a gateway operates on the application layer of the OSI model.

A gateway is required to convert data packets from one protocol format to another before forwarding it, as it connects two dissimilar networks.

### X.25 Standard Interface

X.25 is a protocol for interfacing to a Public Packet Switched Network. It is not a protocol used for implementing a network. Two systems that support X.25 can't necessarily be connected back-to-back. They can only be connected through a DCE in a Public Packet Switched.

International Telegraph and Telephone Consultative Committee (ITTCC) developed X.25 as the standard interface between the Data Terminal Equipment (DTE) and Data Circuit Terminating Equipment (DCTE). This recommendation has been widely accepted as the industry standard for public packet switched networks.

### 10.3.3.1 Types of Wide Area Networks

There are mainly two types of WAN:

- Public Networks
- Private Networks

### Public Networks

Public networks are those networks which are installed and run by the telecommunication authorities and are made available to any organisation or individual who go for their subscription.

### Private Networks

The basic technique used in all forms of private WAN is to use private circuits to link the locations to be served by the network. Between these fixed points the owner of the network has complete freedom to use the circuits in any way they want. They can use the circuits to carry large quantities of data or for high speed transmissions. Private wide area networks can be built using whatever standard technology is available.

### 10.3.4 Metropolitan Area Network (MAN)

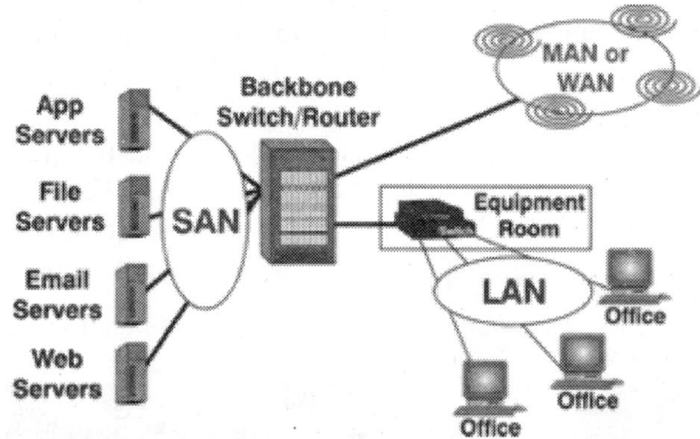


**Fig. 10.5:** Metropolitan Area Network (MAN)

A metropolitan area network (MAN) is a network that interconnects users with computer resources in a geographic area or region larger than that covered by even a large local area network (LAN) but smaller than the area covered by a wide area network (WAN). The term is applied to the interconnection of networks in a city into a single larger network (which may then also offer efficient connection to a wide area network). It is also used to mean the interconnection of several local area networks by bridging them with backbone lines. The latter usage is also sometimes referred to as a campus network.

### 10.3.5 Storage Area Network (SAN)

It is also known by the names like System Area Network, Server Area Network, or sometimes Small Area Network.

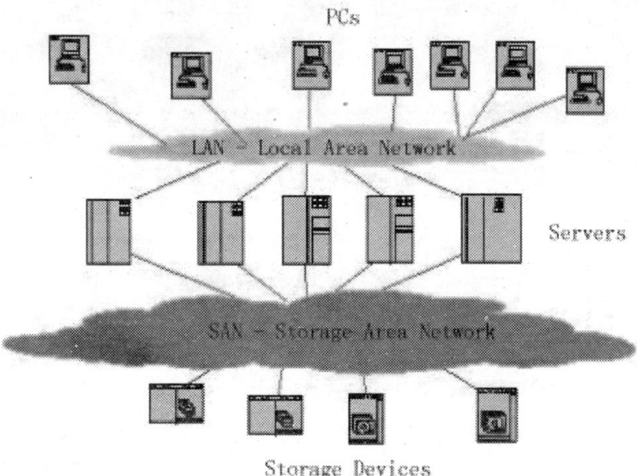


**Fig. 10.6:** Storage Area Network (SAN)

A storage area network (SAN) is a type of local area network (LAN) designed to handle large data transfers. A SAN typically supports data storage, retrieval and replication on business networks using high-end servers, multiple disk arrays and Fiber Channel interconnection technology.

SAN technology is similar but distinct from network attached storage (NAS) technology. While SANs traditionally employ low-level network protocols for transfering disk blocks, a NAS device typically works over TCP/IP and can be integrated fairly easily into home computer networks.

The term SAN can sometimes refer to system area networks instead of a storage area network. System area networks are clusters of high performance computers used for distributed processing applications requiring fast local network performance. Storage area networks, on the other, are designed specifically for data management.

## 10.3.6 Campus Area Network (CAN)

It is also known by the names like Controller Area Network, and often Cluster Area Network.

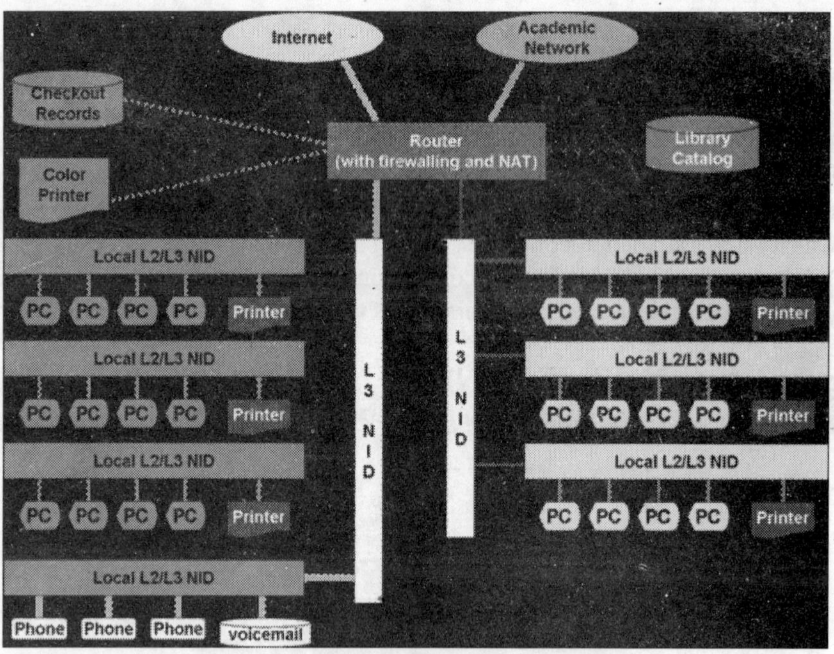


**Fig. 10.7:** Campus Area Network (CAN)

A campus area network known as (CAN) is used to inter-connect networks in limited geographical locality like university campus, military bases, or organizational campuses etc. It can be taken as the metropolitan network that has the specific settings at the small area just like a computer lab in the university.

## 10.3.7 Personal Area Network (PAN)

A personal area network - PAN - is a computer network organized around an individual person. Personal area networks typically involve a mobile computer, a cell phone and/or a handheld computing device such as a PDA.

You can use these networks to transfer files including email and calendar appointments, digital photos and music.

Personal area networks can be constructed with cables or wirelessly. USB and FireWire technologies often link together a wired PAN while wireless PANs typically use Bluetooth or sometimes infrared connections. Bluetooth PANs are also called pico-nets.

Personal area networks generally cover a range of less than 10 meters (about 30 feet).

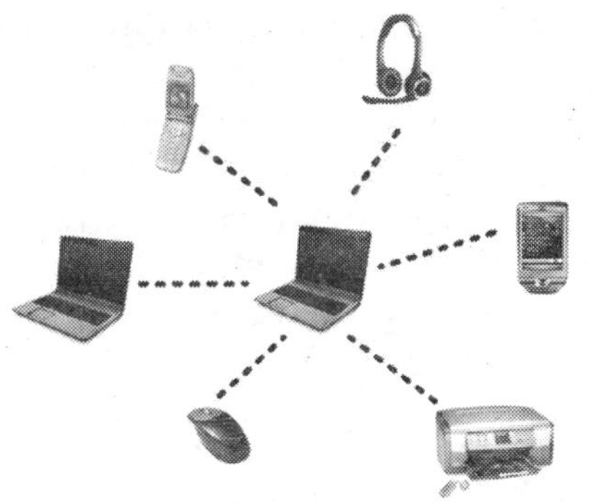

**Fig. 10.8:** Personal Area Network (PAN)

### 10.3.8 Desk Area Network (DAN)

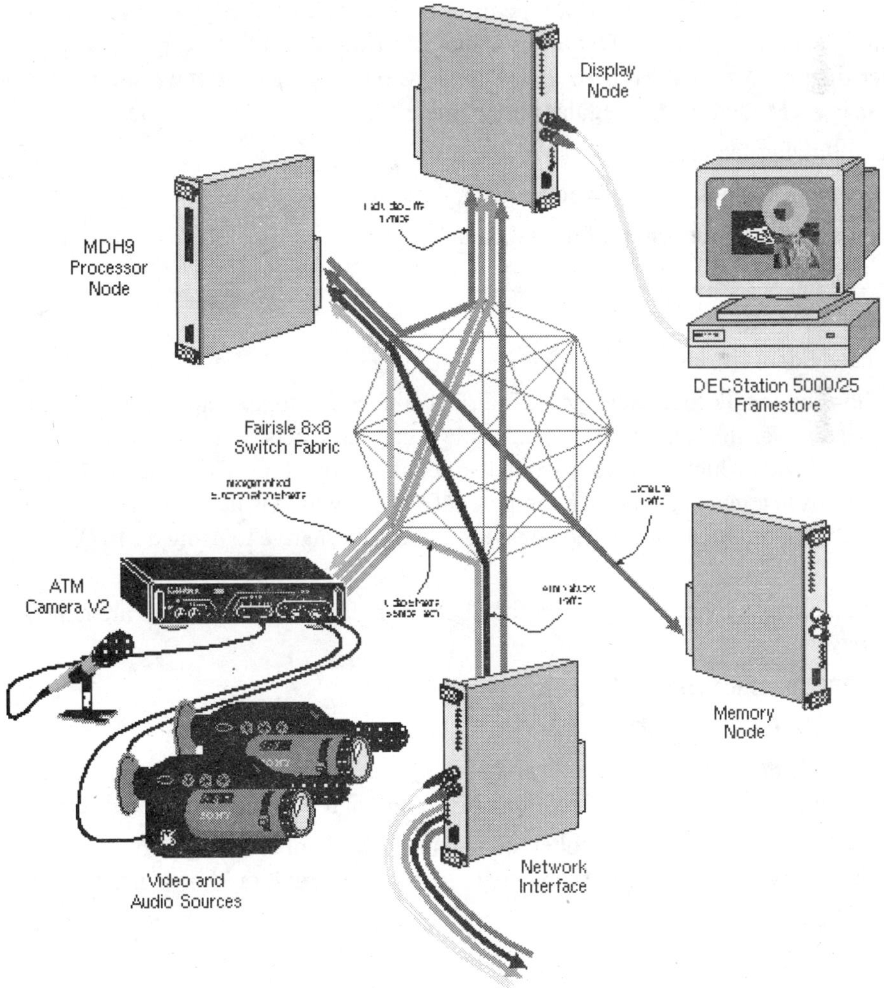

**Fig. 10.9:** Desk Area Network (DAN)

DAN (Desk Area Network) is an interconnection of computer devices around the ATM (Asynchronous Transfer Mode). This exchange of information between various peripherals and CPU is based on the transfer of ATM (Asynchronous Transfer Mode) cells mainly. DAN (Desk Area Network) enables the network to share resources over the network. It also provides the access to foreign devices. This system enables to form A/V connection. DAN (Desk Area Network) consists of A/V software. This software has four main layers. This software is intelligent enough to guide and support the A/V devices. It works on a simple process, when we on a VCR. And put a cassette into it, it is automatically connected to the monitor. VCR and other related devices are often connected to the network in order to built DAN (Desk Area Network).

## 10.4 INTEGRATED SERVICES DIGITAL NETWORK (ISDN)

The ISDN is a networking concept providing for the integration of voice, video and data services using digital transmission media combining both circuit and packet switching techniques. ISDN was first launched in Singapore in 1990. ISDN is a type of telephone service which is an alternative to a regular phone line. The great advantage of ISDN for us is that it allows us connect to another computer at a speed which is faster than even fastest Modem. If ISDN is available in our area, we should consider it as an alternative to using a Modem with a regular phone line.

ISDN has following features:

- Processing of various types of voice, video, data etc.
- Transmission and processing of digital data
- E-mail box
- Tele-conferencing
- Tele-fax, Video-fax, etc.

Users in shops or small offices can use their digital connection to telephone company for transmitting both voice and data over the same twisted pair cable which connects their telephone. In fact, ISDN is a type of telephone service which is an alternative to a regular phone line. The great advantage of ISDN for us is that it allows us to connect to another computer at a speed which is faster than even fastest MODEM. If ISDN is available in our area, we should consider it as an alternative to using a MODEM with a regular phone line.

ISDN is a telephone service provided by the phone company. ISDN services are generally delivered in one of two ways:

- Basic Rate Interface (BRI)
- Primary Rate Interface (PRI)

The difference is that a PRI is an expensive, large-scale service suitable for a company needing to connect many computers and other devices. For a home or small business, we would require a BRI.

A single ISDN line provides a number of channels, each of which offers a specific amount of bandwidth. Here, bandwidth refers to the capacity to transmit information. A BRI provides three channels:

- Two B channels and
- One D channel

### B Channels

The B channels carry the bulk of data viz. computer connections, voice conversations, fax transmissions, and so on. The name "B channel" is short for "bearer channel", because the B channels bear most of the load.

### D Channel

The D channel is used for the control of ISDN itself. It is used for sending the set-up and signalling information back and forth between the telephone system and our devices. The name "D channel" stands for "data channel". This is an unfortunate name, as it implies that the D channel transports our computer data, Actually, the D channel carries the internal ISDN data. Our data is actually carried on the B channels.

Within a standard BRI, each of the two B channels offers a bandwidth of 64 Kbps. We can use these B channels in two ways.

- First, we can combine them into a single large channel and connect it to our computer. This effectively gives you up to 128 Kbps.
- Secondly, you can use one B channel for our computer and another for a telephone. This means that we would have only 64 Kbps in bandwidth for the computer but we would not have to pay for a separate phone line. Moreover, we can use the computer and talk on the phone at the same time and they won't interfere with one another.

The D channel has 16 Kbps, however, it is used by ISDN itself and so it is not available for use with a computer or a telephone.

ISDN is a very important mean for very fast and accurate data transmission, and ISDN truly represents the next generation of the world's telephone service for all forms of telecommunications, including voice.

## 10.5 PUBLIC SWITCHED TELEPHONE NETWORK (PSTN)

Following are the main features of PSTN:

- Low speed
- Analog nature of transmission
- Restricted bandwidth
- Widespread availability

As PSTN is designed for telephones so modems are required when it is used for data communication. The PSTN is most useful in wide area data communications systems as an adjunct to other mechanisms. PSTN connections are usually easy to obtain at short notice, and are widely available and cover almost every location where people live and work. PSTN is most useful for occasional user or as backup to private circuits. It is also used for FAX machines.

## 10.6 PUBLIC SWITCHED DATA NETWORK (PSDN)

The major features of all PSDNs are:

- High level of reliability
- High quality of connections

PSDNs can support both low and high speeds at appropriate costs. Like PSTN, a PSDN is very useful and adjunct to a private network for backup and occasional access purposes. It can also be used to link computer systems and networks of one organisation to several other organisations. PSDN is very popular for connecting public and private mail systems to implement E-mail services with other companies.

I-Net is the first Public Switched Data Network owned by Department of Telecommunication (DOT). This network offers the following services:

- Permitting subscribers to form private network within I-Net
- Communication units across major cities of the country
- Connection provision to other international network

## 10.7 VALUE ADDED NETWORKS

A value added carrier leases communication facilities from conventional common carriers and uses them in conjunction with computers to build a network which offers new types of communication services and tariffs.

In Value Added Services, the provider of such services must process, store and manipulate the data that is carried on the network i.e. add value to it. The technique can be used in specific types of business in which it is advantageous to be able to share information with other companies in the same line.

Electronic Data Interchange is one area for Value Added Services in which two trading partners exchange trading documents such as purchase orders, invoices, transportation etc. using electronic means. In India, VSNL (Videsh Sanchar Nigam Limited) is a service provider.

## 10.8 NETWORK TOPOLOGIES

In networking, the term topology is the way of connecting computers or nodes on a network. There are many ways in which computers are connected together in a computer network. Therefore network topology is defined as: the schemes of joining a number of computers in the form of a network are called Network Topologies.

We know that two or more devices are connected to a link for data communication. Similarly, two or more links form a topology. The topology of a network is the geometric representation of the relationship of all the links and the nodes (communication devices) to one another.

A network can be arranged in one of four different topologies:

- Star Topology
- Ring Topology
- Bus Topology
- Mesh Topology
- Tree Topology
- Hybrid Topology
- Fully-connected Topology
- Multi-drop Topology
- Collapsed-Star Topology

## Criteria for Selection of Network Topology

The main considerations in selecting a particular topology are:

- The availability and cost of physical communication lines between nodes and line bandwidth
- Throughput
- The capability of a node to route information to other nodes
- Delays due to routing of information
- Maximum distance
- Vulnerability to link or equipment failure
- Maximum number of stations
- Cost
- Reliability of communication between nodes when there is a breakdown of a line or a node
- Strategy of controlling communication between nodes in the network centralised or distributed

### 10.8.1 Star Topology

In a star network, each node (computer or other device) is directly connected to the central computer or Hub that provides connection points for nodes on the network. The star topology is the most common topology in use today. In star network, information or data is communicated from one computer to another through Hub. This form of network configuration looks like a star as shown in figure 10.10.

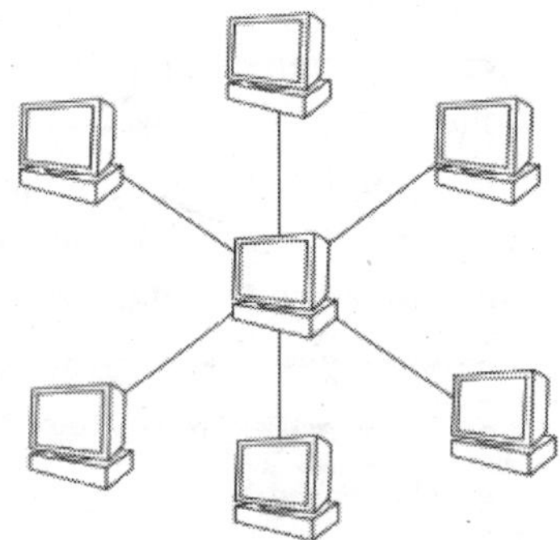

**Figure 10.10:** Star Topology

**Advantages:** The main advantages of star topology are:

- It is easy to install and to maintain.
- You can easily add and remove nodes to and from the network without affecting the network.
- If any node fails, other nodes are not affected.

**Disadvantages:** The main disadvantages of star topology are:

- This type of network depends upon the central Hub. If Hub fails the entire network is failed.
- Each computer is directly connected to the Hub through a cable, so it becomes more costly.

### 10.8.2 Ring Topology

In ring network, each node is connected to two adjacent nodes in the form a closed ring or loop. In ring topology, the last node connects to the first node to complete the ring. In ring topology, each node has a dedicated point-to-point connection only with the two devices on either side of it.

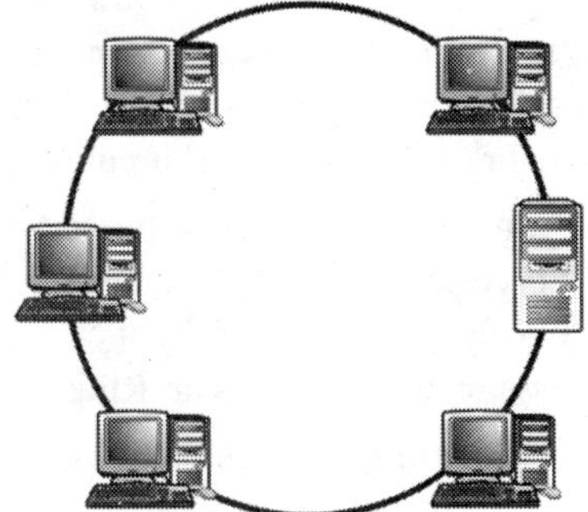

**Figure 10.11:** Ring Topology

In this network, data is communicated in one direction from node to node around the entire ring. When a computer in ring network sends message to another computer on the network, the message travels to each node or computer until it reaches its destination. The ring network configuration is shown in figure below.

**Advantages:** The main advantages of ring topology are:

- It is less expensive than star topology.
- Nodes can be easily added or removed.

**Disadvantages:** The main disadvantages of ring topology are:

- It is more difficult to install and maintain.
- If a node fails, it affects the entire network.

### 10.8.3 Bus Topology

In bus network, all nodes are connected to a common communication medium or central cable. The central physical cable that connects the nodes is called Bus. The data is communicated between nodes in both directions through bus. A bus topology uses the multipoint connection. The central single cable (or bus) acts as backbone to link all the devices to the network.

In bus network, when a computer sends a message to another computer it also attaches the address of the destination computer. In bus topology, a special device called a terminator is attached at the cable's start and end points. A terminator stops the network signals.

In LAN, bus topology is mostly used. In this topology, each computer is assigned a unique address. The bus network configuration is given in figure 10.12.

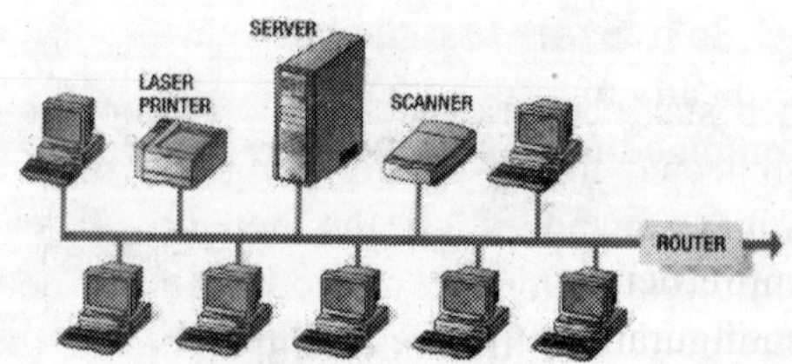


**Figure 10.12:** Bus Topology

**Advantages:** The main advantages of bus topology are:

- It is less expensive and easy to install and maintain.
- When nodes are added and removed to and from the network, the network is not affected.
- If one node fails other nodes are not affected.

**Disadvantages:** The main disadvantages of bus topology are:

- It supports only a small number of nodes.
- Entire network fails if there is any problem in the central cable.

### 10.8.4 Mesh Topology

In this topology, every node has a dedicated point-to-point connection to every other node on the network. A fully connected mesh network has n(n-1)/2 channels to link 'n' devices. Therefore, every device on the network must have 'n-1' input/output (I/O) ports.

In mesh network, each node is directly connected to all nodes on the network. This type of network involves the concept of routes. In this type of network, each node may send message to destination through multiple paths. It means that each node of mesh network has several possible paths to send (or to receive) message, but in Bus, Star, Ring and Tree topologies each node has only one path.

**Advantages:** Mesh topology has the following advantages:

- It has multiple links, so if one route is blocked then other routes can be used for data communication.

- Each connection can have its own data load, so the traffic problem is eliminated.
- It ensures the data privacy or security, because every message travels along a dedicated link.
- Troubleshooting of this topology is easy as compared to other networks.
- Its performance is not affected with heavy load of data transmission.

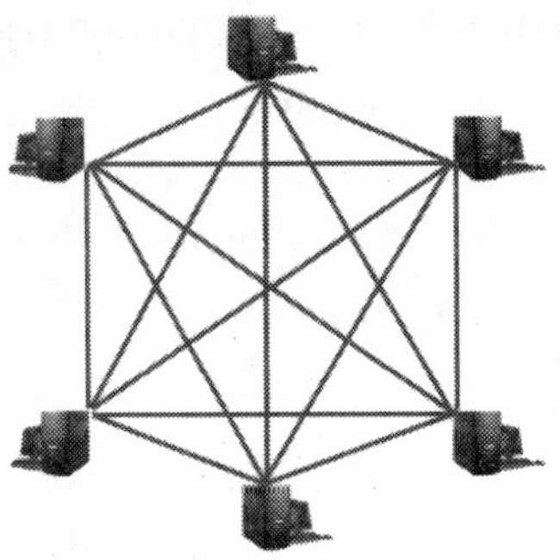

**Figure 10.13:** Mesh Topology

**Disadvantages:** Mesh topology has the following disadvantages:

- It becomes very expensive because a large number of cabling and 110 ports are required.
- It is difficult to install.

## 10.8.5 Tree Topology

In tree network, the nodes are connected to each other in such a way that forms a tree like structure. Typically to form a tree network, multiple star topologies are combined together. This type of network has combined features of bus and star topology.

On tree topology the hubs of each star topology are connected to the central hub that controls the entire network. However, some nodes can be directly connected to the central hub. The tree topology configuration is shown in figure 10.14.

The central Hub in the tree network is an active hub. It contains a repeater (a hardware device), which re-generates the received bit patterns. The secondary hubs usually are passive hubs. The passive hub controls the nodes directly connected to it and exchange data to other devices connected to the other secondary hubs (or same hub) through the central hub. The secondary hub may also be active hub if another secondary hub is directly connected to it. The cable TV network is an example of tree topology, where main cable is divided into, branches and each branch is further divided into smaller branches and so on. The hub is used when a branch is created.

**Advantages:** The tree topology has the same advantages as star topology but it has some additional advantages. These are.

- It allows more devices to be connected to the central Hub.

**Disadvantages:** The tree topology also has the same disadvantages as star topology built has some additional disadvantages such as:

- It because more expansive because more hubs are required to install the network.

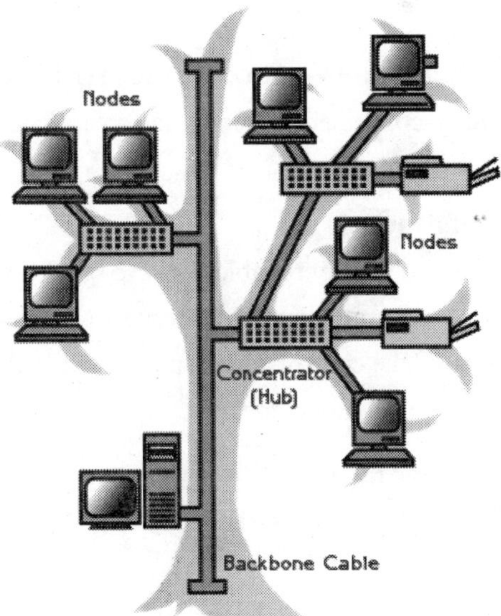


**Figure 10.14:** Tree Topology

## 10.8.6 Hybrid Topology

Hybrid network is the combination of different topologies such as star, Ring, Mesh, Bus etc. For example, if a department uses a Bus network, second department uses the ring network, third department uses the Mesh network and fourth department uses the star network. All the networks of different types (of four departments) can be connected together through a central hub (in the form of star network) as shown in the figure below.

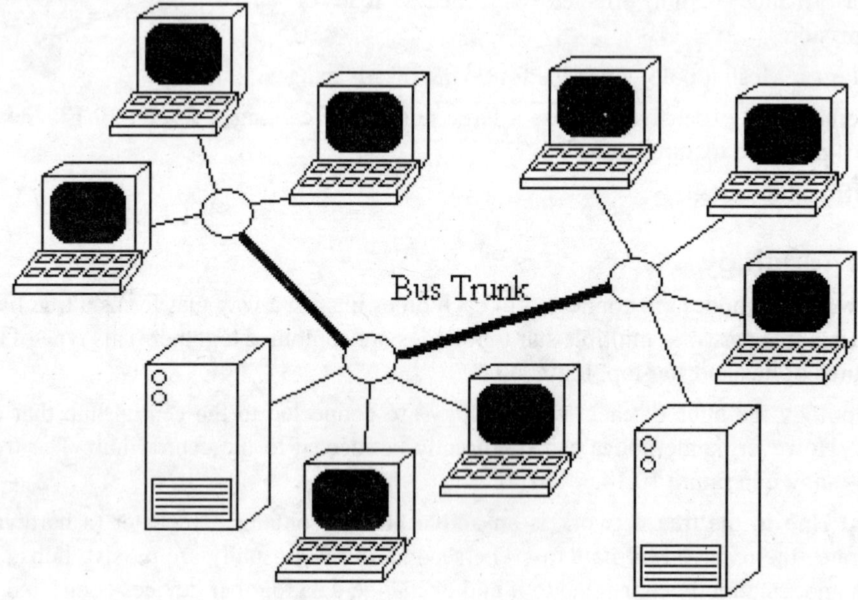


**Figure 10.15:** Hybrid Topology

## 10.8.7 Fully-Interconnected Network

A fully-connected topology has a separate physical links for connecting each node to any other node in the network.

### Advantages

- It is very reliable because breakdown in any line will not affect other links
- Communication is very fast between any two nodes
- The control among nodes is distributed
- Each node does not require individual routing capability

### Disadvantages

- This topology is very costly due to physical links established from each node to every other node in the network
- Addition of any additional node will raise the cost multiple times depending upon the total existing nodes in the network

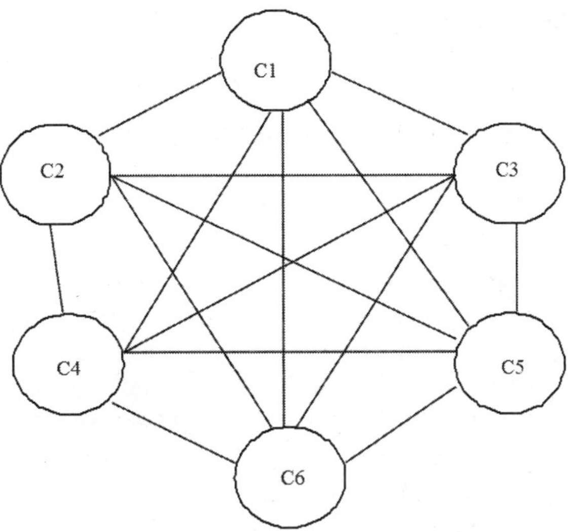


### 10.8.8 MULTI-DROP NETWORK

In this topology only one line is shared by all nodes. Whenever a message is transmitted, sender and destination addresses are associated as Tags and message rides on this single line. Receiver receives it and acknowledges the message through the same line.

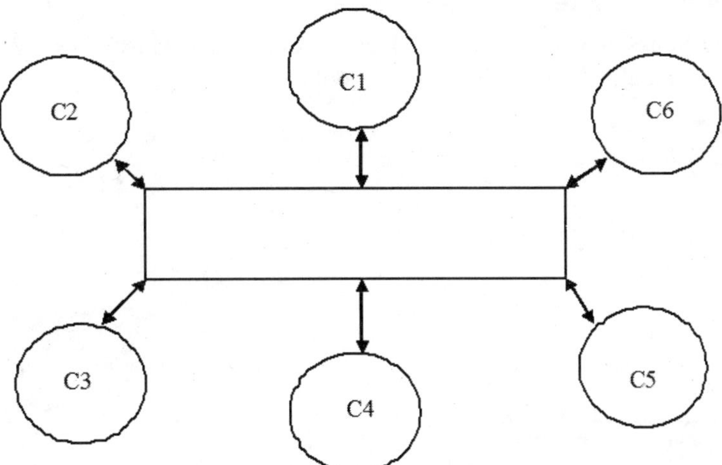


## Advantages

- Cheaper due to reduction in total physical lines
- Relatively higher reliability
- Easier addition of nodes in the existing network

## Disadvantages

- Complete system fails if the single line gets disconnected

### 10.8.9 Collapsed-Star Network

In this topology the multiple ring networks are interconnected. Here, a central backbone is constructed, to which various other ring networks are connected. In this case, each ring is connected to the central ring via a high-speed bridge. High-speed bridge is a device that enables data to be routed from one network to another.

## 10.9 NETWORK CABLING

Cable is the medium through which information usually moves from one network device to another. There are several types of cable which are commonly used with LANs. In some cases, a network will utilize only one type of cable, other networks will use a variety of cable types. The type of cable chosen for a network is related to the network's topology, protocol, and size. Understanding the characteristics of different types of cable and how they relate to other aspects of a network is necessary for the development of a successful network.

The following sections discuss the types of cables used in networks and other related topics.

- Unshielded Twisted Pair (UTP) Cable
- Shielded Twisted Pair (STP) Cable
- Coaxial Cable
- Fiber Optic Cable

### 10.9.1 Unshielded Twisted Pair (UTP) Cable

Twisted pair cabling comes in two varieties: shielded and unshielded. Unshielded twisted pair (UTP) is the most popular and is generally the best option for school networks.

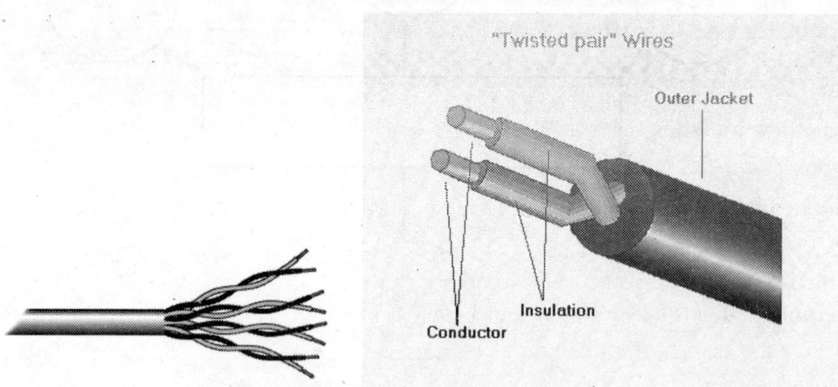


**Figure 10.18:** Unshielded twisted pair

The quality of UTP may vary from telephone-grade wire to extremely high-speed cable. The cable has four pairs of wires inside the jacket. Each pair is twisted with a different number of twists per inch to help eliminate interference from adjacent pairs and other electrical devices. The tighter the twisting, the higher the supported transmission rate and the greater the cost per foot. The EIA/TIA (Electronic Industry Association/Telecommunication Industry Association) has established standards of UTP and rated six categories of wire (additional categories are emerging).

### 10.9.2 Unshielded Twisted Pair Connector

The standard connector for unshielded twisted pair cabling is an RJ-45 connector. This is a plastic connector that looks like a large telephone-style connector. A slot allows the RJ-45 to be inserted only one way. RJ stands for Registered Jack, implying that the connector follows a standard borrowed from the telephone industry. This standard designates which wire goes with each pin inside the connector.

**Figure 10.19:** RJ-45 connector

### 10.9.3 Shielded Twisted Pair (STP) Cable

Although UTP cable is the least expensive cable, it may be susceptible to radio and electrical frequency interference (it should not be too close to electric motors, fluorescent lights, etc.). If you must place cable in environments with lots of potential interference, or if you must place cable in extremely sensitive environments that may be susceptible to the electrical current in the UTP, shielded twisted pair may be the solution. Shielded cables can also help to extend the maximum distance of the cables.

Shielded twisted pair cable is available in three different configurations:

1. Each pair of wires is individually shielded with foil.
2. There is a foil or braid shield inside the jacket covering all wires (as a group).
3. There is a shield around each individual pair, as well as around the entire group of wires (referred to as double shield twisted pair).

#### Advantages:

- As the oldest method of data transmission, trained man power to repair and service this media of communications are easily available.
- In telephone system, signals can travel several kilometres without amplification when twisted pair wires are used.
- This media can be used for both analog and digital data transmission. The bandwidth depends on the thickness of the wire and the distance travelled, but several megabits per second can be achieved for a few kilometres in many cases.
- It is the least expensive media of transmission for short distances.
- The effect on the network as a whole, if portion of twisted pair cable is damaged; the entire network is not shut down, as well as it may be the case with coaxial cable.

#### Disadvantages:

- Easily pickup noise signals which results in higher error rates when the line length exceeds 100 meters.
- Being thin in size, they are likely to break easily.

### 10.9.4 Coaxial Cable

Coaxial cabling has a single copper conductor at its center. A plastic layer provides insulation between the center conductor and a braided metal shield. The metal shield helps to block any outside interference from

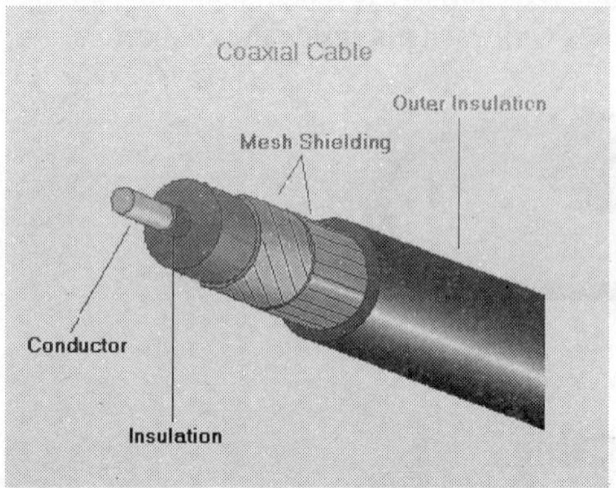


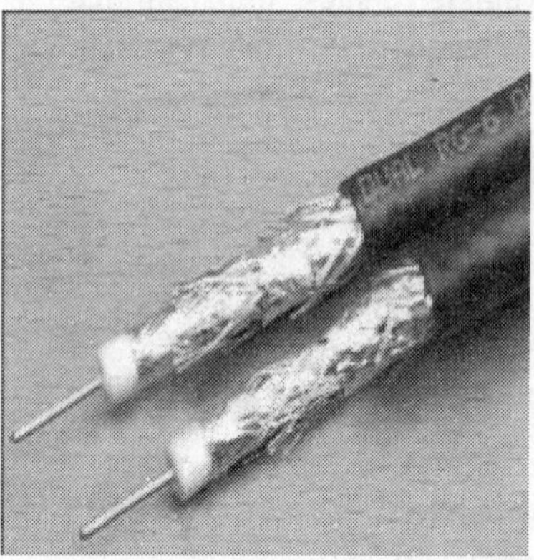

**Figure 10.20:** Coaxial cable

Although coaxial cabling is difficult to install, it is highly resistant to signal interference. In addition, it can support greater cable lengths between network devices than twisted pair cable. The two types of coaxial

Thin coaxial cable is also referred to as thinnet. 10Base2 refers to the specifications for thin coaxial cable carrying Ethernet signals. The 2 refers to the approximate maximum segment length being 200 meters. In actual fact the maximum segment length is 185 meters. Thin coaxial cable has been popular in

Thick coaxial cable is also referred to as thicknet. 10Base5 refers to the specifications for thick coaxial cable carrying Ethernet signals. The 5 refers to the maximum segment length being 500 meters. Thick coaxial cable has an extra protective plastic cover that helps keep moisture away from the center conductor. This makes thick coaxial a great choice when running longer lengths in a linear bus network. One disadvantage of thick coaxial is that it does

### Advantages:

- It has better shielding than twisted pair, so it can span longer distances at higher data bps.
- It can be used for both Analog data transmission as well as digital transmission.
- Coaxial cable has higher bandwidth and excellent noise immunity.
- It is relatively inexpensive as compared to optic cables and easy to handle.

### Disadvantages:

- Coaxial cable is more expensive than twisted pair.
- Coaxial cable emits less radiation which may cause interference with the communication equipment as compared to twisted pair.

## 10.9.5 Coaxial Cable Connectors

The most common type of connector used with coaxial cables is the Bayone-Neill-Concelman (BNC) connector. Different types of adapters are available for BNC connectors, including a T-connector, barrel connector, and terminator. Connectors on the cable are the weakest points in any network.

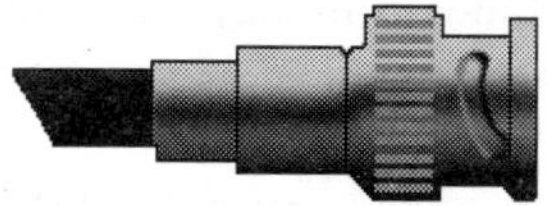

**Figure 10.21:** BNC connector

## 10.9.6 Fiber Optic Cable

Fiber optic cabling consists of a center glass core surrounded by several layers of protective materials. It transmits light rather than electronic signals eliminating the problem of electrical interference. This makes it ideal for certain environments that contain a large amount of electrical interference. Fiber optic cable has the ability to transmit signals over much longer distances than coaxial and twisted pair. It also has the capability to carry information at vastly greater speeds. This capacity broadens communication possibilities to include services such as video conferencing and interactive services. The center core of fiber cables is made from glass or plastic fibers. A plastic coating then cushions the fiber center, and Kevlar fibers help to strengthen the cables and prevent breakage. The outer insulating jacket made of Teflon or PVC.

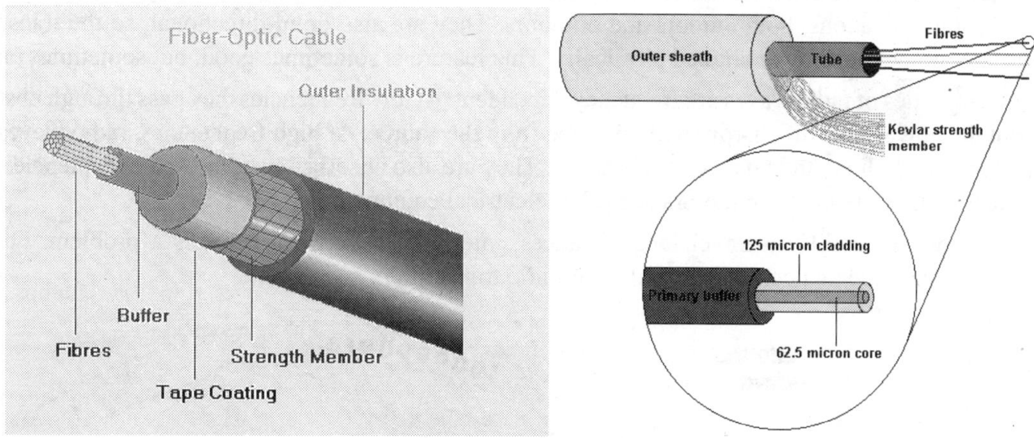


**Figure 10.22:** Fiber optic cable

There are two common types of fiber cables - single mode and multimode. Multimode cable has a larger diameter; however, both cables provide high bandwidth at high speeds. Single mode can provide more distance, but it is more expensive.

**Advantages:**

- It can handle much higher band widths.
- Fibers are not being affected by power surges, electromagnetic interference, or failures.
- Fiber is lighter than other transmission mediums.
- Fibers do not leak light and are quite difficult to tap. This gives excellent security.

**Disadvantages:**

- Fiber is an unfamiliar technology, so requires special skills.
- Since optical transmission is inherently unidirectional, two way communications requires either two fibers or two frequency bands on the fiber.
- Fiber interfaces cost more than electrical interfaces.

## 10.9.7 Wireless Transmission Media

In wireless transmission media, communication devices communicate with each other and data is communicated through the air or space using broadcast radio signals, microwave signals and infrared signals. This transmission medium is used when it is impossible to install the cables. The data can be transmitted all over the world through this medium. The commonly used wireless transmission media are discussed below.

### 10.9.7.1 Radio Transmission

Radio Waves are easy to generate, can travel long distances, and penetrate building easily, so they are widely used for communications, both indoors and outdoors. They are also omni-directional, so the transmitter and receiver do not have to be aligned physically. This feature is sometimes good, but sometimes bad.

The properties of radio waves are frequency dependent. At low frequencies they pass through obstacles well, but the power falls off sharply with distance from the source. At high frequencies, radio waves tend to travel in straight lines and bounce off obstacles. They are also absorbed by rain. At all frequencies, they are subject to interference from motors and other electrical equipment.

Due to radio's ability to travel long distances, interference between users is a problem. For this reasons, all governments license the use user of radio transmitters.

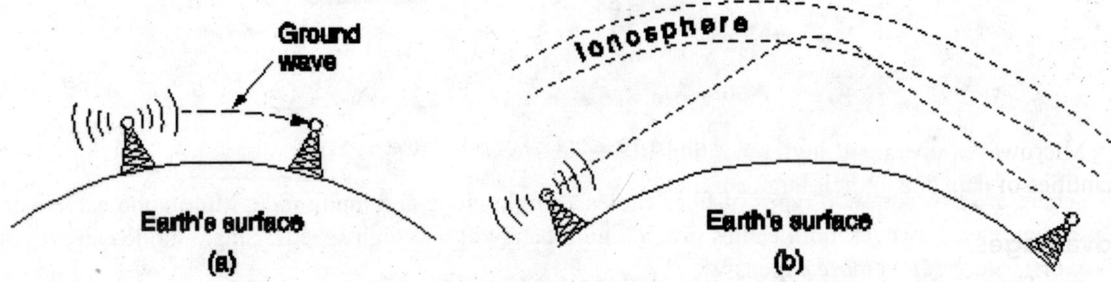


**Figure 10.23:** (a) In the VLF, VF, and MF bands, radio waves follow the curvature of the earth. (b) In the HF they bounce off the ionosphere.

In the VLF, LF, and MF bands, radio waves follow the ground (Figure 7.31(a)) and can be detected for about 1000 km at the lower frequencies, less at the higher ones. The main problem with using these bands for data communication is relatively low bandwidth they offer.

In the HF and VHF bands, the ground waves tend to be absorbed by the earth, but if they reach the ionosphere (a layer of charged particles circling the earth at a height of 100 to 500 km) are refracted (Figure 7.31(b)) by it and sent back to earth. Amateur radio operators use these bands to talk long distance.

**i. Broadcast Radio**

It is a wireless transmission medium that is used to communicate information through radio signals in air, over long distance such as between cities and countries. In this medium, a transmitter is required to send messages (signals) and receiver is required to receive them. To receive the broadcast radio signal, the receiver has an antenna that is located in the range of signal. Some networks use a special device called transceiver used to send and to receive messages in the form of radio signals. The data transmission speed of broadcast radio is up to 54Mbps.

**ii. Cellular Radio**

Cellular radio is a form of broadcast radio that is used for mobile communications such as cellular telephones and wireless modems. A cellular telephone is a telephone device that uses high frequency radio waves to transmit voice and digital messages. Some mobile users connect their laptop computer or other mobile device to a cellular telephone to access the Web, send and receive e-mail etc. while away from a standard telephone line.

### 10.9.7.2 Microwaves Transmission

Microwave transmission is line of sight transmission. The transmit station must be in visible contact with the receive station. This sets a limit on the distance between stations depending on the local geography. Typically the line of sight due to the Earth's curvature is only 50 km to the horizon! Repeater stations must be placed so the data signal can hop, skip and jump across the country.

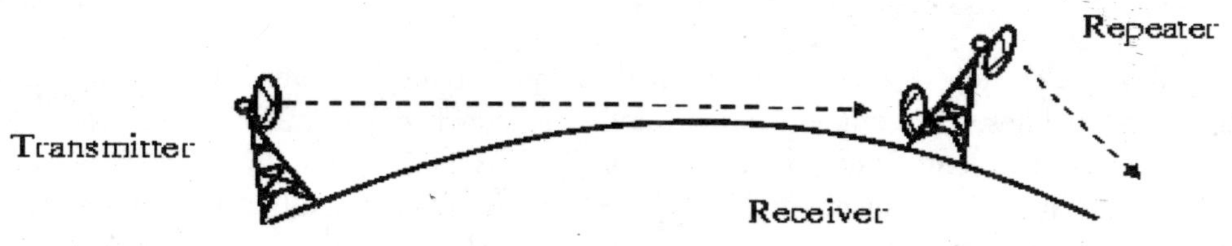


**Figure 10.24:** Microwaves Transmission

Microwaves operate at high operating frequencies of 3 to 10 GHz. This allows them to carry large quantities of data due to their large bandwidth.

### Advantages:

a. They require no right of way acquisition between towers.
b. They can carry high quantities of information due to their high operating frequencies.

c. Low cost land purchase: each tower occupies only a small area.
d. High frequency/short wavelength signals require small antennae.

**Disadvantages:**

a. Attenuation by solid objects: birds, rain, snow and fog.
b. Reflected from flat surfaces like water and metal.
c. Diffracted (split) around solid objects.
d. Refracted by atmosphere, thus causing beam to be projected away from receiver.

### 10.9.7.3 Communication Satellite

A communication satellite is a space station that receives microwave signals from earth microwave station (earth based station). The earth based stations often are microwave stations. Other devices, such as PDAs and OPS receivers, also functions as earth based stations. Transmitting a signal from ground or earth station to a satellite station in space is called up-linking and the reverse is called the down- linking.

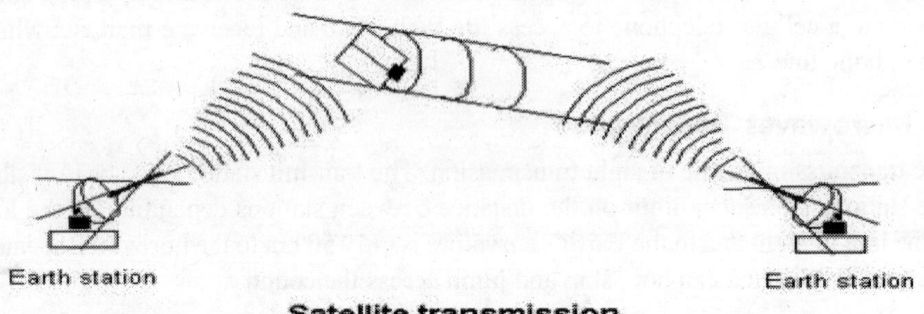


**Figure 10.25:** Communication Satellite Transmission System

Now-a-days, television & radio broadcast, global positioning systems and Internet also use the communication satellites. The communication satellite is launched about 22300 miles (or more) above the earth into space. The communication satellite consists of solar powered, transceiver that receives and sends signals. The signals are transmitted from one earth station to the satellite. The satellite receives and amplifies the signals and sends them to another earth station. This entire process takes only a few seconds. To communicate information from one country to another country more than one satellites are required. The data transmission speed of communication satellite is very high such as up to 1 Gbps.

## 10.9.8 Other Technologies

Infra- red: Infra-red has a wavelength just beyond the visible spectrum. It is invisible to the human eye and is heat sensitive. Infra red cameras can show an image in a totally dark room. New network systems are built around infra red connections.

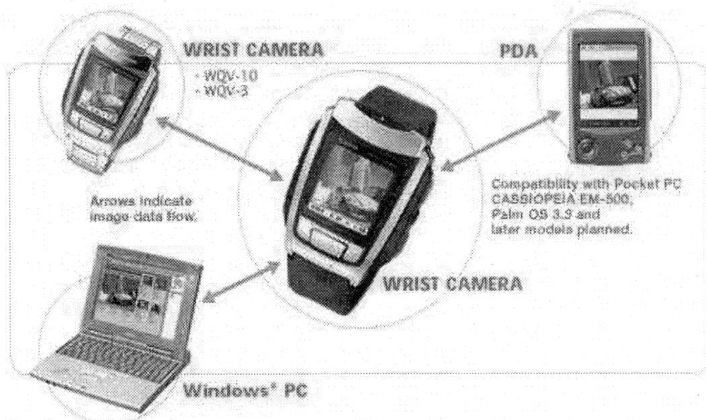


**Figure 10.26:** Infra-red Technologies

WAP: This is the mobile phone technology which can also access the internet and faxes. Been around for a few years now.

**Figure 10.27:** WAP

3G Video phones are just new. At this stage the transmissions are problematic and unreliable but the technology is bound to expand and the problems will be fixed gradually over the next couple of years.

**Figure 10.28:** 3G Technology

## 10.10 NETWORK PROTOCOLS

A protocol is an agreed upon format for transmitting data between two devices. The protocol determines the following:

- What type of error checking is to be used?
- What data compression technique, if any, to be used?
- How the sending device will indicate that it has finished sending a message?
- How the receiving device will indicate that it has received a message?

There are a variety of standard protocols from which programmers can choose. Each has its own particular advantages and disadvantages e.g. some are simpler than the others, some are more reliable, and some are faster.

From a user's point of view, the only interesting aspect about protocols is that our computer or device must support the right ones if we want to communicate with other computers. The protocols can be implemented either in hardware or in software. Some of the popular protocols are:

- TCP/IP
- HTTP
- FTP
- SMTP
- POP
- Token-Ring
- Ethernet
- Xmodem
- Kermit
- MNP, etc.

### Computer Network Architecture

The best architecture ever possible is an Open-Architecture which allows the system to be connected easily to other devices, computers and programs made available by other manufacturers. Such architectures use off-the-shelf components and conform to approved standards. On the other hand, a system with a closed architecture is one whose design is proprietary which makes it difficult to connect the system to others.

Network architectures can be broadly classified as:

- Peer-to-peer
- Client-Server

### Peer-to-peer Network Architecture

It is a type of network architecture in which each workstation (or node) has the same capabilities and responsibilities, meaning that none of these nodes is superior over other nodes.

### Advantages

- Simpler architecture
- Less expensive

### Disadvantage

- Offer less performance under heavy loads

### Client-Server Network Architecture

It is such a network architecture in which each computer or process on the network is either a client or a server. Here, server is having a superiority over other nodes and that's why other nodes will be clients and are likely to be served by the server. Servers must be powerful computers or processors dedicated to managing disk drives (file-servers), printers (print-servers), or network traffic (network-servers) whereas on the other hand clients may be lesser powerful PCs or workstations on which users can run applications. In such network architectures, clients completely rely on servers for resources viz. files, devices, etc.

## 10.11 APPLICATIONS OF COMPUTER NETWORKS

There is a long list of application areas which can be benefited by establishing Computer Networks. Few of the potential applications of Computer Networks are:

- Information retrieval systems which search for books, technical reports, papers and articles on particular topics
- News access machines which can search past news, stories or abstracts with given search criteria
- Airline reservation, hotel-booking, railway-reservation, car-rental, etc.
- A writer's aid: a dictionary, thesaurus, phrase generator, indexed dictionary of quotations, and encyclopaedia
- Stock market information systems which allow searches for stocks that meet certain criteria, performance comparisons, moving averages, and various forecasting techniques
- Electronic Financial Transactions (EFT) between banks and via cheque clearing house
- Games of the type that grow or change with various enthusiasts adding to the complexity or diversity
- Electronic Mail Messages Systems (EMMS)
- Corporate information systems such as marketing information system, customer information system, product information system, personnel information system, etc.
- Corporate systems of different systems such as Order-Entry System, Centralized Purchasing, Distributed Inventory Control, etc.
- On-line systems for Investment Advice and Management, Tax Minimization, etc.
- Resources of interest to a home user
- Sports results
- Theatre, movies, and community events information
- Shopping information, prices, advertisements
- Restaurants; good food guide
- Household magazine, recipes, book reviews, film reviews
- Holidays, hotels, travel booking
- Radio and TV programmes
- Medical assistance service
- Insurance information
- Computer Assisted Instruction (CAI)
- School homework, quizzes, tests
- Message sending service
- Directories

- Consumer reports
- Employment directories and Job opportunities
- Tax information and Tax assistance
- Journey planning assistance viz. Train, bus, plane etc.
- Catalogue of Open University and Virtual University courses

## 10.12 INTERNET

The word Internet is derived from two words 'Interconnection' and 'Network'. 'Network' is a set of two or more interconnected computers that are connected through a set of hardware devices to share information. When a large number of such 'Networks' are 'Interconnected' together to exchange information, using same set of rules and regulations, they constitute the Internet. A user of Internet may feel as if the interaction is carried with single large computer network, but actually it is a Network of Networks.

There are several ways to describe the Internet:

- **From a social point of view:**

  The Internet can be thought of as millions of people communicating, sharing ideas and information. Any individual on the Internet can communicate with anyone else on the Internet. The Internet is a platform where people can communicate with others no matter where they are, their status, or their expertise. People communicate on the internet in a variety of ways: E-mail, Usenet etc.

- **From commercial point of view.**

  The Internet is a vast collection of information that can be searched and retrieved electronically. This collection includes advice on all sorts of topics, data, electronic texts, images, software, commercial activities, and almost anything that a user may need.

  Almost all of this information is shared free of charge, except what one pays to access the Internet, because sharing information and resources is at the basis of the Internet. One of the fastest growing sectors of work on the Internet is in the area of commercial applications. As the Internet use becomes more available and common, it's being viewed as a viable means of doing business and marketing.

- One can access the information or communicate with others on the Internet by using a collection of tools and services that give access to people, information, and resources. There are three basic services: Telnet, FTP, WWW etc.

- **From technical point of view.**

  As discussed earlier, the Internet is a Network of Networks. Every network and every computer on these networks exchange information according to some set rules and regulations which are called protocols. The computers that make up the network may be designed be different technologies or by different companies, but when they all use same protocols they can exchange data or information as a part of same network. Two most commonly used protocols for working with the Internet are Internet Protocol (IP) or Transmission Control Protocol (TCP).

Each computer system as well as each network on the Internet has a unique Internet address called an IP address. These IP addresses are numeric, like 122.35.65.221. Such numeric are difficult to be memorized by humans, so each numeric address corresponds to a name called domain name or host name, such as google.co.in. This address is used to exchange information with, send e-mail to, or use an Internet service that involves another computer system.

Internet is thus one of the greatest inventions of our time. It has given new dimensions to the way of communication. Any amount of data can be accessed and retrieved from any computer on the Internet within no time. Internet has become an inseparable part of not only the computer society but almost every individual nowadays. It brings a wealth of information to us just by a click of mouse.

## 10.13 EVOLUTION OF THE INTERNET

The Internet consists of a network of interconnected computers that transmit data using standard internet protocol (IP). Most people believe that the internet began in the mid-1990s, but in reality, it began much earlier than that.

In 1958 AT&T introduced the first commercial modem. It converted digital computer data into analog signals for transmission across its long distance network. This invention allowed computers to communicate over normal telephone circuits used for standard voice phone calls.

By the end of the 1960s, the Department of Defense constructed one of the first physical networks of computers by linking nodes at the University of California at Los Angeles, SRI (in Stanford), University of California at Santa Barbara, and University of Utah. This was known as the Advanced Research Projects Agency Network (ARPANET), and it grew quickly in the early 1970's, reaching 57 interconnected nodes in the network by July, 1975.

It was only a couple years after ARPANET began that the first e-mail program for the network was created by Ray Tomlinson in 1971. Tomlinson is also credited as the one who decided to use the @ symbol in email addresses. He sent the first email that same year. Five years later, in 1976, the Queen of England sent her first e-mail from a British Army base as a part of a demonstration of networking technology.

It wasn't until 1974 that the term "internet" was first used. The first documentation of the term was in a paper by Vinton "Vint" Cerf and Bob Kahn on Transmission Control Protocol (TCP). TCP is a fundamental protocol for Internet communications, allowing networked computers to create connections to one another, which can then be used to exchange data. These days people sometimes refer to the Internet as cyberspace, and the term "cyberspace" was coined in 1984 by William Gibson in his book, Neuromancer.

Many people think that the World Wide Web (WWW) is synonymous with the Internet, but the WWW is actually just a service that runs on the Internet. Other commonly known services operating over the Internet include email and FTP (File Transfer Protocol), but there are others such as Gopher and Usenet, which are not very popular or well known these days.

The World Wide Web was invented in 1990 by Tim Berners-Lee, in an effort to link scientific research. At the time he was a scientist at CERN, the European Organization for Nuclear Research. As part of the WWW he developed the HyperText Markup Language, better known as HTML, which is the language used to create web pages. In addition to HTML, other specifications such as Uniform Resource Locator (URL) and HyperText Transfer Protocol (HTTP) had to be developed to allow the Internet to expand to handle WWW communications.

In order to view Web pages, computers need programs which have become known as Web browsers. They send a signal to a server requesting a page, and the server responds by sending the necessary data for the web page, which the browser decodes and displays on the computer screen. Naturally, Berners-Lee is the person that created the first Web browser, so that the first web pages could be viewed. This first browser was originally called the WorldWideWeb, but the name was later changed to Nexus in order to be more distinct and avoid confusing it with the World Wide Web.

The first Web site was "info.cern.ch", and it was also built by Berners-Lee. It is worth noting that its address did not begin with the "www" prefix. In fact, there is no technical reason for a website to begin with www. The "www" prefix is a result of the common Internet convention used at the time the Web was developed of giving hostnames that correspond to the protocol they serve. Another peculiarity is that the term World Wide Web is longer to say when it is abbreviated. The acronym WWW actually contains more syllables than any other three-letter acronym in the English language.

It was on August 6, 1991 that the Web became an Internet service that was available to the public.

This was the date that Berners-Lee posted about the World Wide Web project to the alt.hypertext newsgroup on Usenet.

In 1993, the Mosaic web browser was released. Although it wasn't the first Web browser program, it was the first to become really popular due to its incorporation of graphics and the ability to run on the dominant mainstream operating system, Microsoft's Windows. Mosaic was originally designed for a UNIX system running X-windows, but was available for several other operating systems such as the Mac OS and Windows within a year. Almost as soon as graphics became available, the first banner ads began to appear–in 1994 to be exact. Also in 1994, Pizza Hut began to offer pizza ordering on its Web page.

Yahoo!, which was originally named "Jerry and David's Guide to the World Wide Web," was started in February 1994. It was not the first internet directory, but it was the first to become widely popular. By the fall of 1994 it had hit 1 million hits in a single day, with almost 100 thousand unique visitors. During its initial public offering in 1996, it sold 2.6 million shares–33.8 million dollars worth–at $13 each.

As of 2006, according to Internet World Stats, around 70% of the population in the United States is on the internet. Throughout the world, there are almost 1.1 billion users of the Internet as of 2006 and half of them reside in Europe and Asia. Worldwide Internet usage increased over 200% in thesix years from 2000 to 2006, yet there is still plenty of room for expansion considering that less than 1/6 of the world population is online. It is expected that US and world Internet usage will continue to grow.

This growth is often attributed to the lack of central administration, which allows organic growth of the network, as well as the non-proprietary open nature of the Internet protocols, which encourages vendor interoperability and prevents any one company from exerting too much control over the network. The estimated population of Internet users is 1.97 billion as of 30 June 2010.

From 2009 onward, the Internet is expected to grow significantly in Brazil, Russia, India, China, and Indonesia (BRICI countries). These countries have large populations and moderate to high economic growth, but still low Internet penetration rates. In 2009, the BRICI countries represented about 45 percent of the world's population and had approximately 610 million Internet users, but by 2015, Internet users in BRICI countries will double to 1.2 billion, and will triple in Indonesia.

## 10.14 APPLICATIONS OF THE INTERNET

The wide variety of applications provided by Internet can be categorized into following categories according to their behavior:

1. Information Retrieval Services: The Internet has enabled individuals and organizations to publish ideas and information to a large audience online at minimal charges and no time delay. Those ideas can be published in one of the following forms:

   a. Webpages: Internet provides a pool of information through the webpages available on almost every topic. Publishing a webpage involves little initial cost and provides many attractive cost-free services. These websites can be referenced with Uniform Resource Locators (URL's) which allow providers to symbolically identify services and clients to locate websites and access them using Hypertext Transfer Protocol (HTTP). HTTP is a request/response protocol in which client sends a request to the server and the server responds with the requested webpage.

      Webpages are designed using Hypertext Markup Language (HTML) which is a special formatting language that defines the placement and format of text and other objects on the webpage.

   b. Blogs: Web logs or blogs are used as updateable online diaries as journals. Readers can post comments on each journal entry. The blogs are usually arranged in chronological order from the most recent post or entry at the top of main page to the older entries towards the bottom of the page.

   c. Advertisements: The companies and organizations advertise their products via banners on popular websites. Banners are advertisements in the form of graphical images that runs across a webpage. The websites limit the size of the banner to a certain number of bytes so that it displays quickly. The advantage of such advertising is that the marketer can approach the user personally, thus a one-to-one approach between the company marketers and consumers can be established.

2. Communication Services: Internet provides its users one of the most attractive services to communicate over long distances. This communication can be carried out in one of the many forms mentioned here:

   a. Email: Email is a basic communication service provided by the Internet. This is a way of sending electronic text messages between sender and receiver. Images, documents and other files can also be sent as mail attachments.

   b. Voice-over-Internet Protocol: VoIP is a method of transmitting audio over the Internet by encoding analog audio in a digital form, transmitting it over the Internet, and decoding it back to analog form for listening. It carries the voice traffic over the Internet. VoIP can be free of cost or much less cost than a telephone, especially over long distances.

   c. Internet Relay Chat (IRC): IRC enables people all over the world to talk over the Internet in real-time sessions. One can connect to an IRC Server across the Internet through an IRC client application and join a network to participate in world-wide conversations. One can then join any public chat room running on that server. Every message sent in a given chat room is sent by the IRC client application to the IRC server which then gets transmitted to all users connected to that chat room.

3. Data Transfer Services: Retrieving the information is only a first step in the overall transfer of information. Actual data is transferred using specific protocols used in transferring files over Internet. Various protocols used in data transfer are listed below:

   a. File Transfer: File Transfer Protocol (FTP) is the protocol used for exchanging files over the Internet. FTP works in the same way as HTTP for transferring webpages from a server to a user's web browser. It is commonly used to download a file from a FTP server using the Internet or to upload a file to a FTP server.

b. Gopher: Gopher is a menu based document delivery system. An individual uses Gopher to access various types of information such as files, documents, and images. Gopher also allows access to ftp, telnet, and searchable databases. All of this is done by selecting items from menus.

## 10.15 GETTING CONNECTED TO THE INTERNET

An Internet Service Provider (ISP) is an organization that provides user access to the Internet and related services. There are many ISP's available depending upon the area they serve. They can be large national or multinational companies covering large number of cities or small companies serving only limited regions. Like any company, ISP's charge money in exchange of their Internet connection. Besides the standard Internet connection, an ISP provides services like domain hosting, web space, e-mail, instant messaging etc.

In order to access the Internet, one can connect to an ISP using different types of connections available such as dial-up phone, DSL, ISDN, Cable, Satellite and Wireless Internet Connections. Each of them differs in their speed and cost. An ISP provides each user with a username and password and a phone number to enable them to connect to the Internet.

There are many types of ISP's. Some are local ISP's operating at a local level, some are national ISP's operating at National level and some are global ISP's operating at International level. In India, there are total 183 ISP's that are operating at national level. Some of them are BSNL, Sify, Bharti Infotel, Tata Internet services, Reliance etc.

A user can connect to the Internet either by dialing into an ISP's computer or by directly connecting to an ISP. A dial up connection is initiated by dialing into a modem over the telephone link whereas a direct connection is a continuous connection to an ISP through a dedicated phone line. The various types of Internet connections available nowadays are:

1. **Dial-up connection:** Dial-up connection is the most widely used type of computer connection to the Internet. It connects a computer to the Internet using an analog modem as the interface. Dialing up with a modem is the cheapest and most widely available way to connect to the Internet, but because it offers comparatively slower connection speeds, graphics-intensive websites can take a long time to load. The maximum speed at which one can download data is limited by the telephone system's analog bandwidth, the line quality, and the Internet traffic load.

   Dial-up customers usually need to enter a user name and password, as well as the ISP's phone number into a dialog box. The dial-up networking software uses this information to make the connection with the ISP. At the ISP's end, a computer checks the user name and password against a database of active customers. Once the ISP authenticates the information, the user is free to surf, check and send e-mails, download files, and so on. Typical dial-up connection speeds range from 2400 bps to 56 Kbps.

2. **ISDN:** Integrated Services Digital Network is a system of digital phone connections that has been designed for sending voice, video and data simultaneously over digital or ordinary phone lines, with a much faster speed and higher quality than an analog system can provide. ISDN is the international communication standard for data transmission along telephone lines and has transmission speeds up to 64 Kbps per channel.

   ISDN uses two channels for communication which are the Bearer Channel or the B channel and the Delta Channel or the D channel. The B channel is used for data transmission and the D channel is used for signaling and control, though data can be transmitted through the D channel as well.

ISDN has two access options:

i. Basic Rate Interface: BRI is made up of two B channels with a bandwidth of 64 Kbit/s and a D channel with a bandwidth of 16 Kbit/s. It is also known as 2B+D.

ii. Primary Rate Interface: RI has a greater number of B channels, which varies from nation to nation, and a D channel with a bandwidth of 64 Kbit/s.

3. **DSL:** Digital Subscriber Line (DSL) is a technology that allows high speed Internet connections over regular phone lines. In addition to offering significantly better download and upload speed than the traditional modems, DSL offers the benefit of always being on and one does not have to dial up the Internet Service Provider every time one has to get on the Internet. And unlike Cable modems, DSL connections are dedicated, so one does not have to share bandwidth with other users.

   This broadband connection requires special equipment setup at both ends. At the user end, a DSL modem modulates digital information from the computer to send it along phone lines. These signals are then translated by a Multiplexer located at the phone company's nearest central office. The Multiplexer separates the voice from data signals, sending the latter to an ISP and from there to the Internet.

   There are three main categories of DSL:

   **i. ADSL:** Asymmetric Digital Subscriber Line supports data rates from 1.5 to 9 Mbps for downloading and 16 to 640 Kbps for uploading data. ADSL requires special ADSL modem.

   **ii. SDSL:** Symmetric Digital Subscriber Line allows more data to be sent over existing copper telephone lines. SDSL supports data rates up to 3 Mbps. SDSL require special SDSL modem. SDSL is called symmetric because it supports the same data rates for uploading and downloading.

   **iii. VDSL:** Very High DSL is a DSL technology that offers fast data rates over relatively short distances. The shorter the distance the faster the connection rate is. VDSL connection speed ranges from 128 Kbps to 8 Mbps.

   DSL has one significant disadvantage that the farther the user is from the central office, the slower the connection is.

4. **Cable TV Internet Connections:** Through the use of cable modem one can have a broadband Internet connection that is designed to operate over cable TV lines. Cable TV Internet connection works by using TV channel space for data transmission, with certain channels used for downstream transmission and other channels for upstream transmission. Because the coaxial cable used by cable TV provides much greater bandwidth than telephone lines, a cable TV Internet connection can be used to achieve extremely fast access to the Internet. The speed ranges from 512 Kbps to 20 Mbps.

5. **Satellite Internet Connections:** Satellite Internet Connections allow a user to access the Internet via a satellite that orbits the earth. A satellite is placed at a static point above the earth's surface, in a fixed position. Because of enormous distances, signals must travel from the earth up to

the satellite and back again so these connections are slightly slower than high speed terrestrial connections over copper wires. Such connections have a connection speed average around 492 up to 512 Kbps.

6. **Wireless Internet Connections:** Wireless Internet Connections are one of the newest Internet connection types. Instead of using telephone or cable lines for the Internet connection, the radio frequency bands are used. Wireless Internet connection provides an always-on connection which can be accessed from anywhere as long as one is within a network coverage area. It is typically more expensive and mainly available in metropolitan cities.

## 10.16 ELECTRONIC-MAIL

E-mail stands for electronic mail. It is the most popular service or facility provided by the Internet through which we can electronically send and receive messages anywhere in the world. E-mail is a fast and efficient method of communication. It is almost free of cost. The e-mail reaches to the destination in a few seconds. You can also send documents, pictures, audio and video files via e-mail by attaching the file with e-mail. It is also possible to send or receive e-mail messages through a mobile phone.

E-mail is a fast and efficient method of communication. You can also send your important data files or information to your own mail account and download these when required.

### 10.16.1 E-mail Address

E-mail -is sent and received with the reference of e-mail address. Therefore, each Internet user must have a unique e-mail account on an e-mail server, to send and receive e-mails. E-mail address consists of username and his address on the Internet. All ISP companies also provide the – e-mail address when theft membership is obtained.

The general format of an e-mail address is:

username@domain_name

Where **username:** Specifies the name of user or organization. **Domain_name;** Specifies the name of server or ISP of which the user is member. For example, "nasib.gill@mdurohtak.ac.in" is e-mail address in which, "nasib.gill" is the name of user and "mdurohtak.ac.in" is the name of server.

You must type the correct e-mail address to send an e-mail, otherwise it is returned back. When some one sends e-mail to your e-mail address, it is stored in your mailbox. When you login to your account, you will usually be informed if you have new mail. Some mail systems will make sounds and tell you that you have new mail.

### 10.16.2 E-Mail Attachment

Attachment is a powerful feature of e-mail, which enables you to send additional files with your e-mail message. In this way, you can send and receive messages as well as document or program files. You can send documents, pictures or images, and audio & video files via e-mail, anywhere over the network. Attachment size varies from one e-mail service provider to the other.

### 10.16.3 How Does E-Mail Work?

To create, send and receive e-mail, you need e-mail program, also called "email client". Once you send the message, your computer connects to your e-mail server and transmits a copy of your message. E-mail

Server is a host computer on the Internet, which keeps track of information about millions of e-mail account holders. The server checks the address you have typed and finds out where the recipient e-mail server is. It connects to that server and transmits another copy of the message. Once the receiving e-mail server has received the message, the recipient is able to retrieve the message when connected to the server.

Most e-mail clients allow you to attach files to the e-mail message. In this way you can send and receive data as well as program files.

### 10.16.4 Advantages of E-Mail

There are several advantages of the e-mail facility available on the Internet. The main advantages of e-mail are:

1. It is extremely fast and reaches to the destination in a few minutes or even in few seconds. Typically, it takes 1 to 5 minutes to reach a destination in Europe (USA, England etc.) from Pakistan.
2. Its cost is very low. It is almost free.
3. One message can be sent to many persons with a single e-mail.
4. It is available round the clock and round the globe.
5. You can send and receive e-mail from anywhere in the world.
6. You can attach and send any type of files.
7. It is also possible to send or receive e-mail messages through a mobile phone.

### 10.16.5 Limitations of E-Mail

Although e-mail, provides the fast and efficient way to send and messages. It also has some limitations. These are described below.

1. Email is not necessarily private. Your confidential message read by someone such as network administrator.
2. Some email systems can send or receive text files only.
3. It is difficult to express emotions using email.
4. You can receive too much or unwanted emails.
5. You may not know about the person with whom you are communicating.

### 10.16.6 Free E-Mail Account

Although you are provided with the e-mail account when you join any local ISP company. There are also some websites that provide facility to Internet users to create their own e-mail account, free of cost. The most popular websites are:

- http://www.gmail.com
- http://www.yahoo.com
- http: //www.hotrnail.com

To create new e-mail account on the Hotmail, follow these steps.

- Open the Hotmail website.

- Click the Sign-up link for an E-mail account, a registration form will be displayed.
- Fill the form correctly and send to the Hotmail server, your e-mail account is created.

After creation of your e-mail account, you are allotted a. username and password. You can check 'your e-mail account by entering the correct username and password. You can also compose and send the e-mail from your free e-mail account as well as you can manage your mails.

## 10.17 SEARCH ENGINE

Internet is a large source of information and contains almost millions of WebPages related to almost every topic that can be thought of. Initially to search for any relevant item of information, user needed to browse from an initial starting address of a known website, and then begin searching for links from one webpage to another, hoping to reach to the required information. This technique called browsing is a common, sequential way of getting the information. But it is very time consuming and tiring job these days when the internet connections are paid, and time needs to be saved. So many searching tools were developed for the searchers to get the relevant information in minimum time possible with accurate results.

A search engine is a program that searches documents for specified keywords and returns a list of the web pages where the keywords were found. A search engine is actually a huge database that contains references to thousands of web pages on the Internet. The searchers interact with these databases by proving some keywords. On the basis of these keywords, the databases return a list of available web pages along with their titles, URL, several first sentences etc. From these received results, user can choose the webpage whichever seems relevant.

Typically, a search engine works by sending out a spider to fetch as many documents as possible. A spider is a program that automatically fetches Web pages. Spiders are used to feed pages to search engines. It's called a spider because it crawls over the Web. Another term for these programs is WebCrawler. Because most Web pages contain links to other pages, a spider can start almost anywhere. As soon as it sees a link to another page, it goes off and fetches it. Large search engines, like Google, have many spiders working in parallel. Another program, called an indexer, then reads these documents and creates an index based on the words contained in each document. Each search engine uses a proprietary algorithm to create its indices such that only meaningful results are returned for each query.

The information that is received from a database is ranked according to various factors such as location and frequency of keywords in the web page, number of visits to the web page, or some other relevant factors. Redundant references are also removed from the results by most of the search engines.

Although search engine is really a general class of programs, the term is often used to specifically describe systems like Google (http://www.google.com), Yahoo (http://www.yahoo.com), MSN Search (http://search.msn.com), Alta Vista (http://altavista.com), AOL Search (http://search.aol.com) that enable users to search for documents on the World Wide Web.

Hence on the Internet, a search engine is a coordinated set of programs that includes:

- A spider (also called a "crawler" or a "bot") that goes to every page or representative pages on every Web site that wants to be searchable and reads it, using hypertext links on each page to discover and read a site's other pages.
- A program that creates a huge index (sometimes called a "catalog") from the pages that have been read.

- A program that receives the search request, compares it to the entries in the index, and returns results to the user.

## 10.17.1 Components of Search Engines

There are four main components to a search engine which will affect the results of the search.

### 1. Web Crawler

This is the part of the search engine which goes through the pages on the internet and gathers the information for the search engine. Variable features which can affect any search results include:

- **Included pages:** Most search engines will find information by beginning at one page and then following all of the links on that page. It will then follow all of the links on these new pages, and so on. Therefore, if a page is not linked to from another page, it may never be found by a search engine. Authors can include unlinked pages in a search engine by submitting them to each specific search engine.
- **Excluded pages:** Some web administrators may choose to exclude their pages from search engines because they are internal pages or Intranets. Many web pages are also excluded because their content is dynamically generated from a database and a search engine cannot find it.
- **Documents types:** Different search engines will search different document types. All will search HTML documents, but some will also search PDF, PowerPoint, Word, Excel, and more.
- **Frequency of crawling:** An important part of a web crawler is how frequently it retrieves information from pages. Some sites it will visit more often than others.

### 2. Database

The search engine's database is what searcher is actually searching. All of the information that a web crawler retrieves is stored in a database. Every time one uses a search engine, it is this database that is being searched, not the live internet. Variable features which can affect the search results include:

- **Size of the database:** Some search engines will have extremely large databases (~5 billion pages) for one to search, while others will have comparatively small ones (~150 million pages). A small database is not necessarily worse, however, since it may offer more focused and higher quality results than a larger database.
- **Freshness of the database:** The freshness of the database is a direct result of how frequently the web crawler retrieves new information. If the information in the database is fairly old, then the search results will suffer.

### 3. Search Algorithm

Each search engine interprets the terms entered into the search box in different ways. Variable features which can affect the search results include:

- **Operators:** Most search engines allow the use of operators such as AND, OR, and NOT in order to create complex search statements. The terms may need to be entered in upper case. Most of them also use the plus (+) sign to signal that a term must be included in the search results and a minus (-) sign to signal that a term must be excluded from the results.

- **Phrase Searching:** Search engines will generally search for words as phrases when quotation marks are placed around the phrase. Some search engines may use a drop down menu which offers the option of searching the terms as a phrase.
- **Truncation:** Some search engines will automatically truncate the terms you enter. This means that the search engine will not only search for the term exactly as you spelled it, but will also search on that term with alternate endings and as a plural. Some search engines will only search for variable endings on certain common words.

### 4. Ranking Algorithm

How a search engine ranks the results of the search is possibly the most important component of a search engine. Most searches will retrieve thousands of results. Since one probably will only look through the first 1-2 pages of results only, one needs the most relevant results to appear first. Variable features which can affect your search results include:

- **Location and Frequency:** All search engines look at the location and frequency of words in a page. If a term appears near the top of a web page, such as in the title or in the first few paragraphs of text, it is assumed that the page is more relevant than if the term is used at the bottom of the page. Pages where the words appear more frequently in relation to the other words on the page also qualifies the page as being more relevant than other web pages.
- **Link Analysis:** This feature analyzes how pages link to each other and then uses this information to determine the "importance" of each page. If a page is linked to from a large number of other pages, then it is ranked more highly.
- **Clickthrough measurement:** Some search engines also use clickthrough analysis. This means that a search engine might watch what results someone selects from a particular search, and then eventually drop high-ranking pages that aren't attracting clicks, while promoting lower-ranking pages that do pull in visitors.

## 10.17.2 Finding Information Using Search Engine

A user opens a search engine webpage and types the keyword or a criterion that describes the information that is needed. Some search engines allow the use of some Boolean terms such as AND, OR, NOT to further restrict or widen the search results. The user can view the results of search in a search engine by going through the following process:

1. Here we use a Google as a search engine for our example. To open the Google webpage, http://www.google.com is typed in the address bar of the browser. Following home page which is the Google search engine appears:

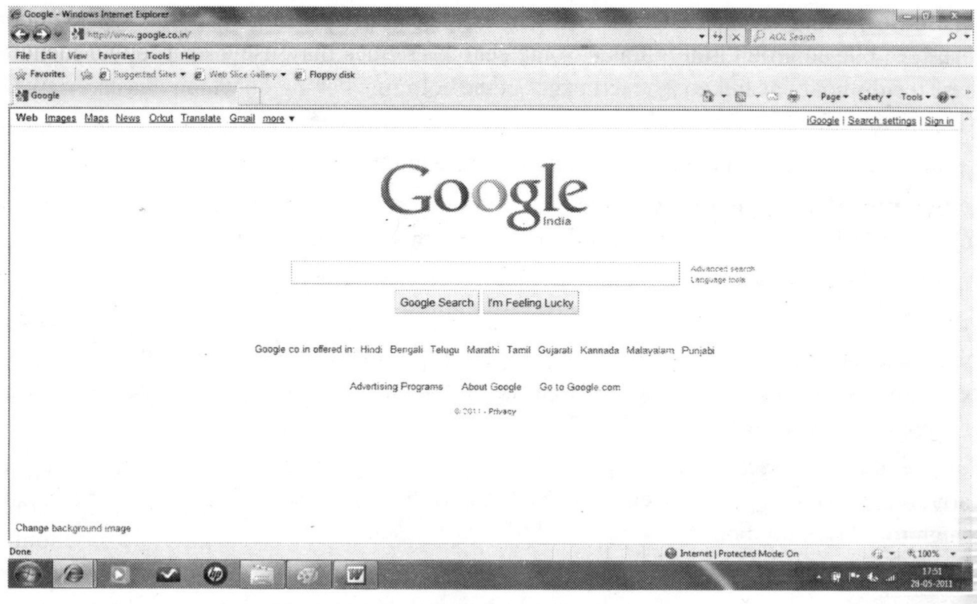


Figure 10.29

2. In the Search textbox, the keyword or search criteria that the user wants are typed. Suppose one needs to find information on Taj Mahal. When Search button is clicked, a new webpage lists all the available WebPages relating to the searched keyword along with a short description about the web site and it's URL.

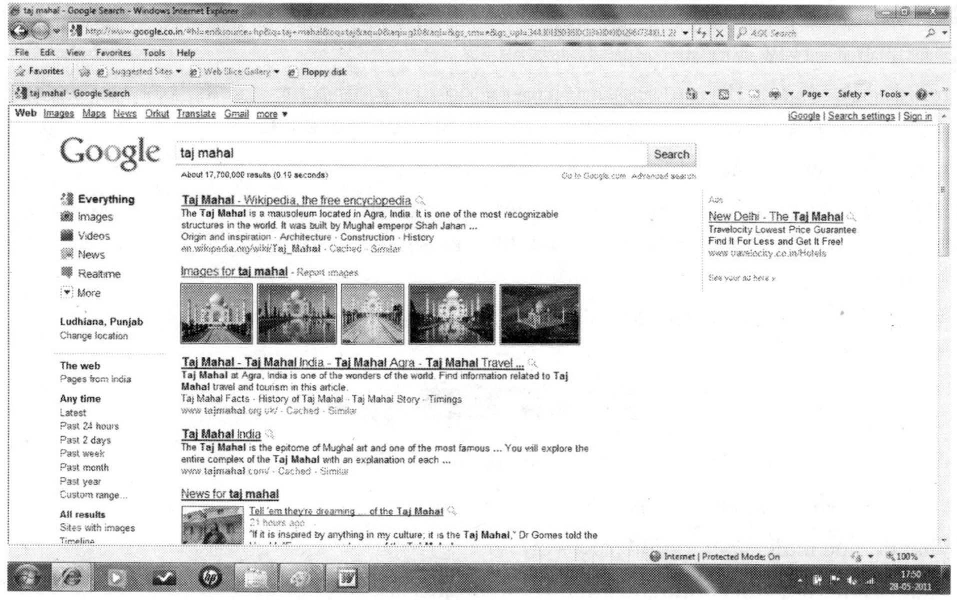


Figure 10.30

3. By clicking on any hyperlink that seems relevant, the searcher can jump to the webpage instantly. There may be hundreds to thousands of matches for a particular keyword. The webpage that lists these results contains link to the next pages at the bottom, clicking on which one can view the next pages in the list.

One should keep the following points in mind before searching for any information:

- **Automatic AND Between Words:** When one enters multiple terms into Google, the search engine will return pages which include all of the terms entered.

  For example: anthrax smallpox botulism plague preparedness
- **Word Variations:** At times, Google will search for variations on the terms you have entered. While helpful, this feature works inconsistently and you need to look at your results in order to determine exactly which terms Google has searched. You can turn off this feature by using a plus (+) sign before each term.

  For example: If a user needs to search for 'Healthy Food', Google automatically considers the variations of 'Health Food', 'Healthier Food' etc. If the user needs to turn off these variations, just search for '+Healthy Food'.
- **Common Words (where, how, you, etc.):** There are a number of common words that Google will ignore. In order to include common words in your search, you can use a plus (+) sign before each term.

  For example: On searching for 'How do you write official letters', Google searches for 'write official letters' only. If one needs to include such words in the search too, adding a + sign before them is a good practice.
- **Searching ("Quotes"):** In order to search for phrases in Google, you need to place quotation marks around your phrase. Phrase searching will also turn off the exclusion of common words.

  For example: "How do you" catch tuberculosis
- **Exclude Words (-):** If your search retrieves too many off-topic results, you can exclude words from your search results using a minus (-) sign before the excluded word.

  For example: emergency preparedness –bioterrorism
- **(OR):** When you need to search for synonyms or related terms, you need to use an upper case OR between each term and phrase. Note that Google will only search for the first ten terms that you enter.

  For example: "earthquake" OR "volcano" OR "landslide" OR "avalanche"

## EXERCISE

1. What is Computer Networking? What are its benefits?
2. When and why Computer Networking is essential?
3. What do you understand by Internetworking?
4. What computing and communication technologies are emerging?
5. What are the aims and objectives of Computer Networking?
6. What are various types of Computer Networks?

7. Differentiate between Public Networks and Private Networks?
8. What is ISDN (Integrated Services Digital Network)?
9. What does WAN stand for? What are the transmission channels for WAN?
10. What do you mean by LAN? Why is it so popular?
11. What are the hardware and software requirements for LAN?
12. What are Value Added Networks (VANs)?
13. What are Servers? Explain the concept through suitable example.
14. What are Public Switched Data Networks?
15. What is meant by a Computer Topology?
16. What are various topologies adopted for interconnecting various computers?
17. What is the criteria for selection of Network Topology?
18. What do you understand by Fully-interconnected Network?
19. What are various applications of Computer Networks? Discuss.
20. What is a Multi-drop Network?
21. What are the hardware requirements for WAN?
22. What are different types of WANs?
23. Differentiate between twisted-pair and co-axial cables.
24. What is meant Fibre-optic Cables? What are its benefits?
25. What are Telecommuting Systems?
26. What do you understand by Communication Packages?
27. What are Videotext Networks?
28. What are the major components of a communication package?
29. What do you understand by Teletext?
30. What do you mean by a tree network? What are its limitations?
31. How are satellites? How do they help in networking?
32. What are Microwaves? How do they differ from satellite communication?
33. What are Public Switched Telephone Network (PSTN)?
34. Can radio-waves be used as a transmission channel in computer networks? Justify your answer.
35. What is Layered Architecture?
36. What is a bus network? What are its benefits?
37. Differentiate between Bridges and Routers.
38. What is X.25 standard interface? Explain.
39. What is 'Distributed Processing'?
40. What are the advantages and disadvantages of distributed processing?
41. What do you understand by gateways?
42. What is meant by Computer Network Architecture?

43. What is Client-Server Architecture? What are its benefits?
44. What are various key-issues of Computer Networks?
45. How does a Peer-to-Peer Architecture work?
46. What are communication channel configurations? Indicate their significance.
47. What is Resource Sharing? How does computer network help in this regard?
48. What are computer network protocols? Indicate their purposes.
49. What is OSI model of network architecture?
50. What are advantages and disadvantages of OSI model?
51. What is an Internet? How did it evolve?
52. What we can do on Internet?
53. Who maintains Internet?
54. What is an Anonymous FTP?
55. What is meant by ISP? Which one is the main ISP in India? Name other ISPs, if any.
56. What are URLs?
57. What is the concept of Cyber-cafés?
58. What is a TCP/IP?
59. What is meant by Shell Account?
60. How do WAIS and Veronica differ from each other?
61. What is E-Mail? How E-Mail works?
62. How does a TCP/IP function?
63. How do we find E-mail address?
64. What is a Web-Browser? How does it work?
65. What is IRC? Is it different from Web-Chat?
66. What is Telnet? Where and how is it useful?
67. Differentiate between Gopher and WAIS?
68. How is IP addressing done?
69. What do you understand by E-Mail Reminder Services?
70. What is meant by Usenet Network? How are they helpful?
71. What is the utility Mail Forwarding Services?
72. What is meant by free ISPs?
73. What is HTTP? How does HTTP work? Explain.
74. What does HTML stand for? State its importance.
75. What is Netscape? How and where does it help out?
76. Is WWW a component of Internet? Explain.
77. What are the various modes for using FTP?
78. What is meant by Hypertext Links?

79. Differentiate between a home-page and a web-page.
80. What are domain names? Also give few examples.
81. Differentiate between host and terminal.
82. What is meant by a protocol? Enumerate protocols available on the Internet.
83. What do you understand by a Web-site? What are its requirements?
84. What is Internet Explorer? Enumerate its capabilities.
85. What do you understand by Search Engines? State their functions.
86. What are various types of files? State the extension of each along with the nature of file.
87. What is meant by Mailing Lists? How do these help?
88. What are the benefits of Mailing Lists? Explain.
89. How an internet can be accessed in a LAN environment?
90. What types of files we can come across on the Internet?
91. Differentiate between dial-up and direct connection.
92. What are the hardware and software requirements for an Internet connection?
93. What do you understand by hyperspace?
94. How can we have a secure internet? Illustrate.
95. What do you mean by uploading and downloading?
96. What are Internet security problems?
97. What is a remote login? Explain.
98. What are the solutions to Internet security problems?
99. What is meant by Internet Addressing? Illustrate.
100. What are the different ways to get an access on to the Internet? Explain.
101. Enumerate the tips and techniques for effective Web-Searching.
102. What are free E-Mail services? Give few examples of such services.
103. What do SLIP and PPP stand for? Explain the purpose of each.

# Computer Applications

## 11.1 INTRODUCTION

Computer is the most powerful tool man has ever created. It made a great impact on every activity of mankind and plays an important role in day-to-day functioning in almost all walks of life. In the early days, computers were only confined to computational tasks in scientific and engineering applications, but now about 80% of work done by computer is of non computational nature. The following are the major areas of computer applications:

- Computer In Desktop Publishing
- Computer Aided Design And Manufacturing
- Computer In Project Management
- Computer Application In Sports
- Computers For Data Analysis
- Computer Applications In Military
- Computers In Design And Research Work
- Point Of Sale Terminals
- Financial Transaction Terminals
- Computers With Visions
- Computers In Artificial Intelligence
- Computers In Banking Application
- Computers In Education
- Computers In Inventory And Quality Control
- Computers In Marketing
- Computers In Medicine And Health Care
- Computers In The Arts
- Computers In Entertainment And Amusement
- Robotics

- Industrial Control And Instrumentation
- Computers In Communications
- Real-Time And On-Line Applications

## 11.2 COMPUTER IN DESKTOP PUBLISHING

Desktop publishing evolved from electronic publishing methods that have been in use since late 1970s. Thousands of books, newspapers and magazines are now produced with the aid of computers. Users of desktop publishing systems are concerned with the quality of the printed images they can get from reproduction of computer outputs. For many printed products, a laser printer is good enough.

**Fig. 11.1:** Desktop Publishing

Desktop publishing systems includes a computer and a number of peripherals with powerful desktop publishing software that can produce page layouts complete with pictures and text printed in a variety of attractive ways. Such pages are used in manuals, bulletins, newsletters etc. They are more attractive and efficient compared to the simple clear printouts. It contains an clip-art library having thousands of pictures which can be selected by the user in his documents. The system contains an output device which can produce text and pictures. Digitizers or scanners may be used to convert art, photo, and text-kind images into suitable format to be fed into the computer. The display monitor used must have a very high resolution.

A powerful PC is used for such an application. Photo typesetter is used which gives better output. For inferior quality work dot-matrix printer or letter quality can be used with desktop publishing package. But these devices do not produce pictures having quality as good as those produced by photo-setter. The desktop publishing package can accept the text which has already been prepared by word processing packages and stored in a file.

***Examples of desk top publishing (DTP) packages are***:

- CorelDraw
- Ventura, and
- Page Maker.

CorelDraw is a very powerful, sophisticated and widely used DTP package.

The desktop publishing package includes a program called page layout program which permits operators to format pages of the text and merge text and pictures on display screen. The operator designs the pages taking suitable pictures from the picture library. He combines pictures and texts and views on the screen. He tries a number of alternatives, then he selects the final design of the page layout. The page layout editor allows him to arrange the text around the picture as he likes. He can add pictures, can remove the position of the picture, can change the style and size of headings, design of borders etc.

When the design is completed, text is entered, the output of the desktop publishing package. i.e., text and images are sent to graphics printer for multiple copies. Alternatively, photo typesetting equipment can be used for output, or a negative can be prepared. The negative is sent to printing forms for mass production.

Any publication that goes into print can benefit from use of DTP techniques. Actually, large periodicals such as mass-circulation newspapers and popular magazines require large-scale computer, typesetting, and printing-preparation capabilities. Some desktop publishing applications are described below.

### Newsletters

A newsletter is a periodical publication produced on a regular schedule. Most newsletters have comparatively small circulations to selected readers and majority of these follow a letter-size format. DTP is an ideal method of producing newsletters. Text and illustrations can be incorporated with a greater ease using DTP software.

### Magazines

Magazines represent a more complex challenge than most newsletters but many magazine publishers adopt DTP methods for this purpose. Major challenge in the production of magazines is due to varying styles of advertisements to be inserted in the magazine at different places. Most of the magazines are published in the letter-sized layout which is ideal for DTP methods.

### Books

Production of books can be carried out with greater ease using DTP technique. The author's manuscript is prepared using word processor on computers and entered text is displayed on the CRT screen and the text may be stored on floppy disks. Generally, laser printers are connected to the computer which produce high quality printouts. Prints of the text are taken out. First proof reading is done in the press. The stored text is retrieved and displayed on the screen. The programmer makes corrections as pointed out by the proof reader. Again prints of the corrected text are taken out. Finally these prints are sent to the author of the book for final proof reading of the book. Error pointed out by the author are corrected again. Then final prints are taken out. Space is left for pasting illustrations, sketches, diagrams etc. Drawing made in black ink are pasted on the pages of the text.

Requirements are more complex for textbooks or other volumes with extensive illustrations, particularly if they are to be printed in multiple colours. However, DTP can be valuable in producing line art through vector graphics techniques and can be used for page composition.

For mass printing, a negative of the document is produced and it is used to prepare plates for offset printing. Nowadays thesis, project reports etc. are also produced using word processor. In case of thesis, project reports, etc. 4-6 copies are taken out using laser printers. Alternatively, only one copy of the text is printed out using laser printer and rest of the copies are produced by photocopying. In educational publishing, DTP techniques are used to prepare most of the study guides and instructor manuals that accompany texts.

### Newspapers

The challenge at most newspapers is to convert large volumes of text to typeset format under extremely tight schedules. DTP techniques are ideal for this purpose. Many newspapers carry out their typesetting on DTP systems. Many of these publications then place the type on page forms that are photographed for printing reproduction. In some instances, plate-making film for printing can be created directly through outputs from PCs. Some laser printers and typesetters are able to generate phototypesetting outputs on paper or film in formats up to 11 by 17 inches. These outputs can be used in printing tabloid newspapers. However, special procedures usually have to be followed for the positioning of advertisements and photos.

## 11.3 COMPUTER AIDED DESIGN AND MANUFACTURING

As the computer has become more powerful over the years, it has become capable of handling more sophisticated tasks than simply processing numerical data. Computers are used in the area of design and manufacturing for the following two practical reasons:

- To enhance productivity
- To reduce costs

### Computer Aided Design

Computer Aided Design (CAD) is the integration of computer and graphics to aid in the area of design and drafting. Computer has started been used a product designing tool. Under CAD systems, a designer or engineer can enter images and/or data to describe a new product. In effect, the computer serves as an electronic drafting tool. It is estimated that most architectural firms use some form of CAD. Architects are able to draw a floor-plan and lay out all structural details, plumbing and electrical fixtures, when designing a room or complete building. Manufacturer of footwear also use CAD systems to design their running shoes. The following are advantages of using computers in product engineering:

- Makes the designing and drafting easier, more accurate and well planned
- Increases productivity as the design and drafting time are significantly reduced

**Fig. 11.2:** Designing and Drafting

CAD operator uses input devices such as mouse, light-pen, etc. in association with CAD package to draw graphical primitives which the user finds even more easier than pencil and paper method as the mistakes can be rectified and redone more comfortably.

### CAD Features

The following are major features of CAD systems:

- Display 3-D and/or color images/drawings on display systems
- Permits the user to move, copy, mirror, erase and rotate objects
- Scales graphical object to any size
- Shows cross-sections of internal portions of a product
- Files drawings in library
- Once a product has been designed electronically, it can be tested mathematically for performance factors such as stress, vibration, and wind resistance
- Testing of designs before any money is spent on tooling and production.

### CAD Applications

CAD systems are applied to the following six general types of applications:

- Mechanical Drafting
- Engineering
- Printed Circuits
- Architecture
- Cartography
- Photogrammetry: It is nothing but use of photographs for precise topographical measurement, mapping and design of such projects as highways)

### Computer Aided Manufacturing

The use of computers to control the factory machines in the manufacturing process is called Computer Aided Manufacturing (CAM).

Computers are nowadays used to control production of certain engineering products, chemical products etc. Take an example of a mechanical industry. Designers use CAD and prepare the design of machines and machine parts to be manufactured. After the design is complete all data, drawings, dimensions are available. This information is available to engineers and operators who are incharge of manufacturing. They use computers to control manufacturing machines such as lathes, drill, milling machine etc. These computers which are controlling manufacturing use design data produced by CAD.

In many industry drawings, dimensions etc. are not needed for manufacturing for example chemical industries. In such a situation information is transmitted from CAD system directly to product manufacturing equipment.

### CAD/CAM

Integrated approach of CAD and CAM is known as CAD/CAM system. The designers design new machines using CAD, and being in integrated system there is a database which stores all data regarding design, drawings, specifications, etc. On the factory floor the manufacturing personnel are on the same computer network. There are appropriate software to get design information from the database and convert them automatically into other programs which activate and control manufacturing machines such as lathes, drills, milling machines etc. Further they control assembly lines and so forth. A series of computer-controlled machines perform the whole task of production. So full automation for the manufacturing of products is achieved in a CAD/CAM system.

### Computer Integrated Manufacturing (CIM)

Automation and integration of an entire manufacturing enterprise is called Computer Integrated Manufacturing (CIM). CIM is used when all the work of a factory is done by computers, such as design, manufacturing, costing, sales management, inventory control, planning and other business and administrative functions.

Manufacturing engineers tend to think of CAM as controlling a single operation or production station. By contrast, CIM applications can be extended to encompass multiple processing stations, including the conveyor equipment that transfers work-pieces. Application of these concepts is expected to expand, particularly with the growth of the robotics field.

### Manufacturing Automation Protocol (MAP)

To integrate all computer-controlled operations and to make sure that the equipment can communicate with each other, equipment manufacturers must agree upon communication links. One such communication link that is becoming the industry standard was developed by General Motors and is called Manufacturing Automation Protocol (MAP). MAP standards can also be implemented in other manufacturing environments.

### Computer Numerical Control (CNC)

A common task in the manufacturing process is the milling of parts. In the early days, all operations of this sort were controlled by individual machine operators. The quality of the end product was often directly related to the skill of the operator. Presently, many of these milling operations have been turned over to Computer Numerical Control (CNC), a system where an operator programs a computer that controls the milling process apparatus.

Often a CNC machine is connected to a CAD workstation and by watching the monitor, the CNC operator can view the part as it is being made by the machine.

### Computer Assisted Materials Requirement Planning (MRP)

Computers have been used to help manage inventories since 1950s. Today, one kind of application program used for inventory management is called Materials Requirement Planning (MRP). A MRP system consists of programs that create files of information about materials needed to manufacture standard product of the company. Such a system also uses files that list the manufacturing operations and time requirements for production of each product.

## 11.4 COMPUTER IN PROJECT MANAGEMENT

Project management software is used on computers to plan, schedule, track, analyse, control manpower, material and other resources for complex and variety of projects related to various professions. Many organisation and departments take up new project work such as installing a new factory, constructing a new building, a power plant, opening a new institute, a hospital and so on. Project management software can co-ordinate all the timing and resources of a variety of projects.

**Fig. 11.3:** Project Management

The Project Manager can establish budgets, arrange schedules, and plan pricing strategy by accumulating data and having all other facts on the basis of which the entire project's plan depend. Actually, the project work is defined as a series of tasks which must be completed in scheduled time period and within the stipulated cost. Computers can be used as a tool to manage such project works with the help of project management software available for such purposes. A project management package may help out to complete the project work in the scheduled time period at reasonable cost. For computer analysis the information required is:

- What are the tasks to be performed?
- In what sequence the tasks are to be performed?
- What is the time required to complete each task?

Due to inter-process dependency, certain tasks can not be initiated until certain other tasks are completed and such type of information is also required to be supplied. The project management software shows the longest sequence of events in the project called critical path. It calculates total project time and checks for tasks which do not stick to laid schedule i.e. either lag or lead or create some other type of mismatching problem.

Most of the project management software employ critical path method. In case a project lags behind the intended schedule, speed can be enhanced to reduce the time of completion of one or more tasks on the critical path to catch up the required schedule. Project management software will show the impact of the delay and will also quickly show the amended schedule. Few software show an automatic resource levelling feature and may show the increased manpower required to catch up the desired schedule.

## 11.5 COMPUTER APPLICATION IN SPORTS

In most sports, computers compile statistics, sell tickets, create training programs and diets for athletes, and suggest game plan strategies based on the competitor's past performance. Following is the brief account of usage of computers in sports.

### Ticketing and Reservations

Today, every major stadium books reservations and issue tickets through a computerised system. The ability to call for reservations and purchase tickets by providing a credit-card number has helped to sell sets by making attendance more convenient and attractive for busy sports-lovers.

### Scheduling

Computers can be used to schedule professional baseball, basketball, and soccer games. Not only does the appropriate day for each game have to be scheduled but also the hour and turf. These requirements create some problems. Now this job takes a fraction of the time and represents only a portion of the work accomplished with the computer.

### Scoreboards

System engineers have developed very good computerised athletic scoring system. Some people have gone for the design of extravagant scoreboards for sports stadiums. Presently, computers create images and slogans, develop and display statistics, and even generate instant-replay videos. Computer-controlled scoreboard displays have become major factors in promoting involvement and enjoyment of audiences at sporting events.

### Biomechanics

Biomechanics is the science used to study dance movements, which is also used to study the movement of athletes. Sports doctors and biomechanical engineers are creating hardware and software that may help athletes to improve their performances. Many devices have been devised for analysing the movement and overall performance of athletes. High-speed video cameras record athlete in performance from two or more angles. Later on, athletes can view the computer screen, see just what they are doing, and can analyse ways in which their performance can be improved.

### Cycling

For 100 years, competitive cycling was a relatively unchanged sport but computer-inspired changes are now taking place. Sensors can be attached to the front wheels of bicycles. Computers collect data from these sensors and calculate figures for speed and distance. This method is better and more accurate than speedometers and odometers. Some computers even calculate the cyclist's time of arrival. The 1984 and 1988 U.S. Olympic cyclic teams wore helmets designed by computers for aerodynamic efficiency.

### Baseball

In baseball, computers determine batting averages, runs batted in, and earned run averages for pitchers. They also examine hitting probabilities between combinations of batters and pitchers. To keep up with masses of statistics, teams employ computer specialities to record pitch-by-pitch data on every game. The statistics are processed by a remote computer and made available immediately to each team's manager and coaches. Computer can analyse data to show a manager what has happened in similar situations during previous games. It can also predict the most likely moves of opposing teams.

### Football

In professional football, computers are being used to prepare game plans, figure probabilities, monitor collegiate players, and log player injuries. As a result, football has become much more strategic than it used to be. Computers are even being used in scouting other teams.

Use of computers in football has generated some controversy. Because coaches can access a wide range of information useful for determining game strategy, professionals feel that coaches with access to computers during games have an unfair advantage over competitors who do not. To overcome these problems, it has been established by various Football Associations that during games computers will not be used.

## 11.6 COMPUTERS FOR DATA ANALYSIS

Computers are widely used for the purpose of data analysis and there are numerous special software for this purpose viz. SPSS(Statistical Package For Social Sciences) package, Lindo Package, SYSTAT package, Spreadsheet package (MS-Excel, Lotus 1-2-3, VisiCalc, etc.), and so on. Data is entered into rows and columns, and using any such package one can tabulate results, calculates number of students in first class, second class, failed student, percentage of students in different classes, list of failure students, average marks etc.

Sales can be forecasted on the basis of required computation pertaining to sales over a period of time ***(see Fig. 11.4 )***. One can prepare product sales, profit, investment computation for an organisation using spreadsheet packages. Year-wise numbers of unit sold, price per unit, production cost, selling cost etc. are entered into the spreadsheet. Revenue are calculated from the units sold and per unit price. Total expenditure is the sum of production cost and the selling cost. Profit is equal to production cost minus total expenditure.

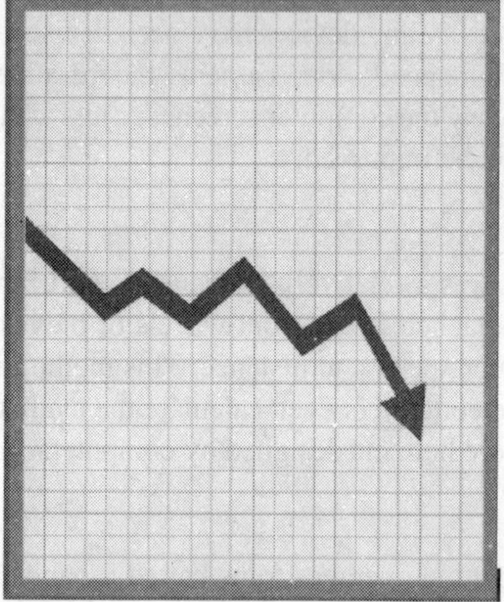

**Fig. 11.4:** Forecasting and Analysis

Similarly, any kind of computation for data entered in the tabulated form can be made using computers with spreadsheet program. Computers are widely used for statistical data analysis. Statistical packages are available for such purposes. They have functions to calculate average, maximum, minimum etc. They can accept data from other files and sort, merge and manipulate data as needed. The spreadsheet programs are also used for accounts, sale analysis, inventory control, financial aspect of business, preparation of budgets etc.

## 11.7 COMPUTER APPLICATIONS IN MILITARY

Computers are being extensively used in defence. Modern tanks, torpedos, missiles, weapons, etc. employ computerised control systems. The following are the four major military areas where a computer has successfully been used:

- Missile Control
- Military Communication
- Military Planning
- Smart Weapons

### Missile Control

A guided missile uses internal computer for its control. Computer's memory holds the detailed map of the target area. Photographs of the target are taken and compared with stirred map before the missile hits the target. Another advantage of computer guided missiles is that they fly faster and turn more quickly as compared to man-controlled aircraft. They can fly into dangerous zones without the risk of pilot's life.

### Military Communication

Computers also play a very important role in military communications. Radar systems employ computers for processing data and for displaying images. Computerised control system provide much more information about range, height etc. of the target.

In near future it is expected that computers will start presenting 3-D pictures of the target. The computer will check the profile and indicate what the profile represents. Nowadays aircraft employ computers for their controls and instrumentation. Fighters are equipped with computers for their quick activity. The X-29A, a fighter has three computers which make about 40 adjustments per second. The computer also allow pilot to interact with.

### Military Planning

The missions of the military services can be described as fighting wars and being prepared to react to hostile acts that threaten wars. Worldwide radar networks and satellite systems monitor the possibility of hostile attack. Computers are used to evaluate the data and plot myriad reactions that can be initiated.

The advanced computer capabilities play a major role in the military operations and planning. For example, Information Systems in the NORAD (North American Air Defence Command) headquarter are linked to radar and satellite monitoring stations that observe the worldwide air-space condition. Computers decode input signals to identify air, sea, and land activities in key areas of the world.

Military commanders can practice making decisions on the basis of realistic situations modelled by computers. For example, Janus simulates a nuclear war. It is used to train high-ranking officers for command positions. This kind of simulation is designed to teach officers to consider the benefits and costs of battlefield strategies in a nuclear age.

Similarly, the U.S. Navy has developed a training device called Navy Technical Action Game (NAVTAG). The game is equipped with three terminals - one for 'them', one for 'us' and one for a 'referee'. Players deal with a number of tactical situations built into the game and can also invent their own. Essential information, such as target location and fuel on hand, is flashed onto the screen and thus players plan their battles accordingly. The referee can add factors to the game. The idea behind it is to make the game realistic enough to enhance skills of the trainees.

### Smart Weapons

Nowadays smart weapons are being widely used in military operations. Smart weapons use microprocessor-based control system which refines the timely functioning, proper calibration, operation, etc. of the weapon.

## 11.8 COMPUTERS IN DESIGN AND RESEARCH WORK

With advent of computers, scientists have started conducting research in hundreds of different ways using it as a tool. Scientific and engineering design and research work involve complex massive computations. In many cases simulation is also required.

### Design

Computers have proved to be as good designing tools. Design of bridges, towers, buildings, generators, motors, electrical transmission network, statistical analysis of molecular structure of complex proteins etc. need complex computations. In some cases massive data are to be processed particularly in statistical analysis. Computers are suitable for both complex computations as well as processing of massive amount of data.

### Research

Research work in different disciplines also require complex computations. Such complex computations are not possible manually now. Nowadays computers are must for this type of work. Varying kinds of researches are being carried out. Computers have made the job very faster and very simple.

### Language Research

Computers may be used to analyse classical literature. A graduate course in the classics requires that students write programs that help them analyse the works of ancient scholars such as Aristotle and Homer. Students program in high level language Ibex that is capable of performing rapid word searches. Students use 20th century technology to conduct research on literature that may date back to the 3rd century A.D.. These studies help them to determine the way a writer's style changes over the course of a lifetime.

### Legal Research

Computers are being used in another project that combines 20th century technology with the work of ancient scholars. A database called Responsa Project stores the contents of more than 250 volumes of statements and judgements legal questions. Responsa are questions and answers about religious issues. The information covers a time span from the Middle Ages to the 20th century.

Scholars use the database to find information about a variety of concerns that affected Jewish life in earlier times but scholars are not the only users of this unusual database. Sociologists, historians, economists, and linguists all have made use of Responsa Project. Information that once would have taken months of devoted research to find can now be located in minutes. Many students consult this database to write dissertations that otherwise would have been impossible because the research would have taken too long.

### Dolphin Research

At the Dolphin Research Center in Florida, scientists have been trying to develop a means of communicating with dolphins. Research has focussed on creating a language that is understood by both dolphins and humans. Whistles voiced by humans are used as commands and are changed by a computer into high-pitched sounds that the dolphins can hear.

The whistle coding is stored in the memory of computer. Thus, the computer reproduces the whistles in precisely the same pitch and pattern each time a command is given. Precision is not the only benefit of using computers-generated sounds but also eliminates the chance that researchers may unknowingly give body signals that would indicate expected actions to the dolphins. The purpose behind such research is that if the intelligent animal does learn to imitate the computer commands, the same animal may someday talk to humans.

### Joint Design

Computers assist in the design and manufacture of artificial joints for humans. The joints are implanted surgically to replace defective or damaged bones. The computer factors into the design such variables as the patient's age, walking condition, allergies, activity level, and other relevant details. The design stage can now be completed in a few minutes whereas earlier it was a very time consuming and expensive process. The surgeon has the final approval of design before the joint is manufactured. Once the design is approved, the surgeon instructs the computer to build the joint.

## 11.9 POINT OF SALE TERMINALS

A ***point-of-sale (POS) terminal*** is a device that reads data at the source of transaction and immediately turns into usable information. POS terminal is used in departmental stores, shops and other retail centres to process sale transaction. Usually an optical bar reader (OBR) is provided with a point of sale terminal and Bar codes or MICR price tags are marked on most packets of commodities to be sold by shopkeepers to identify them.

The point-of-sale terminal is connected to a computer for processing sales. The sold packets are passed through a scanning window. The optical bar reader reads the bar code of the item to identify it. The computer stores its price and other details. The computer prints name of the item, rate, price and other details. If a customer purchases a number of items, the computer issues the receipt for all items after making calculations. It mentions details of all items and the total amount to be paid. It also updates sale records and inventory.

There are various types of bar-coding schemes in use, however, the most common is the ***Universal Product Code (UPC)***. POS terminal is not restricted to reading only bar codes but can also read printed price and other descriptions. If there is no optical characters/bar reader provided with a point-of-sale terminal on PC, salesman enters item number of the item sold. The computer gives the name, price and other description on the receipt corresponding to the item number entered into the computer. All this information remains stored in the computer's memory. If the POS terminal is connected to banks and credit agencies through telecommunication network, it will entertain cheque or credit card also.

## 11.10 FINANCIAL TRANSACTION TERMINALS

Besides online teller terminals which handle customer's withdrawals and deposits, financial transaction terminals are also commonly used in the premises of departmental stores, shops and other retail centres; hotels, railway stations etc. to receive and dispense cash and handle routine financial transactions. A plastic currency or debit card is issued to the customer. The card contains a magnetic strip on its backside to record account number and the amount at his credit. When the customer inserts his card into the terminal, the terminal reads the data on the tape and transmits it to the CPU which processes his account. The customer directs computer to perform financial transaction from the terminal point.

### Electronic Funds Transfer

To reduce demands for handling of paper documents, banks have devised a number of computer applications that make it possible to transfer funds through communication between computers. This technique is known as ***Electronic Funds Transfer (EFT)***.

### ATP (Automatic Transaction Process)

ATP is one of the applications of EFT. The common feature of this kind of transaction is that no money changes hands and transactions are said to be cashless. One account is charged, the other receives a deposit electronically without paperwork. The account holders are normally advised of make transactions only after they receive bank statements. Few banks are attempting to enhance this type of service by making it possible for customers to enter and authorise EFT transactions from home. Users can enter transaction instructions through PCs, under some systems, through push-button telephones.

### ATM (Automated Teller Machines)

Another application of EFT methods is the ATM. ATMs are transaction processing computer terminals operated directly by customers. Access to the computer system is through an encoded plastic card and by entry of a Personal Identification Number (PIN). People don't have to create paperwork but they have to interact with machines to describe details of the transactions.

Fig. 11.5 shows use of ATM.

EFT capabilities are being used to enable some customers to charge retail or gasoline purchases. The ATM card can serve as a key to permit access to specially equipped gasoline pumps. The advantage of using ATM cards is that the money is transferred immediately. When a card is inserted, the customer can pump gasoline and have the purchase amount transferred from his/her account to the gas station operators. The same arrangement is being used in many retail stores.

**Fig. 11.5:** Use of ATM

### Smart Cards

Smart cards have also been developed. They are alternative to magnetic cards. A smart card contains a built-in microchip with memory capabilities. In case of smart cards there are less chances of fraud. How much cash a customer has to credit is stored in the chip before it is issued to him. When the customer uses the card to make purchases, the required amount is deducted from the balance by a special electronic machine used by shopkeepers. The electronic machine used communicate with the card-issuing company's computer time to time for money transactions. Thus a card holder has facility of keeping electronic money with him conveniently and gradually use in making purchases. When his electronic money is used up he can replenish electronic money by depositing money at automatic banking machine of card-issuing company. A record of purchases made by the customer can also be stored in a smart card.

## 11.11 COMPUTERS WITH VISIONS

A computer can be provided with suitable sensors which enable to see its environment. For many applications computers with vision are needed. For example, a computer-based security system is required to look around to see if any intruder has entered the restricted area. It gives warning to intruders not to move further and alerts security personnel. In industries there is a high demand of robots with vision. Some robots with vision can select and sort various components from a random mix. Other robots can lift and position parts on an assembly line. They can also check the quality of assembled products. Still other robots with vision system can recognise, understand, insert and align the various parts required while making assembly of certain items. The development of robots with vision system is expected to allow widespread automation of quality-control, processing, checking and making assembly of certain products in future.

There are several technologies which provide vision capability to computers. They use either of the following:

- OpticRAM cameras
- Video cameras
- Charge-Coupled Devices (CCDs)
- Ultrasonic Vision devices.

### OpticRAM Cameras

An OpticRAM camera contains a 64 KB dynamic RAM. The cover of the dynamic RAM is made of glass instead of metal or plastic. An image of an object is directly focused onto the glass surface of dynamic RAM by the lens on the front of the camera. The dynamic RAM contains 65,536 memory cells. These cells are divided into sections. Each section is a matrix of 128 × 256 cells. Each cell functions as a pixel.

In a dynamic RAM, 0 and 1 are stored as charge on tiny capacitors. As the charge gradually changes due to leakage, a dynamic RAM has to be refreshed periodically. If the light falls on a dynamic RAM cell, the stored charge on the tiny capacitor changes at a faster rate as compared to the usual condition when there is no light falling on the memory cell. A dynamic RAM can be used as an image sensor. For this purpose all memory cells, are first charged to logic 1 level. After certain predetermined interval of time the logic level on each cell is read by a microcomputer. The cell whose logic level has changed from 1 to 0 represents a light spot. The logic level of an OpticRAM can be read and stored directly in the microcomputer memory for processing. The light sensitivity of the camera can be adjusted. It is done by adjusting the time interval between charging up all the cells and reading out the logic levels on the cells. For example, for brighter light a shorter time interval is used.

A Micron Eye camera employing an OpticRAM has been developed by Micron Technology. It contains a printed circuit board with suitable interfacing circuitry so that it can be interfaced to a microcomputer. with this type of sensors bit pattern of images are stored in the computer memory.

An OpticRAM camera is relatively inexpensive. It can easily be interfaced to a microcomputer. It has enough resolution to be applied to robots and other similar applications.

### Video Cameras

Video cameras and TV station cameras contain a special vacuum tube. There is a light-sensitive coating on inside of the face of the tube. This special vacuum tube is called vidicon. An electron beam is swept horizontally and vertically on the face of the vidicon in the same way as on a TV screen. When the beam is at a particular spot of the vidicon the beam current is proportional to the intensity of light falling on that spot. The vidicon gives an analog output signal for each scan line. The magnitudes of the analog signal at various points are proportional to the amount of light falling on different spots along the scan line. To convert analog signals to digital signal A/D converters are used. Corresponding to each dot on a picture there is an output from the A/D converter. Its value determines intensity of the dot. In this way a picture can be stored in the digital form. Video cameras are expensive, have high resolution so they can not be used for all types of applications. For less expensive systems Charge Coupled Device (CCD) cameras are used.

### Charge Coupled Device (CCD) Cameras

A CCD camera is less expensive but resolution is not as high as that of a video camera. It can easily be interfaced to a microcomputer. It is more rugged and smaller in size. It is used in robots to sense images.

CCDs are semiconductor devices. They are fabricated as long shift registers on semiconductor material. There is a P-type substrate. On this P-type substrate there is an insulating layer of an oxide. Finally on the oxide layer there are isolated gates. When a positive potential is applied to a gate with respect to the substrate, a potential well is developed under the gate, the charge will be retained there. If a sequence of clock pulses are applied to the gates, the stored charge will shift under the next gate. In this way a CCD can operate as a digital or analog shift register.

To utilise CCDs in computer vision several hundred CCD shift registers are fabricated in parallel on the same IC. A photodiode is doped in under every other gate. To create potential well all the gates having photodiode under them are made positive. When light falls on a photodiode a charge proportional to the intensity of the light is produced. This charge is held in each well. These charges can be shifted. For each scan line of a picture dot by dot values are obtained by shifting these charges. A CCD register gives video information in discrete samples. As the charge held in a well is proportional to the intensity of light, the discrete samples are in analog form. They are converted to digital form by A/D converters before processing by computer.

### Ultrasonic Vision

Sound waves above human hearing range are called ultrasonic waves. Bats can see in dark. They emit ultrasonic pulses and determine the distance of the obstacle on the basis of time taken by echoes to return. This technique is used by some cameras to adjust distance automatically while taking photograph. Texas Instruments (TI) produces kits for this purpose. Such a kit with some simple circuitry can be interfaced to a microcomputers to provide ultrasonic vision.

Ultrasonic pulses are sent out. When each of the sound waves return they are received by a transducer. The transducer then produces an analog electrical signal. The time between sending out the ultrasonic waves and receiving the echo back can be measured by microcomputer. The distance at which an obstacle is located can be calculated by the computer on the basis of the measured time and speed of the ultrasonic sound waves.

This type of vision can be used in robots. The range of this type range finder is about 10 m and resolution is about 3 mm. For greater resolution optical vision systems are recommended.

## 11.12 COMPUTERS IN ARTIFICIAL INTELLIGENCE

Artificial Intelligence (AI) is that branch of computer science that deals with ways of representing knowledge using symbols rather than numbers and with rules-of-thumb, or heuristic, methods for processing information OR A machine with reasoning, learning and logic capability is said to possess artificial intelligence.

The following are the major areas of research in artificial intelligence:

- Expert Systems
- Natural Language Processing
- Speech Recognition
- Pattern Matching
- Computer Vision
- Robotics
- Intelligent Computer Assisted Instruction (ICAI)
- Automatic Programming
- Decision Support and Planning

### Expert Systems

One of the most common applications of AI is Expert Systems. An expert system is a software which utilises a knowledge base collected from human specialists in a certain area, and helps users refer to this expertise in making their own decisions.

An artificial intelligence system has a knowledge base and programming technique to probe and process the facts represented in the form of a knowledge base. The development of a knowledge base is very difficult and time consuming job. To develop a knowledge base the designers and research workers consult experts of a particular field. They collect facts that are based on the knowledge and experience in that field. Such a collection forms a knowledge base. An expert system uses a knowledge base for its artificial intelligence. Besides expert's knowledge an expert system also uses the decision rules of human specialists to reach certain conclusion and to give recommendations. Natural language may be used to input user's facts and queries. The recommendation made by an expert system is based on the collection of information in the knowledge base. Hence, the knowledge base must be updated regularly. An expert system select one of many opinions depending on input data and information. The machine uses a set of decision rules on logical basis to choose an opinion. The machine is designed to perform such logical functions. It asks users to supply information on a problem. Computer then processes the information and reaches conclusion making use of the knowledge base.

Due to various reasons many organisations want to develop expert systems. If an expert retires, dies or resigns the organisation looses his expertise. So this is a very good reason to preserve expertise of experienced specialists. Another reason is that other person are benefited by specialist's expertise. Some examples of expert systems are listed in Table 11.1.

Table 11.1: Expert Systems

| S. No. | Name of Expert System | Field of Application | Function Performed |
|---|---|---|---|
| 1. | ELF | Oil Industry | Oil Exploration |
| 2. | PROSPECTOR | Geology | Mineral Exploration |
| 3. | MYCIN | Medicine | Diagnose meningitis and bacterial infections |
| 4. | SOPHIE | Electronics | Computer-Aided Instruction |
| 5. | XCON | Computer Science | Diagnosis of Computer malfunction |
| 6. | EL | Electrical Industry | Analyses Electrical Circuits |
| 7. | MOLGEN | Biology | Planning DNA elements and genetic science |
| 8. | DENDRAL | Chemistry | Estimating molecular structure of compounds |
| 11. | PUFF | Medical | To diagnose lung diseases |
| 10. | STREAMER | Training | Teaches navel officers |

## Natural Language Processing (NLP)

The goal of natural language processing (NLP) is to enable people and computers to communicate in a 'natural language' such as English, Hindi, etc. The field of NLP is divided into the following two fields.

- Natural Language Understanding: It investigates methods of allowing the computer to comprehend instructions given in ordinary English so that computers can understand people easily.
- Natural Language Generation: It strives to have computers produce ordinary English language so that people can understand computers more easily.

## Speech Recognition

The primary interactive method of communication used by humans is not reading or writing but it is speech. The focus of NLP is to enable computers to communicate interactively with English words and sentences that are typed on paper or displayed on screen. The goal of speech recognition research is to allow computers to understand human speech so that they can hear our voices and recognise the words we are speaking. Speech recognition research seeks to advance the goal of NLP by simplifying the process of interactive communication between people and computers.

## Pattern Matching

It is one of the most important abilities of artificially intelligent machines to distinguish the objects on the basis of their corresponding patterns. In simplified terms, AI works with pattern-matching methods which attempt to describe objects, events, or processes in terms of their quantitative features, logical and computational relationships.

## Computer Vision

People generally use vision as their primary means of sensing their environment because we generally see more than we hear, feel, smell, or taste. The goal of computer vision research is to give computers powerful facility for understanding their surroundings. One of the most important uses of computer is in the area of robotics.

### Robotics

A robot is an electro-mechanical device that can be programmed to perform manual tasks. The Robotic Industries Association formally defines a robot as "a re-programmable multi-functional manipulator designed to move materials, parts, tools, or specialised devices through variable programmed motions for the performance of a variety of tasks".

### Intelligent Computer-Assisted Instruction (ICAI)

Computer-assisted instruction (CAI) has been in use for many years, bringing the power of computer to bear on the educational process. Now AI techniques are being applied to the development of ICAI systems in an attempt to create computerised 'tutors' that shape their teaching techniques to fit the learning patterns of individual students.

### Automatic Programming

Programming is the process of telling the computer exactly what you want it to do and developing a computer program frequently requires a great deal of time. As part of program development process, a program or system must be designed, written, tested, debugged, and evaluated.

The aim of automatic programming is to create special programs that act as intelligent tools to assist programmers and expedite each phase of the programming process. The ultimate aim of automatic programming is a computer system that could develop programs itself, in response to and in accordance with the specifications of a program developer.

### Decision Support and Planning

The realisation of a complex goal may require the construction of a formal and detailed plan. The development of plans in business may necessitate the collection and evaluation of significant amount of information. Intelligent planning programs are designed to provide active assistance in the planning process and are expected to be particularly helpful to managers with decision-making overheads.

## 11.13 COMPUTERS IN BANKING APPLICATION

Banking is yet another type of business application that benefits from computerisation because of the repetitiveness of the transactions, the accuracy required, and the speed required to handle the large volume of daily transactions. A bank processes huge volume of documents in the form of cheques, loan records, deposit slips, withdrawal forms, saving club coupons, draft-slips, investment source records, and many more. The account balance of every customer must be kept up-to-date. Funds and data must be exchanged among banks. Money transaction may be made electronically which is referred to as Electronic Fund Transfer (EFT). Automated Teller Machines (ATMs), Smart Cards, etc. are nothing but various forms of EFT.

Each teller station has a terminal and operates on-line when accessing accounts to cash cheques or make deposits. Banks use computers for general purpose computations to provide online service to customers who want to perform bank transactions from home terminals and to answer customers at bank terminals regarding their balance etc. Most banks have and branches offices also have installed ATMs (Automated Teller Machines) that dispense asked amounts of cash. Home-banking is also one of the options provided by some banks for customers who have PCs with modems or touch-panel telephones and special home-banking devices.

At bank counters computer allows customers to make withdrawals and deposits. The customer supplies his/her password and makes a few key strokes to enter some other details. To handle cash, banks use Cash Dispensing Machines. Such a machine is a microprocessor based machine. This machine provides cash when identification number is typed in. Money can also put into an account in the same way. The large volumes of cheques received everyday in banks nowadays are processed by computers.

With the use of a computer electronic funds transfer from one account to another has become possible. A customer from his home, office or store can insert his identification number and type the transaction detail on the terminal's keyboard. Immediately the amount he specifies will move out of his account and enter another's account.

## 11.14 COMPUTERS IN EDUCATION

A frequently asked question during 1980s centered on whether computers would replace teachers or not. The answer of course is 'NO'. Computers are becoming valuable and versatile classroom features. Computers can help teachers with their work, supporting such activities as self-paced student learning, preparation of grade reports, and development of tests and other instructional materials. Students can learn at their own pace through computer-aided instruction (CAI), a method of teaching or training individuals or groups where a computer program instructs students through an interactive dialogue.

Most educational application packages incorporate interesting and colourful graphics to hold the student's attention and include programs to increase reading comprehension, improve spelling, build vocabulary, and develop thinking and other special skills. Application of computers in education may be put broadly in the following:

- Drills
- Problem Solving
- Dialogues
- Discovery Learning
- Instructional Simulation
- Computer Aided Testing (CAT)

### Drills

A computer drill, or practice session, lets the student learn at an individual pace by repeating an idea or concept in order for the student to memorise it. The program asks questions, quizzing the student on a particular subject until the student has memorised the material.

Packages for drilling students on multiplication and divisions or on English grammar rules are typical examples.

### Problem Solving

In recent years, various problem-solving packages have gained popularity. These packages allow instructors to assign problem-solving assignments so that students may focus on correctly formulating a solution without indulging into deep and complex computations. The most significant advantage of such problems-solving exercises is that these allow students to work with complex and challenging problems by relieving students of the burden of computations.

Fig. 11.6 shows computer application in problem-solving.

**Fig. 11.6:** Computer Application in Problem Solving

Examples of such problem-solving packages include Statistical Analysis Packages (e.g. SPSS, SYSTAT), Electronic Spreadsheet (e.g. MS-Execl, LOTUS 1-2-3, VisiCalc), and Accounting Packages (e.g. TALLY, WingsLite, MUNIM), and so on.

## Dialogues

The concept of a dialogue between a teacher and student is quite old. Dialogue technique presents the computer as a teacher who possesses knowledge which the students require to learn. Dialogues can be put in the following two types:

- Tutorial Dialogue
- Inquiry Dialogue

## Tutorial Dialogue

A tutorial-dialogue is a teaching method by which a concept is explained to the student, and then questions are asked about it, testing the student's understanding. The student's progress can be automatically monitored as the answers are given and checked for accuracy.

Computerised tutorials have proved to be very useful in adult literacy education. Adult students are usually eager to use the computer; some students in these sessions have been able to improve their reading and comprehension skills. Most of the computer-based dialogues fall under this category. These have been a popular form of computer instruction, but they have been very difficult to write. It requires special programming languages known as Authoring Languages (e.g. PILOT) and differ from other traditional programming languages because the former have special capabilities for handling and analysing English text.

## Inquiry Dialogue

It is a type of dialogue in which the student has to extract the knowledge by an inquiry dialogue made onto the computer which possesses knowledge and information. Students has to interact with the computer in an inquiry-dialogue fashion such as asking questions, selecting the sequence of activities, and taking active steps towards analysis and problem-solving.

## Discovery Learning

It is also one of the CAI techniques applicable in class-room teaching. Class-room teaching involves lectures, exercises, assignments, quizzes, some other short-time activities. Rather than an instructor, discovery learning environment can extend a better control for the above events. Such an environment offers the flexibility to students to choose the time and the manner in which they tackle ideas and concepts. Moreover, simulations represent different types of discovery learning environments.

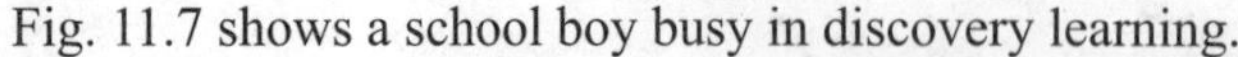

Fig. 11.7 shows a school boy busy in discovery learning.

**Fig. 11.7:** School boy busy in discovery learning

## Instructional Simulations

Simulations provide learning situations to challenge a student's thinking skills. This type of simulation is used to teach students how things work. Simulations use computer modelling to create real-life situations. By creating a model of how something works or behaves, students can change the variables of the program to see how the subject might act. For example, students might conduct a chemistry experiment with computer model instead of using real compounds, which could be dangerous, to observe reactions. These type of simulations are particularly useful in situations where first-hand experience is too expensive, too risky, unavailable or inappropriate.

It may fall into any of the following three categories:

- Task Performance Simulations
- Systems Modelling Simulations
- Encounter Simulations

## Task Performance Simulation

In this type of simulation, realism is must to ensure that end-user learning will transfer to the activity concerned. It may require a good and costly infrastructure in order to make it a real look. Such a simulation helps its end-users to acquire skills related to the specified task. For example, Driving Simulator, Traffic Simulator, Flight Simulator, etc. fall in this category which would require a special arrangement of accessories to be attached with computer.

### Systems Modelling Simulation

These type of simulations are aimed at providing its learners with a meaningful understanding of the systems under experimentation. Actually, the world may be described as a vast network of varying kinds of systems such as Economic System, Weather System, Political System, Air-Traffic System, and so on. Such simulations must contain information and data required to explain the state of a system as well as rules required to govern the activity. Users can use the system modelling simulation for understanding the concepts related to the system and later on can experience its behaviour under the changed parameters, following which user can gain a lot about the system as well as its behaviour.

### Encounter Simulations

These type of simulations are different from system simulations as the experience may not be formalised and structured enough to be represented in a system. For example, Job-interviewing encounters provide the candidates with hypothetical problems and opportunities that require some decision or action. Candidates may learn and gain about such situations after observing the consequences of their actions. Such type of simulations encourage its users for indulging in the activities and experiences which otherwise are very difficult to attain.

Some large companies use all three types of CAI and find them useful to teach new employees their jobs, especially when they involve technical information. It is reported that, on the average, computer-aided instruction cuts a company's training cost by approximately 30 %.

### Computer Aided Testing (CAT)

It is the use of computers to evaluate student learning. The heart of a computer-based testing system is the database containing a large number of test questions as well as a statistical history of the use of each item. Teacher may select questions from the question-bank database. Later on the response sheets from the students is analysed to determine the behaviour of individual test item.

## 11.15 COMPUTERS IN INVENTORY AND QUALITY CONTROL

One of the benefits of using a computer is to generate reports quickly and easily, giving the merchant the most up-to-date picture of sales. Many inventory control programs used in retailing automatically generate purchase orders to reorder stock as soon as the supply on hand is reduced below a specified level. The supplier's computerised system takes the order, prepares an invoice and shipping label, and appropriately reduces the inventory record of the products shipped.

For example, in large textile company, microcomputers are used for quality control and handheld computers check for inferior quality by grading the cloth as it comes off the weaving looms. This type of product control means that substandard goods can be identified. The company also uses computers to create the textile designs and graphics, schedule maintenance of the plant and equipment, and function of the more traditional budgeting and planning areas.

## 11.16 COMPUTERS IN MARKETING

Computers are widely used in marketing operations where they create form letters, generate and analyse market surveys, prepare invoices, process mail orders, and verify status orders.

Computers can also help managers analyse markets and sales and plan marketing strategies. Sales people can be provided with computer-analysed information about their customers, such as what kinds of products they buy, when they tend to place their largest orders, and whether orders are influenced by sale price promotions. Reports can also be created that indicate exactly how well or poorly specific products sell in certain areas; other reports can show each salesperson's bottom-line totals.

### At-Home Shopping

At-home shopping has been made possible through use of computerised catalogues that provide access to product information and permit direct entry of orders to be filled by the merchant. In some parts of the country, purchases can be made through interaction with special TV broadcasts. The broadcasts are carried over cable networks and its viewers can ask to purchase the selected items. In some instances, viewers may have to call special numbers to place orders, which are processed through a computer system by telephone operators. In effect, the computer-processed video signals act as live, interactive mail-order catalogues.

### Advertising

The purpose of advertising is to sell a product or service. With computers, advertising professionals create art and graphics, write and revise copy, and print and disseminate ads with the goal of selling more products.

### Telemarketing

Telemarketing involves ways to reach previously untapped markets, and it has proved to be very successful. Most recently, telemarketing personnel use the telephone and a computer system to make initial contacts. You may have received computerised sales calls on the telephone. In this kind of call, a computer and modem work together, dialling a series of telephone numbers. When the person answers the phone, a pre-recorded message plays. The person may be asked to respond to a questionnaire or sign up for the particular service.

## 11.17 COMPUTERS IN MEDICINE AND HEALTH CARE

When a patient enters a hospital or consults a doctor, a complete medical history must be on hand and in the early days this information was obtained by lengthy interviews but with advent of computers, many hospitals have automated this activity.

Automated system has greatly reduced the amount of time involved in obtaining a patient's history and patients are often more frank with a computer than with a doctor. The medical history can be printed on the slip and sent to the physician for review.

Many physicians and medical researchers enter their fields of speciality not only with a knowledge of physical science, but also with skills in using computers. Besides the usual record keeping and administrative types of tasks in pharmacies, doctor's offices, and hospitals, this combination of knowledge and technology enables doctors and other health-care technicians to:

- Test for and diagnose diseases and illness faster and more accurately
- Design prostheses and reconstruction models
- Build and use devices to monitor vital signs and other bodily functions
- Design and test pharmaceuticals
- Offer choices in life-style and job selection for people who are physically challenged.

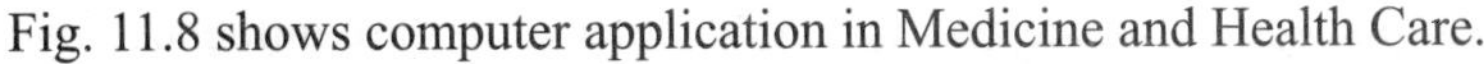

Fig. 11.8 shows computer application in Medicine and Health Care.

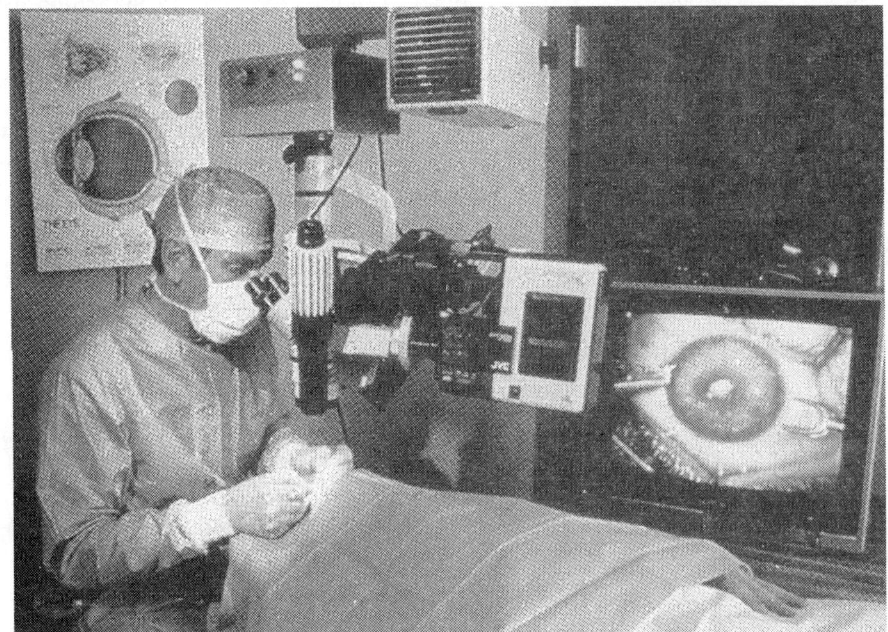

**Fig. 11.8:** Computer Application in Medicine and Health Care

## Computer Assisted Diagnosis

Computer assisted diagnosis helps to provide preventive health care and can complete extensive patient screening tests through non-surgical techniques. Three important applications for computer-assisted diagnosis are:

- Multiphasic Health Testing (MPHT)
- Computerised Axial Tomography (CAT or CT)
- Magnetic Resonance Imaging (MRI)

## Multiphasic Health Testing (MPHT)

In MPHT, computer equipment aids performance of a series of tests and then stores the results and reports them to doctors. In MPHT center, when all data items are entered, the computer system can develop a patient profile by comparing a patient's answers and examination findings with a database that models a range of normal conditions according to patient age, height, weight, and other factors. This information is delivered to a physician before the patient's visit. MPHT allows doctors to spend more time on diagnosis and treatment and can be valuable in preventive healthcare.

## Computerised Axial Tomography (CAT or CT)

CAT is a procedure commonly known as a CAT scan. A computer controls the operation of X-ray equipment and also evaluates the images produced. CAT scan differs from normal X-ray in such a way that a normal X-ray picture is a flat image that presents a view from a single position whereas a CAT scan combines multiple views to produce a 3-D image of an area of the body. CAT is often used to assist doctors in re-constructive surgery, where one of the primary concerns is how the patient will look after the operation.

Ultrasound examination procedures are particularly effective in body areas where soft tissues are encountered. Infrared sensing is the basis of examinations that look for the presence of tumors, which emit greater amounts of heat than normal tissue. Infrared sensing and image resolution techniques are used in testing for breast cancer.

### Magnetic Resonance Imaging (MRI)

MRI technique may be used when a physician needs information on the state of soft- or nerve-tissue areas in a human body. X-ray pass through soft tissue and resolve images of bone structures. MRI procedures can resolve images of soft tissue areas that do not show up at all in radiography.

The source of imaging in MRI system is a series of strong magnetic pulses applied to a body encased in a magnetically shielded chamber. Computer processing delivers an image that can show relationships of bone structures and soft tissue. MRI examinations do not expose patients to radiation.

### Prostheses Design and Reconstruction

Programmers and engineers work closely with physicians using computers to design prostheses and to create models for re-constructive surgery.

Some orthopaedic surgery requires the creation and implantation of artificial limbs and other replacement parts, such as hip joints. By using diagnostic scanning procedures, technicians can digitise an accurate picture of the damaged bone and visually compare it for fit and function. Then the prosthesis is built, usually with the help of computer-aided manufacturing machinery, to ensure the precise measurements are met.

Tooth crowns can be created in the dentist's office while the patient waits. After the natural tooth has been trimmed, the dentists can use a pen-sized laser probe to measure that tooth and the adjacent teeth, and feed the dimensions into a computer. A computer-controlled milling machine, maintaining those exact specifications, creates the crown from metal and porcelain. The dentist then cements the finished crown in place.

### Computer Aided Monitoring

Conditions of few patients, such as those who have suffered from heart attacks, can change rapidly and critically. Close observation and monitoring of these patients is critical and even in ICUs (Intensive Care Units), personnel observation of every patient, every moment is impossible but computers can perform this task.

Computers are used to monitor and report continuously on their vital signs, or life signs. These are the key indicators of health or illness. The vital signs include heartbeat rate, blood-pressure, respiration, temperature, and pulse. Patient monitoring database consists values for normal signs and any deviation from the above signs activates an alarm sounds, which demands nursing staff on an emergency basis.

Computer-controlled devices are used where patients need constant monitoring, such as in intensive care units, post-operative recovery rooms, and premature-baby nurseries.

Premature infants, especially babies whose birth weight is under three pounds, are at high risk of death from strokes that can be caused by high blood pressure. These baby's vital signs, blood gases, and head movements being taken up to 32 times per minute. It would be physically impossible for nurses to obtain the same volume of data.

Researchers are hopeful that causes and prevention of Sudden Infant Death Syndrome (SIDS) can be learned from these computer monitoring tactics.

### Pharmaceutical Design and Testing

Developing a new drug is time-consuming and costly, involves years of research and experimentation and costing millions of dollars. Thousands of compounds have to be made and tested before a new drug can be released for production and human use.

However, compute graphics techniques save drug researcher's time by simulating, in 3-D, the shapes of the molecules. Because the shape of a molecule usually determines its behaviour, biochemists can accurately predict how various molecules should be combined. Some computers are programmed to simulate various attributes of test animals so that checking for toxicity or verifying the safety of certain procedures can be done by computer simulation without endangering human or animal life.

### Help for Physically Challenged

Devices that simulate muscles to move continue to be improved. The computer stores a signal of brain wave muscle patterns, reads the signal, and then gives an electrical stimulation to the appropriate muscle group to cause movement. Tendon injuries are being treated this way, and improvement has been shown in patients paralysed by strokes, accidents, or cerebral palsy.

The Versabraille is a laptop computer that some blind people use to write letters or take notes. There are also braille keyboards, keyboards adapted for those with limited muscle control, and keyboards that can be activated merely by eye movement.

## 11.18 COMPUTERS IN THE ARTS

There are many tools of the trade for persons involved in "the arts" - painting, music, and dance. Today, one tool common to all is the computer.

### Poetry

Computers are being used by linguistic scholars to study word, rhyme, and language patterns. Scholars are able to study style and technique of famous writers in great detail through use of computers. Partly for amusement and experimentation, computer professionals have also devised programs that generate poetic verses. A framework for the rhythm and rhyme patterns of a type of poem is entered into a computer. Then a vocabulary that emulates the word usage of a famous poet is provided.

### Dance

Dance routines are often written in instructions called "dance notation". This notation can be created with a computer by attaching sensors to a dancer.

Another technique is to videotape specific movements. The dancer's moves are transmitted to a computer where they are digitised and stored. The choreographer or an instructor can retrieve these movements on a video display screen, arranging them into the various combinations that comprise a dance routine.

## Art

Using a drawing tool, such as a digitizer or a light pen, and the graphics capabilities in a variety of application packages, an artist can create images on a computer display screen to produce an entirely new form of art. Laser printers can transfer these images to paper with high quality resolution and a great clarity of line and color.

Art historians are using the computer to restore old masterpieces, such as Mona Lisa, by scanning the pictures one dot at a time, digitizing the work, and taking measurements of the intensity of the red, blue, or green color found at each dot. These data are then converted into digital form to be read and analysed through computer enhancement, thus providing information about techniques that could be safely used to clean dirt and remove the discoloration that comes with time.

Film production studios create and animate characters with computerised techniques. 3D and real-life animation are seen in displays at many amusement parks.

## Music

There are many centres where composers, physicists, engineers, acousticians, and programmers work together to create new kinds of music. Fig. 11.9 shows computer application in music.

**Fig. 11.9:** Computer Application in Music

The computer has found its way into music to perform such functions as:

- Creating music and sampling real sounds (Through a musical instrument digital interface (MIDI), computers connected to musical instruments create music by synthesising new sounds and setting and maintaining rhythms).
- Storing and recording (Sounds and musician their digital form can now be easily stored on various kinds of storage media. Once the music is stored, it can be arranged or changed at the computer board).

- Controlling sounds (Computerised musical devices allow a musician to control the timber and depth of various sounds precisely and without loss of clarity).
- Editing musical passages (many musicians create and edit their musical scores with personal computers and synthesisers. Computer editing saves hours of studio recording time)

### Writing

Acceptance of writing using computers has been very rapid. May it be article-writing, newspaper-writing, book-writing, or other, computers with an appropriate word-processing software is most suited for every kind of writing. Most of us what we read today has been written on a computer under control of word-processing software. Often, the published product we receive was typeset by transferring the original text to a typesetting or DTP computer.

## 11.19 COMPUTERS IN ENTERTAINMENT AND AMUSEMENT

Hollywood is well known as the home of motion pictures and TV production, but the same is also becoming known for its use of computers. Motion pictures and TV production relies on computers for:

- Script-Writing
- Special Effects
- Animation
- Sound Effects
- Games

### Script-Writing

The length of scripts is one of the yardsticks of the Hollywood industry. According to one screenwriter, the scripts of screenplays should come out exactly 116 pages long and scripts for TV situation comedies come out to be about 30 pages for ½ hour episode. Any script can be revised in accordance of its market requirement and within a time framework. The script development process also makes use of data communication capabilities.

### Special Effects

The term special-effects identifies any image or sound content of a film or videotape that is added through editing or other post-production processing. Special-effects tools have been developed for motion picture and video production. Special effects include:

- Fading of images between scenes
- Dissolving images between scenes
- Mixing images to create a new reality

and so on.

### Computer Animation

With computer animation complete cartoon images can easily be set up within the computer. Characters and backgrounds can be created as individual stored images. Animation software makes it possible to generate complex sequences of movements for the characters. Additional characters can be blended into scenes from computer storage. Computer animation had its first success in TV commercials..

### Sound Editing

Sound tracks for motion pictures, TV shows, or commercials are composed by mixing multiple elements. The effect is similar to the blending of multiple elements for a picture sequence. To aid in the creation of sound tracks, libraries of special sounds have been released on compact discs. For example, ACCESS sound library includes sounds that range from an automobile crash to chirping crickets. It is a general practice to mix sound tracks from the sounds captured when a film is produced.

### Games

A computer can be the core of home entertainment, running games for all ages and interests, activating toys for youngsters, as well as provide hobbyists with new methods of approaching their hobbies. Computer games generally take one of the two forms:

- Action-oriented games or
- Interactive and thought-provoking games.

## 11.20 ROBOTICS

Robots are computer-controlled programmable machines composed of mechanical hands, legs, and optical sensors to provide vision. A robot contains one or more microprocessors to control its actions. It is designed to move materials, parts, tools, or to perform certain specialised tasks. Robotics will also change as AI develops. Scientist are working hard to develop robots that will be more mobile and sophisticated than today's.

Fig. 11.10 shows application of computer in Robotics.

**Fig. 11.10:** Application of Computer in Robotics

## Deficiencies of Robots

Existing robots are deficient in four areas:

- Vision
- Touch
- Mobility
- Methods of instruction

## Vision

Vision in robots is the most crucial problem to be overcome. Robots distinguish images in black and white, with few shades of gray. Unlike human beings, they do not judge depth. Robot's eyes are TV cameras. Use of fibre-optic eyes as tiny camera to relay images to their computer are also being designed. Engineers are able to program robots to see objects and rotate them until recognition is possible.

## Touch

With development of sophisticated sensors robot touch has significantly improved. Few robots are well equipped with several kinds of hands. A robot researcher has designed a hand that enables a robot to turn a door knob. Other robot hands can pick up an uncooked egg as easily as they can a heavy paperweight. Computer-driven robot arms can feed a bedridden patient and assist in nursing the patient. A voice-controlled robot arm designed by the engineering lab at Stanford university assist the disabled.

## Mobility

Scientists are experimenting with sensors that enable a robot to maintain balance while it is walking. Most of present day mobile robots travel on wheels. Walking robots must maintain their own balance. Research in design of walking robots has been aided by a desk-high robot that bounces around on one leg, as if riding a pogo stick. The longer the robot can keep its balance, the more successful the engineers have been.

## Methods of Instruction

A robot requires an proper way to receive instructions. Personal robots are generally programmed by microcomputers and remote control. Some of the more sophisticated robots come equipped with on-board computers, allowing users to experiment with programming.

## Robotic Applications

The following is a brief account of robotic applications:

- **Industries:** In industries they are used to perform task such as spray painting, welding, stamping, packing cartoons etc. In industry they can perform tasks in the environment where human being cannot, for example, robot can work at places where temperature is too high, they can handle toxic chemicals which can not be handled by human beings; they can perform tasks at places where nuclear radiations are high enough to cause damage to human being, can handle radioactive substances, and so on. They can perform tasks in dirty and unpleasant environments. They can perform tough task, can handle heavy loads and can place certain metallic parts in fireplace for heating and then remove them while they are white hot.

- **Welding Jobs:** Robots can be programmed to perform different jobs at different time. A robot can make a series of spot welding while manufacturing a particular design of a car. It can be reprogrammed to change the welding pattern for other models of the car. When there is no welding job, the robot can be programmed for other job such as material handling. In future more sophisticated robots are expected. They may include artificial intelligence, and hence they can take certain decisions.
- **Homes:** Robots are also used as domestic servants.
- **Hospitals:** Robots are used in hospitals to perform many tasks which are presently performed by nurses.
- **Sorting of parts:** Some robots with vision can select and sort parts from a random mix.
- **Assembling & Quality Control:** Some other robots can lift and position parts on an assembly line. Robots can also check the quality of assembled products. Still other robots can recognise, understand, insert and align various parts while making assembly of certain items. Robots may be provided with artificial intelligence (AI) along with sensing capabilities such as hearing, sense of touch and vision system.

## 11.21 INDUSTRIAL CONTROL AND INSTRUMENTATION

Computers are being extensively used in industry for automatic control of machines, process, measurement and display of electrical and physical quantities.

Examples: Automatic control of

- temperature of a furnace,
- speed of a motor,
- generator's voltage and power,
- boiler's pressure,
- testing of products, etc.

Microprocessor based system or single-chip microcomputers have been developed for industrial control and instrumentation. A microprocessor based system can measure and control any physical and electrical quantities, e.g. pressure, displacement, deflection, force, strain, stress, voltage, current, power, energy, frequency, etc.

It controls the operation of any machine, device, equipment, instrument etc. Take an example of a power house. The microprocessor based system measures and displays the pressure of boilers, temperature of furnaces, voltages of generators, power output of generators, frequency etc. It also controls these quantities. If any fault occurs on any part or the power house it immediately disconnects the faulty part or faulty generator or faulty transformer from the healthy part of the system.

All types of modern instruments contain embedded microprocessor based systems or microcontrollers (or single-chip microcomputer) for their operation and control. Also, computerised controllers for process, equipment or machines are microprocessor-based system or microcontrollers. Many of them are embedded in the equipment or machine to be controlled.

## 11.22 COMPUTERS IN COMMUNICATIONS

Computers are extensively used in sending and receiving information. The information transfer may take place either between two points or throughout a computer network that connects a number of computers or workstations. Data communication packages are available which are used to send and receive information. For communication purposes one must have a computer, a data communication package and a modem. Communication lines are being designed and built in USA, Japan and most of the European countries to transmit digital signals directly. Such systems do not need modems because they do not use analog signals. Until such networks are fully developed, existing telephone lines will continue currently to be in use for data transmission.

Computer communications are being used to send and receive electronic mail, engage in online conferencing (computer conferencing, teleconferencing or videoconferencing); to view and post news on computer bulletin boards; for electronic shopping, banking and brokerage and to get information services etc. This type of information utilities fall in the following three categories:

- Communication Services
  - E-Mail
  - Bulletin-Board Service (BBS)
  - Video-Conferencing
  - Tele-Conferencing
  - Voice-Mail
- Transaction Services
  - Electronic-shopping Services
  - Electronic-banking Services
  - Electronic Brokerage Services
- Information Services
  - Teletext
  - Videotext

## 11.23 REAL-TIME AND ON-LINE APPLICATIONS

A real-time system uses interactive processing or on-line processing. When a computer is controlling certain machine, equipment, process or certain activity, it measures and receives data regarding the equipment, process or activity which is to be controlled. If the measured quantity deviates from its pre-determined value, the computer sends control signal for its immediate correction. This type of computer control is called Real-Time or On-line Control.

In real-time control the computer receives data, processes the received data immediately and gives output to control, direct or change the process or ongoing activity. In such a situation there is time constraint. Suppose a computer is controlling the launching of a satellite. It measures its distance and angle. If it deviates from the prescribed direction, the computer sends control signal for correction. The processing of data, computation, sending of control signals all are to be performed within a prescribed limit of time otherwise the satellite will far off and the project will fail.

## 11.24 APPLICATIONS UNLIMITED

In the survey, we have only mentioned some examples of an ever-increasing range of computer applications. In this chapter, few important and interesting applications have been reported. In fact, the applications of computers are unlimited.

### EXERCISE

1. What is a robot? How does it work?
2. What are financial transaction terminals?
3. What is a smart card? State its utility.
4. What do you understand by real-time application?
5. What are the applications of computers in industry?
6. What are CAD and CAM? State the utility of each.
7. How are documents printed using computers?
8. What is desktop publishing?
9. What is the application of computer in project management?
10. How can computers be used in graphics?
11. How does computer help in communication?
12. What are point-of-sale (POS) terminal? State its principal.
13. What are the applications of computers in banking?
14. What do you understand by industrial control?
15. What does CNC stand for? Where is it used? Explain.
16. Enumerate applications of computers in everyday life.
17. How computers can be helpful in data analysis?
18. How computers can be helpful in education?
19. What is AI? How can computers be helpful in AI?
20. What is an expert systems? Give some examples of expert systems along with their areas of application.
21. What is meant by computer vision? Give some examples of computer applications which need vision.
22. What are on-line systems? Give their advantages.
23. Can a computer help in sound editing? Justify your answer.
24. How can a computer be helpful in language research? Explain.
25. How does computer help in advertising application?
26. How a computer can assist in materials requirement planning (MRP?
27. What is meant by video-conferencing? State its utility.
28. What vital signs or life-signs of a patient in ICUs help in patient-monitoring?

29. What is meant by encounter simulations?
30. What are CCD cameras? How are they helpful?
31. How can computers be helpful in sports?
32. How does a computer support decision-making and planning?
33. What are applications of computers in medicines and health care? Explain.
34. Enumerate the applications of robots.
35. What are the limitations of robots?
36. How can computer be helpful while getting admission in hospital?
37. How does computer perform monitoring of a patient?
38. How a computer is helpful to physically challenged people?
39. What do you understand by computer-aided monitoring? Where is it helpful?
40. What are the applications of computers in arts?
41. What is meant by at-home shopping? How a computer helps in this shopping?
42. How a computer can be helpful in problem-solving?
43. What is automatic programming? How it can be performed by a computer?
44. How is a computer helpful in music-composition?
45. How can computers be applied to entertainment and amusement applications?
46. What is the difference between script-editing and special effects? Are these possible on a computer? Justify your answer.
47. What is telemarketing? State its utility.
48. What are special-effects? How the computer helps in generating these special-effects?
49. What is Multiphasic Health Testing? How does it help?
50. What is Computerised Axial Tomography? Explain its utility.
51. How a computer helps in maintaining scores on the scoreboards? Explain.
52. What is pattern matching? How a computer can be helpful in it?
53. How can computer help in diagnosis of a patient?
54. How does a computer aid in writing?
55. What are the applications of robots?
56. Differentiate between real-time and on-line applications.
57. What is bio-mechanics? How is it carried out?
58. What is meant by task-performance simulation? How is it carried out using a computer?
59. How can a computer conduct tutorial-dialogue?
60. What is the contribution of computer in poetry? Explain.
61. How is telemarketing possible? Why is it becoming popular /
62. What is CAI? How can it be helpful to students?
63. What does NLP stand for? How does a computer contribute towards NLP?

64. How does computer help in pharmaceutical design and testing?
65. What is ICAI? How is it useful?
66. What are Smart Cards? Where and how are they helpful?
67. How a computer can be helpful in newspaper production?
68. What is computer integrated manufacturing? What are its requirements?
69. What are the major areas of AI? State their current status.
70. How does computer in carrying out research work?

# Index

G



H



I



J



K



L



M